To the Edge of the Sky

ANHUA GAO

VIKING

VIKING

Published by the Penguin Group
Penguin Books Ltd, 27 Wrights Lane, London w8 5TZ, England
Penguin Putnam Inc., 375 Hudson Street, New York, New York 10014, USA
Penguin Books Australia Ltd, Ringwood, Victoria, Australia
Penguin Books Canada Ltd, 10 Alcorn Avenue, Toronto, Ontario, Canada M4V 3B2
Penguin Books (NZ) Ltd, Private Bag 102902, NSMC, Auckland, New Zealand

Penguin Books Ltd, Registered Offices: Harmondsworth, Middlesex, England

First published 2000
1 3 5 7 9 10 8 6 4 2

Copyright © Anhua Gao, 2000
The moral right of the author has been asserted

Set in 11.5/13.5 pt Monotype Bembo
Typeset by Rowland Phototypesetting Ltd, Bury St Edmunds, Suffolk
Printed in Great Britain by Clays Ltd, St Ives plc

A CIP catalogue record for this book is available from the British Library

ISBN 0-670-88831-1

This book is dedicated to my parents

Contents

List of Illustrations

SECTION TWO

All photographs are from the author's collection except for nos. 11, 18 and 28, which are from the Hulton/Getty collection

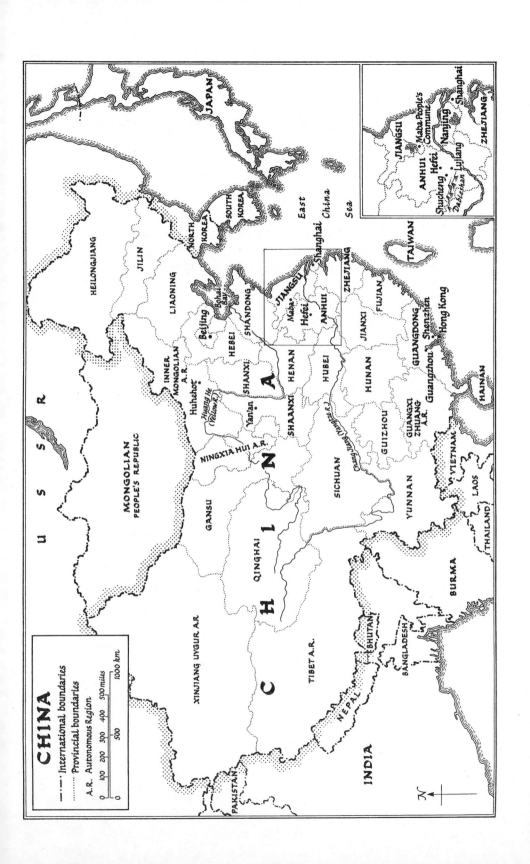

Acknowledgements

It was my respected middle-school teacher, Ming-ya Lü, who first encouraged me to write my life story and urged me on. To him goes my thanks. I also owe a special debt of gratitude to Guanghua (Greg) Chen, a dear friend and a middle-school classmate. He not only shared my feelings and jogged my memory, he gave me his most sincere support and advice – despite living thousands of miles away in America. For this I can never thank him enough. You will meet Greg again among these pages.

To all my family and friends in China who have loved me and helped me during the writing of my book, I am indebted.

Nigel Blundell, British journalist and best-selling author, helped me get my notes and scribblings into sensible order and gave me encouragement throughout the three years it took me to write my story. To him I give my heartfelt thanks.

I was very lucky to find Andrew Lownie to be my agent. He worked enthusiastically and efficiently with the editor at Penguin, Eleo Gordon, who did a remarkable job of editing my manuscript. To Andrew, Eleo and all those who worked so hard to get this book into print, I am for ever beholden.

Harry Bennett, my dear husband, helped me a great deal during the writing of *To the Edge of the Sky* by polishing my English. Without his work and support, this book would not have been possible.

As the Chinese saying goes: 'Good will be rewarded with good, and evil with evil.' I hope my book has done everybody justice.

Anhua Gao
Folkestone, England
September 1999

1. My Parents

Black clouds scudded across the sky that windy afternoon in October 1926. The sounds of battle from the civil war between the warlords were temporarily silenced by the severe weather as the monsoons neared the end of their annual visit. A young man of twenty sat on the south bank of the swollen Yangtze River, staring blindly at the yellow, roaring waters. He had been sitting in the same place without moving for most of the day, trying to make sense of what had happened to him. For one brief moment, he thought of throwing himself into the noisy, rushing waters but instantly dismissed the idea. It took a different kind of desperate courage to kill oneself.

Towards dusk, he rose to his feet. 'I will not give up!' he shouted. 'You will never defeat me!' He raised his fist towards the big sky. 'Under such a large heaven, I will surely find a way. You will see.' With these words, he walked up the steep bank and turned towards the vast greyness of Nanjing to have one last look at the city where he had placed all of his hopes and dreams. Then, with a firm step and head high, despite the rain hammering down, he walked along the riverbank, around the city, and headed south.

That young man was my father.

Gao Dao-pang, my father, was born on 9 February 1906 into the rich, landowning Gao family of Shucheng County in Anhui Province. In those days, the name 'Dao' was given to all children of Father's generation born into the Gao family as their middle name. This instruction was in the ancient writings of the family tree. The reasons for this have been lost in the mists of time, but tradition, particularly in the more important families, was strong in those days. Anhui Province is famous throughout China for the number of scholars and calligraphers born there, and through the centuries the Gao family had spawned a good share of them. The family was well known in the country town of Shucheng, which nestles at the foot of the Dabieshan mountain range, some 500 kilometres north-west of Nanjing.

My father had an elder brother, two younger sisters and two cousins. They were happy childhood playmates but all of them went in terror of my grandfather, who was the head of the Gao family. He was a tyrant and quick to punish every minor offence, real or imagined. The children regularly suffered severe beatings, followed by isolation and withheld meals.

At the age of five, my father was sent to a private school and it soon became evident to his teachers that he was a natural scholar. Nothing seemed beyond him, and soon after joining the school, he was being taught how to write with a Chinese brush. Although it is a difficult art to master, it wasn't long before he impressed everybody with his extraordinarily beautiful writings. By the age of ten, Father was writing articles for the local newspapers and for a provincial paper. He wrote one article about the First World War, criticizing both sides for the way they treated the ordinary soldiers. It was highly praised and he was given the title: 'A ten-year-old child bearing the whole world in his chest.'

My grandfather was pleased to have such a brilliant son. It solved one of his biggest worries. He needed his heirs to manage the vast family estate and business interests, such as a food shop, otherwise everything would be taken over by another branch of the family. Now he need worry no more. Or so he thought.

With the conceit of youth, Father thought he could do greater good for his family by not staying in the same small place, and if higher education was his way out, then that was the route he would take. But although he daydreamed about life in the wider world, getting there wasn't easy. It was considered disloyal for a son not to obey his father, and he was a filial son. He was in torment. He wanted to leave the town but duty compelled him to stay. However, my grandfather's attitude when Father asked him to discuss the problem helped to make up his mind.

Grandfather wanted Father to manage his shop, but Father said, no, he wanted to see the outside world. This was too much for my grandfather. How dare his son answer him back! He beat Father with his fists and then with a thick stick. 'I should have given you this, and this and this, as soon as you began to have these ideas.' Every 'this' was a stroke of the stick until the boy could take no more. The old man was shouting, 'You will not dare to disobey me again!'

Father rebelled. He twisted away from Grandfather, then grabbed the stick and broke it over a chair. 'I am a free man! I will not be your slave!' he said. The old man stared in disbelief. This could not be happening. He had absolute power. Nobody dared to disobey him.

My father hurried towards the door. 'I want to do better things with my life than manage your shop. I am leaving and I will never, ever come back!' He stormed out of the room, hugged his mother and left his home. He had a few coins in his pocket and only the clothes he was wearing. At the age of thirteen years and eleven months he was on his own and on his way.

It was late January 1920 when my father hurried away from everything he knew and loved. There were tears running down his face and his throat hurt. It was particularly hard to leave his mother. She had always been the one to comfort the boys after their father had beaten them for some minor transgression. It was she who secretly brought food when their father forbade them their meals, and shielded them from him. Happiness was his mother. Terror was his father.

He began to make plans. At school he had made friends with two older boys. He had helped them with their work and, although much younger, had coached them for examinations. They both passed and, as a sign of their gratitude, they became blood-brothers to my father and pledged lifelong friendship to him. Soon after leaving school the two older boys had moved to the city of Hefei, the capital of Anhui Province. Father remembered this and decided to make for the city and find them. However, having never left his town before, he did not know that Hefei was 300 kilometres away. As he walked, with the cold and tiredness creeping into his bones, he wished he had not been so impetuous. The memory of his mother laying hot food on the table and her smiling face almost made him turn back. Only the thought of having to kow-tow to his father kept him moving onwards.

Ten degrees below freezing is not uncommon in January and that first night he almost froze to death in the open. From then on, he always found cover, however poor, to sleep under. There was the constant problem of finding food – he became an expert at stealing their food from under the snouts of pigs. He also learned which berries on the trees were acceptable to the stomach and which were not. Birds assisted there: if they ate them, so did he. He found he could go for days without eating much but needed water regularly. He sucked icicles and scraped the rime off the grass and the trees, but it wasn't enough.

Then came his first piece of luck. One evening, as he was crawling into an old temple for the night, his knee hit something hard. He squinted in the gloom, then shouted with joy. It was an old army-style metal water-bottle, cork intact. When he shook it, he heard liquid sloshing around so it had no leaks. Even better, it had a leather strap so he could carry it over his shoulder. He learned that seemingly small things can have great value.

As days became weeks, and weeks became months, life improved for him. He wandered from cottage to cottage, and village to village. Winter became spring, then summer. There was work to be had, enabling him to earn a little money as well as his keep.

One day, Father met a young goatherd of about his own age. As my father walked by, the two boys looked at each other and smiled. Shyly the goatherd invited him to sit for a while and share his small meal. Then he drew some milk from a nanny and offered it to my father. Father remembered that milk for the rest of his life, and I remember him telling me the story: his words brought the scene so vividly to life, I could almost taste that milk myself.

The goatherd was named Sun Zong-de, and the two boys talked all afternoon until it was time to take the goats back to their pen for the night. My father was invited to stay until morning, and a lifelong friendship was born. Zong-de's parents asked him in for the evening meal, then bedded him down under the long kitchen table. He felt part of the family almost from the first moment he stepped inside the door. The next day he accepted an offer of work and decided to stay for a few days.

The 'few days' stretched into autumn, winter and early spring, when he was drawn again to the road. In February 1922, after promising always to keep in touch, he set out on his travels once more. Zong-de waved until he was out of sight.

My father had spent the long cold winter months teaching his new friends to read and write. Zong-de was a quick learner, and was reading newspapers and books by the time my father left. It is strange how life works out: those winter evenings struggling with thousands of Chinese characters would prove to be the making of Zong-de and the saving of my father.

About five weeks after taking his leave of the Sun family, Father was passing through a small village when he saw a scholarly-looking old gentleman writing big characters with a brush on a long strip of red paper. In those days, only a very small proportion of the population could read and write. Many families proclaimed events such as weddings, funerals, the birth of a son or any local festival, especially the Spring Festival, or Chinese New Year (which is as important to the Chinese as Christmas is to Christians), by hanging long scrolls bearing lucky words in front of their doors. Writing scrolls could be a good business for an educated person.

My father went over to offer his services. At first the people standing around the old man would not accept that he could write. He was young, he was dirty, he wore a shabby jacket made from a goatskin given to him by Zong-de. His hair was long and he looked hungry. He said, 'Let me have a try. If I can't write well, I will not charge you any money.' The villagers agreed to see what he could do and from then on his good handwriting ensured that he was self-sufficient until he arrived at Hefei.

My father couldn't find his schoolfriends in Hefei, although he kept a good look-out while writing his scrolls. He rented a room and spent his spare time reading. He was so moved by a book by the famous educationalist Tao Xin-zhi that he decided to write to the author, expressing his theories on how to save China from the warlords. To his delight, Tao wrote back complimenting him on his ideas and making a few observations of his own. They exchanged a few letters, then Tao sent a parcel of books to my father, and through their correspondence he encouraged Father to be a patriot. He put into words what my father had been thinking and feeling. 'Be concerned about the happenings in China and strive for a better future for all of our people.'

Father spent several years in Hefei, working on the scrolls and saving money. One day he heard that his blood-brothers were now based in Nanjing and were officials in the Kuomintang (Nationalist) government. He was overjoyed and set out the following day for Nanjing. He was certain his old friends would help him find good employment. A blood bond was sacred, as strong as if they were true brothers, perhaps even stronger. My father travelled as fast as he could. The weather was bad that year and the monsoons were severe, so the journey took him many weeks until at last he walked through the ancient city wall into the heart of Nanjing.

He found the building where his blood-brothers were working and thought that, at last, his travels were over. His friends would help him find a good job and a better future. Not so! As soon as they saw Father in his shabby clothes, the two men shouted at him to go away. Father refused, so they called a guard and had him removed. The next morning Father waited outside for them to arrive, thinking that perhaps they were not allowed to speak to friends during working hours, but when they saw him they shouted at him again to go away. When he didn't, they picked up stones and threw them at him. This drew the attention of the passers-by, some of whom joined in. He was chased down the street by urchins, shoppers and beggars. He ran round a corner and into the main square. Only the sight of a platoon of soldiers training there stopped the swelling crowd from pursuing him any further. He had been hit several times by bricks, stones and other missiles. Rotting vegetables and dung stuck to him and blood was running down his cheek from a head wound. It started to rain again.

He checked his belongings. Knife, old metal water-bottle, money. Money! Where was the money? He searched the ground around him. Nothing. It had been tied to his belt in a pouch, which had gone. Then he remembered. Two urchins had caught up with him and clung on as he ran. He had pushed them off but now it was obvious that one was having a lucky day. He could hardly believe what had happened to him. 'Nanjing! You can keep it,' he said bitterly.

He was in poor spirits as he went out of the city and down to the Yangtze River. It had taken him years to save that money, which had represented security. What would he do now? He had spent four long years looking forward to this day, and even his blood-brothers had let him down. He was going nowhere and he had nothing to go to. He thought of suicide but recalled a passage from one of the letters written to him by Tao: 'No matter how difficult it is, you can only dedicate your life to your country. It is your duty. Follow your own conscience at all times, and never give up.' He turned, and started his journey to the south.

My father reached Guangxi Province in the spring of 1927. The Communist Party seemed to be everywhere. He had witnessed the Communist 'Peasant Committee' confiscate land from the rich landlords, divide it up and give the peasant workers a section each for their own use. He repeatedly heard the names of Mao Tse-tung and Zhu De as he went on his way. The poor people talked of little else. At last they had hope that their miserable lives might change. They could dream of better times instead of the grinding poverty they endured under the rule of the landowners.

He began to develop a certain respect for Zhu, Mao and the Communists. He admired their stand against the old feudal system and their concern for the poor, but he had no desire to join them. The fledgling Red Army, formed by poor peasants headed by Zhu and Mao, was not like a regular army, more like bandits, so he kept well away from them.

After reaching Guangxi Province he decided to join the Kuomintang army. It was, after all, the army of the official Chinese government. He enlisted at the lowest rank but his education brought him quickly to the attention of the high command. He was promoted to junior officer, and just after his twenty-second birthday he became personal secretary to General Li Zong-ren, a high-ranking officer who was second-in-command to General Chiang Kai-shek, the Kuomintang Supremo. The two generals did not get on well with each other, and Chiang Kai-shek was wary of General Li. He needed the support of the army to show strength against the warlords, who in those days held the real power in most parts of the country. To lose Li might lead to a collapse of his government.

The warlords, with their superior forces, had set up their own government in Beijing in the north and forced the Kuomintang to abandon their capital city of Nanjing and go south. In the meantime, the Red Army was a growing third factor. They had no base and kept to the remote countryside, growing bigger by recruiting from the peasant population. In 1926, in a marriage of convenience, the Communists and the Nationalists joined forces to get rid of the warlords once and for all, and their combined armies began the Northern Expedition against their common enemy. As they moved towards Beijing, it seemed as if the days of the warlords were numbered.

Then came the betrayal. In April 1927 Chiang Kai-shek ordered a surprise, unprovoked attack against the less well-armed Communist forces, which resulted in wholesale slaughter. With the alliance at a bloody end, the warlords were spared total defeat, and continued to be a force in China from their capital city of Beijing for several more years.

From that time on, the Kuomintang regime became the implacable enemy of the Communists. Mao and the other Communist leaders vowed to avenge the betrayal. General Li, too, resented Chiang for his foolhardy actions. Li had wanted to smash the warlords but Chiang had preferred to hunt down the weaker Communists. In disgust, Li took his own personally financed, large, well-equipped and highly trained army and returned to his home province, Guangxi. Shortly afterwards my father arrived there and joined Li's army.

During the years since he had left home, my father had maintained an intermittent correspondence with his mother through a family friend. His mother, he learned, wanted him to return home and settle down with a girl she had chosen to be his wife. He hesitated, but finally he accepted his duty to obey his mother and agreed to the arranged marriage.

At his own request, Father was discharged from the army with honour in the autumn of 1928. As he travelled home to his beloved mother and the rest of his family, he wondered how he and his father could reconcile their differences.

When he walked into the familiar house, his mother hugged him so hard that he could hardly breathe. He held her away from him and looked into her eyes, filled with happy tears, then pulled her to him again. She gazed at her twenty-two-year-old son. He was taller, lean, fit, very handsome, and he still had the winning smile that reminded her of the cheeky child of long ago. However, my grandfather would not speak to him. To my father, the old man seemed to have shrunk. Now Father was at least a head taller than him and he wondered why he had been so frightened of him. He realized that his father was really a very ordinary man. To my grandfather, maintaining face was the most important thing, so he paid for my father's wedding, partly to show the whole county that his son had returned home after serving with honour in the army, and partly because he hoped to woo him into the family business. But his pride wouldn't allow him to reconcile himself with his son.

My father and his bride were strangers. The ceremony was their first meeting. Although he had never been with a woman or tasted love, he had had little desire for marriage until his mother wrote to him. He knew it was his duty to make his mother happy, and that he would wed one day, so he agreed to the marriage with good humour.

It was a sumptuous occasion, held in the large hall of my grandfather's house, which had more than thirty rooms and was the biggest in the district. The guests gathered in the hall, standing along each side, leaving the centre clear. Everyone mixed freely, except the parents of the bride and groom who stood behind a long table at the end of the hall facing the entrance. In the West white is the colour for weddings but in China white means death and red is for a wedding. Everything was decorated in red: red lanterns, red carpets, red tablecloth, and the female guests wore red flowers in their hair.

My father wore a long black silk gown, decorated with embroidered roses. On his head, he wore a round, pointed hat. Over his left shoulder was a red satin sash, which crossed his chest and back. The ends were tied in a lover's knot at the right hip. On the sash was sewn a garland of red satin roses. He stood at the entrance to the hall, awaiting his bride.

At five o'clock in the afternoon, distant music and small explosions could be heard. The bride was on her way. She sat in an ornate red sedan chair, carried by eight bearers. On each side walked a maid dressed in pink, and the procession was led by brightly dressed men blowing trumpets and letting off firecrackers. Townsfolk lined the streets to see the bride go by, and many children followed. A wedding was always a time for happiness, and because such a grand wedding was rare, the whole town came out to watch.

When the sedan arrived at the steps of the house, the chair was lowered to the ground and the bride was helped out by the maids. She was dressed in a red satin jacket buttoned at the side up to the neck, red satin trousers and red embroidered satin shoes. A large red satin veil covered her head and face so that only her hands were visible. My father met his bride in the entrance hall, but still had no sight of her face.

He turned and walked slowly into the hall, followed by her. She was guided by the maids each holding a hand – she could not see anything under the red satin veil. When they reached the table at the far end, the Master of Ceremonies, my uncle Dao-lin, announced, 'The wedding has begun.'

The bride and groom made three low bows: one to Heaven and Earth, one to their parents, the last to each other. They had married. Everybody clapped and shouted, 'Congratulations!' Then, in the final part of the ceremony, my father poured red wine out of a silver goblet on to the floor in a circle around his new wife, to thank their ancestors buried in the ground, to ask for their blessings and, most importantly, their help in making the marriage fertile.

The guests filed into the banqueting hall to eat and drink and enjoy the rest of the evening. The newly-weds went through a side door into a room that had been made into a bedroom: red carpet, red canopy, red quilt, red bed-linen and red candles. There, my father took the satin cloth off his wife's head and at last saw her face. To his delight, she was a beauty.

Her name was Ying, which means Heroine. She had been well schooled in the duties of a wife and had been taught to be gentle and obedient in all her ways. She came from a similarly well-to-do family. My grandmother took to her immediately, and she settled in well. Sadly, the happiness was not to last for Ying died three years later, giving birth to her first baby. A few days later the little boy died too.

Poor Father. At the age of twenty-five, a light had gone out in his soul and he had no desire to stay at home. Also he felt he must do more with his life. He left home and went to Shanghai, the biggest, most modern city in south-east Asia, nicknamed 'the Paradise of the Western Adventurers'. He arrived there at the end of 1931, shortly after the Japanese invaded Manchuria, north-east China, making the 'Last Emperor' Pu Yi their puppet ruler in the region. These were years of critical change for China and also for my father. He took a job as a schoolmaster, and studied the works of Marx and Lenin in his spare time. He also helped popularize and organize the local underground Communists led by Fu Chen-ming (Sister Fu, as Father called her), who became his lifelong great friend.

In 1935, to escape Chiang Kai-shek's constant persecution, the Red Army, led by Mao Tse-tung, travelled 12,500 kilometres (known throughout the world as the Long March) and settled in Yan'an in North Shaanxi Province. The Communists were now considered the real saviours of the poor people from the Japanese and the corrupt Kuomintang regime, in which the landowners had life-or-death control over their workers. Inspired by Sister Fu, Father resolved to join the Communists, and in late 1937 he made his own long march, a journey of several months, to Yan'an. There, after listening to speeches by their leaders, including Mao Tse-tung, he joined the Party, and decided that he should no longer bear the feudalist title given to him by his father. After careful thought, he changed his name from Dao-pang to Yi-lin, which means 'artistic forest'. It fitted with his love of ancient Chinese literature, history, calligraphy and horticulture.

After his basic training, my father was sent by the Party organization in Yan'an to work in the revolutionary base area of the Dabieshan mountain range. In January 1940 he was made regiment leader within the 7th Division of the New Fourth Army. To his great joy, he suddenly came face to face with his old friend Sun Zong-de. The goatherd had come a long way from his origins, and was now a regiment leader within the same division.

The headquarters of this new posting was near Father's home, so he had a chance to pay a short visit to his family. Even after about nine years away, little had changed. His father was as unyielding as ever, and his mother, as usual, was surprised and delighted to have him home. She was a little frail, but still ran the house like clockwork. His sisters had married and were now with their husbands, and his brother Dao-lin had also married and worked in the family business.

Because the area was under the control of the Kuomintang government, my father could not reveal to his family, or anyone, that he was now a Red Army leader. His superiors had allowed him to wear civilian clothes for his visit, so that his family would not suffer because of his political convictions. He went to see his childhood playmates and told them that he was now receiving a good education, was clothed, fed and housed comfortably. It was his duty to recruit wherever possible and he asked his cousins if they, too, would like the same kind of good life he was enjoying. They were pleased and honoured to be asked, because my father was still admired by all who knew him. A distant cousin even stopped him in the street to ask if he could go too. His name was Wang Feng. He was just fourteen and small, but my father remembered how he had felt at the same age, and agreed.

My three uncles, as I called them, joined my father and completed their induction into the New Fourth Army. The two older recruits were assigned to units under Father's leadership. Wang Feng, as he was too young, joined Father's personal staff and was taught the duties of an orderly. In this way, the cousins would have a kindly eye on them for their first few months in the army.

Young Wang Feng found that his uniform was much too big. He had to roll up the long sleeves, and the jacket reached to well below his knees. He was shorter, even, than his rifle! But he felt like the happiest boy in the world: although his new uniform was too big, it was much better than the shabby loincloth he had worn before. He had shared food with the pigs and now he had rice to eat. He did not have the least doubt about the Party, and he was grateful to my father for giving him this wonderful opportunity.

All three recruits were given tests to determine their educational levels. The two older men were fine, but Wang Feng, who had been a farm labourer on the Gao estate, had had no education at all, and Father spent many hours teaching him to read and write.

My father was put in charge of a newly formed Women's Group, consisting of about twenty girls. Although their ages and backgrounds were varied, most were quite young. In the army, men outnumbered women by fifty to one, so the girls were considered very precious. Every female was pursued by many male comrades, but there was a rule in the army: only senior officers who had reached regimental level were allowed to be married. Among the twenty girls in Father's group was my mother, who was then seventeen.

On the women's first morning, they assembled before my father for the customary welcome. During his talk, my father noticed my mother, and was immediately struck by her beauty. However, his army training prevented him from showing his feelings to her, or anyone else. After his talk, he dismissed the women and sent them about their duties. My mother was assigned to work as a nurse in the army hospital. She was surprised at the sight of little Wang Feng in his uniform and found him amusing.

Soon afterwards, the three cousins and my mother became good friends, which brought her into the company of my father. It was soon obvious to everyone that the pair were falling in love and everyone noticed their happiness.

Wang Feng was with my father for six months to get used to life in the army, and to learn to read and write. Then one day, he and the other two cousins were ushered into my father's office. Father passed round a paper bag of sweets, then said, 'You have trained and studied here for six months, and now it is time for you to be posted to your permanent units. I am happy to tell you that all three of you have done very well. However, from now on, I shall not be around to look after you. I have my own orders to report to a new unit, so I may not see any of you again. The best advice I can give you is to study hard and try to make progress every day.'

My father was going off to fight the Japanese. He had been promoted and was to leave for the front the next day. He packed his gear carefully, including the old metal water-bottle, which he always kept with him. He thought of it as his lucky charm. He was to lead three regiments into battle, and couldn't quite believe that he was about to fight for his country at last.

During the hours before dawn, he and his men got into position. As the sky slowly brightened in the east, he looked around and behind him and felt reassured. Like a sea of brown, thousands of men waited for his command. Suddenly the green flares rose into the sky. 'This is it!' he thought, as he rose to his feet, turning to shout to the rear. Arm raised; hand holding a pistol. 'Come on!' he shouted. 'Come on. *Move!*' A thump in his back, and searing pains in his shoulders, his neck, his teeth. He fell, bleeding badly. He could taste the salty blood in his mouth. He tried to get to his feet, but couldn't. He lost consciousness.

When he came round he was in the army field hospital. He had been hit several times. One of the bullets should have killed him, but it had hit the old metal water-bottle, ricocheted sideways and upwards into his chest just below his armpit and out through his neck – chipping his right clavicle as it went – then into his jaw, smashing two teeth, and finally, almost spent, exited again just behind his ear. Three weeks in hospital at the base area of the Dabieshan mountain range, where my mother was nursing, and he was fit for duty.

The two lovers were reunited. Mother was not on the same ward, but she visited him as often as she could. His regiment had suffered heavy losses and the remnants were absorbed into other units. It was decided that he should remain where he was, in the base area. He was awarded his badge of honour for the battle, and was looked upon with respect by the new officers and recruits who had yet to see active service.

When Father returned to duty, he was transferred to the political wing of the army and was promoted to regiment political commissar, a senior rank in the New Fourth Army.

My mother was born on 29 September 1922 into a big family. Her father was the youngest of seven brothers in the Zhou family, based in the town of Lujiang in Anhui Province. All six elder brothers received a good education locally, then left home for careers in the cities. By the time my mother was born, they were all married and had fathered many sons but no daughters, which made Mother the only girl for three generations. The Zhou family were overjoyed when she arrived. If ever a baby girl was loved in China, it was my mother. The whole family doted on her. My mother's father had stayed at home to manage the Zhou butchering business and to oversee the land, as was his duty. He was a filial son, and did not seem to envy his brothers as, one by one, they left home.

When my mother was three years old, her mother died of tuberculosis. Her father had little time to look after her, so he arranged for his father to care for her. Although she was the pearl of the Zhou family, being a girl meant she was not supposed to attend school, which was a pity because she was an inquisitive child and would have done well. She soon charmed my great-grandfather into teaching her to read and write in the mornings, and learned from her grandmother the traditional crafts of knitting, needlework and other domestic duties in the afternoons.

After three years her father remarried and, in time, his new wife produced four more boys for the Zhou family. So my mother was still the only girl, and as there were no other girl babies, she remained the family favourite all her life.

When she was eleven her father arranged her engagement to a boy named Xin Bo-jun, who came from an intellectual family. His parents were teachers in a new progressive school and were ardent supporters of the campaign for equal rights for women. During a discussion about the future of the children, they said they would allow the engagement only if my mother attended school. At first her father would not agree, but finally a compromise was reached and my mother went to the school where the Xins taught in the neighbouring town of Tongcheng. This meant that she had to stay with her future parents-in-law during school-days and at her own home in the holidays. The Xins treated her kindly, and she settled in easily and contentedly. She thought it was her destiny to be a member of the Xin family.

My mother was clever and finished the usual six years of study within two years. After graduating, aged thirteen, she was called back to her own home to help her stepmother, who had been giving birth to and caring for her growing family. My mother washed nappies, made shoes and knitted sweaters for everyone, making up their intricate patterns as she went along. In the evenings, she helped the older boys with their studies by the light of a sputtering kerosene lamp. To all of her half-brothers she was a second mother rather than a sister. She was loved and respected by them all. Many years later, they still came to her for advice on important issues in their lives.

In old China, most stepmothers were often cruel to their stepchildren, and described as 'like a poisonous snake', but fortunately my step-grandmother had come from a well-to-do family, and had been taught to be gentle. Nevertheless, she still treated my mother unequally: she always fed her own children with the best food and gave only leftovers to my mother. But she never dared to beat her – she was well aware that my mother was the favourite of my great-uncle Zhou Xin-min, who had absolute power and control over the Zhou family.

In the summer of 1937, my mother passed the entrance examination to one of the best schools in south-east China. Unfortunately, this coincided with the Japanese launching their campaign for the subjugation of China. The country was in turmoil, and Mother had to abandon her studies and return home. It was a year before she could return to take up where she had left off. As before, she got on well with her courses but she refused to learn English. English was a foreign tongue, and by this time, my mother *hated* foreigners. She hated the Japanese invaders, and from what she had learned of western countries, she hated them too.

They had behaved badly in China, ruthlessly exploiting and spoiling everything they touched, stealing what they could not get by cheating, and killing if necessary to take what they wanted.

As in most schools, an underground Communist movement was quietly recruiting members, and my mother was persuaded to enlist by a friend. With the enthusiasm of the young, Mother was willing to do everything possible to fight the Japanese. In May 1939, aged sixteen, she became a full member of the Communist Party.

The underground movement organized a series of youth rebellions by leading the students out of their classes and on to the streets to demonstrate against the Japanese invaders. The students were enthusiastic and made a great deal of noise, shouting, banging drums, waving banners, and ignored all instructions to return to their classrooms. The teachers and the school authorities were frantic with worry: the local Kuomintang government officials had warned them that failure to control the students would result in dismissals and that the headmaster would be severely punished. The Kuomintang were still persecuting Communists whenever they got the chance and such demonstrations angered them. The school authorities failed to get any satisfactory agreement from the student leaders and decided to dismiss the ringleaders. My mother was expelled at the end of 1939. Also dismissed as the number-one student on the blacklist was the girl who had recruited her, Ye Man-lin, or 'Sister Ye', as Mother called her.

The local Communist Party decided that, for their safety, it would be best to send the disgraced girl students off to join the New Fourth Army, based in the Dabieshan mountain range. The New Fourth Army was part of the Communist rearguard, ready to support the troops fighting against the Japanese. My mother was ordered to change her name to protect her family, and became Hong Bin (Flowing Ice). She did not use her family name Zhou again until she came to Nanjing in May 1949.

After about a year in the New Fourth Army, Mother was promoted and left the hospital where she had been working. She often visited nearby villages to recruit for the Communist Party. She wrote many letters home and also to the Xins, but although her letters to her own family were never returned, her letters to her future in-laws always came back to her, marked 'Moved. New address unknown'. She assumed the Xins must have moved after the anti-Japanese war had started. She lost contact with them and never saw them again.

★

My father was sixteen years older than my mother, and his senior officer was also attracted to her. Of course, my mother was flattered by all the attention but was also embarrassed. She had not encountered anything like this before, and she had to endure much friendly teasing from her comrades.

My father looked after my mother as if he were her big brother as well as her lover, and she fell as deeply in love with him as he did with her. It was a perfect match, despite the difference in their ages. At the end of 1941, my father made an application to marry, but this was refused by the senior officer, who still hoped to win Mother for himself. The extraordinary reason he gave for refusing the application was that he was not convinced the couple were truly in love. He said that as my mother was naïve, she might easily be tricked into marriage by an older, more experienced man. This officer was younger than my father and thought himself a better match for her. In refusing the application, he knew he had abused his power. Nevertheless, he expected my father to accept his decision.

At that time, many girls were selected by the Party organization for arranged marriages to high-ranking Communist officials. They were told that this was 'the need of the revolution', but the Party acted exactly like a feudalist landlord family. The words of the supreme leaders were the law, just as the head of a family's had been. Some of these girls already had lovers within the lower ranks, but they were forced to part from them. If they were reluctant, the lover was posted away, usually to the front, and the leaders would have long talks with the girl – many talks, if necessary, and if she didn't change her mind, they would threaten disciplinary action.

When my father was told that his application had been turned down, he was both frightened and furious. He was frightened for my mother, because she might be ordered to marry someone else, and furious with his superior for misusing his position for his own benefit. He stormed into the leader's office without knocking. He was in an uncontrollable rage, which surprised everyone in the room because he was usually so good-humoured.

He walked to the desk, leaned over it and shouted, 'My love for Comrade Hong Bin is one hundred per cent true!' He snatched up a knife that was usually used to sharpen pencils and chopped off the little finger of his left hand. Everyone was rooted to the spot in wide-eyed silence. Among them was Father's good friend Sun Zong-de. In old China, when people pledged their word, they usually made a small cut in their hand or wrist, let a little blood fall into some wine and drank it, but my father had cut off his finger! Such an action demonstrated beyond any doubt that his pledge to my mother and his love for her were true.

Sun Zong-de put his hand on my father's shoulder to calm him. He told the leader that he and all the other officers present were witnesses to my father's love for my mother, and persuaded the man to agree to the marriage. Otherwise, said Sun Zong-de, my father would leave the army, and that would be a great loss to the Communist revolution. The other officers nodded in agreement. They all knew that the leader was being offered a way to save his face, and he had no choice but to agree. However, because my father had failed to knock on the door of his superior's office, he said he must be punished.

Father was told to write a self-criticism and read it out in front of the whole regiment. In it he confessed that he had, for a moment, forgotten to show proper respect for his leader, which all revolutionaries should do at all times. This punishment was written into my father's personal file, and he also received a disciplinary written warning. Thus, all parties involved in the incident were satisfied, and my parents were married just before the Spring Festival in 1942.

By this time, Sun Zong-de had fallen in love with and married my mother's friend Sister Ye. There was no wedding ceremony, they simply put their two bedrolls together. In those days, it was the usual army way of doing things. Years later Mother told me that she would have loved a 'proper ceremony', but it just could not be. Such frivolity was considered bourgeois, so she did not dare to mention it.

Many battles were fought between the Chinese and the Japanese and it wasn't until 15 August 1945 that the Japanese surrendered uncon-ditionally. By then my mother had given birth to her first child, a girl called Pei-gen (Strengthen the Root). However, shortly afterwards, China was in the throes of civil war, between Mao's Communists and Chiang Kai-shek's Kuomintang.

Both Mao and Chiang wanted to be the undisputed supremo of all China. Chiang was supported by the United States of America and had eight million troops, the most up-to-date aeroplanes, tanks and artillery available to him. The Communists had 'millet plus rifles', according to the propagandists, but in fact they acquired a large amount of arms and equipment left behind by the Japanese. Even so, there is no doubt that the Communist forces were heavily out-gunned and far fewer in number. In the early stages of the war, Chiang had the upper hand.

2. Fight for a New China

In spring 1946, my parents, with their army unit, received orders to withdraw from the Dabieshan mountain range and move north to Shandong Province. By this time, all Red regiments were collectively known as the People's Liberation Army (PLA). Parents were forbidden to take young children and babies with them because the move would involve many nights' marching through Kuomintang-held territory and the cry of a child might easily attract attention. The little ones were handed over to the local Party organization, to be looked after by specially selected poor families. My sister was sent to a peasant woman known as the Widow Liu and her fourteen-year-old son, Liu Qing-yin. Widow Liu's husband had been killed by the Japanese, so she hated all Japanese and loved those who had fought against them. When she learned that my father had been wounded when fighting the Japanese, she could not do enough for my sister. In any case, she and Qing-yin enjoyed having the baby: the widow treated her as her own child and Qing-yin as if she was his sister.

A few weeks after the PLA had left for the north, a young pig-herder rushed breathlessly into the village where Widow Liu lived to warn that enemy troops were on the outskirts. The widow told her son to lift my sister on to his back. Mother and son had prepared for this eventuality, so he knew what to do. She instructed him to hide in a cave they had picked out in the mountains while she stayed at home to deal with the soldiers.

Two hours later, soldiers arrived at her hut where she was alone, cooking a meal for herself. They smashed through her door and grabbed her, twisting her arms behind her back. 'Where is the child? We know you are harbouring an enemy of China here!' The local spy had done his work well. In great pain and terror, the Widow Liu shook her head. They searched the tiny hut and the surrounding area.

'Where is she?' No reply.

'Where is the little bastard?' A heavy blow in the gut. Still no reply.

The men were becoming angrier. 'Where is she?' A bayonet through her thigh. No reply.

They tied a rope around her neck, looped the other end over a beam and pulled her up on to her toes. 'Where is she?' Still no reply.

The widow was slowly choking to death. They beat her with their rifle butts, but not a sound came from her.

This enraged her tormentors even more. It was now a matter of honour that she scream. During the next few hours they broke both her arms and her legs, smashed her face to a pulp. Her teeth were knocked out. Her eyes were gouged out, and her ears cut off. Bayonet wounds covered her thighs, buttocks, back and breasts.

Outside her hut, the villagers waited, unable to do anything. Armed soldiers stood guard, but they could hear everything that was going on, and they marvelled at the widow's courage. After she died, the local medical man could not be sure what had killed her – the prolonged beating, strangulation, or the final act of disembowelment. She had not made a sound.

The Widow Liu is remembered in China to this day. A story and a poem have been written about her, and a film has been made. She died a heroine, and her story is told in schools as an example of a perfect revolutionary martyr. That day the villagers suffered many more atrocities but not one child was given up. After the soldiers left the village empty-handed, the villagers captured the spy and beheaded him.

Similar scenes took place all over the Dabieshan mountains and the neighbouring provinces. The Kuomintang intended to take their revenge on the Communists by murdering their children – or 'cutting the roots', as General Chiang instructed. Some children were found and killed, but most survived to be reunited with their parents. The result was a tremendous surge of new recruits into the Communists from the villages.

To our family Liu Qing-yin was a hero. He hid with my sister in the cave for three days until a runner from the village came and told him what had happened. He was sick at heart at the loss of his mother, and it was clear that he could not return home. He was also full of rage, but the only thing he could do was to leave with Pei-gen on his back. He wandered from village to village, begging for food. They travelled by day, and slept wherever they could at night, usually outside, under other people's roofs. He never left my sister alone for a single minute. He moved as fast and as far as possible from his home village. The further away they got, the safer he felt, but he was wary of everyone he met, and trusted nobody.

As the weeks went by, he became lean, tough and resourceful, but

Pei-gen grew thin, sick and weak. She had to be carried everywhere. Both children were infested with lice from sleeping with animals for warmth. Dogs, cows, horses, goats, pigs – all were host to the two young fugitives. My poor sister contracted a terrible disease of the scalp, which itched constantly. When she scratched, it bled, and her head was covered with painful, festering sores.

Liu Qing-yin (Brother Liu, as we called him) was at his wits' end. He could not stop my sister crying by cuddling her, and worried about her. In the villages people avoided them in case her disease was contagious, so he had to leave her in the safest places he could find while he went to the villages to beg. The best he could hope for was leftovers or spoiled food. Sometimes all he could get was rotting vegetables. The boy and his toddler companion were slowly starving to death. For twenty months they wandered, not knowing where they were, where they had come from or where they were going, never daring to stay in one place for long. But, thanks to Brother Liu, they survived.

One day, as they were approaching a village, they were spotted by a member of the local underground Communists. The Party had circulated instructions to all their units to watch out for wandering children. Hundreds were not yet accounted for, so the local Party members were interested in these two disease-ridden, starving, ragged bundles: a boy of sixteen carrying a scabby little girl of two. When they tried to approach them, the children ran away like frightened rabbits and hid. Only the offer of food lured them out. For a long time, Brother Liu refused to talk, but slowly, as he and Pei-gen were bathed, deloused, clothed and fed, he began to trust their benefactors. When he finally began to tell his story, it was soon clear that they were two of the children the Party was looking for, and a report was passed from unit to unit, until my parents were traced to the East China Army Corps in the Shandong liberated area.

The children had been in safe hands for several weeks by the time Mother and Father heard the news, but it was several more months before they were reunited.

Pei-gen and Brother Liu arrived in Shandong in early 1948. He was in good health, and Pei-gen was on the mend. Her scalp had been treated, but it was still covered in scabs and she was totally bald.

At first, Mother couldn't believe her first-born had been restored to her. As month had followed month without any news, she had convinced herself that Pei-gen must have perished, and she grieved for her. Both my parents were in Brother Liu's debt, and everyone admired his determination and bravery.

Brother Liu joined the PLA and once again my father had a young soldier to protect and care for. Later, Brother Liu had a photograph taken of himself and wrote on the back, 'To my superior Gao. In memory'. Before he left to go to his unit, my parents and Brother Liu were given permission to put on civilian clothes and travel to the village where the Widow Liu had been so brutally murdered. The villagers had given her the best burial they could, and had erected a headstone inscribed, 'Here lies the bravest heart of all.'

Brother Liu laid the ghost of his mother to rest, and my parents spoke publicly of their respect and gratitude for her bravery. Some years later when the old hut fell down, a statue of the Widow was erected on the spot and, as far as I know, it is still there.

In the Shandong liberated area, my father was still the political commissar and my mother was head nurse in the army hospital. The main responsibility of my father was to give lectures on the Communist cause to captured Kuomintang officers. It was considered work of the highest importance. Many eventually joined the PLA. The senior officers were valuable: they had experience of warfare, were well educated and knowledgeable about the enemy. Of course, they were counter-revolutionaries but the more senior they were, the safer their lives. The Communists spared the 'big reactionaries' because they were good for propaganda purposes: news of their capture lowered the morale of the Kuomintang troops. The 'little reactionaries' were usually shot.

My father also talked to new Communist Party members. On one such occasion, he said: 'Chairman Mao is our great leader and a brilliant strategist, but he is just an ordinary man like everybody else, not a god.' He had said it before, but not to new members of the Party or Kuomintang officers. He was reported to his higher leadership at once for uttering a 'political offence' against Mao, then suspended from work and ordered to write a self-criticism.

He might have been punished very severely, but once again his friend Sun Zong-de came to the rescue. Zong-de was responsible for promotion as well as punishments for the Party cadres, and he made sure my father kept his rank and only had a written disciplinary warning put into his file. However, such transgressions were not easily forgotten and my father had to make many verbal self-criticisms at subsequent Party meetings. Yet he had enormous respect for Mao, not only as his supreme leader but as a man. In addition, he was a passionate believer in the aims of the Communist Party and was prepared to give his life for Mao, the Party and his country.

Whilst my father was undergoing his punishment and self-criticism, my mother gave birth to her second child on 17 February 1947. She was named Andong (Tranquil East China). That year the winter was exceptionally cold and Mother slept with the baby on a *kang*, a kind of bed made of bricks with a fire underneath. She wrapped Andong in the quilt, leaving only a corner for herself. As there was not enough fuel, the fire underneath the bricks soon went out and the room became bitterly cold. It was wet and cold all through February and March; my mother suffered severe rheumatism in her legs and her heart was weakened.

Food, along with everything else, was in short supply in the liberated areas under Communist control. All through the winter, the main diet for the East China Army Corps had been apples and soya beans. The army was encamped along the coast where the Yellow River flows into the sea at Bohai Bay. The area had been especially chosen by the Communist high command because of the thousands of apple trees growing there – they would make an excellent source of food for the troops. The senior officers and officials were also given a limited quantity of millet, the best and most nutritious food available at that time.

During her pregnancy, my mother yearned for something other than apples. Apples, apples, apples. How she hated apples! Apples every day, every meal. She constantly vomited acidic water and suffered severe stomach cramps. My father went out foraging for food. His knowledge from when he was on the road helped him find a few things, but he was just one of thousands of hungry soldiers.

In camp, my mother had become friendly with a fellow townswoman, Sister Zhu Li, and her husband, Jiang Jin-yu. In the camps, comrades hailing from the same village, town or city felt close to each other. The army was made up of people from all corners of China, with different languages and cultures, so it was natural that people from the same area would link up.

Sister Zhu had been married for many years but had not conceived. Then she had had cancer in her womb, which meant she would never be a mother. She loved baby Andong as though she were her own, and the two women shared the task of caring for the child.

When Pei-gen and Brother Liu were brought into camp in the early spring of 1948, Sister Zhu looked after Pei-gen, who still had nasty scabs covering her scalp and not one hair on her head. Sister Zhu had been taught many ancient Chinese herbal remedies by her mother and often treated the families in the camp. She washed and massaged the infected area with boiled ginger-water every morning and every night. My sister made a great fuss at first, because the massage was painful, but after a couple of weeks, the scabbing reduced and new skin started to form.

According to Chinese medicine, ginger can be used in cooking and also as a means of killing bacteria. It may also promote the growth of new hair. It cannot work miracles, though. The condition of Pei-gen's scalp had been very serious: now her hair only grew on the sides and back of her head. Nearer the crown the less hair there was, and she was completely bald on top. She had to comb her hair in a certain way to disguise it.

By the autumn of 1947, the Communists began to turn the tide of the civil war their way, and their drive to push the Kuomintang army south continued throughout 1948. Towards the end of that year my mother was promoted to battalion political instructor. She was also pregnant with me. The Communist preparations to cross the mighty Yangtze River and capture the headquarters of the Kuomintang government were complete. 'Nanjing! Nanjing!' was the cry. The troops were in good spirits and ready to go. I was also ready, and was born on 11 March 1949 in the liberated area while plans for the last big push against the Kuomintang were finalized. I was given the name Anhua (Tranquil Flower). My mother always called me Little Flower.

By 20 April, an army of over a million, drawn from all the units of the PLA, was camped along a 300-kilometre stretch of the northern bank of the Yangtze. As the provincial cities and towns were taken, the troops would swing round behind Nanjing to surround the great city. Such a plan was audacious, dangerous and liable to failure, but if it succeeded, it would bring the civil war to a quick end.

The Communists gathered a motley collection of several hundred small boats, mostly loaned by the civilian population. It was impossible to keep the exact location of such a large force a secret – spies from both sides were everywhere. The Kuomintang were better fed, better equipped, well dug in and prepared to defend themselves. However, they did not have the support of the people or confidence. The Communists had those.

At dusk on 20 April 1949 the attack started. All along that stretch of river, the small boats began to cross. Immediately, the Kuomintang army opened fire with machine-guns and rifles. Thousands were killed within the first five minutes before the Communist reserves on the bank returned fire. The PLA had planned to rig up rope pulleys to haul the boats back to their side after each wave of troops had landed, and the first men on the southern bank had the task of setting them up. Many died before they could complete the job, and their boats floated away. But for three days and three nights, the crossing continued.

Hundreds of thousands of PLA soldiers lost their lives or were critically wounded as they tried to cross the river, but that didn't stop others taking their turn. A tide of revenge was crossing the river and nothing was going to stop it. It is said that the blood of the revolutionaries could be seen running down the river 500 kilometres away. In the East China Sea, fishermen found blood in their nets. The following year, the freshwater oysters were found to have pink flesh and were reverently returned to the water. My father was lucky. His boat was not hit and the others in it followed him into battle. In China, that crossing is remembered every year. Re-enactments have been staged in films, on television and in the theatre. Books and poems have been written about those three days and nights. Today the bravery and self-sacrifice of the soldiers still moves people to tears.

Cities and towns fell quickly to the Communists. My father led his troops to the left of Nanjing and around to the rear. Most of the time it was fierce, hand-to-hand fighting, but sometimes a town would be empty of Kuomintang soldiers and ready to surrender without a shot being fired. As the PLA advanced, pushing the Kuomintang back, the people spilled out of their hiding places into the streets, cheering and laughing, urging the comrades onwards.

By the end of the second day, the Kuomintang army, totally demoralized, retreated faster than the Communists could move forward. On the third day, after linking up with the force from the right, my father was in the front line when Nanjing was attacked from all sides at once. The city fell on 23 April 1949. This day is celebrated in Nanjing as Liberation Day.

When a PLA soldier clambered up to the roof of the Presidential Palace and placed the red flag on top, it was the sign for people to come out into the streets shouting for joy. They gave the victorious troops the warmest welcome ever seen in the history of Chinese warfare. PLA soldiers and civilians danced in the streets, in the houses, in the old government buildings and in the squares. Father was there, too, celebrating with the Communist high command – and, for the first and only time in his life, he got drunk.

Shanghai capitulated to the Communists on 27 May. By this time, the Kuomintang government had fled to the island of Formosa (now Taiwan) and had set up a form of government there. Fighting continued in southern China for several more months, until the once massive Kuomintang army of eight million troops was reduced to small marauding bands of outlaws hiding in the mountains. They posed no threat to the new rulers of China but remained a thorn in the side of local people until 1955, when the last of them were either captured or killed.

A few days after Nanjing was liberated, a military committee was formed to govern the city. My father was a member of the Nanjing military government. He found time to trace the blood-brothers who had treated him so shamefully, and learned that they had risen rapidly within the Kuomintang government. They had held high positions and had fled to Formosa with the rest of Chiang's cronies. He was relieved: he felt he was still bound by the blood pledge and he had dreaded meeting them. It would have meant having them shot as part of the old regime, and he was content to know they were now in exile.

A month after the liberation, the follow-up units were drifting into Nanjing. My mother, with we three children, crossed the river. Because of his rank, Father now had a personal bodyguard who carried Andong and me in baskets, one on each end of a long shoulder pole. Pei-gen was brought to Nanjing by Sister Zhu Li, Auntie Zhu as we called her. Her husband was Uncle Jiang. Our family was billeted in the AB Mansion, which had been the United States embassy during the government of Chiang Kai-shek. It was later converted into the East China Hotel and used exclusively by high-ranking military and Party officials.

I was two months old when I was carried into Nanjing and seven months old when the People's Republic of China was founded. On that day, 1 October, everyone was asked to listen to an important radio announcement. As Mao worked at night and slept until late in the morning, all important meetings were held in the afternoons. At exactly three o'clock his voice rang out from the loudspeakers: 'The People's Republic of China has been founded. The Chinese people have stood up!' Everyone was very excited. Crowds filled the streets, beating drums and gongs. Some started dancing and soon everybody had joined in, waving long red silk ribbons. Banners 'Celebrating the Founding of the People's Republic of China' were hastily manufactured and hung from all the tall buildings.

My mother was proud and happy to have given birth to a baby in the same year as the founding of the new China. She took me in her arms, put on my head a little army cap with a red star at the front and carried me into the street. My father followed behind, holding the hands of my two sisters, and the five of us walked through the crowds. We ended up on the south bank of the Yangtze River. For a few minutes, Father looked at the river, which had seen so much carnage, then picked a yellow flower from a cluster growing on the bank and threw it on to the water. 'It is not much,' he said, 'but it is our little tribute to all of you brave comrades. Thank you. Rest in peace!' We stood for a short while, staring at the rushing water, then Father looked around him. 'Ah!' he exclaimed. 'Come, this way.' He steered us to the spot where he had sat so many years before when he first arrived in the city as a very young man. He had returned as a leader, and those who had humiliated him were now defeated.

My parents traced as many of their old friends and relatives as they could, including Father's three cousins who were given good posts. Brother Liu, the most favoured of all our family friends, was still in the army, fighting the remnants of the Kuomintang bandits as a company commander. He was demobilized in 1956 and went back to his village, where he still lives in peace and dignity. If ever there was an unsung hero, it is him. We children adored him and always looked forward to his visits. Mother was appointed chief political adviser to the Women's Federation and was also a member of the Military Committee.

One day my father received a letter from his older brother Dao-lin, the first for many years. At first he was pleased and excited to hear from him. However, tears were soon running down his cheeks. Dao-lin wrote that their mother had died peacefully in her sleep just a few days before the Communists arrived. Father could not go to her funeral – by the time he received the letter, she was already buried – but he packed a bag and journeyed home to pay his last respects. His mother had been the one person who had believed in him and supported him from his cradle to her grave.

The Central People's Government was established as soon as the People's Republic was founded. My great-uncle Zhou Xin-min was selected by Mao Tse-tung to be one of its thirty members. Mao became its chairman and from then on was known throughout the world as 'Chairman Mao'.

For the first time in over a century peace came to China.

3. My Early Years

The peace was short-lived. In June 1950 war broke out in Korea, and in October Premier Zhou En-lai, on behalf of Chairman Mao, announced to the whole world that the Chinese government had decided to send 'military volunteers' to North Korea to resist the 'unwarranted aggression' of the United States of America. Many girls born at this time were given names like Kang-mei (Resistance against the USA) and boys were called Wei-guo (Defend Motherland) or Yuan-chao (Aid Korea). My little brother, born on 8 March 1951, was named Wei-guo.

By the beginning of 1950 the Military Committee had done the job it had set out to do. Order in the city was restored, and services were back to normal and the roads had been repaired. However, there was still much to be done: thousands of buildings awaited renovation to house those sheltering wherever they could. The Central Party Committee decided that the officers of the military should be divided into two groups, one of which would remain in the army to be the backbone of the armed forces, while the other would be demobilized and installed as leaders at different levels of government in the cities and towns. It meant the end of martial law. My parents were instructed to continue to work as civilian administrators in the People's Government of Nanjing Municipality.

Both Mother and Father had mixed feelings about leaving the army. They had lived the army life for so long that the idea of change was a little daunting. It was sudden, and they had expected to remain in uniform until they were pensioned off. But orders were orders, and at least they could settle down in Nanjing to bring up their family. In April 1950 they took off their uniforms.

While the 'volunteers', most of whom were veterans of the wars against the Japanese and Kuomintang forces, were fighting in Korea, Chairman Mao launched his first political campaign on the home front. His instructions were relayed to all parts of China: 'We must suppress all counter-revolutionary activities and punish those who are practising such activities.' His victims included all staff members of the old Kuomintang government, despotic landlords and the bandits who had aided and supported the Kuomintang. A long list of suspects was published and the result was a mammoth witch-hunt. Many old scores were settled, the peasants and workers were happy. All they needed to do was point a finger towards someone they disliked, shout, 'Spy!' and death was certain.

By the end of 1953, hundreds of thousands of people of all ages had been arrested and shot. Their families also suffered by being 'tainted' and were treated badly by all who knew them. After the death of Mao most of the victims were declared innocent, but at the time, Mao had masterminded his first reign of terror. Only he knew that much worse was to come.

After demobilization, Father was appointed director of the Administrative Department of the Environment. His responsibilities included all the places of historical interest, such as the Confucius Temple, the Ming Tombs and the Lingu Pagoda, as well as parks and recreation areas. The mausoleum of an early revolutionary, Dr Sun Yat-sen, was nominated as the key site to be maintained and protected, and Father was allocated a house only fifteen minutes' walk away from it in an area called the Orchard. It was situated outside the east city walls of Nanjing, in an extremely beautiful place. Here we lived in comparative peace. My father described the Orchard in his diary as 'a fictitious land of peace in the turmoil of China'.

Nanjing, with a population of 2.5 million, has a history going back more than 2,500 years. The city is now the capital of Jiangsu Province but for ten dynasties it was the capital city of all China. It was then known as Jin-ling. It was also the capital of China during the Kuomintang regime. That government knew what a capital should look like, and spent a lot of time and money making Nanjing the most attractive city in China. It lies at the foot of the beautiful Zijin (Purple) Mountain on the lower reaches of the Yangtze River. On top of it sits the largest astronomical observatory in Asia where, through a huge telescope, one can watch the movements of the stars, the moon, the planets and man-made satellites. The city wall, built by the first emperor of the Ming Dynasty, is over twelve metres high and four metres thick. It is the longest city wall in the world. Flanking the city is the Xixia (Red Sky) Mountain and several smaller ones. In Kuomintang times, French plane trees lined both sides of most streets to provide shade from the summer heat and there were flowers everywhere. Unfortunately, the battles fought for the city against the Japanese and then during the civil war had ruined all the good work of the Kuomintang. Some of the plane trees were still there but any resemblance to old Nanjing had now almost disappeared. Vast areas had been razed to the ground and almost every building was badly damaged, inside and out.

My father was delighted with his new job: he was surrounded by his passions – ancient Chinese literature and history, calligraphy, horticulture and ancient buildings. His first priority was to recruit experts to help him, and he carefully selected a group of workers who loved the same things he did. Between them, they lovingly restored the buildings to their original glory.

As my father was well known for his skill at brush-writing, he was asked to write the names on all the important buildings in Nanjing and in the suburbs. Some of his work is still there. The beautiful Chinese characters on the temples, the municipal halls, the museums and government buildings were carved or painted by him, and the writings on the Lingu Pagoda, the Aquarium, the Windy Pine Tree Pavilion and the Workers' Cultural Palace are his. I think those days were his happiest. He also wrote signs for traditional-style restaurants: the culture of food is very important in China.

Unfortunately many of his writings were destroyed during the Cultural Revolution, but in Lingu Temple Park a granite pillar stands on the shell of a large stone tortoise. Carved into the side of the pillar are four Chinese characters meaning 'Lingu Deep Pine Trees'. They are painted deep blue and read thousands of times every day. To the side of the pillar, on a board, is the information that Comrade Gao Yi-lin was the calligrapher.

Looking back, the happiest days of my life in China were spent in the Orchard. It had been carefully cultivated to produce fruit for the Kuomintang government officials. There were thousands of fruit trees – apple, peach, apricot, pear, plum and quince. Along one side, there was an enormous watermelon field, and on the other, beautiful gardens. They had been planted and maintained by the Kuomintang for the enjoyment of high officials and foreign visitors and were now under the control of my father. He had been instructed to keep them exactly as they were, but now the area was for the benefit of high-ranking Communists.

Our house was in the middle of the Orchard. It was a three-bedroomed bungalow surrounded by a bamboo fence covered with vines. Fragrant scents wafted through the house and garden all the year round. High summer was my favourite season. In the early mornings, before breakfast, my parents took us all for a walk. I can remember Mother and Father taking deep breaths of the fresh sweet-smelling air and sighing contentedly as they went along hand-in-hand, and it gave me a sense of peace and security to see them so close. It was definitely not wise for a man and a woman to walk hand in hand in public in the China of those days. I enjoyed sitting on my father's shoulders – he was always ready to be my 'horse'. Mother would carry my younger brother on one arm and my sister Andong usually ran ahead of us, chasing butterflies.

Pei-gen attended a weekday boarding-school, which had been founded exclusively for children of officials from the East China Army Unit. She came home on Saturday afternoons and went back on Sunday evenings. In time, all of us children expected to go there, because it had the best facilities and teachers in the province. There were similar schools in all the major cities of China, which ensured a good education for the children of every important Communist. The Party was building a new structure of privilege similar to that of the Kuomintang, thus creating an élite class, exactly what they had fought to eliminate. There have to be people in charge, but when the ordinary people had so little, it was shameful that those in government took so much for themselves. At that time, I think my parents simply took what they were given without thinking about what was happening. They had lived through years of privation, and probably accepted this new, good life as their reward.

Pei-gen never played with us, or went walking. I seldom saw her except at meal-times. I know now that she was an unhappy and jealous child, but then I was too young to understand this. I loved those morning walks, showered in the golden rays of the soft morning sun. In the distance, the Purple Mountain was usually shrouded in mist, and the dew-covered grass sparkled. It was a world of peace, of natural beauty and, to me, a fairyland.

After breakfast, my parents went to their offices. I usually played with my sister Andong and sometimes we looked after our brother while his wet-nurse rested. We were safe in the Orchard, so had more freedom than we would normally have been allowed. We wandered among the trees and in the gardens. Sometimes, a gardener would pick a fruit for us or give us a slice of watermelon. It was heaven, sitting in the soft green grass, sucking the juices and spitting out the pips. We could lie for hours watching the bees and butterflies dancing over the flowers.

Lunch was at noon followed by a nap. We were lulled to sleep by the rhythmic sound of the cicadas outside the window. Sometimes we were woken by thunder as a storm passed over. Afterwards we ran outside to see a colourful rainbow and try to find where it joined the earth. Mother told us that the rainbow was a bridge to help people cross over from earth to Paradise. When the weather was fine, I would blow soapy bubbles to make a rainbow against the sun. Life then seemed tranquil, beautiful and safe.

From May 1950 to March 1953, we lived at the Orchard. Then my father was promoted to be chairman of the Nanjing Municipal Construction Committee. It was a prestigious and important post, but we were sad when the news came through, for we had to move. It was a bad day for Andong and me. For the last time we walked our favourite walks, lay in our favourite places in the grass, said goodbye to the gardeners, and cried. I was only four, but in the broken mirror of my mind, I still cherish the memory of life in those far-off days.

Our new home was 24 Orchid Garden, previously occupied by a Kuomintang high-ranking government official. Father wondered briefly if one of his blood-brothers had lived there. It was a five-bedroomed house with a large kitchen. We had a flush lavatory when most people were still using chamber-pots. Opposite our house, across the road, was an estate of small apartments for non-government working people.

On our first morning in our new home, I was dragged from sleep by a strange shouting, and a foul smell. I hid under the covers, fully expecting the ghosts of long-dead Kuomintang to appear. Nothing happened, however, and at last I ventured to peep out. Andong was beside my bed, staring at me. 'What was the shouting? Did you smell that stink?' she said, as she jumped in with me. We covered ourselves with the quilt and clung together until Mother came to dress us. She and Father laughed when we told them of our fears. 'Don't worry, my darlings,' said Father. 'Keep your windows closed in future and nothing can happen that will harm you.'

This went on until I could contain my curiosity no longer. I just had to know what was going on. One morning, I went out of the back door, across the large courtyard, through the gate and into the street. I was shaking with fear and held on tightly to the iron gate, ready to run inside at the first sign of danger. Suddenly I almost jumped out of my skin and screamed. Something had grabbed my hand! I turned, and there was Andong.

We stood there, looking out, eyes the size of rice-bowls. We watched and waited. Soon we heard the cry, 'Bring out your pots!' and along came the cart. Then, 'Empty your pots!' From out of the apartments on the other side of the street came perhaps a hundred men, women and children carrying chamber-pots. Soon, the cart reached them and one at a time they raised the wooden pot they held and poured the contents into the cart. The smell was awful and we put our hands over our mouths and noses. 'Phew!' we said.

After emptying their pots, the people went to a well about a hundred metres away. Gossiping, laughing and squabbling among themselves, they washed the chamber-pots using long bamboo sticks with a rag on the end. Then they returned to their homes. The stench spread at least fifty metres in all directions from the cart. As it moved on, a man swept up any spillages and put them into the cart. We learned later that the peasants used the human soil as manure for the land. They grew vegetables for the city.

Life in the city was different from anything I had experienced in the Orchard. At first, Andong and I were intimidated. It was noisy, smelly and dirty, just like any other city, but it was also vibrant, busy and exciting. I learned to live with and then to love the vividness of city life and I still do. The streets were full of bicycles, thousands of bells ringing, faces sweating and riders laughing, scolding or cursing.

Crossing the roads as a pedestrian was an experience in itself, because the streams of bicycles never ended. Speed was essential, plus the ability to dodge around the oncoming wheels. The moment a pedestrian stopped at the roadside, the bells began to ring from twenty metres away. In those days, the roads were dangerous.

During daylight hours there were many street pedlars. They came round, every day, doing good business among the houses, the apartment blocks and wooden shacks – cobblers, knife-grinders, mobile stores, people selling pop-rice and sweet rice porridge, dumplings, vegetables, meat, fish and fruit, water-chestnuts on sticks or ice-lollies. They carried their wares in large wicker baskets hung on long bamboo poles balanced across their shoulders. All the time, as they wove their way through the crowds, they shouted or rang hand-bells to attract customers. Donkeys, horses and mules trotted along resignedly, tiny under their loads. Spidery men pulled rickshaws, constantly striving to beat the opposition for any fare-paying passenger. New to the streets was the 'pedicab', a rickshaw attached to the back end of a bicycle. Their drivers pushed on the pedals, muscles bulging, faces straining.

In the centre of all this went the motorized vehicles. There seemed to be no rules: with horns blaring and drivers swearing, the cars, vans and lorries used all the available space. There were frequent crunches of metal, immediately followed by fighting, quickly quelled as the police arrived. Buses stopped whenever and wherever they liked. They were always crowded, and when there was no room inside, people clung to the outside. Sometimes they fell into the road with tragic results.

In those days, chaos reigned, but slowly law and order gained control. Now the mobile pedlars have largely disappeared and there are street markets, but Nanjing still has the vibrancy of old. The modern shops attract large crowds, and they open every day of the week, selling goods from all over the world. Many shops are owned by the State, although there is an increasing number of privately owned shops, restaurants, bars and services. Private enterprise is positively encouraged, these days.

On the day we moved to our new home, Andong was the first to explore the house. She ran from room to room, shouting to us to come and look at each new discovery before moving on. Then she found the bathroom. 'Come and see this!' she called, and this time she waited impatiently, hopping from one foot to the other.

'Well,' said Father, 'look at this. Is there anything in it?' He strode into the bathroom and pulled open the heavy door of a safe. 'It's empty. What a strange place to keep it.' It must have belonged to a high-ranking Kuomintang official. He checked the four drawers. 'There's no key, so it is of no use to anyone. You kids may as well have it.' So we did. Andong and I took a drawer each and stowed away our childish treasures – ribbons, pretty beads, butterfly hairpins and round coloured stones picked up in the Orchard. The door of the safe was thick and heavy. Every time I wanted to open it I had to pull the handle with all my strength, then push hard, grunting, to close it again.

The front courtyard of our new house bore no comparison to the Orchard, but it was quite large with many flowers and trees. I remember a tall sophora tree by the side of the east window, which gave us a nice shady area to play in during the hot weather.

Our neighbours left in April, and the new people came in May. One Saturday, as they were moving in, we all went across to help, even Pei-gen. As we rounded the corner of the house, Father gave a delighted shout. 'At last! You are here!' It was our old and trusted friends Jiang Jin-yu and his wife, Zhu Li. Father hugged his old comrades. 'I knew you were coming. When I heard you had been appointed deputy mayor of Nanjing, I reserved this house for you. We live next door.' That night, after we children had gone to bed, I lay awake listening to the laughter of the adults coming up through the floor and felt comfortable for the first time in my new home.

The two houses were separated by a tall brick wall, with a side gate from our courtyard into theirs. The Jiangs had no children of their own, so shortly after they moved next door they adopted a seven-year-old niece to be their daughter. When she first arrived from the countryside she was dark from the sun and had bad teeth. Also, she was in the middle of a bout of chicken-pox. However, after a few weeks of good food and better living conditions, her skin lightened and her smile improved. She was a pretty girl, now named Jiang Hou-pi, and she used to come to play with us. When it rained, we played in the garage, which normally housed the big limousine allocated to Father for his trips around the city.

Mother had been promoted again, to a level on the Party ladder roughly equivalent to the rank of colonel. She was now in charge of all the industry of the city. She too was entitled to a car, but she preferred to be picked up in the morning and brought home at night. Father, whose rank was at the level of brigadier, had his own driver who lived with us. We thought of him as our protector. He enjoyed his status among us children, and often brought us new things to play with, usually small toys he made himself. One day he brought me a little rabbit carved in wood with red glass eyes. It must have taken him hours to make, and I loved it so much that I wrapped it in a handkerchief and put it with my other treasures in the safe.

Andong and I played with our dolls in the courtyard, under the sophora tree. That, we pretended, was our house and the dolls were our children. We used a handkerchief as a nappy and bamboo knitting needles to inject 'healing medicine' into the dolls when they were ill. When the 'baby' cried, we cuddled it until it fell asleep and then we laid it down to rest in the small bed we fashioned from slats of wood and bits of cloth collected from around the house. We were quite sure we would be excellent mothers when we grew up.

My little brother Wei-guo was toddling now, so he, too, became our child. His nose was wiped so often because of his (imaginary) cold that the tip became red and sore. He had to drink gallons of water, forced on him by his doting 'mother' and 'aunties', but he seemed not to mind and followed us around, wobbling on his little legs as he tried to keep up. When we skipped, using a long rope held at each end, we put little Wei-guo safely out of harm's way until we needed him again to be our 'child'.

My parents often took us to Xuanwu Lake Park. It had been established for many generations, but Father had transformed it into a place suitable for ordinary people. There they could relax and breathe clean air. The main feature of the park was the lake but Father had paths laid and covered walkways built with places of refuge for when it rained. He replanted it, and had the ruined remains of the zoo rebuilt and stocked with animals from other zoos in China. He also had the lake's five islands made accessible by repairing the ruined bridges. There had once been a splendid aquarium, so Father had that rebuilt and restocked. It was a big favourite among us children. Sadly it was ruined again during the Cultural Revolution.

I loved going to the park. We would be put into a boat on the lake and Father would row us out into the middle. I used to enjoy trailing my hand in the water, trying to see the fish lurking below the surface. The lake had always been a good source of fish for the city. When Father got tired of rowing, we would tie up alongside an island and have a picnic. We children would be allowed to run off to explore while our parents lay back on the grass. Little Wei-guo usually had a nap, but if he was awake he wore reins and was safely anchored in the grip of an adult.

Later we would drift back to shore, and cross the bridge to the zoo. I didn't much like the smell of some of the animals, but I loved looking at the monkeys and laughed at their antics. Andong was fascinated by the crocodiles and alligators. She would wait for one to open its mouth so that she could shriek at the sight of its teeth. The aquarium always came next. Mother would point to the top of the door. 'Look. Your father wrote that,' she would say, and we would stop, dutifully but impatiently, and look up before scampering in to gaze at the fish. There were all kinds of fish in the aquarium. I loved the small, multi-coloured ones, especially if they had long feathery tails. But every tank had something of interest to me. I think I preferred the aquarium to all the places we visited. I hated to leave and would turn for one last look before being hurried away.

On the way to the park, we used to stop at the Jiming (Cock Crow) Temple. I think Mother, who professed not to be interested in any religion, felt a spiritual need. Religion is a strange thing: governments and political movements ban it and people declare themselves non-believers, but at the first chance, the churches and temples fill again. In China today, there are well over four million practising Christians, and millions more visit the temples for spiritual sustenance and inner peace.

In the Cock Crow Temple, Buddhist images were ranged around the wall. All the statues were handcrafted and centuries old. In the centre of the temple was Sakyamuni, the Chinese god and founder of Buddhism. There were frightening statues too: images of devils and ghouls looked down from the walls, baring their fangs and waving swords held in their claws. They were the soldiers of hell, waiting for the wicked to come into their clutches to be taken deep into the ground and fried in boiling oil. The Buddhist hell is much like the Christian one.

Until I was five I stayed at home, looked after by a maid. She was a widow with a daughter and the whole family called her Mother Yang. She had been sent to work in our home by the government employment agency shortly after we moved from the Orchard, and her wages were paid directly to her by the government. This was the way things were done in those days. Everything was supplied to us free, such as food and clothes, according to an allowance system. My parents, along with all officials, were given a small amount of pocket money, which was more than sufficient for their needs. All living expenses were paid by the State. We also had a cook, the car and the driver, all paid for. In 1954, though, the old supply system was abolished and replaced with salaries. This meant that my parents had to pay for Mother Yang and the cook. The car and the driver were considered a necessary requirement for work, so they were still supplied by the government. Under the new system, we couldn't afford to keep the cook, so at my parents' recommendation he became chief cook in the restaurant at Dr Sun's Mausoleum.

Mother Yang took over the cooking as well as caring for us children. My parents arranged for her daughter to live with us and to be given a place at the local school. Mother Yang was so grateful for this that she told Mother she wanted to be a servant at our house for ever. She said she would never marry again and intended to remain loyal to her dead husband. This was the old Chinese way, highly praised by the people. Because of this, my mother decided to treat Mother Yang and her daughter as part of our family. She was trusted to run the household and to manage the family finances. Both Mother and Father handed over their salaries to her and she arranged everything for us all. She managed to save some money every month after paying all the expenses and keeping us well fed.

When I was five, Mother Yang complained that she was finding it difficult to care for my brother and me as well as looking after the house. Mother said it was time I began my journey into education anyway, and I was sent to a boarding nursery.

I did *not* like the nursery. I *hated* the nursery! During my first day, I pencilled a lovely picture on the newly whitewashed wall. This, of course, greatly annoyed the 'aunties', as we had to call the teachers. My first lesson that morning had been to draw ducks and chickens on white paper but I decided the fresh white wall needed a nice picture too. I didn't understand that the wall would have to be repainted and that I was being naughty by drawing on it. I couldn't understand what I had done. And why didn't Mother want me any more?

Of course I was punished. An auntie told me to stand on a chair in the corner of the room, facing the wall. I was made to stay there for over an hour. It seemed like years. I had never been punished before, and tears filled my eyes. I tried my best to push them back and keep my sobs from being noticed. I had been taught that a good child must not cry, and I had always tried to be a good girl. I felt homesick and miserable in the nursery, like a little bird in a cage.

The next headache for the aunties was my fussiness about food. Beef and lamb, for example, were left in my bowl, and when forced on me, ended up in my lap or on the floor. All in all, it could be said that I was a most difficult child and eventually the aunties decided to send me home. The senior auntie suggested to Mother that I be enrolled into a daily kindergarten near my home. It was run by the Nanjing Municipality and only children of high officials were admitted. My mother agreed to this, and I was taken there every morning and returned home every afternoon. I was happier with this new arrangement and quickly settled down.

During summer and winter vacations, the kindergarten closed and I stayed at home. At these times we were all there, Pei-gen, Andong, Wei-guo and me. Andong, Wei-guo and I played in the courtyard together. Sometimes other children joined us, but never Pei-gen. She was a solitary child and usually spent her days alone, reading or simply staring into her own private space.

Every morning, Mother gave us drops of fish-liver oil to make our bones strong, but I hated taking it. Mother had to coax me with a sweet in one hand as she spooned the oil into my mouth with the other. It soon became a habit that every time I took medicine, I had a sweet immediately afterwards.

I hated milk too. I remember one particular afternoon when, after my nap, Mother Yang brought milk to me as usual and told me to drink it. She had to see that I drank a bowl of milk every day. I disliked the smell and taste of it. Of course I did not know that milk was a precious commodity in China and that only a small number of children had the good fortune to drink it. Mother Yang had to be patient with me, and every day we had a battle of wills. She usually won, but on that afternoon I flatly refused to drink the milk.

I began to negotiate with Mother Yang, saying I would only drink it if I could have it out of a plate similar to one that hung on the wall with a picture from a fairytale. I thought I was being very clever: Mother Yang could never agree to this, and I was right. She said she had never heard of milk being poured into a plate, but I was adamant. 'Like that,' I said, pointing to the plate on the wall.

'Nonsense!' said she. 'Please, Little Flower, drink your milk.'

I began to cry hard. I was an expert at crying hard. 'I want Mummy!' I yowled. Poor Mother Yang, what could she do? Nothing, and I knew it. But, to my surprise she grabbed my hand and took me to the lavatory next door to the kitchen and locked me in.

Oh, how I cried! Loud, louder and then louder still. I lay on the floor, banging my feet on the concrete until my shoes flew off, bawling at the top of my voice. By now, temper was in control. After the temper came self-pity and I cried hard for over two hours until I was exhausted and fell into a fitful doze. I woke up the moment I heard Mother take her first step into the hall and immediately started crying again to attract her attention, while wiping my dirty hands over my face. I knew exactly what I was doing and made as much noise as I could. She rushed to the lavatory and opened the door to find me sprawled on the floor, with swollen eyes, black face, snotty nose, bare-foot and in a crumpled dress. I was in a very sorry state.

Mother bent down and took me into her arms. To my delight, she sternly admonished Mother Yang, saying she must never do such a thing to me again because it might damage my health. The milk was not drunk that day, and Mother Yang never dared to punish me in that way again.

Unlike my mother, who had a soft spot for me, Father had no favourite child. He loved all of us equally. He had a flute (a typical Chinese musical instrument), and he liked to play it after dinner. We used to enjoy sitting on our stools listening to him, especially when we knew the tune and could sing along. I was three when I first noticed his little finger was missing and asked him how it had happened. He just smiled his loving, sweet smile and said, 'You are too young to understand, Little Flower. I will tell you one day when you are older.' It became a big puzzle to me every time I watched him playing the flute. He had wonderful hands, strong with long fingers, spoilt by the gap where the little finger should have been. Eventually, during one of his evening recitals, I just had to ask the question again.

Father still didn't want to tell me but he finally explained that he had lost it fighting against the enemy during the war. That satisfied me, and I felt proud to have a father who was such a hero. He must have been very brave to endure such great pain. I knew the story of the scars on his body and neck, and to lose a finger as well made me even more proud of him. I loved my father's hands. I loved the look of them and I loved the feel of them when he caressed me. I didn't learn the truth about his finger until after the death of my mother when I read their diaries and autobiographies. The latter were long reports about themselves, a mandatory requirement of all Party leaders.

One day, instead of coming home in the car, Father arrived on an old British-made Royal Enfield motorcycle. He drove into the courtyard in a cloud of smoke with a roar from the noisy engine. He had persuaded the transportation department to let him have the ageing machine. It was noisy, smelly and smoky at first, but after he and Uncle Jiang from next door had worked on it with the help of Father's driver it sounded much better. It was still smoky and smelly, though, so we named it 'the Farter'. Every evening after work, Father rode it in a big circle around the courtyard. He often let Andong or Pei-gen ride on the big seat behind him, their arms tightly wrapped around his waist. Of course, I, too, wanted a ride, so Mother lifted me and sat me behind my father. Unfortunately the moment the engine started and I could feel the vibrations under my bottom, I lost my nerve and screamed to be taken off. Father encouraged me many times to have a ride, but I never overcame my fear. Instead, he would pick me up and run around the courtyard with me on his shoulders.

On Sundays, he would take Mother into the city on the Farter for some shopping. They always returned red-faced, grimy and happy, with presents for everyone. We all adored our father and he adored us. Those were happy days in my golden childhood.

Father had a pistol. All the high-ranking civilian leaders were issued with one by the People's Government. They were issued purely for defence purposes and were to be used if ever a class enemy attacked the house. Mother was puzzled by this because she had never had any trouble and neither had any of her friends or comrades. Father agreed with her, but he had been issued with the pistol and that was that. Neither of them expected to use it: there was almost no trouble in China at that time. Father wrapped the gun in a scarlet silk square and slipped it into the dark brown leather holster issued with it. Then he tucked it well out of reach of us children at the back of the top bookshelf. Every Sunday he cleaned it, checked the bullets and put it back on the shelf.

One day, Father came home early, his face twisted with fury and his lips bloody from biting them. His face frightened us and we kept well out of his way. We had never seen him like this before. He strode to where the pistol was kept and lifted it down. His face was white and his cheeks quivered with anger. He took the pistol from the holster and, through gritted teeth, the cheek muscles showing sharply on his thin face as his teeth ground together, he growled, 'I could kill the lot of them, the bastards!' He banged his fist on the table. 'Japanese devils! They deserve to die. The whole lot of them. It was a pity those atomic bombs didn't finish them all off!'

He sat down, still holding the gun, and slowly the fire left him. His head sank to his chest. Little Wei-guo and I peeped at him through the partly open door. After a short time, my brother toddled into the room, not understanding that Father was upset, and stood unsteadily looking up at him. Father lifted his head, saw me at the door and called me to him. Then he crushed us both to his chest so hard that little Wei-guo squealed, and squirmed to be set free.

Silently he sat us on his knees, kissed us both and nuzzled his face in our hair. 'That can never be allowed to happen again!' he said, half to us and half to himself. Then he let us go and we scampered away, happy that he was not angry with us. He stayed in the same position until Mother came home. She found him so deep in thought that at first he did not notice she was in the room. She kissed his cheek lightly, knowing something was wrong, and waited for him to tell her. That was her way and she understood my father better than he did. She stroked his hair, saying nothing. Later, after he had replaced the pistol, he began to tell Mother what was wrong. The memory brought tears to his eyes and he had to stop from time to time to control himself.

That morning he had been driven to the western suburbs of Nanjing to inspect a building site for a new factory. The area had been cleared and the foundations were to be sunk that day. As the workers dug into the earth, a number of bones and skulls began to appear. They called Father over and asked what they should do. There were about a hundred men digging by hand, plus a bulldozer. By the time Father had given the order to stop work, it was obvious that adults, children and babies had been buried there. Father went to the nearest government building to make some telephone calls and had the old records checked. After a while he was told that the building site was where one of the 'Ten Thousand People Pits' had been dug by the Kuomintang government at the end of December 1937 to bury the victims of the 'Nanjing Massacre'. Father had heard about this but the shock of coming across the horrific remains was almost too much for him.

Nanjing fell to the Japanese on 13 December 1937 and immediately became the scene of one of the most infamous episodes in modern world history. It started when two ordinary Japanese soldiers made a bet, just for fun, and launched a 'slaughter competition' to discover which one could behead the most Chinese in a single day. From dawn to dusk, the two soldiers toured Nanjing and beheaded any Chinese they found, man, woman or child, then counted the heads. The winner on the first day scored 101, the loser 99. The following day, the Japanese press ran the story but made the two men heroes: single-handedly, they had killed two hundred Chinese in the battle for Nanjing.

The next day, every Japanese soldier in the city went on a barbarous killing spree, with the full knowledge and permission of their commanders. They slaughtered countless thousands of civilians and Chinese prisoners-of-war. Headless, mutilated bodies lay everywhere. They raped many women, even the corpses of the women they had killed. If a woman was pregnant, she was raped, kicked in the belly then stabbed to kill the baby before she was beheaded. Sometimes the woman was killed and then beheaded. If her stomach was still moving, her Japanese murderer would insert his sword into her vagina and slice the unborn baby to pieces.

Every Chinese, of any age, was a target. Nanjing was filled with Chinese terror, drunken Japanese laughter and the stench of death.

Within two weeks, an estimated 300,000 innocent people had been killed and twice as many badly injured. At the end, bodies were piled one upon the other, and the streets were red with blood. Heads had been used as footballs. The whole of Nanjing stank of decomposing corpses.

The Japanese high command issued a 'surrender or die' warning to the Chinese, using the massacre as a threat of worse to follow. They expected the Chinese to capitulate, but the inhuman treatment of the citizens of Nanjing made the Chinese nation boil with rage. From that time on, there was no doubt that the Japanese would be defeated.

The remnants of the Kuomintang government still in Nanjing organized the burial of the bodies in the Ten Thousand People Pits – although over thirty thousand were buried in each. They also issued secret instructions to the intelligence department: the two soldiers who had instigated the massacre, their commanding officer and others who had been directly involved were to be kept under constant close surveillance. The Chinese would exact revenge for their crimes after the Japanese had been defeated.

When Mother found Father deep in thought, he had been planning a memorial hall to be built on that site. All work on the factory had now stopped, and the human remains were reverently reburied where they lay. He spent a long time putting his ideas down on paper before he submitted them. I can remember how pleased he was when they were approved. However, because the Korean war cost so much, they were shelved, due to lack of funds. It was not until twenty-four years after his death that work began. The building was completed and opened on 15 August 1980, the thirty-fifth anniversary of Japan's surrender at the end of the Second World War. It is called the Nanjing Massacre Memorial Hall. On its walls are photographs of the Japanese soldiers, who had been executed in 1946 as war criminals.

4. The Death of My Father

My father was often away. I hated it when he wasn't at home, but he had to go. His position called for him to attend meetings in Beijing or other cities, or to tour the increasing number of construction sites in and around Nanjing. When he was away the house seemed unusually quiet: he was always full of fun, and ready to play games with us and any other children who happened to be around.

He enjoyed driving. He often changed places with the driver of his official car: Father would wear the chauffeur's cap and let the chauffeur sit in the back seat, especially when they were going on a long journey. One evening, as I was being escorted home on foot from my kindergarten, Father, in the cap, stopped the car, put me in the seat beside him and drove me home. It was the sort of thing any father would do for his child, but I enjoyed the unexpected ride. In the enclosed car, I could smell him: he had a nice smell, of tobacco, beer and shaving soap.

The next day, Father was requested to go to the office of the deputy mayor. Such a request is more like an order so he lost no time in presenting himself before his old friend and neighbour. It turned out that my teacher had reported him for picking me up. He was told that it was a misuse of the car and was warned not to do such a thing again. The teacher had also reported that he was spoiling me by letting me ride home, and he was criticized for that too. It was only when I read his diary that I understood why he never picked me up again. I remember he passed me in his car several times, waving, and was puzzled as to why he didn't stop.

Such spying and reporting was commonplace in China. A whole network of 'unseen eyes' had been put in place and every citizen was encouraged to report any odd behaviour they observed in others, however innocent. Many people delighted in being informers, as it often led to promotion, sometimes inventing stories about colleagues and neighbours simply to curry favour with their leaders.

One afternoon in April 1954, when I was five, I was playing 'house' in our living room. I was engrossed in my make-believe world when an old man dressed in a long, dirty black gown came into the room. He looked tired and hungry, which frightened me. At the moment he appeared, I was about to have a villain break into my 'house' and the unexpected appearance of this wrinkled face, like dried bark, made me scream for help. He was a kidnapper or a class enemy or something, exactly as I had imagined such a person would look when my mother warned me about them. I never dared speak to strangers because she had repeatedly told me not to. Even someone offering good things to eat must be ignored.

The old man took some biscuits from his pocket and held them out to me. 'Don't be afraid. I am your grandfather. Your father is my son. I have come here to see him.' I didn't take his biscuits. I just looked at him: he didn't seem so bad now that I was gaining my senses, but I was still very frightened and began to cry. Mother Yang came from the kitchen and took the old man to another room. I stayed put until Mother came home.

She arrived at her normal time that evening, and for the first time met her father-in-law. Father came much later. He had been very busy that day, working in the suburbs, and when he got out of his car the weariness showed on his face. Mother had given the old man a good dinner and he sat waiting for his son. I was getting used to this stranger, and Mother had confirmed that he really was my grandfather. I eyed him with great curiosity. I had never seen anyone dressed in a long black coat before, but I had seen them in films: they were always the bad people, despotic landlords, class enemies and the like, so I was still uneasy when I went to my bed.

I was awakened by loud voices. It must have been around midnight. Frightened, I got out of bed and ran to my parents' room. I found them sitting on the end of their bed and the old man lying down. Father, clearly upset, had his back to me as he spoke loudly to his father. I moved closer to Mother, who gave me a quick hug before she sent me back to bed and shut the door. The next day, Grandfather left our house.

Many years later, my uncle, Gao Dao-lin, told me that as my grandfather was a proven despotic landlord, all of his lands and business interests had been confiscated. He would have been shot, but escaped such a fate because his son, my father, was now a senior cadre and an important member of the Party. Grandfather had left his home town and had come to throw himself upon the mercy of my father in the hope that he could live with us.

My father could not allow the old man to stay. He felt honour-bound to uphold the Party discipline, and he also believed he must be loyal to the Party in everything. This was his principle, above all. Many years ago he had severed all links with his exploiting-class background and his father in particular. He said to my grandfather: 'You know I am a Communist Party member so I cannot do anything for you. Otherwise I will be punished by the Party. All I can do is advise you to return to Shucheng and accept whatever reforming treatment the local people and the Party leaders give you.'

I also heard him pacing up and down the room. In his diary he wrote that it was against his nature to refuse help to anyone, but this man, his father, had been a bad landlord and cruel to his workers before 1949, and had been declared a class enemy by the Party. My father had to adhere to the Party's principle and not keep contact with him. 'I'm sorry, but you must go now.' With these words, my father left the room and the house, to stride along the road as fast as he could in his haste to escape his past.

Mother allowed the old man to stay one night and then, after giving him a good breakfast and packing him some food, she sent him on his way with as much money as she could find. (She never told Father about the money.) She explained to him that someone of such importance as his son was not allowed by the Party to keep an ex-landlord parent at home. She suggested that he go to his eldest son, Dao-lin, who now lived and worked in Wuhan at a job found for him by my father. Before leaving, my grandfather stroked our heads and that was the last anyone heard of him.

He never arrived in Wuhan, and it seemed as if he had disappeared off the face of the earth. Uncle Dao-lin tried to find him; he even placed an advertisement in a newspaper asking for news of him but without result. Later, we heard that the body of an old man had been found in the shallows of the upper reaches of the Yangtze River. He had been dressed in a long black coat and was presumed drowned.

In 1954 Mao launched another of his political campaigns. This time, every State-owned industrial and commercial organization must receive 'socialist reform', and all privately owned businesses must now be 'joint' enterprises, which meant that they were nationalized and now owned by the State.

In 1955, when all businesses were nationalized, the trade unions increased in importance in their role of protecting the rights of workers.

They began to exert real influence as more and more companies were taken into State-ownership. A national conference was held in Nanjing with delegates from all over China. Among them was Father's great friend from the old days, Sister Fu. It was an emotional time for him. After eighteen years, he was to meet his mentor again. I can remember his nervous excitement. Clothes were washed and ironed, shoes were cleaned, his cap was brushed. He even purchased a new razor, shaving brush and soap. Mother Yang enlisted two of her friends to help spring-clean the house and the courtyard.

We children looked angelic in our freshly washed clothes. Even Pei-gen consented to wear a red ribbon in her hair. The excitement was beyond words as Sister Fu stepped out of the sparkling limousine, the door held open for her by Father's driver, who also looked smarter than ever before.

I can remember it as if it happened yesterday. My parents were so happy, Father in particular, as they welcomed Auntie Fu, as we children called her, into our home. She was a lovely lady of about sixty, but looked younger, graceful and charming, with a kind face. She was always smiling and she spoke beautiful standard Mandarin. Mother took to her straight away, and Pei-gen adored her. Auntie Fu was one of the few people she could relax with.

We all went with Auntie Fu to visit the Mausoleum of Dr Sun, and took many photographs. In every one, there she was, smiling her gentle smile, with one or other of the family. Whenever he could, Father held her hand. He owed her such a debt. It had been she who had persuaded him to help the Party and, later, to travel to Yan'an where he finally joined the Communist cause. He thought of her as his guide and his saviour. Everything he had become, everything he had, including us, he owed to her.

Some months after her visit, from December 1955 to January 1956, Father was at an important gathering of the highest officials in Jiangsu Province, followed by a study course lasting many weeks, which meant he had to stay in a hotel. He could only come home at weekends and would usually enjoy a hot bath followed by his favourite meal of Nanjing duck, vegetable dumplings, noodles and sweet and sour pork. One Saturday evening, while bathing, he found that the skin of his right thigh had become quite red and tender. He was puzzled. 'Look at this – I wonder what it is?' he said, holding up his leg for Mother to see.

My parents decided the pain and discoloration must be caused by arthritis because his joints had been giving him trouble for a long time. Father took little notice of his condition, other than to put on a pair of extra-thick padded trousers to keep his legs warmer before he left to continue his course.

By early February, after the course had ended, the pain was bad. It had increased steadily each day since he had discovered the red skin, so he went to have it checked in the Workers' Hospital, the best in Nanjing. The doctors there also thought it was an escalation of his arthritis and gave him heat treatment, which only worsened the pain. Soon, he could not walk without a stick. The heat treatment continued and the pain increased, until he could not walk at all. Luckily, a Russian cancer expert visiting Nanjing walked in one day just as he was about to have his daily dose of heat. He stopped the treatment immediately and suggested politely that the Chinese doctors take another look at my father. He strongly suspected that they were dealing with something far more serious than arthritis. Fortunately, he spoke in private, out of my father's hearing. By the time the doctors had looked again, it was too late. Bone cancer had spread all over Father's body.

His condition was reported immediately to the Party committees of Nanjing Municipality and Jiangsu Province. Mother was also told of the seriousness of his condition, but Father was not. By this time, he was in immense pain and did not argue when he was sent to Shanghai East China Hospital. He knew it was the most advanced hospital in China, with the best equipment and medical staff, reserved for high officials of the Party. He convinced himself that he would soon be back on his feet again in such a wonderful hospital.

During the journey to Shanghai, he was accompanied by my mother and his friend, the Deputy Mayor of Nanjing. The hospital had been told to give him the best treatment available to prolong his life. At the same time, the Nanjing Municipal Party Committee and the People's Government were finalizing arrangements for a grand funeral – he might die at any time. He would be the first of the leaders to die while still in high office, and as he had always been a popular comrade, Nanjing intended to celebrate his life by honouring him in death.

The truth was kept from Father right up to the end. Poor Mother – it was so very cruel for her to know that time was running out and have to pretend that Father would soon get better. Their suffering lasted until the end of July 1956. Mother stayed with Father in Shanghai until his last painful breath. Only then did she break down and cry. Her heart was broken in two.

While my father was ill, Mother Yang looked after us children. It was a sad time for us: never before had both parents been absent from home at the same time and for so long. Only Pei-gen appeared to be unaffected – but she just found it impossible to show her emotions. The trauma of her babyhood had damaged her permanently.

At the beginning life went on as normal, but it seemed empty to me, and I think Andong and Wei-guo felt the same. We didn't laugh much any more. At kindergarten, the teachers were particularly kind to me, but I didn't know why. Then, quite suddenly, things changed. Mother Yang started to leave the house early in the morning and not return until late at night, long after we were in bed. I used to wake up to the smells of cooking. Every night, after returning, she prepared a big pot of rice and a dish of vegetables. In the morning, she would feed us our breakfast from the food prepared the night before, then disappear, leaving us alone. Sometimes she left a small amount of pocket money to keep us quiet.

I remember her warnings about what we could and couldn't eat. Terrible things would happen if we broke those rules and her warnings always involved the things I liked best: she told us that the maximum number of ice-lollies we could eat at one go was three. If we ate four we would die. She also said that eating tomato after cucumber was dangerous. When mixed inside our bellies the two vegetables turned into poison, which would kill us.

The result of all her warnings was that I was in constant fear of eating things I liked, in case I died a painful death. I was miserable. Both my sisters and Mother Yang's daughter were at school while I was on holiday from kindergarten and could only play with my younger brother, who was now almost five. He, too, was unhappy. We wandered around the house, bored, listless and hungry. Our lives had gone to sleep.

One day, it was unbearably hot and I could hear the pedlar outside in the street shouting, 'Ice-lolly!' I went out and bought three for me and three for Wei-guo. I demolished mine in no time, and still felt hot and thirsty. I wanted more ice-lollies. The mocking sound came to my ears. 'Ice-lollies! Come and buy your ice-lollies!' I could resist no more. Out I went and bought another, but as soon as I had finished number four, I knew I would soon be dead. I sat down on the sofa, full of remorse, waiting for my punishment. First, I expected a great pain in my tummy as the fourth ice-lolly got mixed up with the other three and turned poisonous. I was sad at the thought of never seeing my mother again and I blamed myself for her unhappiness when she heard of my death. All my fault! But it was too late. I had eaten four ice-lollies. Why had I been so greedy? How stupid I was, I deserved to die. I waited and waited. One hour passed, then another. Nothing happened. I began to cheer up. Perhaps I wasn't going to die, after all. I determined to find out if Mother Yang had lied about other things.

The next day, I was prepared. Before beginning my life-or-death experiment, I had certain things to do. I washed myself all over and put on clean clothes. Then I did my hair carefully, with a nice red ribbon tied to each of my two plaits. If I was to die, then I wanted to look my best. Everyone would be sad when they found me. Such a lovely, clean little girl. What a shame she had to die.

After checking to see that my brother was playing safely, I went to the kitchen to conduct my big experiment. I was quite excited. It was a bit like an adventure because I did not know what would happen. Suppose Mother Yang had only been wrong about ice-lollies? Perhaps she had been right about the other things. But I had to know, I just *had* to know. By this time I had a large red tomato in my hand. I took a big bite. Oh! So tasty. The tomato was soon gone, quickly followed by half a cucumber.

I went into my bedroom and lay down on my back, arms crossed over my chest, hands resting on my shoulders, and closed my eyes. In fact I had been so wound up, I was exhausted and fell into a deep sleep. Of course, I awoke, feeling fine and refreshed. I was pleased. No, not pleased. I was triumphant. I had come back from the dead. I could now eat anything I wished, and I knew that Mother Yang had been cheating us all the time.

I couldn't wait to tell Andong and Pei-gen. Wei-guo wouldn't care much – he ate whatever was given to him. I was proud of my bravery. And, happily, my sisters were suitably impressed too. We were angry with Mother Yang, but I was happy from that time on because I could enjoy eating things without fear.

'Anhua, get up quickly, your father wants a photograph of you.' I was being shaken by the shoulders. 'Come on, Anhua. Get up! I have to take you all to have your photograph taken. Anhua! Get up!'

I opened my eyes, still half asleep. I couldn't understand what was happening. Why was Mother Yang getting me up so early? Why should I have to have a photo taken? We had plenty around the house. Another shake. 'Come on, Anhua. Get up and put on your prettiest dress, we are going to the photographer's. Please, Anhua. It is for your father.' That did it. I jumped out of bed and went to wash.

Later, we learned it was my mother's instruction to Mother Yang to have new photographs of us taken, to be sent to Shanghai for my father. He missed his family and Mother knew he would never see us again. My mother told me years later that when Father saw our photograph, he asked, 'Why are the eyes of my Little Flower so swollen?' He never knew that we had been shaken awake very early to accommodate Mother Yang. He looked at the picture for a long time, then held it to his chest before asking Mother to place it on the bedside cabinet where he could see it.

I was almost twelve before Mother told me the awful truth of those days when she sat and tended my father in his battle for life. She was calm at first, but soon her voice broke and the tears came. She had bottled up her anguish for almost five years when the floodgates opened.

Father was in constant great pain during his last days. Pain-killers had been administered for a long time and the dose had been steadily increased until they were no longer effective. He had torn the sheets as his hands gripped them, and he had gritted his teeth so hard that Mother could hear them grinding together. She was full of sorrow but could not show it to him. She had to force his mouth open to take out the false teeth that had replaced those damaged by the bullet for fear that he might break them and choke himself. In a lucid moment, Father told her the pain was like a thousand saws cutting his body into little pieces. To and fro, to and fro, each stroke searing through him. He asked Mother, 'Why is my arthritis so bad? I have never heard of anyone having it as bad as me.'

Mother choked back her tears and tried to comfort him. The cancer was so advanced she could not even stroke his head or hold his hand, because it hurt him. She felt helpless and her words seemed so inadequate. 'Hold on, darling, you will be all right soon.' As she told me of those terrible days, it was difficult to decide which of them had suffered the most, poor Father, enduring his pain, or my dear mother, so helpless, watching him die.

At the end, she was dozing when he cried out. She jumped awake. 'Oh, my darling,' he said, his eyes wide open, 'I cannot stand it any longer.' He gasped a deep breath, held it, then slowly it left his body.

His eyes were wide open as he died. His right leg, where the cancer had first started, was now two inches shorter than the left. He weighed just over thirty-four kilograms.

It was summer vacation, and I was playing in the courtyard when the news came. Uncle Gao Dao-jun, my father's favourite cousin, appeared. I was overjoyed to see him and cried out to my brother, 'Come, come! Uncle has come to see us.' I ran to him with a happy smile. Every time he came he gave us some sweets, so I was waiting to be treated as usual, but to my surprise there were no sweets this time. He bent down to me and put one arm around my waist and one around Wei-guo and said, 'You must be brave children, because I have brought you some very bad news. You will not be able to see your father again. He is dead.' He bowed his head, holding back his own grief. For a moment, I was stunned. I felt as though a big black hole had opened up at my feet, and I was falling into it. I flopped to the ground.

'Where's Mother?' came a small voice beside me. It was Wei-guo.

I looked up at my uncle's face. 'She is with your father and will be home soon,' he said.

Suddenly I was furious. I jumped up. 'No! It's a lie! Father is not dead. You adults are always cheating us.' I began to beat his chest. 'He can't be dead, he can't. He never said goodbye. You are only joking with us . . . Father wouldn't leave me.' I was convinced that he was playing a grown-up joke on us.

Uncle Dao-jun stretched out his arms again and held me tightly. 'I'm not teasing you, Little Flower. Your father really is dead. I'm sorry, so very sorry.' He clutched me to him and I laid my head on his shoulder, crying.

When Andong came home from visiting a friend, I was still under the tree, sitting on a stool. I looked up and told her, 'Uncle said our father is dead.' I saw her disbelief before she ran into the house. Later, I heard her crying in her room. Only my little brother, who was just five years old, was unmoved. He did not understand how serious it was to have lost our father. As for me, I hated the whole world, and Uncle Dao-jun in particular for bringing me this news.

A few days later, Mother came back, shoulders hunched, weeping uncontrollably. She was accompanied by groups of adults from the various government departments of Nanjing. From that moment, our house was crowded. I was quiet and obedient during those days, looking at my mother anxiously for signs of changes. I had never seen her so sad before.

Years later, she said to me, 'The death of your father was like an icy winter invading our warm home.' She felt very alone. Even we children didn't help her much. She missed Father's warmth, his humour, his love and his inner strength. 'Oh, Little Flower, you are so much like him. It breaks my heart to think that he will not see you grow up.' As we spoke, Mother said she still had his shaving things tucked away in a drawer and his favourite shirt, which she sometimes wore in bed.

Father had once confided to her that he liked western-style suits very much but, as a Communist, he had never had the chance to wear one. After his death, Mother told the Party organization about this and they decided to honour him by granting his wish. A new western-style two-piece suit, with a proper silk shirt and tie were made at the expense of the Nanjing People's Government and Father was dressed in it to lie in state, surrounded by flowers. Draped over the flowers were white ribbons bearing the black characters: 'Comrade Gao Yi-lin is immortal.' In the side pocket of his jacket were the last photographs taken of his family. He was just fifty years old.

My father died on 27 July 1956, still a relatively young man. Though Mother had known it was going to happen, she was not prepared for the tremendous sense of loss that enveloped her the moment he had gone. She felt guilty too because, in a weak moment, she had wished him out of his agony, just hours before he died. It was many months before she was anything like her old self.

She was then aged thirty-three, with four young children. Pei-gen, her eldest child, was still not twelve, Andong was nine, I was seven and Wei-guo was only five. She was at a loss about how to cope. Of course, she still had her government position and Mother Yang could continue as before, but Pei-gen was becoming troublesome. Her school had complained that she was difficult and a disruptive influence in class. Her teachers reported that her work was deteriorating.

Father lay in state for a week, and then a grand funeral ceremony was held for him. The coffin was transferred to the Revolutionary Martyrs' Memorial Hall in Yuhuatai (Rain Flower Terrace). The funeral was presided over by Comrade Peng Chong, the first secretary of Nanjing Municipal Party Committee. More than a thousand people attended the ceremony, including almost all of the officials and officers of the People's Government of Nanjing, and many of his colleagues from the army days.

The coffin had been transported from Shanghai to Nanjing by special train, escorted by the Party secretary of the Shanghai Railway Bureau, He Lin, who had been a fellow-fighter and townsman of my father. He broke the rules of the railway, which stipulated that no fresh corpses should be carried by train during the summer months. The coffin should have travelled by truck, but he arranged for an extra carriage to be coupled to the train especially to carry it. Years later, during the Cultural Revolution, this 'crime' was used as an excuse to brand He Lin a 'capitalist roader' and he was severely punished by the Red Guards.

I can remember the funeral ceremony with crystal clarity. Everyone was wearing a black armband. Peng Chong gave a speech and he was followed by several other important officials, including my uncle Gao Dao-jun. Mother did not speak – she was too weak – and was supported by our neighbour Auntie Zhu. I put my left hand into Mother's and held it tightly.

A special envoy from Beijing also made a speech. He had known my father in the old days when he had been a raw Party member, and he spoke of those times. He remembered how Father had progressed and the increasingly important part he had played in the success of the Party. He remembered the long hours Father had put in when he had helped with the propaganda work before he joined the Party. As he spoke, I could feel Mother stiffen with pride.

After the speeches, everyone filed past the coffin to pay their last respects, bowing as they went by. Some touched the shining wood. Others saluted. A few placed small white flowers on the lid. Many women comrades had tears streaming down their cheeks, and some sobbed loudly, or sniffled into handkerchiefs. I was a cry-baby, tears ever ready, but that day I had been told to be a brave girl and not cry. So why were so many adults crying? Were they not brave? Even Mother was sobbing as she shook hands with each passer-by. I felt numb inside, but later when the tears came, I cried continuously for three days.

When the last mourner had filed past the coffin, it was carried out to a truck covered with wreaths. An enlarged photograph of Father, looking young and robust, gazed out through the windscreen surrounded by black ribbons and white flowers. Before the column moved off, ten metres of white ribbon was unrolled. One end was attached to the front headlight and the other was held by General Sun Zong-de, the one-time goatherd, my father's greatest friend. Then another ten metres of white ribbon was unrolled and attached to the other headlight. The end of this ribbon was held by my uncle Wang Feng, who had risen from a gawky fourteen-year-old to become a general in the air force. I had not noticed him in the crowds and my heart jumped at the sight of him.

Brother Liu was there. He stood with the family, next to Pei-gen. Along one ribbon, holding it with one hand, were the family and along the other were the top leaders of Nanjing, giving the impression that the truck was being pulled forward by us and the leaders. The rest of the mourners followed behind. The driver's view was restricted by the photograph, the ribbons and the flowers, but the truck kept a perfect line and slow speed all the way to the Revolutionary Martyrs' Cemetery.

It took us over an hour to reach the graveside. A tomb had been built with an opening at the rear. The heavy wooden coffin was lifted off the truck by the bearers and gently lowered on to wooden rollers, then pushed slowly and reverently the last few yards into the tomb, with Father's head pointing towards the south. A large granite stone was placed in front of the opening and the tomb was sealed. At the front was a headstone carved with the words 'COMRADE GAO YI-LIN'S GRAVE' and in smaller characters, 'Erected by the Communist Party Committee of Nanjing'. On the reverse was carved a brief account of his life.

The funeral procession had been conducted in total silence, more moving by far than the usual bands, drums, rifle-shots and bugles. Silent funerals were approved by the Party. The traditional funeral music and ceremonial trappings were banned as being 'feudalist superstition'. That lasted until April 1975 when Dong Bi-wu, acting chairman of the People's Republic of China, died. At his funeral, a specially composed piece of music was played.

At their next formal meeting, the Party Committee of Jiangsu Province decided unanimously to recommend that Father be honoured as a Revolutionary Martyr: he was the first high official of the Party to die in Nanjing after 1949. He had devoted the majority of his life to the Communist cause and his commitment could not have been greater. He had cut his links with his despotic landlord father and the wealth that would have been his. He had suffered many hardships and had been wounded fighting against the Japanese. He had bravely led his troops in the battle for Nanjing and had distinguished himself in government, both in the army and as a civilian. It was considered that the long, hard years of privation prior to the founding of the People's Republic were the prime cause of his early death.

A report was sent to Beijing, and the honour was approved within a week. A certificate with the stamp of the Central People's Government was sent to my mother, in which these words were written: 'Comrade Gao Yi-Lin sacrificed his life to the revolutionary struggles and died a glorious death. His outstanding contributions to the revolution are immortal. All his relatives should be respected by the people, and his family should be cared for by the government.' It was signed, 'Mao Tse-tung'. Also, Mother would receive a third of Father's salary as well as her own to help in the raising of her children. My mother framed the certificate, and enlarged two photographs of Father, one taken when he was thirty and the other on his fiftieth birthday, just four months before his death. They were a metre high and she hung them on her bedroom wall on each side of the certificate with the old metal water-bottle beneath. She had them placed so that she could lie down and talk to Father, while his eyes looked directly into hers.

I have always been proud of my father, but one thing made me ashamed of him for a long time. It was the western-style suit he wore on his deathbed. Like all other children in China, I received a political education as well as a formal education. Even in the kindergarten there were politically motivated lessons. We were indoctrinated into the Communist ideals from an early age.

On my first day at school, and then every week, we were shown revolutionary films in which there were always stereotyped images and dress styles. The 'goodies' were always pretty or handsome: the girls had lovely figures and rosy cheeks, and the boys were tall and strong; they were always perfectly dressed and behaved openly and honestly. Then there were the 'baddies': 'despotic landlords' were either tall and thin with a hooked nose or short and fat with a big belly; they were always ugly with bad teeth, mean eyes and sallow faces; they dressed in long black gowns and wore a watermelon hat; they spoke behind their hands, or rubbed them together when about to swindle someone. 'Bandits' wore Kuomintang army uniforms over their too-skinny or fat bodies; they were bullies and usually quite stupid; they robbed, pillaged, raped and murdered without mercy. Later the uniforms changed to look more American, but the stereotyping was the same. 'Capitalists' had fleshy faces, big bellies and greedy eyes; they smoked cigars and wore western-style suits. Their only desire was to make money at any cost, even if it meant the death of others; they also worked their downtrodden and starving employees very hard, treating them with contempt. A three-year-old child could easily tell a goodie from a baddie.

I didn't take much notice of such things. I enjoyed the films and the messages seemed acceptable: good always triumphed and the fat/thin/stupid/cruel/ugly/greedy men, representing the Kuomintang/despotic landowners/capitalists/imperialist Americans/class enemies were soundly beaten by the pretty/handsome/brave/tall/healthy Communists, who had to overcome great odds before winning.

The stereotyping was brought home to me the day I showed a photograph of my father on his deathbed to my classmates. Suddenly one cried, 'Why did he wear a capitalist suit?' Then they all had another look and turned to me with accusing eyes. I quickly hid the photograph in my desk and said, 'My father is a revolutionary martyr and he is immortal. If he wore a capitalist suit, it must be for the needs of the revolution!' But I could see the doubt in their eyes.

I felt a great pain in my heart. Surely my lovely brave father hadn't been a capitalist? He couldn't have been, he had the certificate signed by Chairman Mao. I asked my mother to explain. She said it had been my father's dream to have a western-style suit and as a mark of their esteem for him, the authorities had allowed him to be buried in one. She said that the suit had no political connections. Nevertheless I was still ashamed. I stopped showing the photograph and hid it in a drawer, under my clothes.

When trouble comes, it comes and comes. The day following the funeral, Mother Yang announced that she had remarried during my mother's absence and wanted to leave. This was a big blow to Mother: if ever she needed help, it was during those first weeks after the funeral, but all her appeals to Mother Yang fell on deaf ears.

Now we knew why Mother Yang had been absent so much from our home and why she was in such a hurry to leave. She had spent all the money from my parents' salaries on her wedding and her own house. Poor Mother. She had no time to grieve and adjust to her new life. Of course, her superiors were sympathetic and gave her time off but it was a difficult time for her. Auntie Zhu came every day to help, and she suggested that Mother write to my grandparents and ask if they would like to come and live with us.

Mother thought it was a good idea, but before asking them she thought it would be sensible to check with her leader that it would be acceptable. Her parents had been landlords and belonged to the 'exploiting class', but fortunately my grandfather, instead of being branded a 'bad' landlord, was given the better title of an 'open-minded' landlord. This was in recognition of his help to the New Fourth Army. During the war against the Japanese, at great risk to himself and his family, my grandfather had allowed his house to be used for secret meetings between the New Fourth Army and their supporters. All these things convinced Mother's leader that it would be perfectly acceptable for her parents to come and live with us. Mother contacted her parents and asked them if they would like to move to Nanjing. Luckily they were delighted with the idea, and lost no time in applying for Nanjing registration, which was approved.

As soon as they arrived, my grandmother took over the running of the house. Unfortunately Father's car and the motorcycle had been returned to the transport department. Mother also handed back his pistol. Her father took charge of all the daily shopping and everything outside the house. My grandmother did the washing, cooking and cleaning.

By now, we children were used to looking after ourselves – we had been left alone so much by Mother Yang. We were all glad, though, when our grandparents came to live with us. Our step-grandmother was very good to us, and Grandfather did his best to make up for Father's absence. Pei-gen was as distant as usual, but now that our home life was stable, her schoolwork was back to a high standard. The absence of my parents had affected her more than anyone had realized.

My grandmother was a gentle, jolly old lady and I was very fond of her. I was fascinated by her tiny feet. They had been bound since she was a small child and were only about four inches long. In China such feet were known as 'three-inch golden lilies'. Every afternoon, she washed them with hot water and cut away any dead skin. Sometimes she cut her toenails, which had turned dark grey. I often sat on a stool beside her and watched.

She had long white bandages wound tightly around her little feet, and it took her several minutes to unwind them. Her feet were smelly, and only the big toes were straight. The others were bent and the little toes were stuck tightly to the centre of each sole. The back of her feet bulged out because the bones inside had broken long ago. Her calf muscles were underdeveloped, and her legs were very thin. She could only take small steps and she could not stay on her feet for long. I used to follow her when she was doing the cleaning, imitating her way of walking as she went from room to room.

There is no exact record in history of when Chinese women began to bind their feet. Some said it started during the Song Dynasty, about a thousand years ago, although my grandmother said the custom started around five hundred years after that. But one thing is certain: in ancient times, and right up to the Tang Dynasty, Chinese women had normal feet. They could walk, run and dance like any other female of the world. Then foot-binding came in and everything changed. Women could not walk properly, or dance or run, because they were in constant pain. Grandmother told me that in the old days people thought that the smaller the feet, the more beautiful the woman. From around four years of age, girls' feet were tightly bound with a long cloth to stop them growing. The first binding was left on the feet for two years without being changed. Only after the bones had broken and reset themselves into the required shape was the cloth removed and changed for another, tighter binding. During this time, the child was confined to bed.

My grandmother said that it was terribly painful and she cried all day long. Little girls had to be carried everywhere until they were twelve. Then they were allowed up, and walked like penguins, which was considered graceful, charming and sexy, like a beautiful, swinging willow, in the eyes of men. As they moved along, their feet hidden under their wide trouser-legs, they gave the impression they were floating.

In most families, marriages were arranged. The wedding day was usually the first meeting of husband and wife, and the first thing a groom did, just before the ceremony, was check the feet of his bride. If they were not small enough the marriage ceremony would end, no matter how beautiful the woman. Then she was disgraced, her future destroyed. No other man would marry her. Girls had only their husbands to rely on in those days. If a girl was not wanted as a wife, she was not wanted by anyone, even her parents. After the rejection of their daughter, parents lost considerable face, and as she could not work, they had the unwanted burden of feeding, clothing and housing her. Often, they encouraged her to take her own life.

Dr Sun Yat-sen, the highly respected reformist leader, realized how unfair to women foot-binding was, and made up his mind to put an end to it. He passed the law as quickly as he could after he took power following the overthrow of the last emperor in 1911. However, in China, old traditions take a long time to die, and in many rural areas foot-binding continued. The terrible tradition was abolished once and for all by the Communists after 1949.

5. The Great Leap Forward

A month after the funeral I was sent to school. All children aged seven and over had to go to school and I, as a member of a privileged family, went to one that was open only to children of high officials within the Party. My mother often told me that if it had not been for the war against the Japanese, she would have completed her education by going to university. She said, 'Now I must do what I've always done. Put the interests of the Party first, and devote all my life to it. Perhaps one of you will follow my dream. It would be nice to see at least one child, or all of you, graduate with a good degree.'

My two elder sisters were doing well at school. Now it was my turn to show Mother what I could do. I wanted to do well and I tried hard to learn. I did all my homework diligently. Mother never laughed or sang any more, and I wanted to make her happy. Towards the end of the first term I achieved almost full marks in all my examinations and was chosen by my teacher and my classmates to be the 'Three Good' pupil (good virtue, good study and good health). When I handed Mother my award certificate, her smile lit up my life. She sent me to school the next day with a satchel full of sweets to share with my classmates. In that first year Andong and I won the award three times, and each time Mother would smile and we would go in with sweets. But our success upset Pei-gen. She too did well at her studies but was never popular with her classmates.

Our neighbour Auntie Zhu often came to visit us, and Mother would proudly show her our award certificates. Auntie Zhu praised us and was pleased for Mother. She was disappointed with her adopted daughter Hou-pi, who had been put back a year because she failed her exams. She was now the tallest and oldest pupil in her class, and had become the class bully. She was a big problem for our neighbours.

When I was around nine or ten, I would run home from school as fast as I could. I always did my homework before beginning my 'real work', as I called it. First, I dusted, polished and tidied my mother's big writing table. Then I would sweep and mop the wooden floor. I always timed myself to finish just before Mother was due in from work while the floor was still wet so that she would praise me for my efforts. When she was late coming home, and the floor dried before she could see it, I would pour more water on it to let her know that I was a good child. This was my way of showing her love. Although I didn't know just how hard my father's death had been for her, I did know that she was heartbroken and needed love. Also I needed to see her smile, for her smiles were my happiness.

Mother made many of our school clothes and I marvelled as her fingers fashioned each new garment. As she slowly overcame her grief, her happiness in us showed in the brighter colours she used. The new clothes she made for me warmed my heart. Years later, I enjoyed them all over again when I put them on my own little girl.

In 1956, Mao uttered the famous words 'Let one hundred flowers blossom and let one hundred schools of thought compete.' This was his sign that people were encouraged to speak their thoughts aloud. In June 1957, when I was in the second term of my first year at primary school, the Anti-rightist Campaign began. Mao had tricked everyone. The one-hundred-blossoms speech had encouraged people to talk, and now he used those same words to persecute the speakers. We were told by our teachers that many bourgeois intellectuals wanted to overthrow our socialist system and the Communist Party leadership; therefore such people should be considered our enemies. As usual, a list was published, and we were told to hate the people named. Every day we sang 'Socialism is Good' and our teachers told us to report anything we thought might help winkle out the traitors.

Mother was particularly busy and was often away for several days at a time. She had to visit every factory and organization under her leadership to inspect the progress of the Anti-rightist Campaign. She often came home very tired with red eyes, and flopped into bed where I already was, waiting to snuggle up. It was on such a night that I woke up with a start and a moment of panic. Mother wasn't beside me. I could still feel her warmth, but where was she? Then I heard talking. I jumped out of bed, ever the nosy one, to see what was going on. In the next room, sitting at the big table, was a young man in army uniform, my mother and grandparents. The man's jacket had no epaulettes on the shoulders. They had been torn off. I was puzzled. Why was he crying? And why was Mother holding him?

I was shooed back to bed. In the morning, Mother told us that he was her third younger half-brother. His name was Zhou Ru-sheng and he had been branded a rightist by his senior officer in the army. One day he had said that we Chinese should not copy the Soviet Union in everything. Why couldn't the Chinese follow their own ways instead? That was all he said but it was enough for him to be branded a traitor.

In the 1950s, as Mao did not know how to develop the national economy, he gave orders that China was to copy the Soviet Union. He called the USSR the Big Brother of China and told us we must follow its lead in everything. The number-one foreign language for the whole nation to learn was Russian, and the PLA must follow the Russian system of military ranks. Young soldiers were taught to dance the Russian navy dance and to sing Russian songs. Zhou Ru-sheng was a twenty-two-year-old officer, and doing well in the army. He seemed to have a bright future. Then he was denounced as a rightist because he did not enjoy singing Russian songs and said so.

In the Anti-rightist Campaign, every work unit, including the army, was given a 5 per cent quota. This meant that in every factory, workplace, army unit, hospital, newspaper, school, university, in fact, everywhere, except in the countryside, the leaders had to brand 5 per cent of the workforce as rightists. Mao said 5 per cent of the people were 'rampant class enemies, actively planning to overthrow the People's Government'. Of course, it was difficult to dig out 5 per cent of the workforce and accuse them of being traitors, especially when there were no such people to find. Nevertheless, the leaders must fulfil their quota or they themselves would be branded rightists.

The result of this campaign was that many people, particularly the young who had yet to learn not to utter any criticisms, were branded rightists. The army and the universities were hard hit. Once a person was branded a rightist, he or she was dismissed from their place of work and sent to the poorest rural area to 'receive reform through hard labour'. The work was unpaid and thousands of kilometres away from any big city. Qinghai Province was one such place of exile.

My uncle Zhou Ru-sheng was one of the unlucky 5 per cent. Though his senior officer felt sorry for him, he had to fulfil the quota. My uncle was dismissed from the army. Before being exiled, he was allowed by his officer to pay us a last visit. Mother told him that she would never cut him out of her life. He meant too much to her for her to draw a line between him and us. 'Our door will always be open to you,' she said, as he left, 'and here you will always find people who love you.'

That was his last meeting with my mother and the last time he saw his parents. He was not allowed to attend her funeral when she died in 1961. When I met him again, thirty years had passed. Then he was finally exonerated and had his Party membership restored. His hair had turned snow white and his lined, weatherbeaten face showed the hardships he had experienced. He held a photograph of my mother and sobbed. He had gone away a young firebrand and returned an old, burnt-out wreck.

He was not the only one. Five per cent of the people working in the cities, plus the students and the military, amounted to more than two million people. Over two million innocent young men and women were sent into exile for believing Mao when he said he wanted 'one hundred flowers to blossom and one hundred schools of thought to compete'. Everybody in China had heard that speech and was glad to learn that freedom of speech was a reality. The unjustly exiled knew that it was not. Many of those ruined people had not said or done anything to offend. They had simply made up the 5 per cent quota.

The men were sent to one area, the women to another. They were taken by truck, and those who had not carried food and water had to go without on that long journey. When they arrived, they had to scavenge for food and to build some sort of shelter. Fortunately, the local people were kind and helped all they could. They had little interest in politics and were illiterate – which was the way Mao wanted them. They welcomed these strangers into their midst. In return, many local children and some of their parents were taught to read and write.

All the exiles had to wear black caps to denote their status as class enemies. My uncle remained single because no girl would dare to marry a rightist. He had nothing to offer: no status, no money, no prospects. Most of the married exiles lost their spouses by divorce and lost touch with their children because they were not allowed to correspond. Many killed themselves to escape their unhappiness. The Anti-rightist Campaign destroyed everyone it touched.

June 1 is International Children's Day. It is also the date I joined the Young Pioneers in 1958. I was nine years old and joining the YP was a reward for all my hard work. When I was given the red scarf to tie round my neck I felt very proud. We were told that the Young Pioneers were the reserve force of the Youth League and the Youth League was the reserve force of the Communist Party. Children were not allowed to join the Young Pioneers under nine. At fifteen, with good reports, they progressed to the Youth League. At eighteen, they could apply to become full members of the Party.

Every child applying to join the Young Pioneers had to be tested before acceptance. Those with poor class marks or bad-behaviour reports were rejected. As I had a good record at school I was accepted, and was in the first six in my class to tie on the red scarf. We were told that it symbolized a corner of our national flag, which was dyed red with the blood of the revolutionary martyrs. It was due to their brave sacrifice that we enjoyed such a good life. As my father was a revolutionary martyr, I was convinced that there was a drop of his blood in my scarf, so I treasured it.

After the Anti-rightist Campaign, the Chinese people had been silenced. Their enthusiasm for socialist reconstruction waned to almost nothing, causing great consternation in Beijing. In the spring of 1958 Mao decided to launch yet another campaign in an attempt to save his face and to revive interest in Communism. He called it the Great Leap Forward. He wanted to prove to the world how clever he was by building the Chinese economy many times faster than any capitalist country in the West.

He began by stirring up the people's interest and enthusiasm with such slogans as 'One day of Socialism can equal twenty years of Capitalism', and 'We must march into Communist society at the double. We must run at high speed to pass the US and British imperialistic devils.' His slogans quickly took root. The people awoke from their apathy. Everybody wanted to see socialism overwhelm capitalism.

In the summer of 1958, a few months after his launch of the Leap, Chairman Mao came to Nanjing to inspect work. Mother was then a Grade 13 official, a little above the rank of colonel. She, along with other high-ranking officials, attended the meeting, saw Mao and heard his voice live for the first time. She returned home happy that evening and her face was shining as she said to us, 'I saw our great leader Chairman Mao today!'

It was a great honour for our family, and his visit inspired us to follow his policies with enthusiasm. We all drank a cup of red wine at dinner that evening. Mother looked young and she sang us a song she had learned in the New Fourth Army, 'Get up, children of the Motherland . . .' I was delighted. This was the first time she had sung since Father had gone into hospital.

In the year of the Great Leap Forward, everyone was instructed to eliminate the four pests, flies, bedbugs, mice and sparrows. The first three we dealt with at home and handed over the dead bodies to the neighbourhood committee. In fact, we had no bedbugs or mice so we concentrated on flies and handed over dead ones in hundreds. We had to go outside to deal with the sparrows. That summer I accompanied Mother many times on Sundays when she went to the compound of Nanjing Municipal Government. We took aluminium mugs and spoons with us. Apparently Mao had read that sparrows ate a great deal of grain, which affected the annual yield, so that was why they were included in the list of pests. People were everywhere in the compound, sitting under the big trees, holding basins, metal lunch-boxes and anything else that could be used to create a big noise. All of us scanned the skies and whenever we saw a bird flying across, we shouted at the top of our voices and struck the things we held in our hands. As there were several thousand of us, the overall effect was a cacophony of sound. The birds were frightened by the noise and kept flying. There was no escape for them, because the whole population of the city and countryside was out, doing their bit towards eliminating these 'pests'. Finally, the birds fell to the ground, exhausted or dead. Those still alive were killed, the bodies collected and handed over to the neighbourhood committee for counting. All kinds of birds were killed in this way, and every one was counted as a sparrow. Cuckoos, crows, exotic migrators from other countries, swallows, whatever, all were killed and counted as sparrows. On rare occasions, a bird would be saved and sent to the zoo, but only a few. After this campaign, for many years we never heard the song of a bird in the city. There are not many birds around even now.

Of course, you will think, How stupid! What about all the insects the birds eat? But when Chairman Mao said we should kill the birds, we did it without question. He was always right. We, the people, followed him blindly, as we followed the emperor's instructions in the old days. Mao was our inspiration and our leader. We worshipped him as a god. The Chinese people were not allowed to belong to any religious group, so Mao became the focus of our spiritual needs. He wished it to be so, and it was.

The Great Leap Forward was much more than just killing the four pests: Mao called on the nation to increase production of iron and steel to an extraordinarily high level. He raised the slogan 'Catch up with Britain within fifteen years.' To the Party the tonnage of iron and steel symbolized the industrial strength of a country, and Britain was in the lead in annual output of these commodities. In the same speech, Mao had added, 'Everybody has a share of the responsibility for the fate of this country.'

The newspapers told us how we could all help. We had to collect as much waste iron as possible and send it to feed the furnaces, which were built everywhere in all shapes and sizes. Mother, as a leader of the Party organizational department, had to play a leading role so she contributed our wok. (It was not iron waste, but we had nothing else to hand over.) We found a few nuts and bolts and some bits and pieces of the old motorcycle and handed those over too.

Because people were donating so many of their domestic utensils, public canteens were set up. We had to eat there, too, because Grandmother could not cook without the wok. Soon, though, we got organized. Grandfather fetched our food from the canteen every day and we often went with him to help. Other families did much the same thing. Some had even contributed their stoves.

All over the city we saw the slogan 'Catch up with Britain within fifteen years.' The radio relayed the same message. We, the people, must do everything to help China catch up with Britain. At school, the teachers wrote the slogan on the blackboards. The roads had huge billboards that shouted, 'Catch up with Britain within fifteen years!' All public buildings and vehicles displayed it. Shops had it chalked on boards slung from the ceilings. Huge portraits of Chairman Mao looked down on us, with the slogan written underneath. It was everywhere.

I was curious. We Chinese had to catch up with Britain within fifteen years. Britain was the reason I couldn't enjoy my grandmother's wonderful cooking and had to eat the not-so-good food from the canteen. Where, I wondered, was Britain?

I stood on a chair at home, looking at a map of the world pinned to a wall. There was China in the centre, with the United States to the right. Our friend the Soviet Union lay across the top of China. I knew where Africa was. And Canada, India and Australia. All big countries. My searching eyes found Japan, Chile, Argentina, Mexico and lots of other countries. But where was Britain? I began to feel anxious. Perhaps it was the 'unseen enemy' they were always warning us to be wary of.

My mother came over. 'What are you looking for, Little Flower?' she asked.

'I want to know where Britain is but there is no such country on this map,' I replied.

Mother reached over my shoulder. Her pointing finger went upwards, almost to the top of the map, and way over to the left. It stopped on a little island near the margin. 'There,' she said quietly, into my ear. 'On the edge of the sky.'

The campaign to eliminate the four pests meant that the crops were ruined by insects the following year. Also, millions of peasants had been sent from the fields to produce iron and steel for the Great Leap Forward. There was little to harvest at the end of 1959 and no farmers to collect what there was. The result was a nationwide famine. During 1960, the vast storehouses of grain and other produce emptied and by the middle of the year there was nothing left. Officially, the years of 1960, 1961 and 1962 were known as the three years of natural calamities, and explained away by the Party as something that could not have been avoided. Everything was rationed. We had to carry many different kinds of coupons: for rice, vegetable oil, pork, sugar, eggs, soap, cigarettes, bean curd, toilet paper, coal, cotton, thread and cloth. Each person was entitled to half a metre of cloth per year, and a family of five had to pool their coupons to make one new suit for one lucky person. We also had indus-trial coupons, which included bicycles, sewing-machines, cooking-pots and so on. Some things were not on ration, such as kerosene and leather, but you could never get them. Everything was in extremely short supply. The 'Great Leap Forward' catapulted China back at least twenty years.

Patched clothes became the fashion. The more patches your clothes had, the more praise you earned from your leaders, for clearly you had kept to the revolutionary tradition of plain living. There is no doubt that some people put false patches on their clothes simply to be praised, but cloth was in such short supply that most didn't have enough to make real patches, never mind false ones. Some wives of high officials made clothes out of curtains that had been supplied by the State. During the Cultural Revolution, most of them were condemned as criminals for stealing State property.

In the countryside, the biggest shortage was food. Millions of villagers turned to begging in the cities because they were not given rice coupons, which were only issued to city and town dwellers. They were given permission to beg by the leaders of their respective People's Communes. They received certificates with the stamp of their local government, stating that their region had suffered a series of natural disasters and they had harvested nothing. A nationwide organization of professional beggars was formed. It still exists today.

Many of Mother's distant relatives, who had never contacted us before, suddenly began to appear asking for help. Anhui Province was the worst hit by the famine: millions had died of starvation, and cannibalism was widespread. First they ate the smallest children. If parents could not face eating their own they exchanged them with other families. Then they turned on each other. Finally, those who were left died anyway. Mother would help anyone from her home town by giving them our clothes and letting them stay with us for a few days.

It was upsetting for her, and my grandmother resented them: we had only the same rations as everybody else. She scolded Mother for her soft heart – but that was my mother: she always tried to help people, no matter how difficult it was for her and us. Eventually this was noticed by the local Party organization, and at a special meeting they decided to give Mother some extra rations. They sent rice and vegetables, and even some fish caught in the Xuanwu Lake.

However, the official line was that the country was prospering. The Great Leap Forward was trumpeted as a success. Iron and steel output was up by hundreds of percentage points. The leaders in the provinces made false returns, from which the government made out that the countryside was reaping bumper harvests. The radio was full of good news, praising the population for the way they were assisting the country to reach its targets.

The reality was different: China was heading towards bankruptcy. There had indeed been a tremendous increase in iron and steel production, but the quality of the products was extremely poor. In the countryside, those peasants still able to work the land couldn't because all the farming tools had gone – the metal into the furnaces, and the wood to fire them. Millions of trees had been chopped down and used as fuel for the thousands of home-made furnaces, so now the peasants faced another crisis: lack of wood for fuel and building. The leaders in Beijing knew the truth but dared not speak it for fear of incurring the wrath of Mao.

The Great Leap Forward was over before the end of 1959, and Mao had to act to stave off total collapse of the country. He appointed Liu Shao-qi to be chairman of the People's Republic of China in late 1959 while he remained as chairman of the Party and the Central Military Committee. The first thing Liu Shao-qi did was to announce an amnesty for prisoners-of-war. Old Kuomintang army officers and high officials were released as well as the last emperor, Pu Yi, who was assigned to work in the Imperial Palace Museum in Beijing as a documentation clerk.

Then Liu Shao-qi, with Deng Xiao-ping, attempted to develop the ailing national economy and pull China out of recession. In the cities, they rehabilitated former private owners of many of the factories and businesses that had been nationalized by the Party in 1955. In the countryside, more peasants were given plots of land so that – apart from their collective labour in the People's Communes – they could produce crops and vegetables for their own use. In some areas, Liu Shao-qi scrapped the collective State-owned communes altogether.

This policy resulted in a gradual improvement. Most of the peasants who had begged in the cities returned to their villages praising Chairman Liu. This made Mao jealous: he could not bear to witness Liu's reputation growing higher while his was in decline. Liu Shao-qi became Mao's target at the beginning of his Cultural Revolution. Liu's words about 'red capitalists' and his policy of giving the peasants their own plots became his worst crimes.

Everyone was involved in the Cultural Revolution. Nobody escaped, not even the peasants. Liu's partner Deng Xiao-ping was branded the 'number two capitalist roader' and the two men were condemned as 'holding the red flag to oppose the red flag'. They were imprisoned, but that was not enough for Mao, who also went after their families: Liu Shao-qi's wife and her family were branded 'blood-suckers of the people' and denounced as counter-revolutionary capitalists. The whole family, including distant relatives, were imprisoned and treated cruelly. Some died. The Deng family's fate was less severe because they were protected to some extent by Premier Zhou En-lai, who had been caught by surprise by Mao's attack on Liu's family but was better prepared to render assistance to Deng's.

It was raining as I left school. As soon as I stepped out of the gates, I heard a familiar voice: 'Little Flower!'

'Mother Yang! What are you here for?'

She was standing under a tree, holding a large open umbrella. 'I came to escort you home.' She smiled kindly.

I was taken aback. I was nearly eleven and I had been travelling forwards and backwards alone for a long time. I knew Mother Yang was not really interested in walking me home: she wanted something else.

It had been more than three years since she had left us and I had almost forgotten her. It was a shock to see her after such a long time. She moved alongside and held her umbrella over me. As we walked, she told me how much she had missed me, that she had never forgotten me and thought of me every day. I didn't answer. All I could think of was how she had left Mother in so much trouble and I did not trust her.

Mother was calm when she arrived home and saw her. Mother Yang immediately burst into tears. Handkerchief fluttering, she told us how her husband had died during the famine. She had been forced to sell everything they owned to buy a little food on the black-market. Now there was nothing left. Her daughter had deserted her and she was alone. She had always felt sad at having to leave us, but her new husband had insisted. She loved our family and her daughter had been unhappy from the day they had gone to their new life. She knew Mother was kind, so she had come back in the hope that she could be our servant again.

Mother did not say anything at first, except to be sympathetic about her husband. I hated the idea of having Mother Yang back with us. Somehow, from the day she left, the house had been brighter. As was her way, Mother invited Mother Yang to stay for dinner and gave her a good meal. Afterwards Mother Yang cleaned the table and washed the bowls. She was eager to do all the things she had done before, as if to say, 'Look, what a good servant I am.'

But it was too late. Mother did not mention the money Mother Yang had stolen, or her coldness before she left. All she said was that she could not afford a servant as well as having her parents living with us. Also, there was no room. She gave Mother Yang some money and wrote a letter for her to take to the labour department in the city. We children thought she was too soft. Why help this woman who had let her down so badly? But that was our mother. She could not bear to see people suffer.

Even during those difficult years Mother encouraged us to study hard. She bought as many books as she could, mostly simple Russian and Chinese folk tales, but some were of western origin and were a particular delight to me. These had titles such as *The Ugly Duckling*, *Snow White and the Seven Dwarfs*, *Little Red Riding Hood*, *Cinderella*, and my favourite, *The Little Mermaid* by Hans Christian Andersen. My imagination made me into a fairy with long golden hair and lacy wings, or a princess of outstanding beauty. Mother also let us see films. A cinema had opened near our home and the first one I ever saw was a cartoon, *A Little Red*

Rose, the story of Beauty and the Beast. I went to see it again and again. But one thing puzzled me. Although Mother openly hated the western imperialists, she loved their literature. She tried to explain it to me. She said every country has a cultural legacy that only the foolish will ignore. She had collected a complete set of Shakespeare for us to read when we were old enough (in Chinese, of course) and she took us all to see *Hamlet*. I loved the film, even though I didn't understand some of it. I was nine and it was my first western film with foreign actors, made in Britain. In years to come I enjoyed *Othello*, *Twelfth Night* and *Romeo and Juliet*. I loved western literature. My interest in the West grew: how could countries that gave us such lovely stories be capable of doing the horrible things of which we had been told?

Now that the cinema was open, my vacations were so much more enjoyable. Just before the beginning of our long winter and summer school vacations, our teacher handed out a list of films to be shown in those weeks. Children could go in at half the price of adults and I would tick off the ones I wanted to see (usually all of them). I could see a different film nearly every day. My sisters also made their selections. Mother checked that our choices were suitable, then went to the school and purchased tickets for Pei-gen, Andong and me. Wei-guo was still too young, but he came with us when we went together at weekends.

Andong and I sometimes went on our own, and Mother gave us twenty cents for the short bus ride and three ice-lollies each. Of course, being children, we walked to and from the cinema and used the bus money for more ice-lollies. Pei-gen went by herself. Sometimes we saw her sitting all alone in the darkness of the cinema, the light from the screen flickering over her face. On Sundays, if the weather was bad, the family sat round the table and played games, but never Pei-gen.

In good weather, we went to the park. Mother enjoyed having us run around her, and took pleasure in remembering that Father had planned it all. Pei-gen never came: she sat at home by herself, yet she resented us enjoying each other's company. We could not understand her, and as she grew older, the more complex she became.

During the 1950s most of the films were from the Soviet Union. Among them, *The Gadfly* and *How the Steel is Tempered* were the most famous. Each depicted the strong will of a revolutionary hero, fighting his enemy and enduring great pain but never giving up. In *The Gadfly* the hero fought against religion in Italy. We were encouraged to follow his example by dedicating our lives to the revolutionary cause. I still didn't really understand the difference between 'imperialists' and 'Communists', but I knew I hated the imperialists because I was a revolutionary successor and a Communist Young Pioneer.

From kindergarten onwards, children in China received a fair amount of their education with a revolutionary slant. The films we saw were no exception. The first film the school took us to see was *The White-haired Girl*. It was a bitter story of an eighteen-year-old girl named Xi-er. She was the only daughter of a poor tenant peasant who could not pay the high rent demanded by his landlord. Of course, she was beautiful, the peasant had a pleasing, old-man's face, but the landlord was tall and thin, cruel and ugly. The landlord wanted the girl and tricked the poor uneducated peasant into placing his thumb print on a document passing ownership of her to him. As soon as he realized what he had done, the father poisoned himself.

The girl was taken to the palatial home of the landlord where she was forced to do menial work and was raped repeatedly by him. She became pregnant and, in despair, ran away to the mountains. During the following months, she had such a hard life that her hair turned from shining black to snow white. Her baby boy was born in mid-winter and froze to death almost as soon as he took his first breath. She was found by the PLA (all handsome fellows) and cared for. The despotic landlord was arrested and shot.

This film had been adapted from a stage play, which was written and performed in liberated areas during the civil war. It is said that one PLA soldier was so moved by it that he shot the stage actor who played the landlord. He was forgiven his mistake, as he was 'full of class feelings'.

Our teachers told us that all the labouring people in the capitalist countries were leading miserable lives, exactly like the White-haired Girl. The lowest workers made up two-thirds of the population of the world and it was our duty to help liberate them when we grew up. We were told that Chinese children were the happiest in the world, due to the good works of the Party and Chairman Mao. We were shown photographs of poor American children dressed in rags begging in front of the Statue of Liberty. We believed that capitalist countries were hell for the labouring classes and that we were lucky to be living in socialist China under the Communist Party. Our leaders made Lenin's words 'To forget the past means betrayal' the motto for every school. The political propaganda soaked into our souls, so by the time we entered our teens we shouted, 'Long live Chairman Mao,' or 'Ten thousand years to Chairman Mao,' with conviction.

Our school used to invite veteran Red Army soldiers, who were full of 'great bitterness about life in the past and deep hatred for the enemies', to lecture us on their terrible lives before 1949 and their hard struggle when fighting for a new socialist China. They told us that the Communist Young Pioneers were their revolutionary successors and it was the duty of our generation to continue the fight to liberate mankind. We were the hope for the future. The poor and downtrodden of the world were relying on us. We believed every word and felt honoured to be responsible for freeing the world from the yoke of capitalism. It would be our crusade, guided by our great leader, Chairman Mao.

In May 1959, the chairman of North Vietnam, Ho Chi Minh, visited Nanjing. The day he came, the weather was perfect, dry, warm, clear and fresh. The political instructor of the Young Pioneers at our school sent for me before classes began. 'Go back home and put on your best clothes and return to me before one o'clock. We have an important task for you,' she said. She didn't tell me what the task was, but I obeyed, happy to be entrusted with something important. I rushed into the house, out of breath, and blurted out, 'Grandma! I have to change into my best clothes. I have something important to do for the school.' Imagine my surprise and delight when Mother appeared. 'What are you doing home?' I asked and ran to give her a hug.

'Oh, I have something important to do too,' she said, opening my wardrobe. She laid out a new pink jacket, which she had put by for the end of term, freshly washed and ironed navy trousers, clean white socks, black shoes and my red Young Pioneer's scarf. I looked colourful and smart as I returned to report to my leader.

Another girl of about my age, named Yang Sheng-lian, and I were taken to a large black car and ushered inside. I was puzzled. Where were we going? I turned questioningly to our political instructor. She smiled. 'Don't worry, Anhua. This is going to be a big day for you.' The car stopped and a young army officer got in. We were introduced, then he told us why we were wanted. 'You two girls have been carefully chosen to accompany our great Vietnamese friend Mr Ho Chi Minh when he visits the Mausoleum of Dr Sun Yat-sen. You may call him Grandfather Ho. If you follow the instructions of your political instructor and myself, you will be all right.'

As usual, I was full of questions and excitement but I kept quiet. I noticed, as we travelled through the eastern part of Nanjing, that the whole area had been cordoned off and our car was the only vehicle moving along the road. The streets were empty. The shops and restaurants were closed, and there was not a soul to be seen. I looked up at some windows high above us, and saw a curtain twitch. That was the only sign of life except for the soldiers standing to attention at intervals. I then noticed that from the rooftops armed soldiers were looking down on us.

The other girl and I looked at each other expectantly and smiled. It was very quiet in the car. I could hear the breathing of the officer and smell some sort of cologne. We drove through the Zhongshan Gate, into the suburbs. By the time we were on the approach road to the mausoleum, I was drunk with the beautiful scenery and the lovely day. A gentle breeze blew through the half-open car windows, bringing the fragrance of the flowers. I was proud to be a child of the New China, which, to me, was the best country in the world. I felt so lucky. I was going to visit Dr Sun's Mausoleum with Grandpa Ho, while other poor barefoot homeless children in capitalist countries were begging for food in the streets.

The car drew up at the foot of the long flight of steps and we climbed out. I always enjoyed visiting the mausoleum. This was where Father had worked during the first few years of my life. Our political instructor rehearsed us in what we were to say and do. Yang Sheng-lian wore a lovely lime green blouse, which complemented the pink of my jacket. We must have looked very spring-like as we stood side by side.

At exactly three o'clock, a big black shining limousine swept up to the steps, followed by four police motorcycle escorts. We just stood and stared. Two of the escorts opened the back doors of the limousine: an old man with a white goatee beard stepped out on one side and the governor of Jiangsu Province, Hui Yu-yu, appeared from the other. I knew him, he was a friend of our family, and when he saw me he smiled.

Our political instructor said, 'Look! Look! Who has come? It is Grandpa Ho!' Immediately we ran towards the old man. I was holding a big bouquet of fresh spring flowers and Yang Sheng-lian had a red Young Pioneer's scarf. I can still remember the smell of the flowers as I ran. I offered the bouquet to Ho Chi Minh while making a small curtsy. He took it, then bent down and kissed my left cheek. His beard tickled me, and I can still remember his eyes: they were a deep, friendly brown.

Yang Sheng-lian tied the red scarf around his neck and we both gave him a Young Pioneer's salute. 'Welcome to Nanjing, Grandpa Ho!' we said in unison. I wondered if he could understand us. To our surprise and delight, he replied in fluent Chinese, 'Good afternoon, my children! I am very pleased to see you.' Suddenly I felt very close to him. We walked, one on each side of him, up the steps.

He was only a little taller than I, but he looked healthy, with rosy cheeks. He was in his late sixties, but he climbed the steps like a much younger man. As we climbed the 392 steps, Grandpa Ho asked about our studies, and as we answered him he patted our shoulders and said, 'Very good'. Then, unexpectedly, he gave me a naughty, conspiratorial wink. I felt like I was his best friend.

When we entered the Memorial Hall, we stopped talking. Inside, visitors usually hold their breath in reverence and awe, and Ho Chi Minh was no exception. It was so quiet that we heard Yang Sheng-lian's hairpin land on the floor. Later, she told me she was afraid it had disturbed Dr Sun in his long sleep.

At four o'clock, we left the mausoleum and drove to the Yuhuatai cemetery to pay tribute to the sacrifice of the revolutionary martyrs. The Kuomintang government had always shot captured Communists there. It is said that every inch of the ground has been soaked with the blood of revolutionary martyrs. As we walked through the cemetery, I mentioned quietly to Yang that my father was buried there. Grandpa Ho must have heard, even though I had spoken quietly. He stopped and turned to me, his eyes full of compassion. 'Tell me, where is your father?' I pointed and he diverted his tour to where my father lay resting. He stopped for several minutes to read the inscription on the tombstone. 'Your father was a great man,' he said, and gave a low bow before continuing his tour.

When he had seen everything and asked many questions, we were led to a room where tea was served. Yang and I had slices of apple. Ho Chi Minh asked for a Chinese brush and wrote four beautiful strong Chinese characters in the visitors' book: 'Bi Xue Qian Qiu', which means 'Clear blood for a thousand years'.

I couldn't wait to get home that evening and tell everybody what had happened to me. I rushed in, gabbling my story, and stopped short when I noticed that Mother wasn't there. When she came home she, too, had a story to tell although, like mothers everywhere, she let me tell mine first. She listened intently, shedding a few tears as I described the events in the cemetery. As I came to the end of my tale, she hugged me to her. Then she told of her own day.

She had been one of the organizers of Chairman Ho's visit and her duty was to make all the arrangements for a grand banquet in his honour. As the 'hostess', she was seated between her friend the governor of Jiangsu Province, Hui Yu-yu, and the guest of honour. Ho Chi Minh was an excellent talker, and he soon had Mother at her ease.

Ho Chi Minh was a great friend of Communist China. But a few years after his visit, history was rewritten again by Mao and we were told that Grandpa Ho was not an absolute revolutionary in the international Communist cause – because he kept silent in 1963, when Mao began his open quarrel with the Soviet Union. Ho was criticized by our teachers during our political-instruction lessons for this, and we were told that he was ungrateful: he had received much help and support from China, and it had been expected that he would be a lifetime supporter of Mao.

I could not accept any of the things they said about 'my' Grandpa Ho. Whenever they spouted their propaganda, all I could think of was the afternoon I had spent with him, his mischievous wink. All the propaganda in the world could not make me think ill of Ho Chi Minh – but I did not dare say so.

On 1 October each year, the whole of China celebrates National Day, and in 1959 it was particularly special as that was the tenth anniversary of the founding of the People's Republic. All the towns and cities organized special marches and events to celebrate the great occasion.

That day, I was woken by my mother at five o'clock in the morning. I had been very excited the night before and tossed and turned. It seemed as if I had just gone to sleep. However, I jumped out of bed, washed, dressed and did my hair. My sleepy grandmother had to force a good breakfast into me before I was allowed to leave for my reporting point in front of the People's Government building. Ten of us had been chosen to carry a long, wide banner bearing the words, in red childish handwriting, 'WE ARE ALSO TEN YEARS OLD!'

We stood in the front row of our square, made up from ten rows of ten children. Behind our square were nine more squares of children, all ten years of age, making a thousand altogether. Each child was given two red balloons. We all wore our Young Pioneer uniforms of white shirt, red scarf, navy trousers, white socks and black shoes. We were all excited and proud to be aged ten. The girls were given a special treat.

The teachers came round to each of us and put red blusher on our cheeks, which normally we were not allowed to use. My long hair had been carefully parted into two plaits and tied with red ribbons.

The happiest child there was a girl called Guo-sheng (Born with Motherland). She had been born on 1 October 1949, at the very moment Chairman Mao had declared our new republic. And now she was going to be out in front, all by herself, holding aloft the flag of the Young Pioneers, leading the children. We all wished we could have been her on this special day.

At exactly ten o'clock, Beijing, Nanjing and the whole of China began to march. The processional order was the same everywhere. First came an enormous military band, led by a drum major swinging his mace. The brass instruments sparkled in the bright sunshine. Then came the guard of honour, a specially trained unit of the PLA, with brand-new olive green uniforms, gleaming boots and white gloves, doing small-arms drill as they marched in perfect symmetry. Following them was a square of red flags, held by ten lines of ten gymnasts and sportsmen dressed in red trousers and light blue vests.

After the lone ten-year-old girl, my square was next. We moved forward, heads high, backs straight, proudly holding our balloons and the banner. As we marched, we could see the crowds on the pavements clapping and cheering. The noise was deafening. Huge portraits of Chairman Mao were everywhere. Wherever we looked, he looked back at us.

A decorated podium stood in the central square of Nanjing, just in front of the bronze statue of Dr Sun Yat-sen. All the leading dignitaries were standing on it, waving or saluting, as the parade marched by. As we entered the centre of the city, we released our balloons at a signal from our teachers who were marching alongside us. We all shouted, 'Ten thousand years to Chairman Mao!' as we passed Dr Sun's statue. I had never before heard such a noise. It was exhilarating, and my feet skipped over the concrete. Everything seemed bright and sparkling and shiny.

I looked up and there on the podium was Mother, standing with the other leaders, smiling at me, tears of happiness running down her cheeks. I saw the governor of Jiangsu Province point to me and wave. I knew I was smiling broadly as I waved back.

The workers followed us. They released a thousand white doves into the sky, to symbolize that the Chinese are a peace-loving people. They were followed by the peasants, and then came all kinds of other people, dressed in their working clothes, depicting their achievements in building a new socialist China, many waving rings of flowers. We marched around the eastern part of the city, and ended up, two hours later, back where we had started in front of the People's Government building. As we approached the end of our march, we saw the last square begin theirs: the PLA infantry.

That evening, Andong, Wei-guo and I waited breathlessly for the fireworks to begin. From where we lived in Orchid Garden we had a perfect view, and as soon as the evening meal had finished, we took our chairs outside. At precisely eight o'clock the first fireworks climbed into the sky and exploded in a cascade of brilliant colours. I jumped up in delight and clapped my hands until they were red and sore. The fireworks were bright, noisy, smoky and colourful. The changing patterns filled my eyes with brilliance. A garden of red roses high in the sky was followed by yellow and green chrysanthemums, then white narcissus. Stars and streaks and crystals criss-crossed high above our heads, then a mixture of shapes. Thousands of small parachutes fell from the fireworks all over Nanjing. I was lucky enough to collect one that landed on Mother's hand, with a toy soldier about ten centimetres high hanging from it. I noticed my brother looking at it with 'I want it' written in his eyes, so I reluctantly gave it to him.

The fireworks lasted for over an hour. They changed the whole sky into a magnificent kaleidoscope of colours, which remained in the memory long after they had faded from the eyes. When the last colour had gone, I saw the full moon hanging above our house, spreading silver rays over the earth. The Milky Way seemed to be reflecting the long, watery surface of the Yangtze.

6. The Last Year of My Mother

In 1960 China was in great difficulty. Severe food shortages threatened the whole country, and my grandfather decided to use what he had learned about growing vegetables as a boy living in the countryside. He measured the available ground in our courtyard, then pulled out all the flowers and dug out the grass to make several little plots. It wasn't long before we were eating the results of his labour. We had tomatoes, beans, cucumbers and aubergines in summer, and cabbage, sprouts, turnips, carrots and potatoes in winter.

It seemed strange to me that no 'natural disasters' affected our courtyard, for our vegetables grew abundantly. My grandmother raised a few chickens and we ate all the cocks but one, then had a constant supply of eggs. I can see her now, hobbling painfully on her bound feet, chasing a bird or collecting the eggs. Soon, my grandparents were advising our neighbours how to make the most of their land too.

An increasingly large number of people in the city who lived in blocks of flats and could not grow vegetables or keep chickens began to suffer from severe malnutrition. Their legs swelled and the hospitals overflowed. People were starving to death before our eyes and there was nothing anyone could do to help.

A black-market sprang up all over China. At a price twenty to fifty times higher than in the State-owned shops, the fortunate rich could buy sufficient food to stay alive. This angered everyone, so when the famine was over and a slow but steady recovery from the consequences of the Great Leap began in early 1963, many of the black-market profiteers and speculators were arrested. Some were shot as 'saboteurs of the socialist economic order'. The rest were sentenced to between five and twenty years in prison. Many of those black-marketeers who were imprisoned in the early sixties have become rich businessmen today. They own many stalls in the street markets and they are doing exactly the same thing as they did during the famine. Now they are no longer considered class enemies but contributors to prosperity. They add about 20 per cent to the national economy, and the markets are flourishing everywhere in China.

Despite all our troubles during those years, however, we still believed we were living the best life in the world. News from outside China was fed to us through the propaganda machine. Those who had radios capable of receiving foreign stations found them jammed. Even so, if a radio was found tuned to a foreign wavelength, the owner was sent to prison for years. We believed everything we were told because we knew no better. For example, we knew that the people in the West were starving and dressed in rags. Only the rich had sufficient to eat and gangsters openly killed people in the streets. We cheered the success of the Soviet Union when they sent the first man into space: the Russian astronaut Yuri Gagarin was our hero and their victory was our victory.

We had no idea that most ordinary people in the West already had televisions, cars and washing-machines. Our political teachers said to us, 'With each passing day, we are growing stronger and stronger while our enemies are growing weaker and weaker.' Chairman Mao actually said: 'Rottener and rottener is the enemy.' And everybody knew that our enemy was the West, headed by the USA.

During those dreadful years, soap was almost non-existent, due to the shortage of raw materials such as industrial oil. When I was in grade four of primary school, the teachers gave every child six seeds from a castor-oil plant. We were asked to grow them anywhere we could, then hand over our harvest in the autumn. We were told that it was of the utmost importance that we did our best, because oil from the beans could be used to make soap.

My grandfather helped me choose a small plot in our courtyard. He told me I needed about three square metres of land because castor-oil plants grew so large. He showed me how to dig the soil and plant my seeds. I carefully made six small holes and placed one seed in each. No castor-oil seeds were ever treated so tenderly. Then I watered them, and watched as the water was absorbed into the earth. It was a solemn moment for me because this was the first time I had ever planted anything. And it was also important for my country that I gather a good harvest.

Every morning I ran out to see how my seeds were doing, and became worried when, after several days, nothing happened. My dear grandfather kept reassuring me, 'Don't you worry, Little Flower. They are there, under the earth, happily waiting for the right time to show their heads and say hello to you.' I began to use a small enamel pot at night and carefully poured any urine I produced equally over each place where a seed was planted. I waited, and waited, and waited.

One Saturday afternoon as I entered the house after a meeting of the

Young Pioneers, Grandfather smiled at me and gestured towards the courtyard with his thumb. I dropped my satchel and immediately ran out and over to my garden. Oh! Tender green seedlings! They were out of the ground and greeting me with two lovely little leaves. My happiness was beyond words, and only when I was called in for a drink did I drag myself away.

Grandfather helped me care for my 'babies'. He kept the plot free of weeds and slugs, and the plants began to climb towards the sky. In a few weeks they looked like small trees. Bean pods appeared at the end of June, and I began to pick them as soon as my summer vacation started in July. The plants were so strong that the pods kept coming. When the first harvest was finished, there came a second, then a third. The pods hung in bunches like grapes, but with hard dried shells. There were six to ten beans in each. I threw away the shells and kept the black beans in a big canvas bag.

It was a hot summer and caterpillars began to attack the leaves. They were colourful, fat and poisonous and they were munching my 'babies' away. I hated them! Sometimes, as I picked the ripe pods, the spikes on the back of a caterpillar pierced my skin and caused my arm, hand and fingers to turn red and swell. Grandmother used iodine to treat the infected areas. I was scared of the caterpillars, but it was important that I picked my beans because this task had been given to us by our teachers. Andong and Wei-guo often helped with the harvest, but Pei-gen never did.

The whole of that summer Mother was away in hospital because it had been discovered that she had heart problems. The doctors allowed her to come home at weekends, and whenever she could, she joined us in the courtyard to help pick the castor-oil pods. Her arms were often poisoned by the caterpillars but she continued to pick. When I touched her red, swollen arms and asked, 'It is painful?' she just shrugged her shoulders. 'It's nothing. I'm fine.' We used to laugh at the idea of the doctors wondering what she had been doing during her weekends at home.

In September 1960, at the beginning of the new term, I lugged my big bag of beans to school and handed them over to the teacher for weighing. The teacher checked inside my bag because she did not, at first, believe it only contained castor-oil beans. 'Four and a half kilograms,' she said. 'Well done.' She wrote down the amount in her notebook. Later that day the results of our harvest were announced in front of the school. No one had more than a kilo except me.

As my grandfather and I watched the castor-oil plants grow, our friendship also grew. I had always enjoyed being with him but our joint efforts cemented a special bond between us. To repay him for his help, Mother let me unravel an old black woollen shawl to knit him a long, thick scarf. By the time it was finished, he could wind it over his head, twice around his neck and still have enough to cross in front to keep his chest warm. I also knitted a pair of gloves for him. I worked hard on my gifts and had them finished before the cold weather set in.

When I gave my gifts to him at breakfast one Sunday morning his surprise and pleasure made the effort well worth while. He wore them every winter for the next ten years until he died. In return, he solemnly put forty cents into an envelope and handed it to me. 'Your wages, Little Flower, for knitting me such a wonderful scarf and warm gloves.' I was delighted. My first ever payment for work done. I bought ten ice-lollies with it.

We Young Pioneers had our own flag. The background was the same colour as the red of our national flag. There was a large yellow star in the centre and it was crossed by a yellow torch with orange flames. The star represented the leadership of the Party and the flaming torch meant joining the revolution.

Every Saturday afternoon, after morning school, we gathered in the playground for our weekly Pioneers' parade. I had been made a leader and held the flag aloft as I marched in front of the whole school, followed by three buglers and the drummers. I always felt proud to hold our flag. We would march around the playground for a while, making as much noise as possible. The flag would then be fixed firmly in place, and we would stand to attention before it. It must have been an impressive sight: over twelve hundred children standing still and quiet. As one, we would make the Young Pioneer salute – right hand over our heads with the fingers stiffly outstretched. The salute meant 'The interests of the people are above all.' Then we sang our Young Pioneer song. The last thing before breaking up was for all of us to raise our right arms with clenched fists to the sky and shout in unison the Young Pioneers' pledge: 'For Communism, we are always prepared!' After those meetings I was full of patriotic fervour. The philosophy of the Chinese Communist Party was deeply rooted in my heart and had melted into my blood. I worshipped Chairman Mao above everything, even my parents, and my country and comrades were the best in the world.

Nanjing is a special city in the hearts of the Chinese people. In addition to the Mausoleum of Dr Sun and the scene of the Japanese massacre, there are the killing grounds of the Kuomintang government. A very important political and personal activity for the Young Pioneers and the Youth League every year is the 'Sweeping Tomb Festival'. On 5 or 6 April, all primary-school and middle-school pupils march from the city to the killing grounds in the southern suburbs.

Yuhuatai Hill outside Zhonghua Gate has been a favourite leisure place since ancient times. There used to be many temples, and their bells and chimes were heard far and wide, but it was destroyed by war. After 1927 it was the execution ground of Chiang Kai-shek. Now the hill is covered by pine and cypress trees. People pay homage there to those who died for their country.

The children march to the Yuhuatai Revolutionary Cemetery. It is about five miles from the centre of Nanjing and it takes just over two hours to get there. It was our duty to reflect upon the bravery of those buried there and to show our respect and gratitude for their sacrifice. A solemn silence reigned. Even the naughtiest boy was obedient. Every visitor observed the silence for fear that the slightest noise might disturb the revolutionary martyrs in their eternal sleep.

After laying our wreath on the monument to all the martyrs, we children were free to wander. I usually went to visit my father's grave and was pleased that most of my classmates followed me. On the way, we would pick some wild flowers to scatter over it. On my first Sweeping Tomb Day, imagine my surprise to find some fresh flowers lying there already. I felt good. Someone else had come to pay their respects to Father. I never did find out who it was, but flowers appeared there many times. We cleared away the dead grasses and made everything neat and tidy, then spent a few moments in silence. I felt close to my father and carried this good feeling with me as we marched back.

As often as I could, I went to the hospital after school to visit my mother. She had a small side ward to herself with a sofa beside her bed. Other patients were in larger, shared wards. Whenever I entered her room, Mother's face lit up with pleasure. She would put down her knitting to give me a big hug before handing me some food. She saved the best bits of her meals to give to us children, usually boiled eggs and red dates, or dried longan (like a lychee but smaller) in sweet soup. Such food was supposed to be nutritious and good for the patients, and was rare in 1961.

It was given only to a select few. My mother knew all about the needs of a growing child and had a kerosene stove put into her ward so that she could heat the food for us when we came. Sometimes, as we sat enjoying it, the nurse would come to take her temperature and scold her politely for giving it to us. She also criticized us for eating what had been meant for Mother, and I would feel embarrassed. I usually stopped eating and looked at Mother a little shamefacedly, but she would say she didn't want whatever it was and that 'If you children don't eat it, it will be wasted and I would rather it go into your tummy than into the pig-swill.' We ate all kinds of delicious titbits that Mother put by for us during her two years in hospital. While the rest of the nation starved, my weight increased.

In August 1961, Mother began to feel better and asked the doctors to let her leave hospital and return to work. They did not agree and Mother became suspicious. Were they keeping the truth about her illness from her? She remembered my father, and the way they had kept it from him. Were they doing the same to her? She needed to know and decided to go to the East China Hospital in Shanghai for a thorough check-up. I don't think she would have undertaken the journey had she felt ill but she was convinced she had almost recovered.

She left the hospital without permission and came home to pack. It was probably the first time in her life that she had broken the rules of the Party. As she was packing, she decided to take my brother, Wei-guo, with her for company. They left Nanjing for Shanghai by the first available morning train. The 300-kilometre journey took six hours, and it was midday when they alighted at Shanghai railway station.

Mother and Wei-guo were met by my uncle Gao Dao-fang, a cousin of my father, who had done well for himself and was now president of the Yangtze River Navigation Bureau of Shanghai. It had been my father who had recruited him into the army and given him his start on the road to his present position, so he wanted to repay his esteemed cousin by having my mother stay at his luxurious house in Kangping Road. My uncle was responsible for all the docks and waterways along the 6,000 kilometres of the Yangtze River, from the Himalayas to the East China Sea, and he was away a lot. The day after the arrival of my mother and brother, he had to leave for Wuhan, the largest city and docks in central China, leaving my mother in the care of his wife. She treated Mother and Wei-guo kindly in front of her husband but changed dramatically as soon as he left. She did not want Mother to use hot water to have a bath and kept reminding her that gas was expensive to heat the water, so Mother used cold water.

Mother thought of leaving and staying in a hotel, but that would have caused problems between my uncle and his wife, so she stayed there for the week, waiting for the results of the tests she had undergone. Uncle Dao-fang's wife gave her only one thin blanket to cover herself and my brother at night. Shanghai is on the coast and is usually quite cool at night with plenty of moisture in the air, even in the height of summer. Of course, Mother being Mother, she put all of the blanket on my brother and had none for herself. She found it almost impossible to sleep and lay shivering from the cold and damp.

Her health soon deteriorated. After two years of care in the constant temperature and dry atmosphere of the hospital, the cool damp air affected her delicate constitution. After she returned to Nanjing on 31 August 1961 she felt a terrible pain in her chest and hurried back to the hospital, where the doctors gave her oxygen. The nurses were told to ensure that she was never left alone, and she was not allowed out of bed.

My brother and I went to see her on 3 September, a Sunday. The sun was shining, the new school term began the next day and I was about to start my last year of primary school. When we pushed open the door to her ward, all we saw was an empty bed and beside it, on a table, a note in Mother's handwriting: 'Little Flower and Little Wei-guo, I will be back soon. Please wait here, I have some good things for you to eat. Mother.'

The nurse told us that Mother was running a high fever and had been taken to the treatment room. We sat quietly, until Mother was helped back to bed. As soon as she saw us, she gave us a brilliant smile. Her eyes shone and there was a bright red patch on each of her cheeks. She shrugged off her helpers and hugged us both. 'Come, darlings, I have an orange for you both and some soup.' She heated the delicious egg soup while we peeled and devoured the oranges. I couldn't know, as we sat in the warm, sun-filled room chattering away, that this was the last time I would see her loving smile and hear her gentle voice.

My sister Andong went to the hospital the next afternoon after school. She could not find Mother and was told that her chest problem had developed into pleurisy and she had been transferred to the Gulou Hospital, the largest hospital in Nanjing, which had an excellent chest unit. The pleurisy was followed by a pulmonary oedema, which affected her heart. None of her family was allowed to see her during the next week except Uncle Gao Dao-jun who, like my father, had now changed his name to sever his links with his 'exploiting-class' family. He was now called Gao Peng (Flying Eagle).

Uncle Gao Peng went to see Mother every day. On Saturday 9 September 1961, at about one o'clock in the afternoon, the sun disappeared behind thick dark clouds, which scudded low across the sky. Uncle Gao Peng appeared in my classroom and asked me to go to the hospital with him. It was election day for the Young Pioneers, when we would vote for the next year's committee. Somehow, that day, the Young Pioneers was of no importance to me. All I could think about was that my mother needed me at the hospital and I rushed from the classroom.

We walked in silence all the way to the hospital. I felt my uncle's mood and my heart was heavy. My tummy felt like I had eaten a meal of lead. At the gates of the hospital, I saw my sisters, my brother and my grandparents waiting for us. An auntie from Mother's office came out to meet us. She had red, swollen eyes and her chin trembled as she said quietly in a wavering voice, 'She has passed away. She has gone.' I fainted clean away.

Mother had died twenty days before her thirty-ninth birthday and I was twelve. When I came to, I found myself in front of Mother's bed. I had no idea of how I got there. As I opened my eyes, I saw her pale face. Her mouth was slightly open and her lips seemed almost black in the whiteness of her skin. I realized she was dead. I threw myself upon her body and burst into tears. She was still soft and a little warm. I cried with joy, 'She's alive! Feel, she is warm.' I could not endure this again. First my father and now my mother. Never! Hands took hold of me and pulled me from her. 'Little Flower, Little Flower.' It was my grandfather. He held me close to him, his tears wetting my cheek. 'Little Flower, your mother has gone. She is no longer with us, except in our hearts.' I buried myself in his clothes and wept uncontrollably.

When Dr Ma, the chief doctor and best chest expert in China, entered the room with some nurses, I turned on him in a great fury. I lashed out and my little fist hit the good doctor in his midriff. 'Why didn't you save her? She is my mother – why? . . . Why? Give me back my mother!' I tried to hit him again, but I was held by the wrist. After a few moments I sank back into the loving warmth of my grandfather. I never wanted him to let me go. Then I felt the arms of Uncle Gao Peng around my shoulders. 'It wasn't the doctor's fault, little one. He has done his very best for her. He has not slept for two days and nights and he tried everything he knew to keep your mother alive, but she was too weak.'

I felt I could never forgive the doctor for letting my mother die. I hated him, the nurses and the whole hospital. It was *their* fault she was dead. Dr Ma and the nurses looked at me with sadness and understanding in their eyes. Then, in silence, a nurse drew a white sheet up over Mother's body. I protested and reached out to drag the sheet away, but my arms were held. I watched, horrified, as her beautiful face disappeared. It is this last sight that lives on the strongest in my memory.

In a daze, I remember the nurses transferring Mother to a trolley and my hand being held by someone as we followed it along a dark corridor. The doors at the far end were pushed open. 'Mortuary', said a sign. All of us, tears flowing freely, walked through. Another set of doors: 'Reposing Room'. It had big dark-green metal drawers along one side of the room. A worker dressed in blue pulled one open then slid Mother from the trolley on to the flat bed of the drawer. He closed it with a loud bang, which hit me like a thunderbolt. Sharp knives sliced my heart into tiny pieces. Once again, I fainted. This time, it must have been for a much longer period, because when I opened my eyes I was lying on my bed at home and it was dark outside.

I felt as if I was living my own nightmare. Everything had happened so quickly. How could I have been in my classroom worrying about the election when my mother was fighting for breath? For days I couldn't eat or drink and I kept crying. Time meant nothing. Sometimes minutes were hours and at other times a day passed in a flash. I had a terrible attack of dizziness. My bedroom was spinning. Bright light made me vomit. I kept the curtains drawn day and night and stayed in bed, with my eyes tightly shut. I felt as if I was drifting on a big ocean. The waves threw me up and down, up and down. Then, suddenly, I was dropping from a high cliff down to a deep valley.

I knew that many people came to our house and some sat with me for a while, but nothing registered. Later, I found out that Uncle Gao Peng and his wife had received the visitors on behalf of us children. I knew my mother was dead, but I could not accept that she had left me for ever. Her smiling face would appear and she would tip her head to smile at my father, who drifted in and out of my dreams. But slowly I came to myself, and reality set in with a hard, constant pain. It took years for that pain to go away, but how easily it returns. I can feel it now. The knives are plunging into my chest as I write.

★

A funeral committee was immediately formed by the Nanjing People's Government. Mother's file was scrutinized and telegrams flew all over China. Fellow fighters, friends, comrades, relatives and every other person Mother's life had touched were contacted. They arrived from every direction. All of mother's half-brothers and cousins came, except poor Zhou Ru-sheng who was in exile in Qinghai Province doing hard labour.

My great-uncle Zhou Xin-min was busy in Beijing, and as he had to put the interests of the State before his own needs, he couldn't attend. Instead he sent a telegram of condolence. Later, two letters arrived from him, one addressed to the Mayor of Nanjing and the other to the number-one Party secretary of Jiangsu Province, Jiang Wei-qing, asking them to look after us children in the best way they could.

By the orders of the Central Party Committee, cremation had replaced burial as the official means of disposing of the dead. This was especially recommended for Party officials. The old burial ceremonies were now considered 'feudalist superstition'. The truth, however, was that the famine had forced the authorities to introduce cremation as the best means of body disposal because of the vast numbers dying of starvation, but they never admitted this.

When the founder member of the Party, Lin Bo-qu, died in 1960, his body was burned in the Babaoshan crematorium in Beijing to set an example for all China to follow. Therefore it was a brave decision by the funeral committee to decide that, as my father had been buried in a coffin, Mother should be treated similarly. The chief executive of the funeral committee, Zhuang Cun, was a close neighbour of ours and also a good friend. He ensured that the coffin was made from the very best red pine. The coffin was very thick and heavy, and he ordered the workers to varnish it to a rich mahogany colour. When it was finished, it looked elegant and graceful. Although everything was in short supply Zhuang used all of his skills and contacts to have everything ready within a week. His influence reached as far away as Yunnan Province in the southern part of China, from where he got the best and biggest granite blocks for Mother's grave and tombstone. He jumped the queue for rail transportation to get everything he needed within the shortest possible time. He poured all of his love and respect for my mother into the preparations.

The funeral was held just seven days after Mother's death. It had rained every day since that terrible afternoon at the hospital. At exactly one o'clock in the afternoon, the leaders of Nanjing and representatives of all walks of life in the city gathered for the ceremony. I noticed that everyone was wearing a black armband. Many of the women were weeping and even some of the men. The enormous hall was filled with wreaths and the heavy perfume of the flowers made the damp day seem more oppressive.

As I walked into the hall I almost collapsed. An enlarged photograph of my mother, framed with black silk ribbon, was hanging high up on the white wall with an elegant couplet on each side. On one side were the words 'You have experienced and overcome all the revolutionary storms, always with enthusiasm', and on the other, 'You passed away so suddenly, just when the Party needs thoroughly tempered cadres like you in our socialist construction.' On a horizontal scroll above Mother's portrait were the words 'Comrade Zhou Hong-bin is immortal.'

I was weak after so many days of weeping and not eating so I couldn't stand for long without help. Auntie Zhu supported me. I needed her strength, but I also held my grandfather's hand. I needed his presence. Later the doctors told me that the shock and my intense grief had caused the Menière's disease, which attacked me soon afterwards, and from which I suffered for more than twenty-five years.

Mother was dressed in a white shirt and a new navy blue jacket, ordered and paid for by the People's Government of Nanjing. The leaders of Nanjing spoke over her coffin and so did all of my uncles, but I heard none of their words. All I could hear was Mother's gentle voice talking to me, and I could see only her beautiful young face. I looked at her and a smile appeared before my eyes. All the past happiness appeared too, then slowly faded away. I had lost them for ever.

When everybody had paid their last respects, two men carefully put the coffin lid in place and banged long steel nails through to seal it. I wept my heart out, half dead and half alive. I stretched out my arms, desperately trying to stop them, but Auntie Zhu held me so tightly that I couldn't move.

The coffin was put into a flower-and-ribbon bedecked hearse, with a large photograph of Mother in the windscreen. Three large black limousines led the way, and the hearse followed. Uncle Gao Peng rode with us children in the lead car, and the leaders were in the other two. The close relatives were in other cars following the hearse and more than a hundred more cars came behind them. Then came a long line of assorted vehicles filled with mourners. Two large flat-bed trucks covered with wreaths from the funeral hall brought up the rear. The procession snaked along the road and all other traffic stopped. Even the busy rickshaws came to a halt, their passengers joining the pedestrians, bareheaded, to pay their last respects. All down both sides of the streets people stood in silence, bicycle bells quiet for once. Most of those looking on did not know whose funeral it was but they knew it was someone important and that was sufficient for them to behave respectfully.

The convoy made its way slowly to the cemetery and crept along the narrow lanes towards the grave. It stopped next to where my father had rested for five years. At least they would be together for all eternity. Everything was dreamlike, a horrible nightmare. I had difficulty in focusing my eyes but I remember that a new grave had already been built beside Father's. I can remember Uncle Gao Peng saying to the workers, 'Be sure to put her head towards the south. Let them sleep with their heads alongside each other.' His words gave me some comfort. After being alone for five years, Father was now reunited with his loving wife and best friend. Also, their bodies were whole: this was important to my grandparents because, according to their ancient beliefs, my parents would be able to return and live their next lives when their time came.

The grave was covered with wreaths when we left. On the next Sweeping Tomb Day, I returned with my sister Andong and my brother Wei-guo. By then, I was getting used to being without my parents, but I missed them then and still do.

The day after the funeral was Sunday 17 September. Uncle Gao Peng held a family meeting in the living room of our house. He told everyone that he had been at Mother's bedside during her last painful hours. Towards the end, she had known she was dying. She had held his hands in hers, and silent tears wetted her hair and pillows. She didn't say anything but made a simple gesture. She kissed a photograph of her children and pressed it into Uncle's hand. He understood what she was saying. 'My children are in your care from now on.'

Uncle Peng looked at us. Pei-gen, Andong, Wei-guo and I were sitting in a half-circle before him. 'I loved your parents,' he said. 'Your father was the most honourable man I ever knew and your mother was the very gentlest of women.' He paused and looked at my parents' photographs on the wall. 'I remember your mother when she was just a young girl. Never would she say a bad word about anyone. Not then, not ever. She was the one person everyone could trust and the only person I have ever trusted. Neither of your parents deserved to die so young, but life is never fair.' He paused. 'Your mother was a very brave and strong-willed woman. She never made a sound, even when her pain was very bad. The doctors extracted the bloody water from her lungs with a large syringe twice a day to reduce the pressure on her heart, and she just lay there, silently looking at them. Sometimes, she even smiled. How she could bear the pain so bravely I shall never know.

'Unfortunately, nothing helped. Her heartbeat was very fast and erratic, over 240 beats a minute, which made breathing difficult for her, and she needed oxygen. She never complained, only wept if anybody mentioned her children. At the end, when she was asked if she wanted to see you all, she shook her head. This must have been the hardest decision she ever had to make, and her tears broke my heart. She knew that the sight of her, nearing death, would upset you and make things worse for you.'

He looked at us. 'You are my children now. I owe your parents a great deal and you also owe them a debt. They gave you everything they had and you can only repay them by continuously working hard at your studies, and by being good. Let your mother rest in peace beside your father, free from worries.'

The Nanjing People's Government and the Party Committee decided to reward Mother for all her hard work, honouring her as a revolutionary martyr. She was the youngest senior official to die and she had earned the respect of everyone.

The decision was approved by the Beijing authority and the certificate was sent to Nanjing. Uncle Peng accepted the award on our behalf. He had it framed and hung it on the wall beside Father's. Then he held another meeting with our three uncles and Mother's half-brothers, except Zhou Ru-sheng. There was only one item on the agenda: how best to care for and bring us up. There were three options: (1) Let our grandparents continue to care for us in the same house that we had lived in for so long. (2) Send us to be cared for by my parents' good friends and comrades-in-arms. (3) Each of our three uncles to take a child into their homes. Pei-gen was now sixteen and could live in her middle-school dormitory.

My three uncles rejected the first suggestion immediately. It was just not possible to leave young children in the care of a member of the old 'exploiting classes', even an 'open-minded' landlord like my grandfather. He had old ideas and would be a bad influence on us. The second suggestion was also unacceptable: I was in my last year of primary school and it was important that I continue to study there, to ensure the best possible chance for me to pass the entrance examination to a good middle school. Also, after what had already happened to us, it would be better to keep us together.

At last those gathered around the table came to a decision. We three younger children were placed in the care of Uncle Peng for a year. The local government would contribute a third of Mother's salary towards our keep. After I finished primary school, I was to go to Shanghai to live with Uncle Wang Feng, now the commanding general of the air-force headquarters there.

In the end only my brother and I went to live with Uncle Peng: he said it was too much for him to have all three of us. Andong went to live in the junior middle-school dormitory. The People's Government allowed my grandparents to continue to live in the old house, but reduced their accommodation to just one room. They had to share the kitchen, toilet and bathroom with two lower-level cadres and their families. With the death of my mother, our family was destroyed.

I felt sad to see strangers move into our home. We had lived there for eight years and I wanted to stay with my grandparents, but we children had no say in what was going to happen to us. Nobody asked us what we wanted or how we felt. Uncle Peng's wife checked all of Mother's belongings and made a list: furniture, clothes, suitcases, a large camphor-wood trunk, personal belongings, mementos and bank account. The list and everything on it was handed over to the organizational department of the Nanjing Party Committee. The huge photographs of my father, the old metal water-bottle and the framed revolutionary martyrs' certificates were taken down from the walls and sent into store with the other things. We were told that as our grandparents were from the 'exploiting class' they had no right to keep anything, not even a small token of remembrance.

I couldn't understand why there had been no problem for them to live with us when Mother was alive and now they had no right to look after us. My uncle explained that, with Mother in charge of the household, there had been no political difficulty: she had been a senior Party official and could give us guidance. Now, without her influence, it was too dangerous for us to live with our grandparents. We were 'revolutionary successors' and could not be allowed to live under the influence of a landlord. The Party Committee took on the responsibility of looking after our property in their warehouse until we grew up. One good thing was decided: as my grandparents had a revolutionary martyr for a daughter, they were given a small living allowance, payable monthly, for the rest of their lives.

Uncle Gao Peng lived a long way from our school, in the southern part of Nanjing. Every schoolday morning, my brother and I had to leave the house very early to walk to school. It took more than an hour to get there and we had to walk back in the afternoon. Wei-guo was only ten and I was twelve, and at first we found it hard going because we were not used to walking so far. The first week, when we returned to school after the funeral, our legs ached and we developed painful blisters on our feet, but we soon toughened up.

My teachers were understanding and helped me all they could, but that made me feel worse. Every kindness made my throat constrict and the tears flow. To show our love for Mother, my brother and I wore the black armband for many weeks, and only at the request – order, really – of Uncle Peng did we reluctantly take them off.

Wei-guo was in grade four, so we were not separated during our first year as orphans. We had lunch in the high officials' dining room and many of Mother's old friends had their lunch there. They often came to ask how we were. And we always answered, 'Very well, thank you.' It seemed to be the best way. I was not happy living with my uncle, but I kept silent for fear it would bring shame upon him. Sometimes they understood and sighed. A few also shared their good food with us. As time went on, I adapted to my new life and learned to control my grief. Wei-guo soon settled back into his easy-going ways.

I had changed. Now my classmates never heard me laugh. I no longer went to the Children's Amateur Physical Training School and I stopped going to the cinema. I became a serious student. The only thing I wanted to do was study hard. My gymnastics coach came to see me at school and asked me to continue training. She said I had a great future if I wanted it. I was sorry, I said, I had no time for anything but my studies.

I was on a mission. My only desire was to fulfil my mother's wish: I must enter the best middle school and then the best university. Nothing else mattered to me. Looking back, I was dealing with my grief in the only way I could: I retreated from the real world and buried myself in the safety of study. People could hurt me, study couldn't.

My brother and I tasted the hardships of life as we walked to school every day but we were never late. We trudged through snow, hail, rain and sun. It made no difference to us how hot it was in summer or how cold in winter: we got to school before classes started. We were often soaking wet when we arrived. Our little umbrella could not protect us from the windy storms, the splashing of the traffic, or the sideways slant of the rain. Our trousers and socks dripped water and we often felt icy cold during our lessons.

We were sensible children and even my lazy brother, in his own way, wanted to bring honour to our parents by good attendance and hard study, although his idea of hard study was just a few minutes' concentrated effort. The nicest thing was that during that year we never quarrelled. We were often praised by the teachers for our attendance and punctuality, but it had little effect on me. My hidden sorrows were too strong. I had nightmares that woke me at night in terror, but which I could not remember in the morning.

As our old home was on our way to and from school, Wei-guo and I often dropped in to see our grandparents. Grandmother cooked delicious dishes for us and Wei-guo would play games with Grandfather. The old ones were lonely after the hustle and bustle of looking after us and they, too, were suffering: not only had they lost their daughter, they had lost a whole family. Sometimes I caught their sadness in a look or a sigh, and I would cuddle up to them. I don't know if it helped them, but it certainly helped me. Occasionally we were allowed by Uncle Peng to spend a weekend there. My grandfather would sleep in a single bed, and Grandmother, Wei-guo and I snuggled together in the big double bed. I enjoyed that: I had few opportunities to feel the trusted warmth of another human being, and Grandmother felt very dear to me during those visits.

In early July 1962, I took my final examinations at primary school, and I achieved high marks in all my major subjects. Uncle Gao Dao-fang was transferred from Shanghai to Wuhan as chairman of the General Yangtze River Navigation Administrative Bureau and my brother was sent to live with him. As soon as the term ended and I had graduated from primary school, I went off to the air-force headquarters to live with Uncle Wang Feng. Pei-gen passed the entrance examination and entered the Hydraulic Engineering Institute in Beijing. Only Andong stayed in Nanjing with Uncle Peng. Now our family was dispersed, hundreds of miles apart from each other.

That was the end of my childhood.

7. Living under Other People's Roofs

Uncle Wang Feng lived in married quarters in the compound of the Shanghai air-force headquarters. His wife, whom I called Auntie, worked in the navy hospital. The military had much better supplies of food and everything else during the economic crisis and life at my new home was comfortable enough. A single bed had been prepared for me in a servant's room beside the kitchen. Uncle Gao Peng had brought my own quilt from Nanjing, which made me feel more at home. It was the one Mother and I had shared, and I had not wanted to be parted from it.

Shanghai was, and still is, the largest and most modern city in China, and is governed directly from Beijing under the leadership of the Central Party Committee. It is almost impossible for ordinary people not from Shanghai to obtain registration to live in the city. There never has been freedom of movement: everyone must live and work where they are registered. Before I left Nanjing, my registration was transferred as an exception to Shanghai by the Public Security Bureau, because I was the daughter of two revolutionary martyrs. It was an important concession because it meant I would be issued with ration coupons in Shanghai.

Uncle Wang Feng contacted the best middle school there and arranged for me to take the next entrance examination. About 99 per cent of the students went on from there to good universities. People in Shanghai used to say, 'If you get one foot into this school, your other foot is already in the university.'

I arrived at Uncle Wang Feng's home on 12 July, and five days later I was escorted to the school by a smart young air-force officer to take the examination, which was in two parts: mathematics and Chinese. I remember feeling relieved that the first wasn't too difficult. Then came the Chinese exam, in which we were asked to write a composition under the title 'On the Eve of the Examination'. I thought for a while, then put pen to paper and poured out my heart. I started simply: 'Whoo-whooooo! The train huffed and clanked out of Nanjing railway station, taking me towards Shanghai and a new life. I turned and looked back through the window. Nanjing, my Nanjing, the beautiful city where I grew up and spent my precious childhood was gradually fading out of sight. I was travelling away from all I knew and loved. My beloved parents were buried there. My sobbing grandparents, whom I had left on the platform, would now be making their way to the house that was still their home, but was my home no longer. Tears filled my eyes as the train hurried me further and further away. I took out a small box in which I had put several rain-flower stones collected from around the graves of my mother and father. They were all I could carry with me.'

In mid-August, the letter of acceptance for me to enter Fuxin Middle School came. My uncle admitted that he had been more nervous about my results than I was, but after reading the letter, he had turned to me and cried joyfully, 'You've done it! You're in!'

Uncle bought me a bus pass, and on 1 September 1962 I made my first solo journey to my new school. I found my way to my classroom where many students were already sitting and staring around them. Some knew each other, but most were strangers to the rest. This school drew only the cleverest children from every part of the city and the surrounding countryside. A young woman teacher was sitting in front of the class with the blackboard behind her, collecting the tuition fees and registering the children. (All schools, at every level, charged for tuition.) I was in a short queue. When I reached the desk, I handed over the fees and my photographs with my name on the back. The form teacher was bending over, busy writing. Her name was Zhao Pei-qiu. She looked up, flashed me a warm smile, and I knew I was going to like her.

My new school was the key to educational reform in Shanghai. The years of study had been reduced in both the junior and senior departments while the level of achievement was increased: more teachers were employed, new teaching materials were introduced, and students were expected to graduate within five years instead of six. My school had the best teachers and the best facilities. It boasted the finest student science laboratory in China.

I had more than ten subjects to study, including Chinese, maths and politics. Later, due to the 'needs of the revolution', English was added. I began to learn history and geography properly, and everything I heard about Britain was bad. Mother had been right: the British people had been aggressors since ancient times and had conquered many lands, treating the inhabitants as slaves. Also, in addition to algebra, trigonometry and geometry, we began to learn about atomic and molecular structure. I found the work hard, challenging but stimulating, and I managed to keep up.

It was a big school, founded seventy years before. The imposing buildings were in the British colonial style as it had been opened to educated the children of the eight foreign imperialist countries who had set up their colonies around Shanghai in the late nineteenth century. The big windows reminded me of the pictures in the fairy-tale books bought for me by my mother.

There were eight classes in each grade and each class contained about fifty students. Half of the classes in each grade were taught Russian and the other half learned English. I felt fortunate to take English. We had two English periods each week and I struggled with the strange characters. Chinese seemed so easy compared to ABC.

Shanghai is the largest city in Asia and the most important industrial base in China, but it has only a comparatively short history of a little more than a hundred years. It lies on an alluvial plain formed by the mud and sand deposited at the mouth of the Yangtze River, where the waters flow into the East China Sea. For many centuries the area was known to the Chinese as the Shanghai Beach. The world simply calls it Shanghai, which means 'going to the sea'.

It was just a small fishing village when, at the end of the nineteenth century, the eight western imperialist countries, headed by Britain, invaded China. Before the invasion, the largest building in the area was a fair-sized family house with an enclosed garden owned by a landlord named Yu. In due time, the garden became known as Yu-yuan Garden. There is a much older building called Chenghuang Temple, which in recent years has become a favourite tourist attraction as many small restaurants are dotted around it.

The British thought Shanghai would make an ideal port, and they were right. The small colony flourished, many tall buildings sprang up and the small port grew into the premier harbour of all Asia. Shanghai developed at breakneck speed. It attracted large numbers of foreign investors and rich Chinese businessmen, all needing houses, hotels, shops, factories and multi-storeyed office blocks. There were many foreign churches too. By the 1930s Shanghai had become a large, modern westernized city. Many westerners brave enough to try their luck became millionaires by importing and exporting goods through Shanghai, or by exploiting the cheap labour force of women and children in their factories. It wasn't long before Shanghai was nicknamed the Paradise of Western Adventurers.

The invaders treated the Chinese as second- or even third-class citizens. Such arrogance was typified by a wooden noticeboard put up at the waterfront entrance to Wampoo Park. It said, in Chinese and in English, 'NO ADMITTANCE TO CHINESE AND DOGS'. This was a great insult to the Chinese and it has never been forgotten. The term 'dog' is used as the worst kind of insult in China. To call someone a running dog, a dog's turd or a dog's bark is the supreme Chinese curse. All children are told the story of the noticeboard at school and although it no longer exists, photographs of it are displayed in the Shanghai History Museum.

The busiest section of Shanghai was, and still is, the Nanjing Road. The long thoroughfare runs for over ten kilometres, starting from the harbour in the east and cutting across the centre of the city to the outskirts in the west. It boasts the biggest shops, the grandest houses, the most expensive hotels and the tallest buildings. They line both sides of the road, which has been internationally famous since the 1930s for the neon lights that come to life as dusk falls.

By the time I arrived to live with Uncle Wang Feng in the summer of 1962, Shanghai had a population of over ten million. The standard of living there was the highest in China and the influence of capitalism was everywhere. When my uncle took me to see the Nanjing Road for the first time, it was so different from Nanjing that I thought I had crossed a border into a foreign country. There was the 'English Sector', the 'Japanese Quarter' and 'French Town'. The Shanghai dialect sounded like a foreign language. Fortunately, Mandarin was spoken at school. If it had been 'Shanghai-ese', I would never have learned anything!

The first lecture given to us when we began our day at Fuxin Middle School was a political warning. The same warning was repeated time after time, year in, year out. We were told always to be on our guard against the 'bullets coated with sugar'. It was, in fact, a quotation from Chairman Mao: 'The enemies with guns have been defeated, but the enemies without guns still exist. We can easily be shot by the bourgeois bullets coated with sugar.' By 'bullets', he meant the tempting aspects of the western lifestyle. To fall under a hail of these 'bullets' might destroy one's revolutionary will. So Shanghai was a dangerous place for us youngsters. The dazzling lights and hundreds of shop windows in the Nanjing Road displaying luxury goods from all over the world were the bullets coated with sugar. Uncle Wang Feng never allowed any of his family, including me, to window-shop.

War raged between the proletarian class and the bourgeois way of life for the hearts of the young, but when I arrived in Shanghai, I was such a fervent Communist that the idea of being exposed to such decadence filled me with revulsion. In addition, the Party had set up a good example for us to follow. The Eighth Company of the PLA guarded the Nanjing Road. All the soldiers of this company had resolutely resisted the corrupting influence, and kept to plain living at all times since entering Shanghai in 1949. Chairman Mao called them 'the Good Eighth Company in Nanjing Road'. Their story was recorded in a book, and then in a stage play, *The Sentry Under the Neon Lights*, which was performed everywhere in China. Later a film was made, and I was impressed with the strength of will shown by the simple soldiers. In Shanghai every school arranged for its students to see the film and the stage play. So did all work units, factories, shops, offices and public departments, because the people of Shanghai were at the centre of the anti-capitalist front.

The story-line was simple. A company of soldiers was given the task of guarding the Nanjing Road soon after Shanghai was liberated by the PLA. It wasn't long before a platoon commander named Chen Xi was drawn towards the bright lights at night and the shops in daytime. He was from a poor peasant family but that didn't stop him wanting a better lifestyle. The first thing he did was to throw away his old cloth socks and buy a pair of new knitted cotton ones.

When his wife, who was also a Communist Party member, came to see him and found the cloth socks she had made for him in the dustbin, she burst into tears. She was upset to discover that her husband had abandoned his lowly background and she wrote him a letter. In it, she recalled the past and said it was a shame to throw away the old socks. However, she went on, 'It is not a question of a pair of socks. It is what was behind your action. You are in danger of throwing away the glorious revolutionary tradition of plain living, which is exactly what our enemies wish you to do.'

Chen Xi was severely criticized by his company commander and his comrades, and he was reminded of his bitter past. His wife's letter was read out to the whole company and he felt so ashamed of himself that he threw himself on his knees, crying bitterly. He told the meeting that he realized how wrong he had been and deeply regretted what he had done. Then he retrieved his old socks and threw away the new ones. Thus, he had thrown away the bourgeois life. The actor was especially good when he threw away the new socks: with his screwed-up face, he looked as though he was getting rid of a handful of dog-shit. But as I saw the new socks disappearing into the dustbin, it crossed my mind that this was a terrible waste and contradicted Mao's anti-waste instruction.

For the whole of my stay in Shanghai, over two and a half years, I never had a new pair of socks. My uncle only gave me darned ones, which I took without complaint. Of course, I often wished for just one pair of new socks – but then I felt ashamed of myself. Neither did Uncle ever allow me warm, padded winter shoes. I wore his old 'liberation shoes', which were home-made from old uniforms and car tyres. My feet were icy cold all winter long, and when I sat in the classroom they were so numb I could hardly walk between lessons.

In our political classes, we were constantly told that two-thirds of the world was under a capitalist regime and that the people were living in an abyss of suffering as if they were in 'deep water and scorching fire'. We must never forget our duty to liberate them when we grew up. However, just one tiny thing bothered me: if the countries of the capitalist bloc were suffering so much compared to our happy lives in China, where did all those wonderful clothes, the jewellery and other things displayed in the windows of the Nanjing Road come from? It was a puzzle to me, but sensibly I kept that question to myself.

Shortly after my second term started, on 5 March 1963, Chairman Mao called on the whole nation to 'Learn from Comrade Lei Feng.' Mao's own handwriting was printed in all the newspapers and magazines, which made this call particularly important. Lei Feng was an ordinary soldier of the PLA based at the Shenyang Army Unit. He was a fellow townsman of Mao and had come from a poor peasant family in Hunan Province. His father had died before he was born, and his mother hanged herself after being raped by her landlord, so he was orphaned at the age of seven. In the China of those days young orphans had little chance of survival.

He spent his first few months as an orphan wandering along the Xiangjiang River begging for food. Then he had a stroke of luck. The area was liberated by the Communists and he was found, starving and close to death. The local Party took him into their care and from that time onwards he told anyone who asked that it was the Communists who had saved him from the vicious old society and certain death. He was grateful to the Party and Chairman Mao for giving him a new life. At seven he committed himself to the Communist cause. He was sent to school, where he worked hard to master reading, writing and arithmetic.

When he grew older, he worked diligently at all his jobs and he performed whatever was assigned to him with a good heart.

Lei Feng spent many years around the army and he expected to join when he was old enough. When he applied, though, he was turned down because he was too short. He was bitterly disappointed and it showed on his face when the recruiting officer told him the bad news. The officer was a wise veteran with many years' experience. He suspected that there was more to this earnest little fellow than met the eye, so he invited him to sit down for a chat. It wasn't long before the boy was telling the officer all about his bitter life in the old society and how his life had been saved by the Communists. His story was so full of class feelings that the officer was moved to accept the young fellow into the army as a special exception. Lei Feng completed the basic military training in the top half of his platoon, despite his lack of inches, and was accepted into the Communist Party.

He was a good soldier and Party member. In his off-duty time, he often helped the local people. He was also the political instructor to the nearby primary school, and he studied the works of Chairman Mao every day. The only clues to his life were contained in his diary and no one ever saw that – until, at twenty-two, he was killed in a freak accident when a lamp-post fell on to the cab of his lorry while he was driving supplies through the city. His diary was found among his belongings and sent to his commandant, then to the central military high command and eventually landed on Mao's desk. It was published as a pamphlet and everybody in our school was told to buy a copy. I bought one and was much moved by it.

I felt genuine respect for Lei Feng, and I started to keep a diary of my own. Every day I carefully recorded everything that had happened. At the end of the second term, my teacher asked if she could read it, so I handed it over. She sent it to the Youth League Committee in Shanghai, and soon after that it was printed in the *Liberation Daily*, the official local newspaper of the Party, and with my photograph in the *Youth Weekly*, published by the Shanghai Youth League. During the next few days, the radio broadcast my words over the air. News reporters kept calling on me and also visited my uncle in his office.

I was asked if I would like to talk to other children in different schools and even to adults in the evenings. I felt honoured and agreed enthusiastically. The topic was always the same: I was a daughter of two revolutionary martyrs and I had to follow in their footsteps. I must study hard and carry the revolution through to the end. I would learn from Comrade Lei Feng and, like him, dedicate my life to Communism.

A few days after my diary was published, one newspaper paid me five yuan *renminbi* (Chinese currency, called People's Money). It was a good sum for those days, but as I had only been doing what I considered my duty I handed it to my form teacher, along with a suggestion for its use – that she purchase a full set of hair-cutting tools. I had read in the pamphlet that Comrade Lei Feng had never had his hair cut by a barber and usually the soldiers cut each other's hair. From that time on, the boys had their hair cut every Saturday afternoon in our classroom. Not the girls. We preferred to keep our hair long.

In the summer vacation of 1963, a delegation of Algerian children visited Shanghai. They had all lost their parents in the struggle against the 'French invaders'. I was one of the Chinese students chosen to accompany these children of 'revolutionary martyrs' and was coupled with a pretty girl named Sofia. She was twelve, two years younger than I but much taller. She had lovely long black curly hair, big black eyes and a warm smile. We could not communicate in her language or mine, but managed quite well in English. With the aid of signs and drawings, we could understand each other. An interpreter was attached to their party, but we had no need of her and enjoyed each other's company. During the four-day visit, the other Chinese students and I stayed with our guests in the Shanghai Children's Palace, which had been built by Madam Soong Ching-ling, wife of Dr Sun Yat-sen. We went sightseeing and sat on top of an official double-decker bus, used only for visitors. For the first time, I sat on the top deck and saw the whole of Shanghai fly past the window. It was as new to me as it was to Sofia. In the evening we attended a banquet in honour of our visitors held in the imposing banqueting hall of the Jinjiang Hotel. The leaders of Shanghai were present and each had to give a speech of welcome. Then the visiting adults gave their responses. It took quite a long time for each speech to be completed, because every word had to be translated, but at last they were finished. Not that I minded: this was my very first banquet and I enjoyed every moment of it. When the food was served poor Sofia had a terrible time with the chopsticks.

The next day, we were taken aboard a navy gun-boat. It must have been daunting for the sailors to have two dozen excited children descend upon them, but they coped well. The boat started off with a loud roar, and we whooshed down the Wampoo River at great speed, and out into the East China Sea. Naturally, a few felt seasick, and were held firmly as they hung over the rails. All the time Sofia and I were hand in hand. A long table stood on the deck with all kinds of fruit, juices and biscuits on it, and those who could still eat soon reduced the spread to pips, cores, skins, crumbs and empty cups.

The boat moved very fast, vibrating from the thrust of the engines and bouncing over the waves. I was fascinated by the long white wake trailing away behind. The foaming water made me think of white flowers appearing and disappearing. I gingerly touched a cannon on the after-deck. The official cameraman saw me, and took a photograph of Sofia and me in front of it. After about an hour, when we had quietened down, the sailors asked us to sing and dance. When my turn came, I sang a song from the film *The Heroic Little Eighth Route Soldiers* called 'We are Communist Successors'. A few years later, this song became the new anthem of the Young Pioneers.

Sofia said she would dance and we all applauded, but the moment her body began to move, I put my hand over my mouth to prevent myself crying out in astonishment. She danced with her belly! Her upper body remained still, and only her bottom moved, swaying from side to side. Naturally, the sailors were interested in such a spectacle, because we Chinese would call it a 'rascal dance' and it was shocking to us. We thought it very low behaviour to move one's bottom in that way. But out of courtesy no one said anything, and we applauded politely. The sailors clapped much more enthusiastically than we did.

Eventually it was time for Sofia and her party to leave Shanghai for Beijing. We all went to the railway station to see them off and Sofia showed me the photograph taken with me on the gun-boat. I felt sad because I had not been given a copy and had nothing to remember her by. She understood how I felt, took out a picture from her bag and signed it on the back in English, 'To Anhua, my dear new friend. Sofia', and gave it to me as a souvenir. It was a picture of a graceful foreign lady. 'Isn't she beautiful? Like a film star,' she said, just before she boarded the train.

I worshipped this lovely lady from the first moment I laid eyes on her, even though I didn't know who she was. I did not tell my teacher or anyone else about the picture. I knew all foreigners were a bad influence and that I should have handed it in but I took it home and put it in my drawer. It was my secret. I used to take it out from time to time and look at the lady sitting there in a lovely white gown, so upright and composed, with the pretty jewels on her ears, neck and wrist, sparkling in the light.

In September 1963, a few days after the start of my second year, our political teacher asked us to listen to the radio that evening, saying that there was going to be an important news bulletin that we must not miss. At eight o'clock, the Central Radio Station began to broadcast to the whole country. It was 'An Open Letter from the Chinese Communist Party to the Communist Party of the USSR'. It lasted for more than an hour and officially announced that the Communist Party of the Soviet Union headed by Khrushchev had turned: they were now revisionist renegades.

There were many political sentences I couldn't understand, even though I listened intently, but it was Chairman Mao's decision, therefore it must be right. The next day, during our political period, our teacher explained it all to us. The third generation in Russia had changed their colour from red to grey, therefore our responsibility as third-generation Communists had become even greater. The eastern European bloc countries and even Cuba had turned their backs on China by allying themselves to the USSR. As Kim Il Sung of North Korea and Ho Chi Minh of North Vietnam had 'assumed an ambiguous attitude', there were even more difficulties on our revolutionary road. 'We must break through the brambles and thorns and march forward unshakingly towards Communism,' was his conclusion.

I was puzzled by all this. Why had our friends changed so quickly? Just one year ago Cuba had been our firm friend and now Mr Castro had betrayed us! How could that be? I dared not ask. I forced myself to swallow everything the Party fed me.

The day after the open letter our teacher said, 'We will still follow the economic system of the Soviet Union because it was formed by Lenin and Stalin, who were always our great friends during their lifetimes. Mr Khrushchev has betrayed them but we must adhere to the system. We still need five-year plans to make our economic development a success.' As far back as 1953 China had had five-year plans and they were exact copies of those in the Soviet Union. In 1962 we were in the last year of the second five-year plan, and our political teacher said that our country had fulfilled it 'in the main' and would begin the third one soon. We never knew what 'in the main' really meant, and we were never to know how much of the current five-year plan had been left unfulfilled, but we knew we had achieved great success under the wise leadership of the great, glorious and correct Communist Party. It crossed my mind to ask if the famine had caused any problems but, like my classmates, I had learned to keep silent during political periods.

Just before my fifteenth birthday, my class teacher told me it was time for me to apply to join the Youth League. I wrote out my application and handed it to her. On my fifteenth birthday, 11 March 1964, I joined the Youth League, sponsored by my teacher. I took off my red scarf and pinned the Youth League badge to my blouse. The next step would be to join the Communist Party on my eighteenth birthday.

In October 1964, just a month after the new term started, the first Chinese atomic bomb was exploded. We watched the mushroom cloud rise high into the sky in a documentary film shown in all the cinemas. The commentator told us proudly that China was only the third country to have the technology to be able to explode an atomic bomb. The USA had been first, then the USSR and now *China*! What an inspiration to us all.

The constant effort to do everything to the best of my ability was affecting my health. I was hardly sleeping. It was a rule at air-force headquarters that nine o'clock was the time for 'lights out', so I got round this by spending many night hours under my quilt working with the aid of my torch. I must study hard to get to a good university as I had promised my parents I would at their graveside. I was pale, thin and weak. I started to run a fever.

I continued the mad merry-go-round of study, political meetings and social gatherings until even my uncle had to agree that I needed a rest. My tonsils were so swollen that I often had difficulty in speaking. During the summer vacation of 1964, he sent me to the air-force hospital where I had them removed. He then made sure that I was kept away from public life for the rest of the school holidays. By the time school started again, I felt much better.

Though I was still being awarded the 'Three Good Student' certificate every term, I never received any praise or a reward from my uncle. He didn't give me any new clothes either. I had to alter his old uniforms and underwear for myself. I was now in my middle teens and becoming conscious of my appearance.

I never said a word about my feelings, but I missed the warmth of my mother's love more and more. Time had taken the sharp edge off my grief, but without my mother I felt unloved and unappreciated. When our teacher asked us to write a composition of our own choosing, I wrote 'My Mother'. It began: 'Whenever I see other children clapping their little hands and running happily towards the loving embrace of their mother, my own mother appears before me. Her kind, smiling face looks at me, just the way I always remember her.' Then I wrote about her good deeds, her virtues, her loyalty and devotion to the Party and her kindness towards other comrades. My last sentence read: 'Dearest Mother, may your memory be like the evergreen pine trees and remain fresh for ever. Your spirit is immortal.'

During 1964, Chairman Mao and the Party called on the educated young people to settle in rural areas to help build 'a new socialist countryside'. This would solve the problem of too many graduates from the middle schools chasing too few jobs in the cities, they thought. Countless enterprises that had sprung up during the Great Leap Forward were closing down due to shortages and famine, and the problem of large-scale unemployment was dealt with by moving the superfluous labour force. The local authorities began by forcing the peasants who had flocked to the cities during the famine years to go back to their villages. Then they 'encouraged' the city-born students and young graduates to leave their homes and go to the hungry countryside.

No one knows exactly how many people were transported to the country. Most estimates range from fifteen to twenty million. So many young lives were changed, perhaps ruined, for ever. Moreover, the enrolment policies of the universities and even many middle schools began to follow a 'class line', giving priority to children from 'a good family background'. Many otherwise first-class students could not enter university or a good middle school – perhaps they had a landlord in their background – even though they had passed the entrance examination with flying colours.

A daughter of a professor in Tianjin named Hou Jun was set up as an example for all the educated young people to follow. She was eighteen, a good student at middle school, but her family was considered 'unreliable' so she lost hope of entering a university. She decided to abandon her comfortable life in the big city and go to the countryside. Her story was broadcast in all the cities and published in the newspapers to encourage more young people to follow her example. They were trucked out as fast as transport could be arranged and given the grand title of 'Socialist New Peasants'. The Party propaganda machine did a good job: suddenly, going to the countryside was made to sound like the most glorious and patriotic thing a young person could do.

We younger middle-school students also had to learn how to labour in the fields and I had my baptism into the harsh world of the countryside in the autumn of 1964. The authorities of Fuxin Middle School organized a two-week stay for all the students in a People's Commune in the countryside near Shanghai. We were to help the peasants gather in the harvest. We had to walk the forty-five kilometres from Shanghai to the commune. Our bedrolls were slung across our backs and the rest of our luggage was draped around us. Try to imagine about twelve hundred young people singing revolutionary songs at the top of their voices marching along: 'We are walking on the big road, high-spirited and vigorous. Chairman Mao leads our revolutionary team. We clear out obstacles and march forward towards our great goal!'

When we arrived at our destination, the leader of the People's Commune came out to welcome us. He gave the teacher a list of poor or lower middle-class peasants who were reliable, and a list of ex-landlords and bad elements. We could make contact with the former but we must avoid the latter. Even in the countryside we had to be on our guard against class enemies. Nine other girls and I were sent to a poor peasant home where they had prepared one room for us. There were no beds, only hay spread thinly over a floor of hard mud, but we were so tired that simply to lie down was a luxury.

There was a lot to get used to. For example, there was no toilet in the house; our host placed a large wooden bucket with no lid in our room. Every morning, we took turns to empty it into a stinking pit behind the house. The bucket was washed with water fetched from a nearby pond, but the room stank anyway.

The first night, I was disturbed by a terrible smell. One of the girls had a tummy complaint and used the bucket again and again. None of us got much sleep that night. Of course, we were all embarrassed, but after a few days, and a lot of joking, we got used to it. Often, in the middle of a conversation, one of us would use the bucket without interrupting our flow of words. The time I hated most was when I first entered the room after being in the fresh air and the stench hit me.

There was worse to come. In the fields, we had to use a big hole in the ground surrounded by a woven reed fence. A pole was nailed to an upright at each end for us to pop our bums over. I hated it. It was the most unpleasant place I have ever encountered in my whole life, but I had to use it: it was strictly forbidden to go elsewhere.

There were millions of flies. Of course, with no birds, the flies multiplied to plague proportions. Whenever I was forced to go to the 'toilet', millions of flies rose to greet me. No words can adequately describe such a place. I began to feel so sorry for the rest of the world. If this was 'heaven' in China, how bad was the 'hell' they had to put up with? But we dared not complain. We had to put up happily with the 'Three Togethers': live together, eat together and labour together, with the poorest of the poor people.

There was a pond near the village, the only source of water in the area – it served both humans and beasts. The villagers used the water for cooking, washing and laundry. Animals used the pond the way animals do. It was not long before the girls in our room, including me, were suffering from diarrhoea, along with just about every member of our school. I hated the idea of drinking the water from the pond. It was not clear like city water, but a murky brown. Despite boiling every drop of water on a small stove, we still had severe pains in our stomachs and could not control our bowels. We were up for most of every night, either comforting others or being comforted. Our supply of toilet paper was quickly disappearing, and once it was gone . . .

Our first working day began with 'class education'. We had to attend a meeting arranged by the commune leader, called 'Remembering the Past Bitterness and Thinking of the Present Sweetness'. An old and very poor peasant woman gave us a report on her bitter life in the old society under the Kuomintang government. She had been born into a poor tenant peasant family and became a child wife at the age of twelve. She was made to do all kinds of hard labour, but never had good food to eat. She had no shoes and went barefoot all the year round, even in the icy winters, and she was beaten regularly by her cruel landlord. She cried as she remembered those terrible times and her audience, including me, felt sad about her unhappy life as compared to the sweetness of our own.

However, it was not long before we noticed something wrong with her report. She dwelt on the terrible hunger of 1960 to 1962, which had occurred under the Communists! She was clearly unaware of her mistake, because she was illiterate and could not distinguish between the Kuomintang and Communist governments. All she knew was the hard life she had endured, and to her the old past and the recent past had blurred into one. As soon as the leaders realized her mistake, they led her away from the meeting. The commune leader explained that she was too old and sad and her mind was muddled; everyone in the village knew that all of her unhappiness had happened under the Kuomintang regime. I don't think many of us were fooled but, as usual, nothing was said.

After the meeting, we were divided into groups to be taken around the commune to visit the poor and lower-middle-class peasant families. I was astonished to see the terrible conditions these people were living in. Of course, we were guided only to the poorest houses. To visit the better homes might cause us to come into contact with a class enemy. The homes I saw had mud floors with chickens and dogs running around, and shit everywhere. The roofs were made from hay spread across wooden slats. Filthy children, sucking on dirty chicken bones or even dirtier fingers, crawled around and every house smelt bad. For the first time, I began to question all I had been told, and all I believed in. Was this the 'happy life' I had heard so much about? If so, how had they existed in the bad old days? And was this really better than conditions in the capitalist countries? Could anything be worse than this?

The next day we went into the fields for our first lessons in harvesting. Some were assigned to pick cotton bolls, and I was among those chosen to cut down the rice. By the time the grain was ready to be harvested, the fields were dry. My experience of the wet paddyfields was yet to come, but not during this visit to the countryside. I was given a sickle and shown how to cut the rice stems. I had to bend over all the time, and by lunchtime, I was running with sweat and exhausted.

As I sat eating my meagre meal and drinking the brown boiled water, I wondered how on earth I was going to get through the rest of the day. Two of the fingers on my left hand had deep cuts that wouldn't stop bleeding, but the pain blended in with the aching of the rest of my body. I couldn't stand upright and my arms and legs felt like lead.

The afternoon was worse. I cut myself again, and my injured fingers were swollen and painful. The girl next to me had cut her fingers too. Like the rest of us, she bore her pain without complaint. I wondered why we couldn't get the cuts dressed, but said nothing.

I looked at the sun, praying for it to set quickly, but it was glued to the sky. Time seemed to have stopped. My arm hurt every time I swung the sickle. How I hated that sickle! I winced every time it came down, in anticipation of another cut. Fortunately, I was learning to keep my left hand well away from the blade. Both my hands were raw and blistered, and some of the blisters had burst. I bled from those too. I glanced at the girl next to me. She, too, was leaving a trail of blood on the cut stems. Her face was red and awash with sweat, and her neck was badly burned by the sun. How I hated the sun. Would it ever go down over the horizon? At long last it did, and a whistle sounded. The first labour day was over. Only twelve more like it. Then we could march back to the city.

All that I had experienced so far – the bucket, the pit, the water and the work – were as nothing compared to the fleas. That night, my whole body itched and red lumps appeared all over me. I could not sleep for the itching and the pain. I felt as though I was being eaten alive.

I was scared of life in the countryside. I hated everything about it. We had been told that the countryside around Shanghai was the best rural area in China. That meant other places were worse. We were expected to be prepared to live and work in the countryside after finishing middle school. Our teacher said, 'Everybody must have one red heart for two preparations, entering university or going to the countryside according to the needs of the revolution.' But now I only wanted one preparation: to enter university! I said to myself repeatedly: 'I shall never come back to live in the countryside. I must enter university!'

A shiver ran through me at the thought. My firm pledges to the Party were collapsing. I felt ashamed of myself, because I doubted whether I could show loyalty to the Party if the Party needed me to settle in the countryside. The Party had given me many honours and I was an advanced student, but I wanted to stay in the city. I didn't care what the Party wanted or if the revolution needed me to be in the countryside! Of course, other students must have been having the same thoughts but as they said nothing, I kept silent too.

The two weeks in the countryside had seemed like two years to me. At last we were going home. We were filthy. I was desperate for a bath. The peasants only had the odd wash in the pond in summer and for special events such as a wedding. All of us were one red rash and there were many stops to allow students to relieve themselves. By this time, all of us were unconcerned about appearances and privacy. All we wanted was to get home. My fingers were lumps of festering inflamed flesh and my palms were covered with calluses and fresh blisters, but I had never been so happy in my life; I was leaving that hell-hole of a place, and going back to civilization.

★

After the countryside and my return to school, I wanted to spend more time on my studies – to ensure that my future would be in education, not agriculture – so I asked my teacher to arrange for me to be excused all social activities. Fortunately, we had become quite close and she was very supportive. She told everyone that my health would not allow me to do as much as I had before. It was impossible for her to have all the meetings cancelled but she reduced them and I settled down to regular concentrated study.

Though I had been the youngest daughter in my own family, I was the oldest child in Uncle Wang Feng's home. When I arrived there, Uncle's son was eight and he had two younger sisters, one aged five and a newborn baby. Uncle Wang Feng had been in the military for most of his life and he was a serious man. He thought it his duty to mould me into an 'ideal person'.

His problem was not me but his own children. Where they were concerned, he had a blind spot. He had told me, on my first day in his home, that I should behave like a big sister to them. That meant I should help them with their studies and play with them. He expected me to devote all my free time to them. When they misbehaved it was my fault because I was not doing a good job to guide them. If the boy refused to do his homework, that was my fault too. In fact, everything they did wrong, even the crying of the baby, was because I had neglected them. This put enormous pressure on me: I was only thirteen. Uncle Wang Feng was just and generous towards his comrades, but he spoilt his children. His own early life had been so miserable that he was determined his children would have the best he could give them.

Uncle's dream of seeing his children enter Fuxin Middle School never came true. To begin with, they failed the entrance examination. When he tried to use his position to get them in through the back door, the headmaster steadfastly refused to let them in – he knew how badly they behaved. But that was all in the future – I had to cope with this situation from the first day I walked into his house.

I was too young to be in control of children. I had no idea how to help them with their studies. I tried to teach them how to read and write, but it was no good: they just couldn't, or wouldn't, concentrate. Eventually I gave up because I had better things to do with my time. This annoyed my uncle and he scolded me many times for shutting myself in my room and doing my homework instead of helping his children. On several occasions he even summoned my teachers to his home to watch me do self-criticism. He made me stand in front of them while he accused me of being selfish by ignoring his children. I had to call myself all the nasty names I could think of as tears ran down my cheeks. 'I am selfish and full of personal vanity'; 'I am only concerned about myself'; 'I do not appreciate my good fortune to live here'; 'I am wrong to do the things I do. I must change my ways'; 'I am not like a big sister to my younger cousins'; and many, many more. On it would go, for up to two hours at a time. My misery flowed out of me as I stood before them in hand-me-down clothes, and shoes made from old uniforms and car tyres, gulping out the words of my failure, knowing I would be taunted by my cousins after their father had finished with me. Once it was over, I always gave a little bow to the teachers and to my uncle before escaping to the kitchen where I would sit, weeping my heart out. The worst part was the knowledge that the episode had not helped me to teach his children and that I could expect the whole thing to be repeated sometime soon.

It was at these times that I missed my mother most and I cried even harder. The servant was sympathetic and kind – she would try to cheer me up with a big steamed bun with lots of sugar inside it. Wang Feng's wife was kind too and never scolded me, but she was a typical Chinese wife: whatever her husband did, she supported. When her husband scolded me, she kept silent.

During my stay in Shanghai, I kept in contact with my siblings by letter. Andong and Wei-guo wrote regularly to me, but Pei-gen never did. This was no surprise to me, but I continued to write to her. As Pei-gen was the eldest, I thought of her as the nearest thing to my mother, and filled my letters with my unhappiness. It seemed easier to open my heart to her because she never replied.

Wei-guo had an even more unhappy time, but the source of his misery was the nasty wife of Uncle Gao Dao-fang. When he was there my uncle was kind to my brother, but he was usually away inspecting work at different docks spread along the banks of the Yangtze River. In Dao-fang's absence Wei-guo was ill-treated both by his wife and by her children. Influenced by her, they considered Wei-guo an intrusion into their lives, a nuisance who robbed them of their father's attention.

My brother felt no warmth in their home and hated going back there after school. He took to wandering along the riverbank until it was dark and everybody was in bed. Eventually, after several late nights, he found the door locked when he got to the house. No one responded to his knocking, so he spent the night sitting on the cold concrete stairs. His request for a key was refused with a cuff around the head. He was just eleven when he was sent to Uncle Dao-fang's home, and over the next two and a half years, he changed from a pleasant, gregarious boy to a solitary, bad-tempered lout. He was discovered by a neighbour on many a morning curled up on the landing, shivering with cold.

Eventually, Uncle Dao-fang was told about the bad treatment my brother was getting and he remonstrated with his wife, but she wouldn't change her ways. Her bad attitude was finally reported to Auntie Chen, one of my mother's oldest and closest friends in Nanjing. Auntie Chen had some business in Wuhan and, on her way back to Nanjing, she went to my uncle's home to take a few gifts to my brother. She was horrified by what she found and hurried back to Nanjing to report to the Municipal Party Committee.

The news spread fast within the Nanjing People's Government and many of my mother's old colleagues and friends felt indignant about the ill-treatment of her son. Soon, a delegation demanded the return of Wei-guo to the safety of Nanjing. When Andong heard about it, she asked to have her brother with her. She said she was lonely and needed his company. She also argued that, at eighteen, she was now old enough to look after him and said that he would be happier with her.

My uncle knew he could not protect Wei-guo because he had to be away most of the time. Also, he was losing an enormous amount of face: he was becoming known as the man who could not control his wife and children, and the man who badly treated the son of two revolutionary martyrs. Eventually, he bowed to the pressures and sent him back to Nanjing.

This raised another problem. I was still at Uncle Wang Feng's home. If Uncle Dao-fang sent my brother back to Nanjing he would appear to be neglecting his duties, because he would be the only uncle not taking responsibility for the raising of us orphans. Such is the Chinese way of thinking. The three uncles had a meeting. It was clear that my brother could no longer stay where he was. Uncle Wang Feng was not happy either: in his view I wasn't helping enough with his children, so he didn't argue against sending me back to Nanjing. Andong was supposedly cared for by Uncle Peng in Nanjing, but in fact she was independent. She spent all her time at school on her own except for some weekends when she stayed at Uncle Peng's home. The Uncles finally agreed that we could all lodge with Andong. Thus the problem was solved in the Chinese way.

In January 1965, a few days before the end of my fifth term at Fuxin Middle School, Uncle Wang Feng told me that he and the other uncles had decided to send me back to Nanjing as soon as I finished the end-of-term examination. I was stunned. I might have been unhappy at home but I loved my school and I had pinned all my hopes on graduating from there. But I had no say in deciding my own destiny. I had to leave, whether I wanted to or not. I packed my things into a suitcase and shaped my old quilt into a bedroll. Uncle purchased a train ticket for me, and early the next morning he and his wife took me to the railway station.

When we got there, it was still dark but my teacher and at least thirty of my classmates were waiting to see me off. I was crying, my teacher was crying, the girls were crying and my auntie was crying. Even Uncle had red eyes as we said goodbye. Everyone told me to take good care of myself and asked me to write to them. I leaned out of the window and waved and waved, long after I could no longer see anyone.

8. High School in Nanjing

As I alighted from the train in Nanjing, I heard the voices of Andong and Wei-guo as they pushed through the crowds. 'Anhua! Anhua!' We were all excited and happy to be together once more and we danced around, hugging each other. My brother was now much taller than me. He took my bedroll and slung it over his shoulders. 'Let's go home!' he shouted, above the noise of the crowds.

A big lump grew in my throat and tears threatened. 'Where is our home now?' I asked, as normally as I could, but without fooling my sister.

She came back to give me another hug and said into my ear, 'Don't worry. We are together again and this is better than anything else. We will stay in my dormitory at school for now.' She linked arms with me and the three of us threaded our way through the crowds and out of the station.

The school Andong was attending was called 'School Attached to Nanjing Normal University' and was the premier middle school in the whole of Jiangsu Province. It had been built in 1902, with money supplied by foreign diplomats, and was used initially to educate the children of the Nanjing élite classes, such as rich Chinese, Kuomintang high officials and the many foreigners then living in the area.

By the time I was transferred there, half of the students were children of high government officials and senior military officers, and the other half came from the families of professors, engineers and scientists. Children from labouring families had almost no chance of being accepted as students and the people of Nanjing had nicknamed it the School for the Aristocrats. When we arrived that day it was quiet – everyone was away for the winter vacation. My brother was now a student there too. Normally he lived in the boys' dormitory but during the vacation he was allowed to stay with Andong.

Andong and I sat up talking almost all of the first night. She had a small stove and some coal, and we sat near it, in a corner of the room near a window, because there was no chimney. These coal stoves were used extensively in China. They were a good source of warmth but also very dangerous, many people losing their lives by breathing in the fumes or setting their homes on fire. After I had settled in, Andong boiled some rice and vegetables on it for the three of us. Then Wei-guo grumbled his way to bed, which gave Andong and me an opportunity to whisper our hopes for the future.

The first thing I did after returning to Nanjing was to buy myself a pair of new cotton padded shoes and two pairs of nylon socks. My mother had been dead for over three years, but Wei-guo was still wearing the tank-top knitted by her long before she had gone into hospital for the last time. It was much too small and tight so I gave him a sweater of mine while I unpicked the tank-top to salvage what wool I could, then bought some more and knitted it all up into a nice, warm cardigan that buttoned up to the neck. Andong and I shared the responsibility of looking after our brother. Andong made him settle down to serious study, ignoring his complaints, and I took care of his food, clothes, and making sure he kept himself clean.

On the third day, we went to see our grandparents. My dear old grandfather was now very frail and had to use a walking-stick, but his eyes still had the light of mischief in them. I had brought two egg pies for him as I knew he loved them but as he took them his hands trembled badly, and I realized it would not be long before I lost him too. I knew how sad he had been since Mother's funeral, and he knew how I felt too. He opened his arms and I wrapped myself around him, tears trickling down our faces.

Before we left, Grandfather asked us to spend the Spring Festival with them, and we agreed. However, two days later, our old neighbours, Uncle Jiang and Auntie Zhu, came to see us. They had made a special journey to warn us not to visit our grandparents too often because they had been landlords. It was important that we obey, because we were now relying on the charity of the people, and if we defied the Party we would destroy our future.

We were still obedient children, so we did not see our grandparents during the Spring Festival, but my heart was with them. In China, the Spring Festival is a time for unity of the family, and I had been looking forward to us all being together. I was beginning to resent the constant interference in my life of people spouting politics. Everything that gave me pleasure was not allowed by some obscure Party ruling. Why was it bad for me to visit my grandparents?

That same day, I received a letter from Uncle Wang Feng. He said he felt empty after I had left, that something of importance had gone from his house. He wrote warm words, but all I could remember was his ill-treatment of me. Nevertheless, I wrote back. I said I was doing fine, emphasized my independence and how good I felt about it. I finished by thanking him and his wife for caring for me, and promised I would always keep in touch.

I still had my ambition to graduate from middle school within five years. Students of my age, which was nearly sixteen, were in junior three at this school, but I needed to join senior one to graduate a year early. Andong collected a full set of books for me and, to my relief, I found that mathematics and chemistry would not be a problem. However, in English and physics, I needed to catch up so I settled down to study hard.

I got up early every morning and pored over my books from six in the morning to ten in the evening. I read and practised my English, and even Andong's English improved as she coached me. She also helped me with the physics. It was obvious that she was destined to enter university soon, and she said she would like to become a teacher.

On 12 February, the first day of the new term, the director of teaching gave me an oral examination in English and physics. I read out the English text quickly, and when I had finished, I looked at him, feeling proud of myself. He said nothing, simply started a conversation in English. That was harder, so I chose my words carefully, and coped well enough. The physics was easier, and I passed the oral section without any problems. Then came the written examinations, and I passed those too. He checked my student report, which I had brought with me from Shanghai, and a smile lit up his face.

'Very good,' he said. 'Of course we have heard about you from your sister. You can study in senior one, but if you cannot keep up, I will have to put you back to junior three.'

The director accompanied me to my classroom and introduced me to my new classmates. I was a little intimidated because they seemed so grown-up. I was going to be the youngest pupil in the class, and also the smallest. However, my worries disappeared when I was given a warm welcome by everyone during the break. After lunch my new teacher surprised me by announcing that I had been appointed a Youth League cadre, responsible for class propaganda and the school blackboard newspaper. Suddenly, Shanghai seemed a long time ago.

At the end of the holidays my brother and I had moved out of Andong's dormitory. I shared a room with eleven of my classmates: six double-decker beds, three on each side of the room, with a small wardrobe each for our clothes, and a tiny bedside locker for our bits and pieces. Andong, Wei-guo and I each lived in a different dormitory, but we met every evening around Andong's small stove to do our homework. Andong and I continued to look after our brother. We spent half our money on food and some on coal. I felt more secure now that we had control of our finances. I had more pocket money than ever before and could now buy some of the things I had always wanted, without being scolded by an adult. Soon, I had a small library of my favourite books and some decent clothes. 'Plain living' was all very well, but I was growing up and felt a need for pretty things.

Food was still rationed. In the school dining rooms, every student was given a fixed amount a day. Boys and girls had equal portions. Every morning we had one bowl of rice porridge and a small steamed bun, which was enough for the girls, but not for growing boys like Wei-guo. He was always hungry by ten in the morning and so were the other boys. I constantly heard them grumbling during the breaks. 'I'm starving!' was the morning chorus. I remembered how my mother had saved her food for us while she was in the hospital so I began to give Wei-guo my breakfast bun.

Wei-guo was so tall now that Andong and I thought he looked older than us. At the beginning of every term, we challenged new pupils to say which of us was the eldest. Most thought it was Wei-guo, until they saw us enter our respective classes.

In those days, foreigners were rare in China, but as our school was a showcase for the provincial educational system, we regularly had foreign visitors from friendly countries. I was happy in my new school. It was easily the equal of Fuxin Middle School in Shanghai. Students were encouraged to use their brains, instead of simply being fed information. The teacher gave us brief details of a subject, then it was up to us to learn all we could through self-study. An examination followed, and our marks went towards our end-of-term results. If we got into difficulties, we were always able to ask the teachers for guidance, either in or out of the classroom.

The boy who sat at the desk in front of mine was named Chen (he later adopted the English name Greg) and he, too, was a child of a revolutionary martyr. His father had been one of the first Red Army soldiers, and had taken part in the Long March. He had fought his way through China, first against the warlords, then the Japanese and finally the Kuomintang. Like my mother, he had died of heart trouble. Greg's mother was a leader in the local People's Government, and she and my mother had been friends. She still lived with her children, including Greg, in the house given to her husband. Greg was a handsome boy, with a quick, clever mind. He raised all sorts of questions for the teachers, and was often cheeky. He was popular and I secretly adored him.

Another boy, called Tian, had transferred from Beijing when I had come from Shanghai. He was the son of a high official, and I liked him too. Both Greg and Tian were much involved in school activities, but neither was in the Youth League. That seemed odd to me. Soon, I found out the reason.

The League secretary of my branch was a tall, strong girl named Zhang, who could beat the boys at carrying two big buckets of water on a shoulder pole. She was proud of her strength. Looking at her, it was hard to believe she was the 'Little Precious' of a senior professor who lectured at Nanjing Normal University. She was clever too, so she was highly praised and admired by the school authorities. They said she was an excellent example of a child from an 'undesirable' family, who had been able to 'remould herself through hard labour'.

I was one of only five members of the Youth League leadership in our class able to recruit new members, and I badly wanted Greg and Tian to join. I found out that they had sent in their completed application forms but had been refused membership. Apparently, Zhang and her best friend always voted against them, saying, 'Greg and Tian are too undisciplined and too naughty. Also, they shun those from bad family backgrounds, so they don't help in uniting all the people to take part in the revolution.'

Another girl and I voted for their acceptance. The meeting always included five people, and the fifth girl abstained so as not to bring trouble on herself, so the votes ended up as 2:2 and the applications were turned down. I felt sorry for Greg and Tian. I knew they wanted to be members, but I had to be cautious and play my cards carefully.

The school policy was that students in senior grades should be divided into two groups; half should concentrate on physics and half on chemistry. I was lucky to be in the half to study chemistry. I had been well taught in Shanghai so I was allowed to study alone during the chemistry lessons. This meant that most of the time when I should have been learning chemistry I was working on my English. I began reading simplified versions of stories written by the great English writers, like Charles

Dickens and Shakespeare. I read *Great Expectations* twice and *Oliver Twist*
three times. Shakespeare was much harder going and I had to push myself
to plough through his works. Then I discovered the Brontë sisters. Their
books fired my imagination and I made myself a promise that I would
try to see the places I could only read about now. *Jane Eyre* was my
favourite. I hugged it to my chest after reading the last words on the last
page, full of romantic dreams.

I adored English literature. I plundered the school library and scoured
the local shops for any book by an English author. I found Thomas Hardy,
George Eliot, Thackeray, and many others, until my own collection of
books had doubled and then doubled again.

Political study was still the most important subject. The education authority repeatedly demanded that we students 'put politics in command'.
'Class struggle' was continually emphasized by the Party and must be
thought about 'every year, every month, every day, every hour, every
minute and every second of our lives'. We must never forget that the
US imperialists and their 'running dogs', such as the British, had occupied
many countries that did not belong to them. At that time, our friend
Vietnam had been invaded by the USA, so we must support the Vietnamese people to wipe out the US aggressors and their running dogs. A
vision of the charming Ho Chi Minh came to me, and I felt real hatred
for the Americans. We went on school-sponsored demonstrations in the
streets, denouncing the USA, shouting our slogans, beating our drums
and waving our flags. I joined in with great enthusiasm, waving my fist
in the air, shouting, 'Down with the US imperialists and their running
dogs! US imperialists and all their running dogs, get out of all the places
you have robbed! Get out of Vietnam!'

Britain was considered the chief running dog of the United States,
because it supported everything the US did. This pained me, because I
was growing attached to the country on the edge of the sky. But how
could I feel so drawn to our enemy? My parents had fought for our
freedom, and Britain wanted to take it away and again put chains around
our necks to work us like oxen. I was so mixed up but I could not talk
to anyone. Nobody must know how I felt. If they did, I knew the
punishment would be severe, that was certain. So I kept silent, and tried
to make sense of my confusion.

We were constantly urged to remember the four 'Never Forgets':
never forget the class struggle, never forget the proletarian dictatorship,

never forget the continuation of the revolution, and never forget to hold high the great banner of Mao Tse-tung thought. The four 'Never Forgets' had been raised by Lin Biao, Minister of National Defence. In 1965 he had published quotations from Chairman Mao's works for the whole army to study: *The Little Red Book* was covered in a red plastic jacket. In the foreword, he wrote, 'Mao Tse-tung thought is the greatest Marxism and Leninism in the modern era,' which was set to music and broadcast every day over the radio.

The Little Red Book was to spread across China during the Cultural Revolution, but until then it was not in the book stores. Some children of important military officers managed to get a copy from their fathers, which earned them the admiration of other students. Greg's family was well connected with the Nanjing Army Unit, so he got one. Soon, Tian persuaded his father to give him a copy. As my parents were dead, I didn't think I would ever own a copy of *The Little Red Book*, and I wanted one so badly. Greg and Tian kindly let me hold theirs and riffle their pages.

In April 1965, another soldier was made a hero for the whole nation to learn from. Wang Jie had sacrificed his life to save a young militiaman during a military training exercise. He was training a group of young soldiers to throw live hand-grenades. One recruit was nervous and dropped his as he pulled out the pin. The seconds ticked by as he stared, transfixed, at the grenade lying just inches from his feet. The other trainees threw themselves to the ground, but Wang Jie flung himself forward and covered the grenade with his body just before it exploded. His chest was blown to bits, but his action saved his comrades and the young recruit was unharmed.

While he was packing Wang Jie's belongings, the company sergeant found his diary. In it he had written, 'Soldiers armed with Mao Tse-tung thought are all-conquering. For the revolution, I fear neither hardships nor death.' Chairman Mao was so impressed by this, he raised another call: 'I'm for the slogan, "Fear neither hardships nor death."' Then he lengthened it: 'Fight against egoism and denounce revisionism.' This became the main slogan for us students to follow. We were told to think only of the revolution. No personal needs and feelings were allowed. We must 'regard Mao Tse-tung thought as our food, our weapon and our steering-wheel, and always act according to Chairman Mao's instructions in our daily life', as Lei Feng had written in his diary.

In the early summer of 1965, our political teacher told us, 'According to Chairman Mao's teachings, China is surrounded by international class enemies. A Third World War is unavoidable and could begin at any time. Therefore we must always be prepared for war.' All work units, factories and government organizations formed their own militia units. Even the smallest farming communes trained for war. Hoardings emblazoned with 'Fear neither hardships nor death!' sprang up everywhere, and the people went about their daily lives in fear. Mao also said, 'We must make every citizen a soldier and put the entire nation under arms.'

Our political teacher told us this was Chairman Mao's great theory of 'people's warfare' so we students formed our own company of militia. The *People's Daily*, the official newspaper of the Communist Party, published an editorial under the heading 'Long Live the Victory of People's Warfare', and the same editorial was broadcast to the nation. From then, and for many months, the paper printed a series of similar 'important editorials', which were also broadcast, keeping the notion of world war at the forefront of everyone's mind, and the militia companies constantly ready for action.

At school, we got up early every morning, while it was still dark, and began our morning drills. We ran round the school campus, shouting, 'One, two, three, four!' in time with our steps, like the regular PLA soldiers. I always got a sharp pain in my forehead as I breathed in the cold morning air, and ended up with a stitch in my side, but somehow I went the distance. I had to, because it would have meant ridicule if I had dropped out.

In the afternoon, after two periods of study, we formed up in the playground for bayonet practice. We had no real rifles or bayonets, of course, so we used broom handles, shoulder poles or pickaxe handles instead. We were expected to show our deep hatred of the enemy by shouting at the top of our voices, 'Aaaaaaahhh, *kill*!' as we lunged at a dummy.

Greg did well in those drills. This gave me a good reason to propose him again for the Youth League. The girl who did best was Zhang, the League secretary. She had a voice like the engine of a tank, and her thrust forward with the shoulder pole made us all wince, as though it was us she was cutting to shreds. I didn't like bayonet drill. With my tiny voice, I could barely be heard by those behind me, and my 'deadly' thrust with the pole was more like a friendly tickle. I also had trouble with grenade throwing. The chunk of brick we used in place of a grenade was too big for my hand, and I frequently dropped it as I tried to hurl it towards 'enemy lines'. And my aim was appalling. My comrades kept well clear when it was my turn to throw. On the odd occasion when I got the brick to fly in the general direction of the target, the others would cheer ironically.

I tried my utmost to be good at the drills – my throat would be sore after shouting as loudly and as gruffly as I could when attacking the dummies, and my arm always ached after grenade throwing – but I was never going to make a good militiawoman. It was at these times that I was glad I was a girl. When war came, it was the boys who would march off to do battle. We girls would be kept in the rear, doing female things like nursing, cooking and administration. My worry was my brother. He was growing broader and taller every day, and was sure to be one of the first chosen to go. He was looking forward to it. He was ever ready to fight other boys, and he was often punished for his short temper and loutish behaviour.

I hated eating a 'Bitterness Meal'. In order to remind us of the old society, when China was ruled by the Kuomintang and the black-robed landlords, the school kitchens produced brown buns made of rice husks which, we were told, were the basic food of the labouring classes in days gone by. We were made to eat them with 'good class feelings', and were told we must always remember the past and be thankful for the present. The 'Bitterness Meal' was hard to swallow, so I used to throw half of it down the toilet and flush it away. I suspect that half the school did, but it was I who was discovered by the ever-vigilant unknown reporter and severely criticized by the teacher at the next militia meeting.

However, when I renewed my efforts to have Tian and Greg accepted into the League, the girl who had abstained was persuaded to vote in their favour. At the next elections, both boys and I were elected to be members of the leadership.

One result of 'denouncing revisionism' throughout our country in 1965 was Chairman Mao's decision to abolish the system of military ranks that China had taken from the Russians. All the epaulettes on the officers' uniforms showing their ranks disappeared, and so did the army-style peaked caps. Army men and women changed into a one-style uniform with one plain red oblong pinned on each side of the collar, and a red metal star in front of the soft peakless cap. The shirt buttoned up to the neck, and officers and men looked the same. The officers kept their ranks, but from then on they were not saluted in the streets. It was explained that officers and soldiers in the Chinese People's Liberation Army were now equal, and it was 'a very bad thing' for any soldier or officer to have ambition or hopes of promotion. Such personal desires for advancement were considered 'shameful and selfish, full of egoism'. Few understood the reasons for the change. Even high-ranking officers were puzzled, but if Mao ordered it, it must be right. It was really the first salvo of the Cultural Revolution. Mao was laying the foundations of his next – and most horrific – campaign.

The new-style uniform was called a 'revolutionary red star over the head and the revolutionary red flags flying from both sides'. By this time everything about the USSR was bad, worse even than the USA, and billboards and hoardings vilified it. I was very confused. Only a few years before, everything about Russia had been good. When I saw Uncle Peng in his new army uniform, I thought it was ugly. He had come to say goodbye to us because he had been transferred to the Anhui Provincial Army Unit to be the new political commissar.

On the last Sunday in April 1965, I visited Uncle Jiang and Auntie Zhu. They confided that they had decided not to go to their respective offices any more because, officially, they were not in good health. He had high blood pressure and she was suffering from a gastric ulcer. Then Uncle Jiang smiled and gave me a crafty wink. 'To tell you the truth, Little Flower, we are fed up with those everlasting political meetings, but we dare not say anything, so we invented the excuses that we are not well.'

Their ailments were real but they had played up the symptoms so that they could stay at home on permanent sick leave. They were not the only ones. All over China, old soldiers and freedom-fighters were becoming disappointed with life under Mao. The continual political slogans and campaigns were meaningless to them, just empty words. Of course, they could never say how they felt, so they simply withdrew from their offices, and lived quietly at home, out of danger.

I was astonished to hear Uncle Jiang's explanation, but I was happy too. This was the first time I had been treated as a grown-up and an equal. And I felt honoured that they trusted me with their thoughts – I could easily have caused trouble for them. I also felt a surge of relief in discovering that I was not alone when I mentally questioned what was going on.

Uncle Jiang and Auntie Zhu still enjoyed all the special privileges as high officials. Their adopted daughter Hou-pi was now a student in the Nanjing Foreign Language School, majoring in English. However, she still couldn't concentrate on her studies and was left far behind. Uncle Jiang sighed and shook his head as he told me this.

He had always been overweight, but now that he was not working, he had developed a big belly, which made him look like a jolly old Buddha. I liked him better like that, and enjoyed watching his chins wobble and his tummy shake as he laughed. He was good company and I felt I could trust him and Auntie enough to tell them my own thoughts. I began by telling them about my school life, and how I resented the morning drills and the long-distance run. Those students living at home did not have to do this and I thought it most unfair. Immediately, Uncle picked up the telephone and dialled. He waited a moment, then surprised me with the best present I could have wished for. 'I need a two-bedroomed flat. It is for Comrade Gao Yi-lin's three orphans. You must get it done tomorrow . . . No, that's not good enough. Suppose it was for your own children, what would you feel? . . . Tomorrow? . . . Good. I will check back with you tomorrow evening to see what you have accomplished.'

The next day at lunchtime Andong ran to me. 'Anhua, guess what. We have been given a flat in the compound of the Nanjing Municipal People's Government.' And that afternoon, we moved in. A polite young official was there to ensure that everything went smoothly. As we watched, three single beds, some bedding, a gas stove – a real luxury indeed – and pots and pans were carried in. Andong and I were to share one bedroom and Wei-guo had the other. I unpacked my things, and stuck my foreign film star postcard inside my wardrobe door as usual. My books had to be kept on the floor of our bedroom until I found an old bookcase for them.

The flat was on the second floor of a block and we could hear the noises of normal living going on all around us. Soon our neighbours knocked timidly and introduced themselves. Andong and I investigated the mysteries of the gas stove and cooked our first meal. Then we each had a long, luxurious bath. Thanks to our kind Uncle Jiang, we had a new start.

Spring turned to summer, and by the end of June it was hotter than usual. Time flew by as we enjoyed our new freedom. School became much easier now that we did not have to do the morning drills and runs, although we still had to attend bayonet practice and grenade-throwing. The three of us helped each other with our studies. Poor Wei-guo was finding it more and more difficult to concentrate. His mind never seemed to be on the tasks in hand but somewhere else – like playing ping-pong, which he loved. He often threw down his pen in temper, and thumped out of the room, but Andong and I kept going.

During the last week of June, we heard inspiring news from the radio: 'Our great leader Chairman Mao has again been swimming in the Yangtze River.' He was about seventy-two then and we saw photographs of him on the front page of the newspaper, swimming with just his head showing above the water. Almost every summer, he swam in a big river or the sea. This time, under his photograph was his call, 'Go and train yourself to swim in the big rivers or sea!' In the editorial it said that swimming-pools were a 'bourgeois recreation' and 'the greenhouses of the bourgeois flowers'. The rivers and the sea were the places to swim now.

Most middle-school students enjoyed swimming, but none wanted to be a 'bourgeois flower' so the swimming-pools were suddenly empty. Our political teacher said that, according to Chairman Mao's teachings, we revolutionary younger generation should be like eagles and sea-gulls, who bravely withstand the power of the thunderstorms, and encouraged us to swim in the river. Which we did, in our hundreds, and then in our thousands. Every afternoon almost all the students cycled down to the banks of the Yangtze to swim. It was one way of getting out of bayonet drills and grenade-throwing.

One day a classmate, Qiao Yi, a boy of seventeen, came up to me at the end of the second period of afternoon study. 'Anhua, would you like to go and swim in the Yangtze River?'

I looked up. I wanted to review my lessons, and had planned to hide myself away in the local park. 'No, I'm sorry, Qiao, I need to study. Besides, I cannot swim and I don't feel well.' This was true.

But he continued, 'Don't you want to be a true revolutionary successor? I can't swim either, but we can learn. You know that I have had to miss my schooling for several months because of illness, but I intend to go. We must all strive for a healthy and strong body, and swimming is the best thing to build up our muscles.' This, too, was true. He had been ill for a long time. His small, thin, pale body was even thinner and whiter than usual, and his eyes looked enormous behind his thick glasses. I was irritated by his persistence, but he had hit a nerve: I felt guilty at my lack of response to Mao's call. Not only that, I was beginning to realize that I was never going to be a 100 per cent revolutionary successor. I hated the countryside. I hated rough living. I hated the morning drills. I hated bayonet practice. I hated the rice-husk buns of bitter living. And

I hated being away from my landlord grandparents. I was a bookworm. I loved my books more than anything else in life, except my family. So I refused, with a curt shake of my head and a dismissive shrug of my shoulders. 'Swimming is not compulsory, so I shall not go today. Perhaps tomorrow.' I was ashamed of my anger and softened my words with a smile. He nodded, disappointment showing on his face, and left to join the other students rushing to the river. Andong, Wei-guo, Greg, Tian, Zhang and almost all the others went off to swim while I stayed behind reading.

By dinnertime, everyone had come back, except Qiao Yi. He was missed at bedtime, and the teachers took about a hundred students to the riverbank to look for him. It was a little after ten o'clock that evening when they found him. His body was lying in shallow water several kilometres downstream. He was rushed to the nearest hospital where doctors said he had been dead for several hours.

Qiao's death shocked us all, and a lesson was learned. There had been no teachers or coaches supervising the students, which had made it dangerous. Thousands were going down to the riverbank every day and randomly choosing a place to jump into the water, with no regard for safety. Qiao Yi had picked an unsuitable place for a non-swimmer – full of small whirlpools and a strong current.

I felt awful. If I had gone with him, perhaps I could have saved him. Or maybe I would have drowned too. I felt sad for him and his parents. I had liked him. He was the only son of an intellectual and although he had been quite delicate he had tried hard in all the military drills and to increase his strength. He had applied to join the Youth League and had been turned down because of his family background. Now he had given his life by answering Chairman Mao's call to swim in the river.

The day after the tragedy, the headmaster spoke to the whole school over the loudspeaker system. 'From today, no student may swim in the Yangtze River unless there is a teacher or other qualified escort. And no student may go swimming in any river, pond or lake unless it is a school event organized by the teachers, and authorized by me.' It was a clever speech: he did not say that swimming in the river was prohibited because that would have directly opposed Chairman Mao's call. He simply said that swimming must be organized and properly supervised. However, he never arranged a swimming session in the river. Instead, he had a floodlit outdoor swimming-pool built within the grounds – ours was the only school in Nanjing to have a pool for the safety of the inexperienced. It took three weeks to complete, and two weeks after that I swam my first length. Students of other schools continued to swim unsupervised in the Yangtze River or in Xuanwu Lake, and hundreds of young people drowned during the summer of 1965.

When the summer vacation came round, Uncle Jiang and Auntie Zhu invited me to spend my holidays with them. They said they were worried about me, because I looked too pale, and suspected that I was suffering from anaemia and needed looking after. I had to admit to them that I had been feeling unusually tired and weak for quite a long time.

They decided to improve my general health by giving me the best food they could supply. They put a bed in Hou-pi's room for me, and every morning I was given a fried egg with rice. Most food was still rationed but Uncle Jiang bought eggs on the black-market to ensure that I had one every day. They also made sure I ate plenty of peanuts, which were reputed to be good for the blood, and every afternoon I had a big chunk of watermelon, which is rich in vitamin C. Once a week, they arranged for a doctor to test my blood, and under their care, I soon began to feel better.

Every afternoon during my stay at Uncle Jiang's home, we played cards. Another high official who lived opposite, called Wang Bin, often came to join us. He had once been a grade six lieutenant-general, stationed in the headquarters of the National Defence commanded by Marshal Peng De-huai. When the news came that the marshal had been accused by Mao of being the head of an anti-Party clique, Wang Bin had gasped in astonishment. 'What? Marshal Peng is anti-Party? No! It is absolutely impossible! He is the most loyal person I have ever known.' And that outburst signalled his downfall.

Fortunately, he was kept out of prison by friends who were still in power, but they couldn't prevent him being demoted. They advised him to leave Beijing for his own safety, and that of his family and friends, and arranged for him to transfer out of the army before his move to Nanjing. He was given the position of deputy mayor of Nanjing, but he had no power. (There were four deputy mayors at that time, and Uncle Jiang was one of them.) The two men had liked each other from their first meeting, and soon became friends.

Wang Bin was glad to take off his army uniform because he, too, disliked the never-ending political slogans and campaigns. In fact, he was so unhappy that he had been ready to resign from his position and even the Party. Fortunately he met Uncle Jiang, who convinced him that it would be better if he simply feigned sickness and stayed at home. His 'illness' was TB, so every six months he went to a good sanatorium for a supposed period of convalescence.

When Wang Bin was introduced to me, he turned to Uncle Jiang and smiled. 'This little lady is really very pretty – quite lovely!' I looked at the floor, my face burning. Such compliments were rare in China and it was thought improper for a man to say such things to or about a young maiden. But, as far as I was concerned, Wang Bin couldn't have said anything nicer! I was sixteen and needed to be thought attractive.

Auntie Zhu must have been reading my mind because she bought a sewing-machine and taught Hou-pi and me how to use it. This was a big asset to me: it was much cheaper to make clothes at home rather than to buy ready-made. We could also use it for mending. Although cloth was still rationed, we could now get enough for two new pieces of outdoor clothing and several items of underwear every year.

An armed uprising was led by Zhou En-lai against the Kuomintang on 1 August 1927, and that date is known throughout China as 'Army Day'. In 1965, the thirty-eighth anniversary, Uncle Jiang sent for Andong and Wei-guo so that he could take us all to a special song-and-dance show being held in the Nanjing Great Hall of the People that evening. The mayor, Shu Bu, and his wife, Auntie Lee, had arranged for us to sit beside them in the front row. Auntie Lee had once worked in the office where my mother was the leader, and they had been friends.

Shu Bu had received orders to take over as mayor of Xi'an City – where in 1974 the terracotta soldiers were found. Mao had decided to change all the mayors of major cities, to avoid them forming their own personal cliques, he said. Uncle Shu Bu let us three children stay in his home for several days before he left Nanjing for Xi'an. On our last night, he called us to his office, where he and his wife sat us down with cups of best-quality tea. They confided that they had wanted to care for us themselves when our mother had died, but matters had been taken out of their hands by our uncles. 'We are sorry we shall not see you grow to adulthood and help you on your way through life, but we sincerely wish you every success. Please take care of yourselves and study well. We can see that you are growing into fine young people, and we think your parents can now rest in peace. Good luck to you all.' I felt sad at their words, and gave them both a hug before shaking hands goodbye.

On 5 August Shu Bu and his family left Nanjing. No one could see into the future and the terrible fate that awaited them in Xi'an. Neither could we have guessed that Mao was making his plans. The swimming had been a test, to find out how the young would respond to his words. They hadn't disappointed him. The moving of the mayors ensured an uncoordinated regime in all the major cities, and the denouncing of the army marshals and government members effectively removed any threat to his authority in Beijing. These things were all part of his plan. But no one knew it at that time.

In the middle of August, Andong called for me at Uncle Jiang's house. She said Pei-gen had come from university to spend part of her holiday with us. I agreed to go back with her, and promised Uncle Jiang and Auntie Zhu that I would return soon. On our way home, Andong told me that Pei-gen was angry with me for staying with Uncle Jiang. She had said it wasn't proper for a revolutionary successor to enjoy such good conditions, and that I should have kept to plain living. She had added that although Uncle Jiang deserved a good life because of his past sufferings I certainly didn't. She was even more upset when she saw me dressed in a nice skirt and blouse. I didn't care. She had her life and I had mine.

Andong and I were suspicious. Pei-gen wanted something, that was for sure, but we couldn't think what we had that might interest her. We soon found out. There was no pleasant family reunion. As soon as we arrived at the flat, she sat us down to talk. 'I want us all to go to the People's Government,' she said, 'to take back the things which were stored after the death of Mother.' Ah! I had almost forgotten about them, and thought this was a good idea. Pei-gen was twenty, Andong was eighteen, I was sixteen and Wei-guo was fourteen, so we were old enough to have them now.

Pei-gen was cold towards me, and ignored almost everything I said. I put it down to her displeasure at my staying with Uncle Jiang. She became even angrier when she found out that we had stayed with the mayor, but it was me she rounded on. 'I bet you really enjoy yourself here in Nanjing, living the soft life. You are nothing but a bourgeois decadent!'

I was stunned at her outburst, and almost broke down in tears as I remembered those sad plain-living years in Shanghai. Then I thought she was just reacting to all her political education. I reasoned that she was angry with me for my own good because she wanted me to become a true revolutionary successor. So I looked at her understandingly and said that I would honour my promise to go back to Uncle Jiang's for a few days but then I would return to plain living.

She didn't answer as she bent over, sewing a new pair of knickers. I said, 'If you give that to me, I will sew it with the sewing-machine when I return to Uncle Jiang's house.'

She didn't lift her head as she said quietly, 'I don't need your help. Hand-sewing has always been good enough for me.' Her tone hurt me. It was our first meeting for over four years, and the first time she had been in touch. She had sent no letters, made no visits, and had had no contact with any of us. She had never acted like a big sister. Now, when we were trying to show her how happy we were to be together again, she was doing her best to destroy it. I never understood why she acted as she did, no matter how hard we tried to be nice to her.

Andong inclined her head and swivelled her eyes towards the bathroom. She left the room and I followed. 'She has only come back for the things Mother left for us and she hates to see us getting on so well,' said Andong, cocking her ear for any sound of movement. 'Wei-guo and I tried to be friendly, but it's no use, she is just cold. Never mind, she won't stay long.' We agreed to make the best of things during her visit, and went into the kitchen to cook the plainest-living food we could. I winked at Andong. 'Perhaps we should give her a bitterness meal of rice-husk buns,' I whispered, as we stood giggling like two naughty children.

The next day the four of us went to the organizational department of the Nanjing Municipal Party Committee where, after Pei-gen had filled in the inevitable forms, it was agreed that we could have our inheritance. We were led to an enormous warehouse where thousands of items were piled to the roof, twenty feet above us. There was a strong odour of mould and mice. The custodian took us down a dark, steep staircase into the cellars, where the damp hit our faces like a cold fog.

In the dim light I immediately recognized the camphorwood trunk. There, too, were the bookshelf, the four leather suitcases, Father's leather swivel chair and the big photographs. Everything was there, covered with thick dust, which made us sneeze, but perfectly usable. We claimed what was ours and Pei-gen signed a receipt. Then the whole lot was put on to a cart and taken to our flat.

We cleaned our heirlooms lovingly. As I wiped the frames protecting the photographs of my father, I was dismayed to find mould spots behind the glass, spoiling the pictures. I cleaned it all away and was pleased to find that his face was almost undamaged, so we hung them on the wall beside one of Mother. Andong placed the bookshelf beside her bed and the camphorwood trunk beside mine. I liked the smell of camphor, and enjoyed breathing in the aroma every time I lay down.

Inside the trunk, we found a feather-and-down padded quilt, several of Mother's coats, some books and all the files containing the writings of my parents. The clothes were too big for me, so my sisters divided them between them. Pei-gen claimed the largest suitcase and packed it with some of Mother's clothes and shoes. Andong was content with the two smaller suitcases and the rest of the clothes, and Wei-guo was happy to accept a small round table, Father's leather chair and a suitcase containing a few things that had belonged to him. We had fun that night when Wei-guo tried to shave and cut himself several times. Pei-gen also wanted the quilt, so we agreed that she should have it. I laid claim to the photographs, including the big ones which had once hung on the bedroom wall, the certificates of revolutionary martyrhood and the files of our parents' writings. I also wanted a share of the books, and added a few new titles to my library. A book of poetry by Pushkin was one. They gave me the camphorwood trunk too, so I could store my new treasures in it. I have it still. It continues to waft camphor into my face every time I open it, and it holds my little keepsakes.

Finally it was time to divide the money Mother had left us. Altogether it came to 1,300 yuan, enough for one person to live comfortably for at least five years. We divided it up fairly. Each of us got 200 yuan, and with the rest we bought a bright new bicycle each. It was a real luxury to own a new bicycle in those days and we proudly rode them home from the department store, showing off every sparkle of the chrome and flash of the new paintwork. The bells tinkled loudly and the pumps gleamed white, drawing many admiring glances from passers-by.

Pei-gen went back to her university a couple of days later, and we saw her off at the station. She had seemed much more approachable after we had sorted out Mother's effects, and as we helped her load her things on to the train and saw her bicycle safely tucked away in the goods van, she looked almost happy. She even leaned out of a window to wave goodbye as the train pulled out of the station.

That evening I returned to Uncle Jiang's home. A young PLA soldier was in the living room. Uncle introduced him to me as Hui, the son of a high official in Anhui Province who had known my father. Hui was twenty-two and he had been in the army for four years, following his graduation from middle school. He was on his way home for two weeks' leave, and had dropped in to visit Uncle Jiang whilst changing trains.

Hui stared at me, it seemed for ever, but it was more like a minute as we shook hands. Our fingers seemed reluctant to part as I returned his look before dropping my eyes. Uncle looked at us with amusement, then he laughed delightedly. This was the first man he had seen me take any notice of, and he was pleased. He stood between us and put one arm around my shoulders and other around Hui's before looking seriously at us. 'Believe it or not, I was once young myself. I know all about your feelings, but please, don't think of love now. Be friends. Anhua, you are still too young, and you have to finish your studies. Hui, you are on your way home. Go now, but call again on your way back to camp.'

I was embarrassed and shy. My body was talking to me in a language I couldn't understand, and strange but wonderful feelings zipped up and down my spine. Hui blushed, too, as he replied, 'Of course I won't do anything which is not proper. I was just taken by surprise, that's all. I'm now a Party member, so I know what must come first.' Then he turned to me: 'I have heard about you from Uncle Jiang. I hope we can be friends. Pure friends, good and true. Perhaps we can help each other on our road to revolution.' I nodded, pleased that this handsome young man liked me, because I liked him too.

Ten days passed as I waited impatiently for Hui to return. Then his tall frame and handsome face were before me at last. I felt love burst out from my heart and fill my chest. It was glorious.

Hui spent the last few days of his leave with me. We talked every day for hours, walking the crowded streets of the city, but oblivious to it all. The days flew, and too quickly it was time for him to go. We went sadly to the railway station, accompanied by Uncle Jiang, and said goodbye. Before he left, he gave me his address and asked me whether I would reply if he wrote to me. If he had not asked me, I would have begged him! I clutched the small slip of paper in my hand as I stood waving, long after the train had left the station. Hui was my first boyfriend.

Soon after I had seen him off, I began my studies in senior two. I rode my new bicycle to school, flanked by Andong and Wei-guo on theirs. A week later, the first of many letters came from Hui. I opened it with a bumping heart. In it he told me about his life in the army. He filled every page with his vitality and enthusiasm, so that his comrades became my friends, and his daily doings were as familiar to me as my own. We wrote to each other about literature, and learned that we both loved the English classics. He said he wanted to leave the army and work in Nanjing, and was simply waiting for his chance. Also, he said he knew about my past, and his father approved of our friendship. He repeated in every letter that he would always help me, anytime and anywhere. All I had to do was to ask.

My letters to him were more restrained. I didn't dare write what was going on inside me. My first letter to him was also my first letter to a boy, other than my brother. I thanked him for his concern for me, and I told him about my school life and my family. Of course, we sprinkled our letters with plenty of revolutionary slogans to please his censors.

He had his photograph taken and sent it to me. As we middle-school students were not allowed to have love affairs, I tried to restrain myself, but in the end I just had to send one of myself to him. I kept my correspondence with Hui a secret from everyone, even Uncle Jiang. His letters brought me sunshine. He made my life more colourful.

The Mid-autumn Festival came in September that year. Like the Spring Festival, it is a time for the unity of the family. People enjoy looking at the full moon on that night while eating 'moon cakes'. A woman who used to work with Mother, whom we hadn't seen since the funeral, called at the flat with a box of them. She also brought us about six metres of white cloth, saying it was given by the city leaders to help us make new quilt covers. I felt very warm inside: Mother had been gone for over four years yet we still enjoyed her legacy of goodness. In fact, throughout my life, I have always felt her beside me, helping me from her world.

As Wei-guo was growing fast, Andong and I decided to use the cloth to make him two new shirts and some underwear. He was embarrassed as we girls went over him with our tape-measures but submitted because he would soon have some new clothes. The next day, after school, I went to Uncle Jiang's home with the cloth, and spent the whole evening making one of the shirts. The following evening I made another, and the next day, a Sunday, I made two vests and two pairs of pants.

When I watched Wei-guo put on one of the shirts, I knew why Mother had been so happy when she dressed me in clothes she had made herself. I felt the same now and to let Mother's soul rest in even deeper peace, I promised her that I would look after her youngest child.

★

In early October, our school authority decided to 'run the school in an open-door way'. It was part of the educational reforms and meant that we must go to the countryside to be educated by the poor peasants in the fields. Our school leader chose to send us to Jiangning County, fifty kilometres away from Nanjing. Different grades would go to different communes, so Andong, Wei-guo and I would be separated and sent to different villages for a month.

The entire school set off at dawn. We had to arrive at our destination by the evening of the same day and we had a fifty-kilometre march ahead of us. We carried our luggage on our backs, just as before, and we sang the same revolutionary songs as we marched. I was not looking forward to the next month. Even though I was older my dislike of the countryside hadn't changed. We stopped to rest at an army institute half-way to Jiangning County to eat our lunch. I had known what to expect, and I took time to rest my feet, attend to my blisters and change my socks. Most of the students had blisters, but only a few had come prepared. When I had seen to my own feet and helped Andong and Wei-guo do theirs, I made them lie back, using their bedrolls as pillows, until it was time to move on.

Zhang strode along as if she was on an afternoon walk in the park, encouraging everyone else. 'Comrades! Compared to the 25,000 *li* [about 12,500 kilometres, as 500 metres make one *li*] of the Long March this will be nothing extraordinary.' She did an excellent job in cheering us up. She made us laugh with her jokes and led us in the singing. On our way that afternoon, she shouted revolutionary slogans, which we repeated.

It was already dark when we split up and each group went off to their commune, and pitch black when we arrived at where we would spend the next thirty days. How our teachers had navigated the way was a mystery to me. We were met by a guide from the village. We needed our torches to follow him to the commune leader's office. There was no electric light, only a smoking kerosene lamp hanging from the roof. I remembered that there had been electricity in the countryside around Shanghai, but not here.

Our group was divided into sections of eight and we were led to our quarters. My group was led by Zhang, and I was appalled to find that this was a much worse place than before. It was so backward – only a short distance from Nanjing and there were no proper roads and only a candle in the bedroom. One thing was the same: the bucket. I couldn't understand why these people did not have a toilet in their homes. China has a history of civilization going back five thousand years, but the peasants still lived as they always had.

I made my bed, then sat down on it to take off my shoes. At least I had decent shoes this time. I remembered the footwear I had trudged around in the last time I had gone to the countryside: just strips of old uniform and sections of worn-out car tyres. But I couldn't take off my socks. They were soaked in dried blood, so I went to the kitchen and found some hot water in a big pot on the stove. Our host must have thought about our discomfort, and left it for us. Beside the stove was a big baked-clay vat of cold water carried from the pond. I used my mug to scoop some hot water into an enamel basin, then some cold, and put my feet into the water. It was very painful, but after a while, I was able to peel off my socks. My feet were a mess, big blisters all over, but bathing them felt wonderful.

The other girls did the same, except Zhang. How she could walk all those extra kilometres, moving up and down the column, and not have damaged feet, I never knew. But there she was, walking about as if she was still in Nanjing, organizing the room. My respect for her increased, especially when she knelt down and helped one girl with particularly bloody, painful blisters.

The peasant woman of the house was kind. She taught us how to deal with our unbroken blisters. She pulled out a single hair from her head and pushed it through a blister on a girl's foot and told her to leave it: the liquid would drain away without the skin breaking. It was an effective way to reduce the pain and speed up the healing process. When the woman had gone, Zhang said, 'We must learn from Lei Feng and do something nice for our host family.' So we did. Every day, we carried water from the pond and filled the large clay vat. Also, we stopped using the candle supplied by the peasant woman because Chairman Mao had written in his famous text 'The Three Main Rules of Discipline and the Eight Points for Attention' that we must not use anything belonging to the people, even a piece of thread. We must pay for it or buy our own elsewhere. Every girl in our room gave Zhang a little money and she purchased some candles.

After a simple dinner we settled down to sleep. I was exhausted, but as soon as I felt comfortable and drowsy, the itching began. Then I remembered. The fleas! They were biting me to bits. My neck, back, arms, legs, tummy. These fleas were even worse than those in Shanghai! I could hear the groans of the other girls as we scratched frantically. It didn't help when Zhang quoted from Mao: 'The cleanest people are the workers and peasants. The dirtiest are the intellectuals.' As for me, I would have sooner been a dirty intellectual tucked up in clean sheets any day!

It was raining hard the next morning, but the work had to be done. Our first task was to fetch water for the vat. The muddy road to the pond was slippery, and our feet sank into deep holes as we struggled with the buckets. The mud clung to our feet as we squelched our way along. Being small, I had a hard time: the deep mud held my legs almost up to my bottom, and I had to use all my strength to get one leg out and forward. Several times I fell with a *shlump* on my bottom or my face as I made my way to the pond, and it was even worse coming back, holding the heavy bucket with both hands. By the time I got back to the kitchen, the bucket was almost empty. So off I went to do the whole thing again.

By this time all the girls were fed up. Nothing was said – our faces did the talking. We looked like eight clay sculptures when we had finished and we were soaked to the skin. We stood looking at each other, then burst out laughing.

Soon we began to shiver in our wet clothes and had to take them off. We discussed whether we should wash them, but decided against it – we would have had to fetch more water from the pond. So we simply hung them up to dry. Most of us only had two sets of clothes, so we scraped as much mud as possible off our bodies, put on our clean clothes and wrapped ourselves in our quilts. During that month we washed our clothes just twice. We simply changed from dirty wet clothes into dirty dry clothes. We never washed our bodies.

Our form teacher Mr Yao had recently graduated from Nanjing Normal University. During our stay, he lived with Greg's group in another part of the commune. He appeared in our hut to see how we were getting on and found us in our quilts. He laughed, saying he had just left a similar scene in the boys' hut. He hadn't fallen in the mud, because he knew what to do – he came from a poor peasant family. He had worn a pair of straw sandals, which were easy to make and helped reduce the slip and grip of the mud.

He found some straw and taught us to make sandals. He also had good news. Our headmaster had said that during this month in the country the students must, of course, do manual labour, but must not be allowed to neglect their studies. The rule was that we would spend half the day

labouring and half the day in study. He had also said that the younger
children should not do as much labouring as the older ones, who in turn
should do less than an adult, because their bodies were not fully developed.
He was a kind, considerate man – whose kindnesses were turned against
him during the Cultural Revolution. He was branded a 'capitalist roader'
and severely beaten by his own students. Not the hard-working students,
but those he had punished for their bad behaviour.

When the weather was fine, we helped the peasants construct a new
reservoir. Some of us were given spades and hoes to dig out the thick
red mud. Others filled large round rush baskets shaped like soup bowls
with it, and the rest carried the baskets to where the dam was being built.
We were supposed to take two full baskets each, one at each end of a
shoulder pole. As I was the youngest in my form, and by far the smallest,
those filling the baskets put just enough mud in my baskets for a half-load,
but even with less to carry, my shoulders ached and blisters burst under
my clothes.

After the first afternoon working on the reservoir, we helped each
other to soothe our aching bodies. The carriers had broken blisters on
their swollen, red and blue shoulders. Sweat had poured down us and
our clothes were sodden. Some had bleeding hands and burnt necks. No
one had escaped, not even Zhang. We couldn't bathe so we just washed
away the blood, and gently cleaned the damaged skin.

When we came to put on dry underwear, we found it had not dried
from the day before. It was late October, and the night temperatures
dropped to near freezing, which made sleeping even more difficult. If
we managed to forget the fleas, we shivered under our quilts. Many of
the students caught colds and flu, but nobody dared to complain. None
of us wanted to be ridiculed or branded 'backward' or 'afraid of hardships
and seeking bourgeois comfort'. One small complaint might mean
becoming an outcast, or being given a bad political report, which would
severely affect one's future.

After we returned to Nanjing, it took a month for the blue bruising
on both my shoulders to fade away. The angry red flea bites took six
months to disappear. And I couldn't bear the thought that one day I
might be sent to live permanently in the countryside. Millions of young
Chinese had already gone, and I hoped with all my heart that I would
not be another.

We had to go to the countryside again during the second term of
senior two. In April 1966 the whole school set off for Xuyu County in

north Jiangsu Province. This time we had to walk 100 kilometres with our bags and bedrolls. The headmaster had chosen this particular place because a graduate of our school had settled down there. Her name was Yuan, a daughter of a professor, and she had given up her chance of university to go to the countryside. She had been proclaimed a good example by the Youth League of Jiangsu Province for all the educated young people to follow. I admired her for following her revolutionary conscience in going to live with the poor people, knowing full well that I could never do the same.

It took us two days of hard marching to get there. We slept in the classrooms of a middle school that first night, half-way to our destination. This time, our feet were still hard from the previous march so we coped better. The girls put all the desks together to make a big bed, and we slept on that. The boys did the same in another classroom. We got up early the next morning to continue the march.

The trees had just turned green, and I saw a beautiful picture painted by nature. The tall trees standing guard around green fields bright with wild flowers, with the hills in the background, filled me with pleasure, and the soft, fresh spring air felt good as I breathed deeply. I was happier this time. It looked as if our headmaster had chosen a better place for us.

Sadly my good mood soon faded. The further north we marched, the more barren the fields became, and by the time we got to Maba People's Commune where we were to stay, the scrubby yellow land was inhospitable. There were no crops, and when the wind blew, sand stung our eyes. Later, we discovered that there was always a wind, and sometimes heavy storms, when the wind speeds increased and stones flew like bullets, wounding animals and humans alike. This was one of the poorest places in the province, which was why Yuan had chosen to go there.

By now I was an old hand, and knew what to expect. The only good thing was that we eight girls who had been together before stuck together this time, and our hut was a lot closer to the pond. The bucket was in its usual place, so were the fleas, and the pit was in place beside a field. But there was a big difference in the conditions: life here was worse than ever. The grubby children ran around naked. There was just a thin reed mat for our host family to sleep on in their small mud hut, and they all slept together under a dirty black quilt. The room had no windows, just a small hole in the wall to let in some light, which was sealed in winter. Every house was dirty and smelt of urine and animals. The adults had just one set of clothes and never wore underwear. They sewed pieces of old cotton into their clothes for the winter, and took them out for summer. They had never seen a sheet or a woollen blanket and they never bathed. A 'good wash' was a rinse of face and hands in the water bucket. No soap, of course.

I remembered a propaganda film we had once been shown at school, describing the life of the black people in Africa. We were told that they lived under the bullying rule of the imperialists and were shamefully exploited. I tried to put the idea out of my mind, but it persisted. There was no doubt there were many similarities between the film and the commune I was now expected to live in for thirty days.

In the countryside near Shanghai, almost all of the peasants could read and write, but here 90 per cent could not. I realized now that I had been lucky to have lived in such good conditions near Shanghai.

A 'Socialist Education Movement' had been launched by Mao in the spring of 1964. Educated city dwellers were being sent to rural districts to check on the leaders of the thousands of communes. Mao suspected that the cadres were cheating the mass of the uneducated poor out of their fair share of food and 'work points'. The peasants were not paid in cash, but earned points depending on the amount of work they did. After the harvest, food was distributed to them according to the number of points they had earned, and stored in their huts. Mao also suspected the cadres of stealing from the State. Therefore, he used the city people, as 'Production Brigade Checkers', to look into the financial accounts and the production records.

It was the first time Mao had attacked the countryside people politically. His plan was to discredit as many grass-roots leaders as possible, leaving the simple peasants virtually leaderless, ready for when he launched his Cultural Revolution. In fact, although the people of China, and the world, did not realize it, the Cultural Revolution had already begun and China was about to erupt into chaotic disorder.

Many of the commune leaders were found guilty of crimes against the people, and severely punished. It was common for them to be strung up by their thumbs and beaten many times by the peasants over several days, before being thrown into prison. A few were tortured to death. It is not possible to say how many people were guilty, but in almost every commune the leaders became the victims of the poor.

Some of the educated young people who had been sent or had volunteered to go to the countryside were living in a small settlement near the Maba People's Commune. The girl we had come to meet,

Yuan, was also living there, so we went to visit her. The first noticeable thing was that these young people were living in much better conditions, not because they had more money but because they were better organized. Four city girls from 'undesirable' families lived in one room. They had sheets, decent hand-made quilts, and the rooms were clean. Their job was to help with the building of a new reservoir about ten kilometres away from the settlement. Reservoirs were being dug all over China at that time to improve land irrigation. One lucky girl had been appointed teacher to the children in the commune so she did not have to work on the reservoir. There was no classroom so she had to teach them in her own room with a small blackboard she had bought with her own money. Although the lessons were free, she had only three pupils: most peasants thought education was of no value to their children, and would rather have them working in the fields. For the sake of amassing work points it was important for them to do their share. Even a toddler had to make a contribution to the survival of the family. There was never enough food, and yet these people were feeding the whole of China.

Like the peasants, none of the young city people were paid any salary, just work-points, which could be changed for food after the harvest. So every month, they received money from their parents in the cities. Without this support, they would have died of starvation.

Yuan had been a schoolmate, so we were interested in how she was getting on. We asked her about her experiences in the countryside, and how we could build real 'class feelings' for the poor people, as she had. To our surprise, she said she had nothing to tell us about her 'thought reform', and that after a whole year of very hard labour she still lived on money sent by her parents. The work-points she had been given to last for twelve months earned her just enough food for two weeks! As she was talking, I was idly turning the pages of her diary which lay on her desk – a wooden box – when one line caught my eye: 'I hate it! I hate everything here!' I closed it quickly and slipped it under her pillow. It would get her into trouble if it was found by the wrong person. I now understood that, despite everything we had been told, poor Yuan had been forced to come to the countryside because she had seen no hope for herself in the city. Now she could see no future in the countryside either. (Fortunately, many years later, after the death of Mao, when she was in her forties, she passed the entrance examination to a university and came back to Nanjing after she got her degree.)

I was becoming more and more disillusioned. It seemed to me that no one was happy in China, and everywhere there was discontent. That entry I had read in Yuan's diary lingered in my head. 'I hate it! I hate everything here!' It seemed so wrong that she had to stay here after twelve years of schooling. Now I decided that, somehow, I was going to go home. I was not prepared to spend a month in this place. I had to think of a way to be sent home. I remembered Uncle Jiang. 'Of course! Why didn't I think of it before?' I whispered to myself, as I lugged a bucket of water from the pond.

From that instant I became ill. It was really so simple. Uncle Jiang and his wife were doing it, so was their friend Wang Bin. So why not me?

I staggered into the hut and collapsed dramatically on to my bed, complaining of a bad pain in my belly. I refused to eat, and for two days I lay on my quilt, groaning whenever anyone was in earshot. I had always been pale, even when I was in the best of health, so it was not difficult to make the teacher believe I was very ill. Finally, I heard these wonderful words: 'I think we must send you back for a complete medical examination. There is nothing we can do for you here.'

'I'm sorry,' I said, earnestly. 'I hate to make trouble.'

The next day, my teacher carried my bedroll as he walked, and I hobbled, to a nearby town, where he put me on a bus. 'Take care of yourself, Little Gao. I hope you will soon feel better.'

I looked at him with all the pathos I could muster. 'I'm sorry I cannot continue with my revolutionary work here.'

Four hours later, I was soaking in a lovely hot bath. After a nap, I went to visit Uncle Jiang and Auntie Zhu. I rolled up my trouser legs to show them the flea bites. Uncle Jiang said, his chins quivering with indignation, 'This is ridiculous. Why should students like you have to suffer by being sent to the countryside? The duty for young people should be to study.'

Then he looked at me straight in the eyes. 'Don't worry, you will surely have a bright future.' In a conspiratorially low voice he continued, 'Our country desperately needs reliable interpreters of foreign languages, and outstanding students can be recommended by the leaders for admission into the Foreign Language Institute in Beijing. Any student who is recommended under this directive will not have to take an entrance examination.' It seemed that two vacancies had been allocated to my school, and I was to be recommended for one of the places. I was overjoyed, and tried to give the fat old fellow a big hug, but my arms would not go round him. So I kissed him on the cheek. He looked pleased, as if I had given him a present, and he was obviously delighted at my response. This meant that I would be entering university after the summer vacation and my mother's dream would come true at last!

Uncle Jiang said my acceptance depended on fulfilling three conditions. One, good family background – well, that was no problem. Two, good marks in all subjects at school – that was going to be no problem either. And three, good looks – my face fell. He laughed heartily, his belly shaking. 'Don't worry, Little Flower. You are exactly what they are looking for.'

I smiled, excitement coursing through me. If I did well at the Foreign Language Institute, I would be working in the Ministry of Foreign Affairs after graduation. Uncle Jiang said a good-looking face and figure would be an important requirement for my future career as part of the diplomatic service. Then he warned me not to tell anyone about this, not even Andong and Wei-guo, until it was announced at school just before the summer vacation. Suddenly, from being full of despair in the countryside, I was full of hope in the city! And no more fleas – ever!

9. The Cultural Revolution

It had been a lovely dream while it lasted, but it wasn't long before my hopes for the future vanished like soap bubbles in the wind. In early June 1966, the Cultural Revolution officially began.

As early as January 1965, Mao Tse-tung had proclaimed the necessity of a new ideological campaign, specifically designed to further the cause of true Communism. He quietly launched it on to an unsuspecting nation in October that year when he made a vitriolic attack upon the deputy mayor of Beijing, Wu Han, and his play, *The Dismissal of Hai Rui*. Wu Han had used as its basis an ancient Chinese fable that told of how a good and loyal official was forced by his emperor to give up his post because he dispensed fair play and justice to the ordinary people.

The play had become a great favourite in China but Mao didn't like it. He convinced himself that it hinted at the unjust dismissal of Marshal Peng De-huai and therefore made veiled accusations against him. He denounced the play and its author, then ordered the persecution of the whole Wu Han family. This resulted in the death of every man, woman and child. The Wu Han family tree stopped for ever. In the 1990s, a television drama was shown on Chinese television called *Wu Han*, which told the dreadful story of their persecution and death. It left most viewers in tears.

Not only Wu Han but the entire Beijing leadership was replaced, entirely from Mao's most intimate inner circle of supporters. The leader of this new group was his wife Jiang Qing.

In May 1966, when my schoolmates returned from the countryside, there was already no normal education in the schools. On 16 May, the call for a far-reaching purge of the Party was broadcast to the whole nation. The targets this time were the officials who were taking the 'capitalist road' within the Party, headed by 'China's Khrushchev'. At first, nobody knew who this meant, but it soon became clear that this was none other than our chairman Liu Shao-qi, who became the number-one 'capitalist roader' in China after Mao branded him 'a renegade, a traitor and a scab of the working class'.

Every day, the *People's Daily* published a new quotation from Chairman

Mao across the top of the front page, which would read something like this: 'SUPREME INSTRUCTIONS: The class struggle is the key link. Once it is grasped, everything is solved.' The daily saying was also broadcast dozens of times on the radio, and others screeched silently at us from billboards and posters.

In June, education ceased. The students were made to attend school to study the editorials of the *People's Daily*, which only reported what Chairman Mao authorized. Then, in the second week of June, the fateful editorial entitled 'Sweeping Away All Bull-devils and Snake-demons' appeared in the paper, and was broadcast repeatedly. Overnight every billboard and poster was changed and the editorials officially announced: 'The Great Proletarian Cultural Revolution has been launched and led by Chairman Mao. The essence of this revolution is to touch everybody's soul.'

The glorification of Mao had started in the late 1930s and had gathered strength from that time. There had been a dip during the Great Leap Forward, but it was now stronger than ever. His words were the supreme instructions for everything. Now the Cultural Revolution, which would last ten years, had arrived, and grew to envelop the whole of China, which comprised 9.6 million square kilometres and contained 800 million people.

Zhang collected money from every student in our class and went to the bookstore to place an order for *The Little Red Book* and we waited impatiently for our copies. Demand was far too great for the printers to satisfy, even by running the presses twenty-four hours a day. It was not easy to produce around 700 million copies, and it was a month before ours were delivered. Every day, we sang a song about Chairman Mao, written, it was said, by a poor peasant, entitled 'The East is Red'.

> The east is red,
> The sun rises,
> Chairman Mao emerges in China.
> He brings happiness to all of us,
> He is the great saviour of the people.

There was no vacation that summer, although the school closed, and there was no mention of whether or not I would be accepted at a university. It was obvious now that learning had become the least important duty of the young. At first we students, whatever our backgrounds, took part in the revolution with enthusiasm. On 5 July, a teacher at Qinghua University made a 'big-character poster' – large Chinese characters written with a brush on a big piece of paper. At the top, it read: 'FIRE BOURGEOIS HEADQUARTERS'. At first the teacher was attacked for putting up the poster without Mao's consent, but when Mao heard about it, he wrote, 'How well written is the first Marxist-Leninist big-character poster in our country! There are thousands of Marxist theories, but in the final analysis, one sentence stands out: Rebellion is Reasonable!'

Less than an hour after these words were broadcast, our school campus was filled with big-character posters. Large white sheets of paper covered in writing hung on every possible surface. It seemed that every student had something to say.

In the beginning, the writings were just grumbles about teaching methods or other complaints. Then, on 8 August 1966, everything changed after the broadcast of 'Solutions by the Central Party Committee on the Proletarian Cultural Revolution', among which was: 'All education in China since the founding of the People's Republic is denounced as being under "a counter-revolutionary revisionist educational line" which has poisoned the minds of the children for seventeen years.' The harsh, grating voice continued: 'We will no longer allow the bourgeois intellectuals to rule in our schools.'

On the same day as the broadcast, posters appeared with larger characters and drawings criticizing the educational system. Then came even bigger posters mentioning certain teachers by name. Soon every teacher in our school had been vilified in at least one poster. I felt uneasy about this, as did a great many other students: it was common knowledge that most of the posters censuring the teachers had been written by non-achievers.

Within a few days, writing defamatory posters was no longer enough for them. The poster-writers were strutting around the school, ready for mischief, and it pained me to see my own brother among them. It wasn't long before the students were in control of the school, and the rabble was in charge of the students. Then the first beating occurred.

It came, as these things usually do, from nowhere. A teacher came into school and discovered her students tearing pages out of a book from the school library. She tried to take it from them, failed, and was pushed to the floor. The students laughed, and one girl picked up a torn-out page. '*Eat!*' she shouted, and pushed the paper into the face of the

1 My father (right), my mother (centre) and my uncle Gao Dao-fang in
the headquarters of the New Fourth Army in 1942

2 My mother (centre), at the age of
seventeen, arrived at the headquarters of the New Fourth Army
in February 1940

3 My father in 1926, aged twenty,
on his journey to Nanjing

4 My mother holding me (almost seven months old) on 1 October 1949 by the Yangtze River

5 My parents and myself in 1950

6 My elder sister Andong and me (aged two) in the Orchard, summer 1951

歡送周洪冰同志臨別紀念一九五三年于幹部療養院

7 Staff members bidding farewell to my mother (third from the left, second row) in 1953 before she was promoted to her new post

8 My father and mother in 1949

9 My father (centre) and his colleagues in his office in 1951

10 My parents, my brother (held by Mother), my sister Andong (centre) and me in 1953 after we moved from the Orchard to Orchid Garden in Nanjing

11 Kuomintang soldiers and civilians visiting Dr Sun Yat-sen's Mausoleum, Nanjing, c. 1948

中共江苏省委高幹自修班第一期结叶纪念

12 My father (third from the left, bottom row, in his padded trousers to protect his leg) on completion of the study course for the high officials in Nanjing, 16 January 1956

13 Sister Fu (centre, in dark jacket), who encouraged my father to go to Yan'an in 1937, during her visit to our home in 1955. My mother is on the far right

14 My father died on 27 July in 1956. My mother had dressed him in a western suit to make his dream come true after death

15 The leaders on the left, and our family and relatives on the right, holding ribbons to lead the truck that carried my father's coffin to the burial place. My mother (first on the right), with me next to her and Andong behind us

16 My mother and two of her half-brothers in May 1957. Uncle Zhou Ru-sheng (right), the young air-force officer, was branded a rightist two months after this photo was taken

17 Mao Tse-tung in his special train on a trip to Nanjing to inspect work in 1957

18 Nanjing University during the Anti-rightist Campaign in 1957

19 My mother, sister, brother and me in 1960
during the famine

21 My mother's funeral in September 1961

20 My mother, Andong, Wei-
guo and me (on the left at the
back) in front of a monument
which bears my father's handwriting, 1961

22 My parents' tombs at Yuhuatai (Rain Flower Terrace) Revolutionary Cemetery

teacher. '*Eat this!*' She forced the page into the mouth of the teacher, and made her chew it, urged on by a few slaps across the face. Then one of the boys punched her. Punching became kicking, which progressed to a full-scale severe beating. Only the intervention of several other teachers saved her.

It was expected that the students responsible for the beating would be punished, but they weren't. So more and more students, wanting to settle old scores, joined the gang, and every day we had to watch as one teacher after another was beaten up by the students. Also, teachers from 'undesirable' backgrounds had half of their heads shaved so that everyone would know they were one of the 'black gang' of either Bull-devils or Snake-demons.

I dared not read English now, or do any kind of study, because I was a typical example of those students who had taken the 'white academic road'. However, I wasn't attacked by other students, like so many of my classmates, because I was protected by the certificates of revolutionary martyrs. They shielded me from danger for many years.

In one Beijing school, an organization calling itself the Red Guards was formed by students from the families of high officials. Soon the movement had spread across the country. On 18 August 1966, Chairman Mao, dressed in army uniform, received the leaders of the Red Guards on the terrace of the Tiananmen (Gate of Heavenly Peace) building, which stood to one side of the famous square. The reception was followed by the first of eight gigantic rallies.

At the beginning of the rally, Mao was given a Red Guard armband by a young girl. He allowed her to slip it over his left sleeve and up his arm. He stood beside her for a while, then when the girl told him her name was Bin Bin, which means 'gentle and polite', Mao turned to her and said, 'Apply violence!' The girl Red Guard immediately changed her name to Yao Wu, which means 'apply violence'. This is the only known direct order given by Mao to a Red Guard, and his words travelled across the vastness of China like a thunderbolt.

Representatives of different schools at the rally each gave a short speech from the terrace, which was broadcast to the whole country. All the speeches ended with the same call: 'Ten thousand years to Chairman Mao!' It was a supreme example of total worship. Mao was our god. One of the speech-makers was a student of senior three from our school. The son of an air-force general based in Nanjing, his name was Li

Tian-yan. He stood beside Mao throughout the rally and the radio commentator mentioned him by name. The school was soon buzzing with the news, and our own brigade of Red Guards was immediately established. Li Tian-yan was unanimously elected our leader because of his closeness to Chairman Mao.

Students were divided into two groups. We were either a 'Red Five' or a 'Black Five', according to our backgrounds. The Red Fives were from the families of workers, poor and lower-middle-class peasants, PLA officers, revolutionary officials and revolutionary martyrs. The Black Fives came from the families of landlords, rich peasants, counter-revolutionaries, bad elements and rightists. Shortly afterwards, the Black Fives became the Black Sevens when renegades and traitors, and enemy agents were added. Then came the Black Nines, which included capitalist roaders and the intellectuals, known as the Stinking Old Number Nines.

Only the Red Fives could become Red Guards, so I was given a red armband and became a founder member of our brigade. I had to be in it, because I did not want to be linked to the Blacks. I wore my armband – not with pride but to stay safe.

At home that night, I thought about my parents. I knew they would have been unhappy. All their ideals and everything for which they had fought so long and so hard was being ground into the dust. I felt sad, because they had been betrayed by their own countrymen and had suffered for nothing. Even Pei-gen had suffered for nothing. She was still living with the effects of her babyhood both physically and mentally. Suddenly I understood her pain and felt compassion for her.

When the leader of our Red Guard brigade, Li Tian-yan, returned from Beijing, he declared that our unit should be called the Red Rebels Army because we were children of veterans of the old Red Army. We were pleased with the title and we called him Commander Li. We also agreed with his decision to change the name of our school to the Military School Prepared for the Third World War, because one of Chairman Mao's daily editorials had said, 'We must always be prepared for war.'

Most of the students from 'undesirable' families became 'Red Surroundings' of the Red Guards, but a handful were not even allowed to join the Surroundings. These were the children of Black families, who had relatives outside China. All overseas relatives were considered 'enemy agents'. We had a simple pecking order: children of heroes were themselves considered heroes, but children of reactionaries were bastards. They must do continual self-criticism and attend the numerous denouncing meetings, which were springing up everywhere. Hatred was deliberately built into the political campaign, which eventually led to prolonged, violent and pitiless factional fighting.

Now the slogan 'Ten thousand years to Chairman Mao' was not enough. We had to think of him as 'the red sun in our hearts that never sets', and every morning, as soon as we heard the song 'The East is Red', we were expected to sing as loudly as we could, facing the east, waving *The Little Red Book*. Finally, we shouted, 'Endless life to Chairman Mao!' Ten thousand years was not enough for Mao: now he wanted to live for ever!

Army uniforms were the most fashionable clothes. Almost all Red Guards acquired one from their parents and every Red Guard wore an army cap, but with no red star to differentiate them from real soldiers. Of course I had my uniform too. I couldn't get a real one because my parents were long gone, and the old uniforms I had worn in Shanghai had been consigned to the rubbish. I bought white cloth and had it dyed olive green, then asked the tailor to make three imitation army uniforms, one each for Andong, Wei-guo and myself.

During the same month, Chairman Mao called upon the Red Guards to begin the destruction of the 'Four Olds': old culture, old traditions, old customs and old habits. His words were: 'We must not only be good at destroying the old world, we must be good at constructing a new one. But destroy the old first, and the new will automatically be there.' This was the signal to the Red Guards throughout China to behave like bandits. Inspired by Mao's words of violence, there were countless raids on the homes of Blacks, such as intellectuals, because it was well known that they had collections of old books, paintings, ceramics and furniture. Thousands of precious items were confiscated and destroyed. Some writers committed suicide after they were forced to witness years of work being burned in front of them. Books and manuscripts of all kinds went up in flames, along with works of art. Jewellery and antiques were stolen, and what couldn't be taken away was smashed beyond repair. Whole families of Blacks were beaten and tortured.

The beautiful temples were 'old', so they were destroyed too. Jiming Temple, where Mother had often taken us, was smashed with hammers. The centuries-old statues of the Buddha and his eight warriors were reduced to a pile of powder, and the monks were beaten. No old building was left alone. Everything of value to the people was smashed, all in the name of the people.

★

The Party leaderships of Beijing, Nanjing and every other city were alarmed by the chaos created by the Red Guards so they sent work teams, made up of local government staff, to all middle schools to guide the students and get them to behave themselves. But as soon as Mao's wife, Jiang Qing, heard of this, she branded the teams 'ruthless killers trying to suppress the new revolutionary emerging things'. The Red Guards attacked the local-government teams and the teachers. Many were taken to denouncing meetings and made to kneel before a portrait of Mao and say, over and over and over, 'I am guilty. I deserve death ten thousand times over.' If any refused, numerous fists thumped hard on their skull until they succumbed.

During these meetings, dirty water and spoilt food were poured over the heads of the victims. Our headmaster, Mr Sha, was dragged to one. His hair was pulled so that he had to bend forward, but his arms were lifted backwards. It was a favourite way to inflict pain, called 'flying a plane', and was used extensively to punish capitalist roaders. A long list of his 'crimes' was read out to him, not least of which was the building of the swimming-pool, now closed, which had sabotaged Chairman Mao's call to swim in the big rivers and the sea. Other charges included 'growing the revisionist seedlings', which referred to the students with good marks.

He was forced to crawl on all fours around the big playground, barking like a dog until his voice became a croak and his hands and knees left a trail of blood. Then, with other teachers, he was paraded through the streets. They had to wear pointed witches' hats made of white paper, and big cardboard squares hung round their necks, bearing their names. A bright red cross went through each name, the mark of a condemned criminal.

One morning, hundreds of leaflets were distributed all over the school campus reporting a talk between Chairman Mao and his niece Wang Hai-rong. Mao was reported to have said to her, 'The more books you read, the more stupid you become. In my opinion, it is quite enough for children to be able to read and write letters.' He also said, 'We must destroy the reactionary age-old tradition of respecting the teachers, which has existed for several thousands of years.' The result was that more and more teachers were beaten. Those who had not yet been shaved by the Red Guards did it to themselves to avoid having it done by the students. It didn't matter whether a teacher was male or female, they were all treated the same. Many were knocked senseless before they had their feet tied to a rope and were dragged around the playground, the students taking turns to pull them along.

And still they turned up every morning, ready to give lessons, bruised and battered, lips cut, noses broken, fingers crushed. Many limped or leaned on sticks, even crutches, but they were upright and proud.

My mathematics teacher, Madam Tao, was the highest-grade teacher in our school, and an acknowledged beauty. When she had been a student under the Kuomintang government she had once been chosen as the 'University Flower'. She had had many admirers among the Kuomintang officials until she finally married Zhang Yu-zhe. He was a learned man, a member of the British Royal Academy and the president of the Nanjing astronomical observatory situated on top of the Purple Mountain. The students accused her of having had illicit affairs with Kuomintang officials. Women who had affairs were called 'worn-out shoes' and traditionally it is the worst thing to call a woman: it will destroy her reputation and her future. The students taunted Madam Tao and called her 'a big worn-out shoe' as they beat her mercilessly. Then she was forced to take off her shoes and hold them in her mouth. Her tormentors tied her to a rope and walked her barefoot into the street and paraded her around the city. When she protested, she was beaten again. The experience haunted her for the rest of her life. Her husband, of course, was a 100 per cent running dog of the British imperialists, because he had graduated from Cambridge University in the 1930s and was a world-famous scientist. Fortunately, Premier Zhou En-lai had sent instructions to protect him so the Red Guards did not dare touch him, but they repeatedly tortured his wife. She never gave up, though, and returned to teaching at the end of the Cultural Revolution.

One morning a teacher called Gao Hong-kui was found dead. He was hanging on the door of his classroom and it was assumed that he had committed suicide. However, when the doctor checked his body, he declared he had been beaten to death. His body was covered in terrible wounds and his back was a mess of cuts and weals. He had been hung up after his death to make it appear that he had taken his own life. It was murder, but the police refused to handle the case: the dead man was a 'class enemy'.

There was news from other schools. In Number 13 Middle School, a woman teacher had been forced to crawl head first down ten flights of stairs after being severely beaten. Her tormentors knew she had high blood pressure but didn't care, and she died of a heart-attack before reaching the bottom. There was no investigation. Many murdering young thugs escaped punishment during the ten years of the nightmare because the judiciary system had been smashed by the Red Guards under the orders of Mao's wife, Jiang Qing.

In the last week of August 1966, there was a big demonstration by the workers of many factories in Nanjing, protesting against the local Red Guards after they had beaten a man called Wang Jin to death. The victim was a worker in a printing house and the Red Guards found out he had relatives living outside China. The Red Guards did everything they could to force him to confess his supposed crimes but he resisted all their efforts. They beat him with the buckle ends of their leather belts for over two hours until he died. The ringleaders were two students: Guan Hu-ning, son of an army officer, and Hou-pi, the adopted daughter of my beloved Uncle Jiang.

Hou-pi had been the worst student at her school, both academically and behaviourally. She had constantly been criticized by her teachers but now she was one of the leaders of the school Red Guards. The news of the murder spread quickly among the workers of Nanjing, who demonstrated in the streets to demand the death sentence for the two students. Both were shielded by their parents and dispatched to the army to become PLA soldiers. Their crime was explained away as the excess of revolutionary fervour and hatred for the class enemy.

It was at this time that girls were having their hair cut to ear level or even shorter like the boys, to look more 'revolutionary and aggressive'. I cried as my tresses came off and I kept the long plaits in my camphorwood trunk for several years afterwards. Although I was still wearing the armband of a Red Guard, I was appalled and sick at heart as I saw or heard about what was going on, and did my best to keep away from it all.

I stood out of sight at the back of the denouncing meetings. I had always been keen to participate in all school activities (except trips to the countryside) but now the past was denounced as wrong. Even the Young Pioneers had disappeared, along with the Youth League. The Pioneers in the primary schools became Little Red Guards and wore armbands instead of the beautiful red scarves. Many good things of the past were branded as revisionist. Advanced workers were branded the 'Loyalty Party' of the capitalist roaders. I did not understand any of it. Why was the past so wrong? And I hated to see the teachers treated so badly. I did not go to see Uncle Jiang for months after Hou-pi had escaped to the army, because I was angry with him for shielding her. I did not know then that I would never see him again.

By now the Red Guards had taken over the city. Buildings were wrecked and every neon light was broken. Shop windows were smashed, and looting was widespread. In the schools, hardly a window was left intact. The Red Guards smashed everything, even the toilet bowls. They continued to terrorize the Blacks, breaking into their homes in the middle of the night to do as much damage as they could. Nothing was done to stop them.

Many students, including Red Guards like me, stayed at home in case they became involved in the acts of destruction. The city was grinding to a halt, as it became more and more dangerous to be out on the streets. No Black was safe, and everywhere, day and night, there were beatings. Loudspeakers hanging from the tallest buildings continuously blared out the works of Chairman Mao and inflammatory editorials from the *People's Daily*.

Andong had become friendly with a girl student from senior three. She was the only daughter of Wang Ye-xiang, who had been my father's best friend when he arrived in Yan'an. Uncle Wang had sponsored Father into the Communist Party and his wife, Auntie Shi, was chairman of the Women's Federation of Jiangsu Province. Unfortunately she was the first person to be denounced as a capitalist roader in that organization. She was suspended from work, instructed to stay at home and write a full confession of her 'crimes'. Andong went to live with them to help Auntie Shi write her self-accusations and her so-called confession.

Both Uncle Wang and Auntie Shi had been given pistols by the Party organizational department when my parents received theirs, and still had them. Auntie also had many photographs, which had been taken in Moscow in the early 1950s when she was a member of the Chinese Women's Delegation. Now the pistols and photographs would be used as proof of her crimes. The Soviet Union was our enemy and the photographs would prove her guilt as a class enemy.

Andong asked me to hide the pistols and the photographs to stop the Red Guards getting their hands on them when they raided the house. I put them in my camphorwood trunk. They would be safe there: we were children of revolutionary martyrs so nobody would raid our flat.

Andong and I said nothing about the pistols and the photos to anyone, not even to our brother. He was out with his friends most of the time, doing goodness knows what, so we could not trust him. It grieved us both to know that he had helped persecute the teachers and joined in the raids on the houses of Blacks. However, after a while, he, too, realized that what he was doing was wrong and went travelling with a few friends to 'stir up the revolutionary fires' in quieter parts of China.

All trains and buses allowed Red Guards to travel free of charge, so as there was no school I decided to get out of Nanjing for a while and visit my old classmates and teachers in Fuxin Middle School in Shanghai. The train was crowded with Red Guards. I managed to find a seat, and soon began to talk to my travelling companions. I had been to Shanghai before, so I was asked many questions by those travelling with me. None of them had been out of Nanjing so this was a big adventure for them, and the journey passed quite pleasantly.

I arrived in Shanghai at lunchtime on 2 September 1966 and reached my old school at about one o'clock. To my astonishment, I was surrounded by hostile students, who were not from my old class. They shouted at me as if I was a class enemy, pushing and prodding me with their fingers. At first I just stood there, transfixed. This was a new, terrifying experience for me.

Slowly, the words they were shouting at me began to make sense. They were angry with me because, although I had left some years before, I had been set up by the teachers as a good example for them to follow. Those same teachers had been denounced as having carried out a 'revisionist educational line' and I was now a target for punishment. They pushed their faces into mine as they shouted. They came so close I could smell their bad breath. 'Steadfastly smash the old system of education! Confess your mistakes!' I was in a panic, but I still noticed 'mistakes' not 'crimes' and relief flooded through me. I said nothing, looking directly at them, until there was a lull in the shouting. 'I, too, am a victim of the past,' I said, as calmly and quietly as I could.

At this moment my old classmates came to my rescue. They pushed their way through the mass and got me safely to my old classroom. Fortunately, they still thought of me as their good monitor and a friend, but I was feeling frightened and stayed only for an hour. Several of the girls accompanied me a safe distance from the school before wishing me a good journey. I was sad. My old life had disappeared.

In the dormitory of the institute where I stayed, I met a group of students from the universities of Beijing. They were four or five years older than I, and they had been sent by Premier Zhou to help push along the Cultural Revolution in Shanghai. Most were sons and daughters of high government officials or army generals. They were friendly, and I found it easy to talk to them. When I mentioned that I was the daughter of two revolutionary martyrs, they accepted me into their company. I soon made one or two special friends in the group, among them a handsome boy called Pei Jin-jun (Marching Army), whom everybody called Old Pei. He introduced me to his two friends. All three boys had stood close to Chairman Mao on the terrace of Tiananmen at the 18 August Rally. They proudly showed me a photograph of them standing with Mao and Premier Zhou, and I felt honoured to be accepted into their company.

'I wish I could see our great leader Chairman Mao,' I said wistfully, and Old Pei laughed.

'Don't worry, little sister, just follow us. We will take you to see him.'

I couldn't believe it at first. How could I be allowed to see Mao? They said again that they would take me. I was overjoyed, and agreed to travel on to Beijing with them.

On 6 September, at four o'clock in the afternoon, we climbed on to the no. 14 express train heading for Beijing. I was in high spirits, and we sang revolutionary songs, chatted and laughed until I fell asleep, my head resting against the window.

The train crawled into Beijing station at around lunchtime on 7 September. I was so excited, I felt my heart would beat itself out of my throat. Now, at last, I was in the centre of the world revolution, where our great leader Chairman Mao lived! I walked in a daze along the platform, oblivious to the noise and movement around me. All I could think of was the nearness of everything I had ever believed in. Beijing! It all came from here, every morsel of food, every inch of cloth, shoes, our houses . . . everything. My parents had fought for this chance for me to be here. Without them, and the millions like them, our lives would have been so different. And at their head was Chairman Mao. It was his genius that had guided everything, and he was guiding us now. Who was I to question such a man? My mother and father had followed him through untold hardships, and so would I.

The students said goodbye to each other and to me outside the station, before parting to go their separate ways. I followed Old Pei and was eager to see Tiananmen. We got on a bus and alighted just before it reached the square. As we approached, I realized just how vast it was, and I could easily imagine a million people gathered there. Everything seemed so familiar to me: I had seen the square and the buildings thousands of time in books, magazines, films and newspapers.

There was the main building of the ancient emperors. I felt disappointed because it was not kissing the sky as we had been told – in fact, it was barely as tall as a block of Nanjing flats. Nor did it shine 'splendid green and gold' as described in all my textbooks. It looked rather dingy, with dark red walls and a greyish yellow roof. The buildings in Shanghai were much taller and brighter. I felt cheated, and told Old Pei. He smiled. 'Never expect too much of anything, little sister, then you will not be disappointed in the future.'

Old Pei took me to his home in the army barracks. His father was a general and commanded the National Anti-chemical-warfare troops. Both he and his wife, who was also in the army, were kind to me and welcomed me into their home as though I was an old family friend. For the first time in my life, I saw a television. It was an eighteen-inch black-and-white set, and I couldn't take my eyes off the flickering images. Beijing had the first television transmitter in China.

The next day, Old Pei's friends, Ya-dong and Yan-wen, came. They told us it would be unsafe to go to the city centre today as thousands of Red Guards were marching in the streets, shouting anti-British slogans. Apparently they had surrounded the British embassy for several days, and now every Red Guard in the city was marching towards it. But I wanted to see what was happening. My curiosity about Britain had not abated and I wanted to be there.

The three boys agreed reluctantly to take me to watch the demonstration, and we set out for that part of the city. After a bus ride and a walk, we could hear the noise long before we got to the road where the embassy was situated. 'Down with the British imperialists!' 'Burn down the embassy!' 'Shoot all foreign spies!' Never had I seen so many people in one place. There were thousands of Red Guards of all ages from about twelve to twenty-five. Many were carrying big-character posters, which they intended to hang on the embassy fence, but it was covered already in posters and red flags. 'Why are they demonstrating against the British?' I asked a nearby Red Guard.

'Because the British are the ancestors of the number-one enemy of the people, the USA, and Britain has always been the real perpetrator of world invasion and war,' was his reply.

It was true. Britain *was* the biggest invader of the modern world, so it was natural, now that the Americans had abandoned their embassy, that the British should be thrown out too.

Suddenly a large black car, with Chinese flags fluttering from each wing, edged its way through the crowds and stopped in front of the embassy gates. A man got out of the front, then opened the rear door and stood to attention as a tall, almost regal Chinese woman, dressed in a smart army uniform, climbed out. From where we stood, we could see little and hear nothing, but a fierce argument took place between the newcomer and a group of Red Guards. Then, as quickly as she had come, the woman got back into the car, and the vehicle pulled away.

The crowds had quietened and it wasn't long before we heard people shouting, 'Premier Zhou En-lai has said we must not touch the British or the embassy. We must leave the area.' I was filled with curiosity and turned to Old Pei, who seemed to know everything. 'Come on, little sister, I will tell you about it as soon as we have got ourselves out of here.' Thousands of Red Guards were moving down the street away from the embassy, but they were still shouting slogans and looking for trouble.

As soon as we were clear of the crowds, Old Pei told me that Britain had been the first western country to establish diplomatic relations with the People's Republic of China. The British government no longer considered Chiang Kai-shek's Taiwan administration as the legal government of China and they had been the first of the western allies to recognize the government of Chairman Mao. 'Oh! They are quite good,' I cried, pleased to hear something favourable about Britain for once.

'Sssh!' Old Pei put his finger on my mouth. 'Be careful. Don't let anyone hear you.'

We were still quietly discussing Britain's role in Chinese affairs when we arrived at the Summer Palace built by the empress dowager of the last Qing Dynasty. Once again I was disappointed. Its gate was sealed with white paper scrolls criss-crossing it: 'Real revolutionaries should not tour the bourgeois scenic spots!' I was dejected. Why was a visit to this building such a political problem? Then I felt ashamed of the thought.

Old Pei tilted his head to Ya-dong. The two boys went up to the Red Guards on the gate. From where I was standing I could hear nothing, but after a while there were smiles all round. Old Pei waved to Yan-wen and me to follow him, and we were allowed to walk through a side entrance into the palace grounds. As I entered, the sight took my breath away. I had never seen anything so lavish and so beautiful. The gardens stretched out in front of us, covered with thousands of flowers of every conceivable hue. And in the distance was the palace, standing proudly in the bright sunshine on Longevity Hill, showing off the reds, gold and greens of its façade. 'How beautiful!' I exclaimed, as I stood, clapping my hands with pleasure. 'What did you say to the guards?'

Old Pei laughed quietly. 'Everything is possible if you know how,' he said. 'I told them we were a special squad of Red Guards sent by Chairman Mao to inspect work inside and to search every corner to make sure there were no bourgeois intruders hiding in here!'

We spent two hours in the Summer Palace. The lake was much bigger than Xuanwu Lake in Nanjing, and the buildings on Longevity Hill really were of 'splendid colours of green and gold', exactly as my teachers had described them. The architecture was exquisite and I felt a surge of pride in our ancestors. Once again bad thoughts came to me as I wandered around. 'Why should old things like this be wrong? Surely it must be good for everyone to keep the best of the past for us to enjoy in the present.'

After lunch, we went to the Xiangshan Mountain to see the beautiful maple trees. It was early autumn, and the leaves had turned red. Thousands of maples covered the mountains and the valleys, and their shimmering reds were dazzling against the golden rays of the bright sun. Autumn is the best time of year to be in Beijing, before the cold weather drives in from the north.

We came down the mountain at sunset and left for home, but soon the real world came to spoil our peaceful mood. When we returned to the army headquarters, big-character posters covered the outside walls of the barracks. We stopped to read in the dim light of the street-lamps. One said: 'Chairman Mao teaches us, "I'm for Marx's motto: Doubt everything." This means all of us Red Guards should follow Chairman Mao and doubt all leaderships. Revolutionary comrades, let us take up our pens as weapons and concentrate our fire on the Black Gang!'

Suddenly I thought, Doubt everything? Can I also doubt Chairman Mao? If it really is everything, then it should include him. I felt a shaft of panic cut through me. I was frightening myself with my own thoughts and moved on quickly to read another poster. Then I remembered something I had once heard on the radio: 'Chairman Mao is the only person in the world who has always been proved correct, and he has never made a single mistake.' Who was I to doubt him?

On entering Old Pei's house, his father told us Premier Zhou had sent for the leaders of the Red Guards who had attacked the British embassy, and had given them instructions not to organize similar demonstrations. Instead, they made their protest by changing the name of the road in which the embassy stood to 'Anti-imperialist Road', and that's the way it stayed for ten years.

From the start, Mao's wife Jiang Qing had been hailed as the Standard Bearer of the Great Proletarian Cultural Revolution. She stood beside Mao at the mass rallies, and almost every day received representatives of the Red Guards. Each time she had the earnest young people in front of her, she denounced more leaders, reading their names from a list with their 'crimes'. Most were simply accused of being capitalist roaders, which was sufficient for them to be guilty. The Red Guards, mostly middle-school louts of both sexes, took immediate action. They raided the houses of the accused, beat them up, then dragged them to a denouncing meeting. Usually their families were severely beaten too. More and more government leaders were losing their positions after being beaten almost to death. In this way Madam Mao settled all of her personal scores and those of her husband.

It was novel for me to be able to say what I felt at this time without fear. Old Pei had taken me to meet his friends at his university. There, the Red and Black factions mixed freely and there was no bullying. Sometimes they argued fiercely but without coming to blows, exactly as I had always imagined university life. Also, I found out that most of them resented Mao's wife. Even at this early stage of the Cultural Revolution, they dared to criticize her openly in the campus. I was years younger than any of them, but they listened intently to everything I had to say, and I was flattered. Nobody made a secret report. I don't think they knew how, unlike the ordinary people. The peasants, workers and the poor were mostly illiterate, therefore it was easy to get them to betray each other. While the rest of the nation was following Chairman Mao blindly, Old Pei and his friends had lost their belief. Not in Communism, perhaps, but definitely in Mao.

On 10 September 1966, Ya-dong and Yan-wen told us they had arranged a meeting with Premier Zhou En-lai. I jumped with excitement. The meeting was scheduled to take place at two o'clock that afternoon in the Beijing Workers' Gymnasium, so we had to get going.

When we arrived, Yan-wen showed a card, and the guards opened a heavy iron door to let us in. About two thousand Red Guards from all over China were already sitting in rows on folding chairs. Our seats had been reserved. Old Pei, Ya-dong and Yan-wen were old hands at this, and had met the premier many times, so they fixed it for us to have special invitations as distinguished guests. We made our way to our seats near the rostrum. I felt slightly uncomfortable as I was ushered along.

At exactly two o'clock, Premier Zhou En-lai entered, dressed in army uniform. He was only about ten metres away from where we were sitting and I felt overwhelmed to be so close to him. He was a handsome man, with a tremendous presence. Thunderous applause broke out, which went on and on, then a deafening shout: 'Endless life to Chairman Mao!' I stood up and clapped too, full of my old Communist Party fervour.

The atmosphere was electric. Yan-wen had done well to get us such good seats. The roar from behind me added to my euphoria. Premier Zhou En-lai had a healthy, rosy face, and his voice was clear and firm. Unlike Mao, who used a dialect, the Premier spoke Mandarin.

The purpose of the meeting was to guide these middle-school Red Guards in their next assignment: they were about to 'stir up the revolutionary fires' in the Xinjiang minority region, thousands of kilometres away from Beijing. Premier Zhou spoke of the religion and customs of the ethnic groups they would meet, and asked them to behave respectfully towards their new hosts. 'We do not want any conflict with them. We don't want them to have any reason to split away from China. We need their support, and we want to keep the unity of all ethnic groups. It is important that they know we support their way of life and religion. And you must always be friendly. I have been to Xinjiang several times, and I hate horse milk, but when the local people invited me to their feast, the first thing was to drink milk from a horse. It is their highest courtesy, so I just had to hold my nose and gulp it down. It tasted like the worst kind of medicine to me, but I pretended I had drunk the sweetest honey.' He punched the air in front of him with his right arm. 'And you will have to do the same!'

I was moved by his humour, and I wanted to hug and kiss him. Instead I just sat, entranced by every word. He spoke for about two hours, then paused. 'Any questions?' he asked.

'Yes!' I shouted, surprising myself. He turned and smiled at me. 'I want to see Chairman Mao!' I said loudly.

He smiled and said, 'Chairman Mao will have another review of the Red Guards in Tiananmen in a few days. Everybody has a chance to see him.' A roar came from the audience. Then Premier Zhou shouted, 'Endless life to Chairman Mao!'

The cheering and clapping went on and on, for perhaps ten minutes, until we heard the music to the revolutionary song 'The Voyage on the Sea Relies on the Helmsman'. We sang it at the tops of our voices. Then came the final chants of 'Endless life to Chairman Mao! Our Great Leader, Great Teacher, Great Supreme Commander and Great Helmsman!' We all sang and chanted with great revolutionary zeal – except my companions. They were noticeably quiet.

The third mass rally was scheduled for 15 September. I really wanted to go, but unless I got a good position I would see nothing. I was only one and a half metres tall, even though I was now seventeen, so I would be lost among the million Red Guards demonstrating their allegiance to Mao. However, I needn't have worried. Old Pei was aware of my problem and he solved it.

His university had been allocated a few places on the reviewing terrace, and he managed to secure one for me. He told me that his fellow students were not keen to see Mao – they had seen him many times – and would be content to stand in the square, so I was welcome to use one of the spare tickets. He explained that, as a daughter of two revolutionary martyrs, I had a right to go, and the Red Guard commander agreed.

On the evening of 14 September, we gathered in the university and spent the night in the students' dormitory. We rose at four the next morning and mustered in the university grounds. A young woman with a Red Guard armband announced various points of attention and discipline before marching us off in ranks to Tiananmen Square. The rally was due to begin at ten o'clock, but when we arrived, at just after five, there were already crowds of people. The young woman led the university company to the place reserved for them, then called out the names of those who had tickets for the terrace. 'Follow me,' she said, and marched away.

We had to push our way through the crowds towards the main building, and up on to the terrace. The square was filling up fast, and the nearer we got to the front, the more difficult it was to move forward. Our guide had disappeared. Then she reappeared above us on the terrace, looking down over the parapet. I was soaked with sweat, my toes were sore from being trampled on, and I was wondering if I would ever reach the terrace. Tears of pain and frustration stood in my eyes, as I elbowed my way forward. I had lost Old Pei in the crowds. Then I heard his voice: 'Little sister, where are you?'

'Here!' I yelled. 'Over here!'

Old Pei grabbed my hand and forced a way through the mass of young people, until we were stopped by armed soldiers. We showed our tickets, and they allowed us to cross the Golden Water Bridge leading to the Tiananmen building. We went through an open door, up some steps and out on to the terrace.

It had taken us almost three hours to reach it and I was exhausted. 'Come and sit over here,' said a voice. It was our woman leader. She took my arm and led me to a space where I would see everything. She smiled and disappeared into the crush. I never saw her again.

After I had rested for a while, the music of 'The East is Red' blasted out through a thousand loudspeakers, and a roar came from the crowd. I stood up, dusted myself down and looked around. The noise was deafening as a million throats roared: 'Ten thousand years to our great leader Chairman Mao!'

There he was! Just yards from me. Mao was stepping forward, followed closely by his nominated successor Lin Biao, Mao's wife and other State leaders. I almost fainted. He was really there, before my eyes: big and strong, dressed in a perfectly fitting army uniform. He looked magnificent.

Then I was knocked backwards by an excited boy who thrust his way in front of me. Before I could recover my balance, I was behind a hundred backs, all with arms waving *The Little Red Book*. And that was it. Chairman Mao was out of sight. Gone for ever. By this time, my back was against the rear wall of the terrace, but I didn't care. I had seen Chairman Mao.

Suddenly the voice of Lin Biao boomed around the square and across the terrace. I don't remember much of what he said, just the ending: 'We must carry the Great Proletarian Cultural Revolution through to the end!' followed by 'Endless Life to Chairman Mao! Endless life to Chairman Mao! Endless life to Chairman Mao!' From that day, it became a rule to shout this slogan three times at every political meeting.

On my way back to Old Pei's home, many children of primary-school age stood on both sides of the main streets, asking the same question: 'Have you seen Chairman Mao?' They stretched out their little hands. 'Please shake hands with me if you have shaken hands with Chairman Mao,' they said earnestly. They just wanted to share our happiness. A boy of about ten gripped my hand with both of his, and walked alongside me. He looked up at me, and said, 'How happy you are to have seen Chairman Mao.'

Children were not allowed to attend the big rallies but, just like my generation, they were being brainwashed to worship Chairman Mao. I told the boy that I had indeed seen Mao, and had been just a few metres away from him. His eyes widened with admiration. 'Thank you for letting me hold your hand. I must go back now.' And, with a wave, he skipped back towards his home. He now had a big story to tell his pals.

Suddenly I had a flash of memory and saw my ten-year-old brother Wei-guo walking beside me on our way to school after the death of our mother. Where was he now? I felt a need to see him. I did not know it until I returned to Nanjing, but Wei-guo *and* Andong were in Beijing and had been at that rally too.

National Day was coming, and I wanted to spend it in Beijing because I had heard many stories of how enjoyable the celebrations were in our capital city. I counted the days impatiently, spending the time seeing as much of Beijing as I could. Many places were closed, and it saddened me to see the damage done to our ancient temples and relics.

National Day is 1 October and Old Pei's friend Ya-dong had arranged a complimentary ticket to allow me to visit the Great Hall of the People for the occasion. As I was escorted to my seat, many curious eyes stared at me. It was rare to see a young female Red Guard on her own, being taken to a seat normally occupied by a high official. I sat down and looked around. Premier Zhou and Mao's wife were sitting in the front row, and a thrill went down my spine. I turned the other way, and almost cried out. I was sitting next to Uncle Sun Zong-de, my father's oldest, most faithful friend.

'Uncle?' I said timidly. After all, he was a general and had come a long way from his days as a goatherd. 'Uncle, do you remember me?'

We looked at each other. His warm kind eyes stared questioningly at me, then his face lit up. 'Little Flower? Is it really you?' His delight warmed my heart. How I loved this man! He had given his support to my father without question, and he and his wife had kept in close touch with Mother. We had lost contact with him after her death.

We sat through the concert, and although I enjoyed it very much, I was impatient to talk to Uncle. He was now commanding the armies of Anhui Province and was just three steps away from being promoted to marshal. As soon as the show finished, we turned to each other, gabbling excitedly. Although he was almost sixty, he acted like a boy. I told him my news quickly and he told me his before he was whisked away to attend an official function. And that was the last I saw of him. He was denounced by Madam Mao, along with others about six months later, and died under interrogation.

When I arrived home in early October, I found the door still bolted and barred, exactly as I had left it. So my brother had not returned. I found Andong in Auntie Shi's home. She was still helping Auntie to write her confessions. Andong was disgusted at what was going on. She told me she and Wei (Auntie's only daughter) had been to Xi'an and had spent two days at Uncle Shu Bu's home, where he had lived since he had become mayor of Xi'an. Now he was under attack by the Red Guards.

When Andong and Wei had arrived it was dusk, but Uncle Shu Bu told them not to turn on the lights. The family remained in the dark, to give the impression they were not at home so that the Red Guards would not come in the middle of the night to take him away. He told the two girls it would be better if they didn't stay. They went on to Beijing, then returned to Nanjing. To their sorrow, when they entered Auntie Shi's home she told them Shu Bu was dead.

Not long after Andong and Wei had left, the Red Guards had come for him, and hauled him off to a denouncing meeting. He refused to confess to any crimes so they kicked and punched him while he lay on the ground shouting his innocence. Then they dragged him up to the fourth floor of the building and threw him out of the window head first. He hit the ground and died instantly. Soon afterwards the Red Guards held an inquiry at which they condemned him to death in his absence for 'resisting against the people by committing suicide'. He was also branded an 'unrepentant capitalist roader'. In the records of his 'trial', these words were written: 'Even death will not atone for all of his crimes.'

Years later, after the end of the Cultural Revolution, his murderers were arrested and shot, and Uncle Shu Bu was named a revolutionary martyr. It is difficult for me to describe adequately the horrors of the Cultural Revolution. All I can do is write what I know to be true. You will have to imagine the terror for yourself.

Wei-guo came back to Nanjing in mid-October, without a coin in his pocket. He, too, had encountered cruelty. While in Beijing, he had twice visited our great-uncle Zhou Xin-min, the eldest brother of our grandfather. The first time was in early September, and by that time our great-uncle had been confined to his home to write his confessions. His house had been raided many times by the Red Guards and stripped of everything. As he was accustomed to attend meetings at the highest level, including the negotiations with the Kuomintang before 1949, it was his nature to behave in a polite and courteous way, even when the Red Guards invaded his home. He bowed and said goodbye as they left, but his good manners were condemned as 'Kuomintang-style' and he was severely beaten. He was seventy and could not understand why he was being treated so harshly: he had spent his entire life in the service of his country and this was his reward. He told my brother he had done his best to placate the Red Guards by writing the story of his whole life, thinking it would be sufficient as his 'confession'. He wrote only the truth, describing how bravely his comrades-in-arms had fought for Communism. He included the names of about three hundred people in his life, mentioning that Premier Zhou En-lai and Comrade Dong Bi-wu were his friends, which probably saved his life. The Red Guards continued to drag him to denouncing meetings but they did not kill him.

A month later, before he left Beijing, Wei-guo returned to see how he was getting on. He found a broken and defeated man. Our great-uncle had lost his senses: he could remember nothing and recognize nobody, not even his wife. Only when Premier Zhou En-lai's name was mentioned did his eyes show a spark. He never recovered his wits but, with the loving care of his wife, who made a full recovery from her beatings, he lived to a ripe old age. He was eighty-three when he died in 1979. His obituary in the *People's Daily* covered two full pages.

Wei-guo stayed at home for just a week then went on his travels again. Andong was still with Auntie Shi, so I was alone in our flat. At first I missed their company, but once I got used to the solitude, I enjoyed it. A knock on the door was an intrusion into my privacy, and I resented the presence of visitors. I hated going out; there was too much unhappiness everywhere.

One day while I was hurrying to the shops, I came across Zhuang Cun, who had arranged my mother's funeral, and was a near neighbour of Uncle Jiang. I didn't recognize him at first: he was dressed in dirty rags and was sweeping the courtyard of the municipal government compound. I stopped when I heard a small, frightened voice behind me: 'Is that you, Little Flower?'

Zhuang was holding a big bamboo broom. He was old, very old. His face was wrinkled and his hair was almost white. 'Oh! Uncle Zhuang, how you have changed!' I cried out, as I felt a stab of pain in my heart. 'What has happened to you?'

He looked furtively around him as he told me that he had been condemned for shielding the children of a counter-revolutionary. His eldest brother had been shot by the Communists as a despotic landlord during the campaign of 'suppressing the counter-revolutionaries' in 1953, leaving two young children aged under seven. Zhuang had taken them to live with him, declared them to be his own and had sent them to school as the children of a revolutionary official. That was his 'lofty crime'. Now, he was reduced to sweeping the roads in the big compound, for the smallest wages, barely enough to stay alive. His wife was in detention and he didn't know where the children were.

Zhuang didn't talk much because he was afraid for me. 'Please, Little Flower, don't be caught talking to me. You could easily be accused of something,' he said, waving me away.

By this time I had lost all interest in taking part in the Cultural Revolution. All the people I loved and respected most were dead or in disgrace – my teachers, uncles, aunties and friends. None, as far as I knew, had done anything against China, or the Communist Party, or Chairman Mao. The teacher with the lovely smile, who had interviewed me after my return from Shanghai, was dead. He had been tied to a desk and his life had been slowly bludgeoned out of him.

Though I had my twin shields in the certificates of revolutionary martyrs, I felt I was not far from being a Black, and that if they had lived my parents would have been Blacks too. My father would have been murdered, that was for sure. He had enlisted in the Kuomintang army before joining the Communists. And Mother, with her landlord father, would probably have been killed too.

On 28 November 1966, the Chairman of the People's Republic of China, Liu Shao-qi, was placed under house arrest. He was officially denounced as the number-one capitalist roader in China, 'a hidden Khrushchev sleeping beside Chairman Mao'. His second-in-command and closest friend, Deng Xiao-ping, was denounced as the number-two capitalist roader. Mao was using the Red Guards to consolidate his power base and to destroy the top leadership.

The revolution grew ever more insidious. Children of former high officials were encouraged to expose the 'crimes' of their parents. In many families, husbands and wives accused each other, and ended up as mortal enemies.

Mao's next targets were China's regional governments. In a radio broadcast, he urged, 'The revolutionary Rebels should seize power from the bourgeois headquarters.' Thus, in January 1967, the Rebels of

Shanghai attacked and ejected the People's Government of the city. It wasn't long before the other cities fell to their local Rebel groups. Then the various groups fell out with each other and street battles were rife. Stupidity was the norm. For example, one group wanted to change the traffic-lights: they said the colour red was good, and therefore should be used for 'Go' not 'Stop'. Green should be used for 'Stop'. Fortunately, the suggestion was turned down by Zhou En-lai. He explained that traffic lights were used all over the world with the same colour code so the enemies of China had to stop for red! This didn't satisfy the Rebels, but they had to obey the premier. Not to be outdone, the opposing group demanded that everybody should drive on the left and walk on the left. Left was good, right was bad. This was also refused. Britain and Japan drove on the left, so we should not. Again the Rebels had to withdraw their demand.

Rebel power struggles were taking place in all the major cities of China, and after the fighting there were always two factions of about equal strength left – in Nanjing we had the 'Red Nanjing' and the 'August 27th' groups. The ordinary city folk thought the fighting was terrible, but they were to experience an even more terrifying episode. In the spring of 1967, Mao said, 'Both factions are revolutionary left wings. The army should support the left wing people.' Thus both factions, in every city, were supported by some of the PLA troops. In fact, the PLA commanders had split up into two different factions too. The Rebels were given weapons, and war broke out between the two groups, which was to last for several years.

Most of the members of the Rebels gangs were working people employed in factories, industrial complexes, the coal mines and the like. And it wasn't long before all production in China completely stopped. It must have given Mao great pleasure to see people fighting each other in his name. He did not seem to care about what he was doing to the Chinese economy, as long as he had absolute power. Many thousands of people lost their lives in the meaningless struggle. They were willing to die because they genuinely believed it was they, not the other faction, who were fighting to 'safeguard Chairman Mao's revolutionary line'.

The original Red Guards from the middle schools had virtually broken up, their revolutionary role replaced by the Rebels. They had lost interest in politics, and spent their time wandering the streets or gathered in groups with nothing to do. In February 1967 the army began to recruit the sons of officers, so our Red Guard leader, Li Tian-yan, and my old classmates, Greg and Tian, joined up and left Nanjing. So did many of my brother's classmates. By the time Wei-guo returned to Nanjing at the end of March, after a pilgrimage to Mao's birthplace, he found himself almost alone. It was only natural that he would want to join the army too.

There were just the two of us at home. Andong was still with Auntie Shi and came to see us once in a while. Every day my brother complained about not being able to join the army and asked for my help. 'What is the use of having an older sister if you cannot help me when I need it?' was his constant grumble. But how could I? All our contacts were either dead or in detention. He did nothing to help himself, choosing to sit around the house or stand on street corners with the remains of his gang. However, he was my younger brother, so I felt responsible for him and decided I would try.

An armoured troop headquarters, where many of our schoolmates were now based, lay about fifty kilometres outside Nanjing and this was where I determined to seek help for my brother. On 5 April, I got on the first morning bus out of the city and alighted in Tangshan County town. I asked for directions to the army base and was pointed in an easterly direction. I walked, and walked and walked. I tramped along the narrow mountain paths all day and my feet were bleeding by the time I found the place just before dark. I went up to the heavy iron gate and asked a guard for help. He could see I was almost dead on my feet, and took my arm. It was then I discovered that I had taken the long route – there was another road from the town that ran as straight as a bamboo pole!

I was led to the guardroom where a soldier brought me some food, which I demolished in no time. If this is army food, I thought, munching away, Wei-guo will enjoy army life. So would I!

I asked to see Liu Li-min, a friend of Wei-guo who had been recruited only a month before. He soon arrived, accompanied by an older, more seasoned-looking soldier. At first they said my brother did not qualify for the army at present, but then, as they observed my distress, they came up with a plan. The older man took out a piece of paper, wrote down the address of General Xiao Yong-yin, who was the commander of the Nanjing Armoured Division, and handed it to me with some good advice: 'Be sure to cry. He cannot bear to see girls crying.' The general had been a ten-year-old orphan when he was found by soldiers of the

Red Army in the early 1930s, and joined as a little Red Army soldier when he took part in the Long March. He was known for his quick wit and intelligence, as well as his compassion. 'Don't be afraid of him,' said the kind soldier. 'Be sure to tell him you are orphans. It is his soft spot.'

After a restful night in the army hostel and a good breakfast, I returned to Nanjing, a journey which, by the main road, took just half the time. I wrote a long letter to the general about my parents and my brother, and his strong desire to become a revolutionary successor by following our parents into the army. I enclosed the precious revolutionary martyrs certificates, and delivered the big white envelope at the house of the general the next morning with the message that I would return later for an answer.

How pushy of me, I think now, as I look back. But it worked! When I returned, taking Wei-guo with me, we were ushered into the general's presence. He was a short, straight-backed, healthy-looking man, with bright, intelligent eyes and one of the kindest faces I have ever seen. 'Who wrote this letter?' he asked.

'I did, Comrade General,' I admitted, prepared to cry if necessary. But when he looked at me, I knew I could never fool this man.

He sighed. 'It's a pity we're not taking girls.' Then he looked at my brother.

Wei-guo was standing stiffly to attention, with only his eyes moving. Finally the general wrote in a notebook, then tore out the page and handed it to me with the certificates.

The general had written, 'Please recruit Gao Wei-guo,' followed by his signature. I smiled at him, and real tears ran. 'Go to our headquarters in Zhanyuan Road, and show my note to the guard. Your brother will be a PLA soldier,' he told me. Then he turned to Wei-guo. 'You have a good sister. Be sure you don't let her down or me. Be a good soldier. This is my command.' He walked out to his car and waved to us as he was driven away.

My brother became a soldier in the PLA that very afternoon. He was given a one-day pass to travel back to Nanjing on the following Sunday, with the order, 'Go back and see your sister.' But Wei-guo did not come straight home. He went to see his mates first, strutting proudly in his new uniform. I only knew he was in town when some of his friends told me, 'We have seen your brother in his army uniform! Doesn't he look smart?' I went to Auntie Shi's home. Andong was there, and we knew our brother would eventually turn up to show himself off. And he did, at four o'clock in the afternoon, just before he was due to return to the base. I had to admit he looked good. Then he spoiled it all by saying, 'I have come to warn you both that I don't want you to come to my army camp to see me because you look too delicate and squeamish, like bourgeois decadents. If my comrades see you wearing your skirts, they might think bad of me, having such unrevolutionary sisters. You will shame me and influence the army against me. I am sorry you look like you do. I wish you were stoutly built, and looked more revolutionary!' He spun on his heel and left, without saying goodbye.

I was astonished. After all the kindness I had experienced from those I had met in the army, and my efforts to have him accepted as a soldier, this was his thanks! I thought of my blisters, still healing, and my aching legs. Andong and I looked at each other. 'I can't believe it!' said Andong. 'He must have felt ashamed of our smallness all the time we were looking after him.'

'And our clothes!' I added. 'He never once said anything, but he must have wished we were big and strong and wore shabby clothes!'

Of course, we soon forgave him. He was the youngest, after all, and a product of his time.

10. Five Golden Flowers

I was alone at home now. Every day I slept late and wandered around the house dressed, or not, as I pleased. Every Monday I went to school to see if there were any changes, but things were only getting worse. I shopped and read big-character posters. They were mostly crude and poisonous, these days, and did not have the subtlety of the earlier efforts. I was reading the posters one morning when I felt a tug on my sleeve. I turned, frightened it might be the Rebels, but it was Hui, my boyfriend.

He had just been demobilized by the army and assigned to work in the Nanjing Youth League, where there was no job now. Every member of his working unit had joined the Rebels of the Red Nanjing and so had he. He lived in a dormitory and invited me to go with him for lunch in his dining room. There, I found some books and riffled through the pages. They were the stories of Sherlock Holmes, translated into Chinese. I had not opened a book for nearly a year, and to me they were like ice-lollies on a hot summer day. Hui let me borrow them. He had more in his room, detective stories about Russian and German spies in the Second World War, and some about India by Rudyard Kipling. I took them home too.

The books were my friends during the terrible days that followed. During the latter half of 1967 factional fighting broke out everywhere. For several months the streets were as dangerous as they had been during the Japanese occupation. People ventured out only if they had to, and then were cut down by a hail of bullets. It was often impossible to buy food. The shops closed, so did the restaurants and markets. But Hui looked after me, and brought me everything I needed.

A hot and humid July brought a lull in the fighting, and Hui took me to see his uncle in the Military Academy. As we entered the gate, we came across a corpse lying on the concrete, surrounded by big blocks of ice. A large slogan had been written on a board and placed in front of it: 'We must take our revenge for our revolutionary martyr Comrade So-and-so.' Now the Rebels were honouring their dead with the title of revolutionary martyr!

Hui's uncle told us that the body had been there for three days. The man had been shot at midnight during a skirmish. Many had been wounded too. A new phase had begun: Rebels from other cities were coming to Nanjing in large numbers to bolster the Nanjing groups. The classrooms of the Military Academy had been turned into sleeping quarters for the reinforcements. Men and women slept together in the same rooms, and often in the same bedrolls. Lovemaking between the Rebels was common, and blessed by Chairman Mao. Everyone found a bedmate after Mao announced, 'Such affairs in life are minor, as long as their main revolutionary orientation is correct.' Many unmarried women became pregnant, and a large number of love-children were born during the Cultural Revolution and never knew who their fathers were. Millions died during the ten years of nightmare, but the population of China did not reduce.

There had been no peace in the military compound since the arrival of the Rebels, Hui's uncle said. The local people hated the fighting and were continually frightened. Their normal life was ruined and they complained that the revolutionary Rebels were worse than the Kuomintang bandits had ever been. As we chatted, a radio broadcast was pounding through the compound's loudspeakers. We could hear the voice of the announcer as clearly as if he were in the room with us: 'Our great leader Chairman Mao has recently inspected both north and south of the Yangtze River, and gives his latest comments: "The present revolutionary situation in our country is very good. It is not a little good, but extremely wonderful!"'

It was too dangerous to go home so I spent a sleepless night with Hui and his uncle. The Military Academy was attacked, and the three of us cowered on the floor. Glass rained down on me as a hail of bullets came through the window and smashed a mirror. We heard people running past the house and shouting. The next morning, everything was quiet. The Rebels had melted away in the light of dawn, leaving behind shoes, torn clothes, broken sticks, bricks, shell casings and blood. I wanted to vomit.

As I was hurrying home, I was tapped on the shoulder suddenly. I almost jumped out of my clothes, then warily turned round. Relief flooded through me. It was a girl classmate from my primary school days, named Fang. Her father had been a lecturer in chemistry at the Military Academy, so Fang had lived with her family in the compound all of her life. Mao had given strict instructions to the armed forces not to take an active part in the Cultural Revolution. The supply of arms to the Rebels was all he allowed. Mao said the P L A was the 'Great Iron Wall' protecting China, and must be ready at all times to carry out his orders. However, the students and teachers in the military academies must take part in the revolution, just as in every other centre of learning.

Fang told me tearfully that her father had been dismissed by the Rebels in charge of the Nanjing Military Academy and, after a severe beating, had been sent in disgrace to his home village thousands of kilometres away from Nanjing to do hard labour. He had fought long and hard against the Japanese and the Kuomintang but that counted for nothing. He was from a landlord family, so he was a Black. Poor Fang was as good as orphaned because her mother had been forced to go with him, leaving Fang and her four younger sisters to fend for themselves in Nanjing. The girls had been nicknamed the Five Golden Flowers by all who knew them, but had had to give up most of their home to other people, leaving just two rooms for themselves.

When Fang reached the end of her story she was crying her heart out on my shoulder, and I was doing my best to console her. It was a strange sight in those days to see a Red Guard comforting a Black, and perhaps it was too much for someone. A crack echoed among the buildings, and a bullet hit a nearby wall. We looked around, terrified, then scuttled into a doorway. As we crouched down, I saw the blood. It was all around our feet, still tacky. I retched. Someone had not been as lucky as Fang and I. We made ourselves as small as possible, but there were no more shots, so after a while, we left the area in a fast, crouching run.

A couple of days later, Hui called for me and we ventured out to buy some food. The shops had little to offer but we found enough for a few days. We were wandering around, happy to be with each other, when we bumped into Fang. She invited us to her home, where her sisters were delighted to see me – we had been friends since we were little. Then I introduced Hui, who looked a little uncomfortable: it was the first time he had been in a Black home, but he relaxed when the girls made a fuss of him. They danced attendance on him: one handed him an ashtray, another gave him some green tea, then came the matches and finally some roasted peanuts. I had almost forgotten how nice it was to be treated as an honoured guest.

Fang was a good cook and we had a delicious lunch, accompanied by much laughing. I was happy with these warm, good-humoured girls. It had been a long time since I had enjoyed myself so much. Then Fang surprised me by shyly asking me if I would like to stay with them that summer. Her sisters clapped their hands. 'Please say yes,' said the youngest. 'You could live in one of the empty rooms. Nobody would say anything.' The idea sounded good to me. I was starved of female company, but I needed a little push to make up my mind. I turned to Hui. He nodded with a smile, so I agreed.

After lunch, Hui and I went to my home to pack a suitcase. I locked the flat securely then went to see Andong to tell her I would be staying in the military compound for a few weeks. She told me that Pei-gen had come to Nanjing from her university with the Rebels. She was living in a classroom in the same military compound as me and Andong warned me to be careful: our sister was dedicated to her Rebel faction, and would not like the idea of me living with Blacks. She would scold me for my lack of revolutionary dedication. I felt a little worried when I heard this, but decided to keep to my plan. After all, I have a life too, I thought, and the Rebels have no place in it. Pei-gen will just have to accept that we are now travelling down different roads. I was eighteen and able to decide my own fate.

The summer of 1967 was exceptionally hot. Every morning Pei-gen went off with her Rebel friends to march in the streets. There were many thousands of Rebels on each side, and they often clashed as they marched around the city. They shouted insults and slogans at each other and tried to smash the banners the other side carried. Only the pictures of Mao were safe. Pei-gen would return, triumphant, late at night, to eat and sleep in the classrooms. Then, as soon as it was dark, the armed fighting began.

All day long, rival loudspeakers churned out propaganda at full volume, and the Rebels attacked anyone they suspected of not being sympathetic to their brand of Maoism. At night, full-scale warfare broke out, and by morning hundreds of dead and dying lay in the streets. There seemed to be no end to it all. The bullet that had missed Fang and me so narrowly had made us girls cautious, and we went out only if we had to. Fang or I did the shopping for at eighteen we were the oldest. The youngest was not yet seven. Fortunately we had Hui, who went everywhere with us, which made us feel safer.

We heard that the conditions in the classrooms where the Rebels were housed were bad. As one lot went out to demonstrate and fight, the others returned to sleep. There was no hot water for washing, and they were poorly fed. Fang urged me to invite Pei-gen to her home for a hot bath, a good meal and to wash her clothes. Though Pei-gen had never shown the slightest concern for me, I was, nevertheless, looking forward to seeing her.

The next morning Fang helped me prepare some soup and rolls, and just before noon, I crossed the compound with them. The sun beat down, and it was unbearably hot. Sweat ran down my face, and the food I was carrying became heavier and heavier. I had to stop and rest several times, but I thought only of how delighted Pei-gen would be when she saw the food.

I entered the classroom and there she was. It had been over two years since she had come to Nanjing to sort out the things left behind by our mother, and I felt a pang of distress at the change in her. She looked like an old woman: her face was creased and lined, and her sparse hair was already turning grey. She was dressed in an old patched army uniform, which badly needed washing. I placed the two big pots on a table and smiled at her, inviting her and her room-mates to eat.

'Take that food away!' she screamed. 'We do not need your charity! What kind of shame do you want to bring to me with all this food? We have no need of such luxuries!' I stood at the doorway in shock. 'When everybody else is following Chairman Mao and sticking to his revolution- ary line, you are learning how to cook at home!' She turned her back on me, her legs wide apart, her hands on her hips. I was stunned, unable to utter a word.

Her room-mates looked at me, at the food and at her. Then they gathered around Pei-gen, saying that it was a good deed for me to think of her and go to so much trouble. They were sure Chairman Mao would forgive just one bite. After all, they were heavy pots for someone so small. And the food smelt so good.

I waited, holding my breath, hoping for some sign of a change of heart in my sister. It seemed like an hour but was probably nearer twenty seconds before she turned round. I could see the torment she was going through: longing, repugnance, hostility and want flashed across her face in quick succession. It was the first time I had ever seen her show any real emotion, and my heart went out to her. I imagined her mouth watering while she fought temptation. If anyone was a true devotee of Chairman Mao, it was she. Then, with a look that meant 'Don't you dare say anything,' she snatched a steamed roll, opened her mouth and took a big bite.

The other girls joined her, and soon the pots were empty. Then each woman left, smiling their thanks, until only Pei-gen and I remained. I stayed silent, waiting for her lead. 'It has been a long time since anyone has done anything nice for me,' she said. Her words came out like bullets, and I could see how difficult it was for her to make this small apology. 'But I don't want anything else from you. I need to keep to my chosen revolutionary path. It is my sworn duty.'

'I came with an invitation,' I said, trying to sound casual. 'My friend Fang and her sisters invite you and your room-mates to their home for a good bath and to wash your clothes.' Suddenly, the anger was back. 'We are not bourgeois decadents like you! Cold water is best for us!' She turned away, the old bitterness back on her face. 'Go!' she shouted. 'Go! And never come here again. You are too soft and I am ashamed to have such a decadent sister! Get out!'

Once again she had hurt me, but this time I was determined to stand my ground. 'I'm sorry we have chosen our different ways. You have yours and I have mine, but we both follow the teachings of Chairman Mao. I have no wish to shame you, so I will not come here again. You are my sister, and you cannot escape that. And I don't think being clean will damage your beliefs, so you are always welcome, if you change your mind.'

I had picked up the pots while I was speaking, and then I marched out of the door. Our family was now split asunder, exactly as China was being split, four siblings living their different lives, and all convinced that their way was correct. Andong was hiding away, not wanting any part in the political activities, my brother was in the army, Pei-gen was slavishly following her Maoist road, and then there was me.

My sadness covered me like a shroud as I trudged across the compound. I felt a mixture of sympathy and resentment towards Pei-gen. I was beginning to hate Mao, and I detested the Rebels, and the strident voice that assailed my ears from the loudspeakers. At that moment I hated almost everything about my life but I could not hate Pei-gen. Her fanaticism and her blind worship of Mao and his politics would never make me love her less, and never would I hold her beliefs against her. However, my way of thinking was beyond anything Pei-gen could tolerate or understand, and I knew she hated me for it.

As I reached my temporary home, I did not know that I had seen Pei-gen for the last time.

A couple of days later Andong came to see me with her new boyfriend, Zhan Pin-cheng, a student at another Nanjing military institute. He looked good in his uniform and the Five Golden Flowers made just as much fuss of him as they had of my Hui. He was a handsome young man, and my sister had fallen in love with him at first sight when she had stopped outside his base to read some big-character posters. He had been coming through the gates, and they had smiled at each other as he walked past her, and that was that. Since that day, Andong told me, her life seemed full of sunlight. Her face shone with happiness, and so did his. I was happy for her.

Zhan was not only nice-looking and intelligent, he was also a first-class cook. We didn't notice when he disappeared into the kitchen because we were too busy gossiping but suddenly we could smell tantalizing aromas. Then the five sisters came in, each bearing a dish – vegetable dumplings, fried rice, chow mein, fragrant lotus roots and red pork – followed by Zhan, red-faced from the heat of the kitchen. Andong looked at him adoringly, and I was delighted for her. She deserved something good in her life.

After the meal, the five sisters begged Zhan and Andong to tell them about how they had got together and, little by little, the story came out. Zhan was shy with women and Andong had initiated their love-affair, which was unusual in China. Boys pursued girls, not the other way round, yet bold Andong had chased shy Zhan. However, even she had been too bashful to speak out about her feelings, so she wrote him a note. 'I want to be your girlfriend. Please give me your answer within ten minutes. I shall wait under the trees opposite the camp.'

Zhan had never received such a note, and his face turned crimson as he read it. He looked up and squinted in the bright sunlight, trying to see her in the shade of the trees. She was hiding, appalled at her daring. Zhan didn't know what to do. Although he was attracted to Andong, he had not expected anything to come of it, and he was at a loss. He wanted a girlfriend, and he was pleased that a girl as pretty as Andong had made it known she liked him, but he was rooted to the spot in a panic. His mouth was dry. He needed a drink. He shuffled from foot to foot. He must do something quickly. If he didn't, he would miss his chance. He looked again into the trees, but could see nothing, so he moved nearer, then nearer, his feet dragging through the summer dust, and there she was, standing in front of him. She, too, looked uncomfortable.

'Well?' she said, fearing the worst. The note fluttered in his hand as he looked at her. He wanted to say yes. He wanted to shout yes, but nothing came out. He just nodded. 'You want to?' breathed Andong.

'Yes,' he mumbled, looking at the ground. 'Yes, I think it will be good.' And the two of them stood wordlessly facing each other, blushing profusely, wondering what to do next.

We all laughed, and I warmed to this quiet, shy, decent man. Andong went on to tell us that she went to see Zhan almost every day, to take care of his room and to wash his clothes. She had found that he had only two army uniforms, and nothing else. He was an orphan from a poor family, but he was the best student in his class, and she was proud of him. She never worried about his lack of money, and spent hers on him. She bought him some summer shirts and trousers. Zhan confessed he had never owned anything new in all of his twenty-three years. My sister had changed his life and given him the future he had always wanted, so he promised to look after her for as long as she needed him.

When I told them about my distressing meeting with Pei-gen, Andong sighed and told me that our sister had become the leader of the Rebels in her university, and had twenty thousand followers. I had had no idea that she had become so involved or that she had risen so high. Andong went on to explain that Pei-gen tried in every way to be like Chairman Mao. His words were her religion, and in his name she had persecuted a great many people. She never made allowances for any opinions that were different from her own. At this I felt a great pain. As an innocent child, Pei-gen had suffered greatly in the name of politics. Now she was making history repeat itself by persecuting others.

During the confusion and chaos of 1967, I spent several months in the home of the Five Golden Flowers. The flat was a haven of sanity in a mad world. We read books, and did our best to continue our studies. I tried to repay the girls for letting me stay with them by teaching them basic English. We spent many hot afternoons playing cards, and I learned how to cook. I seldom went out but Hui visited us regularly, and time passed.

In early December Hui told us there was nothing to do in his office. Almost every workplace had closed down, and those workers who did not want to join the Rebels called at their workplace only to collect their salaries. He asked me if I would like to go with him to visit his eldest brother in Beijing.

The strange thing was that despite the constant yelping of the loud-speakers, the fighting and killing, life was settling down to a kind of normality. The ordinary people were adjusting to the madness, and getting on with their own lives as best as they could. A few weeks before, I had been terrified at the idea of going out, yet here I was agreeing to travel with Hui to Beijing.

Hui gave me a new army uniform, which I wore over my padded winter clothes. I still wore my old Red Guard armband for protection, but the journey was uneventful. During the nineteen-hour train ride, and the two-hour river-crossing, Hui told me about his brother Tao, a senior army doctor at the headquarters of the PLA General Staff in Beijing. He was in the team of private physicians assigned to tend the health of the top echelons in the government and in 1964 had been hand-picked by the marshal commanding the special regiment of men assigned to protect Mao and his family. Tao was given full charge of Mao's son, Mao An-qing, who had severe schizophrenia. He was the son of Mao's first wife Yang Kai-hui, and had become ill after hearing about the death of his mother at the hands of the Kuomintang. Since then, he had got steadily worse, until Mao, fearing his image would be tarnished, had confined him to a secure room. At one time, Mao had sent him to Russia for treatment, which seemed to do him good, but he relapsed when he learned of the death of his favourite elder brother in Korea. He craved the love of his family, but Mao was always too busy to see him. So he just sat, heavily medicated, not speaking to anybody except himself.

Each morning, before the medication took hold, he wrote a long letter to his father, always ending with 'Great Father Chairman Mao, I want to see you.' The letters were never delivered. On the orders of Mao, they were filed away and used by the doctors to try to help their patient. Mao showed little interest in his son. He visited him once every six months for an hour or so, and afterwards An-qing would be in good spirits before he slid back into his private hell.

At the military compound where Tao lived, behind Tiananmen Square in the centre of Beijing, he took out the file on Mao An-qing and showed me a photograph he had taken of Chairman Mao and his son. The two men were sitting side by side on a large sofa in the son's living room. The resemblance between father and son was extraordinary, but where Mao looked interested and alive, An-qing didn't. His loneliness came out of the picture as clearly as if I was in the room with them. Tao told us he felt uncomfortable in caring for the young Mao, because Jiang Qing delighted in finding any excuse to persecute the doctors and nurses.

Madam Mao was an excitable woman who lost her temper easily, for no reason. A number of nurses and doctors had been bullied by her before Tao was chosen to care for An-qing and every one of them had taken their job seriously and had looked after him with kindness and consideration. However, Jiang Qing had accused them all of 'attempting to murder Chairman Mao's son', and they had met a painful, miserable end.

Tao told us quietly that he had no peace in doing his 'glorious job' and had tried hard to find a way to be transferred. It was dangerous not to obey the orders of the Party, but in Tao's case it was also dangerous to obey. Every day he went to tend his charge, nervously expecting to be Jiang Qing's next victim. Hui had made it plain to me many times how proud he was of his brother. But now, after hearing what Tao had to say, he felt anxious about him. Hui and I stayed with Tao for over a month, and the whole family, including me, worried about him the moment he left the house in the morning and sighed with relief when he returned in the evening.

Fortunately, Mao's wife was then busy with the Cultural Revolution and paid less attention to An-qing and his attendants. This gave Tao the chance he had been waiting for. He pulled a few strings within his profession, and was transferred to an army hospital without her interference. The night Tao ended his last day tending An-qing, we sat down to a celebration dinner, and I was happy to witness two drunken brothers, arms around each other, singing lustily, very out of tune.

Hui and I went to the Summer Palace in the western suburbs. The last time I had visited it was with Old Pei in the autumn of 1966. Now the gates were wide open and anybody could go in. The whole complex was in disorder, dirty, with overgrown gardens and lawns and litter everywhere. Nobody cared for it, and vandals had smashed their way into the buildings. The lake was frozen, and hundreds of children were skating on it. We, too, went on to the ice, and crossed the two kilometres or so to the other side. I could see the green weeds in the water beneath my feet clearly as we balanced ourselves on the slippery surface. It seemed as if we were walking on a big sheet of glass, and I felt it could break at any moment.

We went home by bus. Some services continued as normal, and the bus service was one. On the way, we passed the zoo. The gates were locked. An image from the past flashed into my mind of my family enjoying themselves, and I felt a momentary pang of sadness. Those days had gone, except in my memory. Now, where there used to be happy people relaxing, there were political slogans. The zoo was plastered with them, and so were the surrounding streets. The most commonly repeated of Chairman Mao's words were: 'Rebellion is reasonable!' As the bus drove past the slogan, I thought, Rebellion is not at all reasonable. It is meaningless fighting and death.

When we got home that evening, Tao told us there had been a big fight on the lake at the Summer Palace and the ice had cracked as thugs slugged it out. Several had drowned. I was glad we had left when we did, or we would almost certainly have been dragged into it. The Chinese lost their tempers over the slightest things in those days, and fought fiercely among themselves. Disinterested onlookers had to become involved too, or be denounced for something. We had narrowly missed being badly injured or killed. It was a bad ending to a lovely day.

Hui and I returned to Nanjing at the end of January 1968, just before the Spring Festival. In those days, nobody dared celebrate because it was an 'old' tradition and must be abolished. For the duration of the Cultural Revolution, the people of China dared not even mention the Spring Festival. The traditional unification of the family could not take place anyway because so many had been split apart: millions of people were missing, in prison, detention or exile. Hundreds of thousands of families were never reunited.

I was riding my bicycle across the compound after a visit to my flat when the news hit my ears. It was March 1968 and now I barely noticed the strident voice bellowing from the loudspeakers; it had become part of the constant background noise of the city. But I heard this titbit loud and clear, and almost fell off my bicycle. In shock, I stood beside it, shaking from head to foot, hoping against hope that I had misheard what the announcer had said. I listened intently, as he went through the rest of his script. And there it was again. It was the worst news I could possibly have heard. I was to be sent to the countryside, possibly for ever. I fainted clean away. When I came round I was in bed, with the Five Golden Flowers in the room, looking anxiously down at me. Hui was holding my hand.

Mao had decided to send all middle-school graduates, both lower and upper departments, of the years 1966, 1967 and 1968, numbering some forty-five million young people aged sixteen years and upwards, to the countryside. Most were to go to the poorest regions of China and, even worse, the rest to the most remote areas, way up in the deep mountains 'to receive re-education from the poor and lower-middle-class peasants', trumpeted the announcer, as if he was giving us news of a great victory.

'I'm finished!' I said. 'I'm going to the countryside.' I burst into tears.

The others knew how much I hated the countryside. We had no secrets from each other, and all of us dreaded the thought of spending our lives rotting away in the middle of nowhere. How could I get out of this?

Many of my female schoolmates from army families had joined the PLA and had been trained as nurses, administrators, secretaries and telephone operators. That might be my escape route. How could I join the army? I would be safe there. I would receive regular wages, clothes and food. Desperation made being a soldier very desirable. Just a few months ago I would have sneered at any suggestion that army life might appeal to me. I still remembered my feeble attempts to throw the hand-grenade and my puny efforts during bayonet practice. Now all I wanted was to join the army. But how to achieve it?

Ironically, it was Mao Tse-tung who came to my rescue. When he was certain he had got rid of all possible opposition and felt himself secure as absolute leader, he wanted his followers to stop the factional fighting and restore order. In early 1968, he changed the tone of his daily 'thoughts' to a more conciliatory line, using less inflammatory language. The new instruction was: 'Inside the working class, there is no actual conflict. All mass factions are revolutionary organizations and should work together towards peace and unification.' The Rebels were confused: they had been fighting each other, and hundreds of thousands had died defending Mao and his thoughts. Suddenly they were to stop fighting and become friends. Slowly, a sort of peace came and the streets filled with people again.

A new organization calling itself the Revolutionary Committee was set up in Beijing, quickly followed by similar committees in all the communes, villages, towns and cities throughout China. The local leadership consisted of middle- to high-ranking army officers, Rebel leaders, and a carefully selected group of the old officials, who had been 'liberated' by Mao and freed from detention. At the head of these new committees were the local army commanders or political commissars, who became the local chairmen.

On 6 April, the Revolutionary Committee of Jiangsu Province and Nanjing Municipality was established, and the inauguration ceremony was held in Gulou Square. The commanding officer of the Nanjing

Army Unit, General Xu Shi-you, was the chairman and Peng Chong, who had been the number one Party secretary in the old Nanjing Party Committee, was appointed by Mao himself to be the deputy chairman of the new leadership.

Peng Chong had been severely punished by the Rebels. They had branded him a capitalist roader and, after beating him almost to death many times, they had imprisoned him and his family in a 'cowshed' – a place of detention, or prison. His appointment by Mao came as a surprise to everybody, especially Peng. Only days earlier, he had suffered yet another beating from the Rebels, and his whole family had been herded through the streets in disgrace. The Rebels had tied ropes around their necks and pulled them along, while others beat them with bamboo sticks. Yet now he had been 'liberated' by Mao and his status changed from class enemy and capitalist roader to important leader!

On his appointment, General Xu sent one of his senior officers to where Peng Chong's family was confined. At first, they thought it was time for their execution and they stood up, almost pleased that their ordeal was over. Only when the officer smiled and saluted respectfully did the family begin to hope that their luck had changed. A limousine was waiting to take them home. After a bath and a change of clothes, Comrade Peng Chong would be driven to meet General Xu.

Peng Chong looked at his wife, then addressed the officer: 'Tell the driver to meet me at my house. We will walk.' And the whole family, dressed in their rags, dirty, cut and bruised, walked the five kilometres home along the same streets they had been dragged through just four days previously. They sang revolutionary songs as they went, and soon a large crowd was following them, cheering, laughing, clapping and singing. This was the first time that any prisoners of the Rebels had been set free, and almost everybody felt a surge of happiness. Only the Rebels, glowering helplessly, refused to join in.

When I heard of the release and appointment of Peng Chong, I was surprised and delighted. He had been a close friend of long standing to my family. It was he who had presided over my father's funeral, and he had always shown a kindly concern for us children, especially after Mother died. Even during my time in Shanghai, he had kept a friendly eye on me. Perhaps Mao, without knowing it, had given me the means with which to escape the fate he had chosen for me.

I was among the onlookers in Gulou Square as we watched the inauguration ceremony of our new provincial and city government.

Peng Chong looked dapper in his new clothes. I guessed he must have been about fifty but his recent experiences had etched deep lines into his face, making him look much older. He was terribly thin, and the marks of his recent beatings still discoloured his face and neck. He stood straight and proud as he was sworn in as deputy chairman.

The next day I went to the offices of the new leadership, in a splendid building that had once housed the American ambassador to the Kuomintang government. The soldier on guard at the gate stopped me as I tried to walk through. 'Excuse me, Comrade, do you have official business here?'

'I should very much like to see my uncle, Comrade Peng Chong,' I said, with as much dignity as I could muster. I was quaking in my shoes, fearful I would be turned away.

A young junior officer sauntered across, obviously newly promoted, and full of himself. 'Comrade Peng Chong is very busy. He cannot be disturbed.'

His loud, rude tone almost unnerved me, and only my desperate need to escape the countryside kept me from walking away. 'He will see me,' I said, with false authority. 'He is a good friend of my father and I have important things to tell him.'

My apparent confidence frightened him, and he straightened his back. His voice was more respectful as he asked, 'Can you tell me what it is you wish to tell him?'

I took a deep breath. 'Certainly not, but you can take this note to him.' I pulled out my notebook and hurriedly scribbled: 'Dear Uncle Peng Chong, I am the daughter of Comrade Gao Yi-lin. I would like to see you. Anhua.'

The officer had no idea who Gao Yi-lin was, but dared not delay in case I had been sent by another important leader. It wouldn't look good for him if he blundered during his first week in his new job. The names of leaders were changing all the time and nobody could keep track of who was whom, so he walked away with my note.

A few minutes later Uncle Peng was hurrying towards me with a wide smile on his thin face. The young officer was following him and this time he gave me a smile before moving away out of earshot. Uncle Peng took my hand in both of his. 'Anhua! It is a pleasure to see you looking so well. What a nice surprise.' He took me into his imposing office and waved me to a chair. The officer started to follow, but Uncle Peng stopped him. 'Please arrange some tea for my little guest,' he said, and the officer walked away. He reappeared with a servant who carefully placed a full teacup in front of me.

When we were alone, Uncle Peng sat down facing me. 'Tell me your news.'

I told him everything about my brother, how Andong and I were getting along, and about Pei-gen. Uncle was particularly interested in her activities because of his own experience at the hands of the Rebels. 'What a shame,' he said. 'None of you have had the life your mother and father wished for you, but they could never have guessed what was in store for us all. Now tell me about yourself.'

I knew instinctively that I could speak freely to him but even so I began hesitantly, telling him of my experiences and my dislike of the countryside. Soon, though, the floodgates inside me opened and I told him everything. By the time I got to the prospect of being sent away again, perhaps for ever, the tears were streaming down my face. Uncle nodded, with compassion and understanding, as I gulped my way to silence. By this time, he was holding my hand, and as I looked down, I could see white marks on his skin where I had gripped him so tightly.

'I think you are right,' he said, after a pause. 'You would be better off in the army. At least you would be safe there.' Hope sprang up, and I waited with bated breath. 'I will have a word with the general. Don't worry, Anhua, you will not be going to the countryside. It is not what your parents would have wished, so I will be pleased to help you.'

He stood up. Our meeting was at an end. 'I am sorry to hurry you away, Anhua, but there is such a lot to do. Everything is in chaos, as you can imagine, but I shall find the time to take care of your problem today.' He walked with me from the office building right up to the gate, about a hundred metres away, to see me off. The young officer was standing in the courtyard, hands behind his back, and smiled at me. The warm greetings from Peng Chong had made him think I was someone of importance and he came to attention and saluted as we went past.

When I got home, I thought I had better write to the general too. In the letter, I told him about my parents and that Comrade Peng Chong knew me well. I asked him to give me permission to join the army, and scattered plenty of revolutionary slogans among my words. When I had finished, I rode my bicycle to his home and handed it over to the bodyguard.

I thought it might take time for something to happen, so I went back to Fang's home in the military compound and carried on with my life.

As usual, the following Monday I went to my school to have a look round. I was reading a new set of big-character posters when I saw a message written in chalk on a blackboard hanging from a nail on the door of what had been the reception room. 'Comrade Gao Anhua, please go to the army headquarters immediately.' The school gatekeeper had resumed his duties and told me that an army officer had come to the school three times looking for me.

I hastened to the army headquarters, where a staff officer led me to his office and told me, 'Your request to join the army has been granted by General Xu Shi-you. Here is the form, please fill it in.' He then pulled out a 'Recruitment Notice' from a drawer, stamped it with a big red star and put his signature across it. 'Take this notice to the headquarters of the Rear Services department at Xin Jie Kou Square and show it to them. They will tell you what unit you have been assigned to.' And that was that.

I called in to see Andong and told her what had happened. She thought it would be a good idea for her to join the army too – until she remembered she wanted to marry Zhan. If she had joined the army, she would not be allowed to marry because of her age: twenty-one was, and still is, considered too young for a woman to marry but, like most things in China, it is possible to bypass the rules by knowing the right people. Not long after I joined the army, Zhan fiddled his way into marriage to Andong with the help of an influential friend.

We discussed what to do with our flat, and agreed it was no longer of any use to us. Andong was now living in Zhan's dormitory and Wei-guo was in the army. As I was about to follow him, we decided to return the flat and furniture to the authorities. I sold most of my books to the wastepaper depot and moved my camphorwood trunk and my bicycle to Hui's dormitory. That was my property sorted out. I told Hui about the pistols and the old photographs belonging to Uncle Wang and Auntie Shi, hidden in my trunk. To my surprise, he insisted on me handing over the revolvers to the new local government in case they were found in his room. I wasn't happy, but I had to agree. Then came the hardest part: saying goodbye to the Five Golden Flowers.

After a tearful farewell, I reported to the Rear Services headquarters on 12 April 1968. A courteous officer escorted me inside. Here I was welcomed into the People's Liberation Army of China. I was proud to be a part of it. I was given a female uniform, underwear, a white shirt, a new pair of shoes and a pair of cotton socks. A girl soldier sewed a red cloth badge to each side of my jacket collar, and pinned a red metal star to the front of the cap. Then came a moment I will never forget: I slipped behind a screen and donned the uniform of my country. It fitted me perfectly, and I strutted around the room for a few seconds, enjoying the feel of the new clothes and the stiffness of the shoes.

The officer and the girl had already made up a bedroll for me from a new quilt and a bed-sheet. In it were another uniform, a pair of shoes, more underwear, two more shirts and a raincoat. She gave me a satchel with a long strap to be carried over one shoulder, and a water-bottle to be carried over the other. I thought of the old metal water-bottle, safely stored in my camphorwood trunk. I was also issued with a tin mug, two towels and two more pairs of cotton socks. Everything except the towels and the shirts was a drab olive green, yet to me it looked beautiful.

I put my own clothes, the towels and the other things into the satchel, and tied the mug to the strap. Then, with some help from the officer, I lifted the unfamiliar bedroll on to my back, and was escorted to the gate. The whole thing had taken about twenty minutes, and the same guard grinned hugely. He had seen a timid schoolgirl go in, and a soldier come out. As I passed him, he gave me a little wave and whispered, 'Good luck!'

Then the officer summoned a pedicab — half-bicycle half-rickshaw — and I climbed in. He instructed the driver to take me to the army training camp in the southern suburb of Nanjing and paid the fare. We waved goodbye to each other and I moved off towards my new life.

11. In the Army

I sat in the pedicab in high spirits heading towards my splendid future. I looked around me, back straight, as the houses, shops, trees and people moved in and out of my vision. Many people we passed stared at me with interest and admiration: every young person wanted to join the army then, but only a tiny proportion would do so – least of all, girls. It was a rare sight to see a young girl wearing a brand-new uniform. How lucky I was! The sun seemed to shine with an extra brightness as I rode along.

Half an hour later, I was in the army camp where I was to undergo my basic military training before being sent to my permanent posting. A guard directed me towards a large parade ground where I joined over a hundred other girls, all new recruits, waiting to be told what to do next. As girls do, we soon began talking. It seemed to me that every girl except me was the daughter of a high-ranking serving officer.

A man with the loudest, nastiest, rudest voice in the whole world began to give orders. Exactly what Loudmouth was shouting I had no idea. Nor, it seemed, did the others, as we milled around like a flock of frightened sheep. But, slowly, we were formed into lines, and divided up. Later I learned that we were one company, divided into three platoons, with each platoon made up of three squads.

After a few hours everything began to make sense and I was soon taking the whole thing for granted. I learned that the company commander and the political instructor were male officers, and so was the company sergeant (Loudmouth) – I will call him a sergeant because his real title won't translate from Mandarin. The rest of the leaders were women. They had been carefully selected and posted in from different military hospitals all over Jiangsu Province, and they were in charge of the platoons and squads. I was in the third platoon, squad eight, with eleven other girls, who looked as confused as I was.

I selected a bed and thankfully dropped my bedroll. It had begun to feel heavy and my shoulders ached. The girls on either side of me had done the same, and we laughed as we rubbed our necks. We introduced ourselves: on my right was Wang Xiao-ping (Little Ping), a daughter of Lieutenant General Wang, the Chengdu Army Unit commander, and on my left was a shy, pretty girl named Tsao Lin (Jingle Bell), whose father was also a general. The three of us quickly became known as the Three Tiddlers because we were fairly small and very slim.

Little Ping was the only recruit in our intake from outside Jiangsu Province. Chengdu, where her father commanded his regiments, was the capital city of Sichuan Province, where there was still heavy factional fighting. It was a hazardous place to live and she was glad to be out of it: she had lost a brother in the fighting and had narrowly escaped death herself several times. Little Ping was twenty-one, the oldest in our squad. I was nineteen and Tsao Lin eighteen. We held similar views, and as time went by we confided to each other our secret feelings, including our hatred of the countryside.

At noon a whistle sounded and we looked at each other, mystified, until our squad leader walked into our hut and told us to follow her. It was time to eat. We were lined up in ranks and told to sing songs made up from Chairman Mao's quotations on the short march to the dining hall. Before eating, we had to recite a selection of Mao's thoughts, chosen beforehand by our platoon leader. This happened at every meal, three times a day, every day. Thankfully, the food was worth it.

During our first afternoon in the camp, each of us was given a brand new copy of *The Little Red Book*, and a round aluminium badge showing the head of Mao, which we pinned on the left breast of our uniforms. We were told we had a tight timetable to follow, and that all our activities were governed by a whistle. Then we were taught the three basic rules: '1. Obey orders at all times, without question, whether you understand them or not. 2. Never argue with your leaders. Their orders are law. 3. There must be no talk of love during the first two years of army life.' It was made clear to us that any infringement would result in disgrace and severe punishment.

Discipline was strict, and we were harried from morning till night. An old and experienced comrade – aged at least twenty-four – told us that this was so that they could build us into real soldiers, trained to fight any aggressor. They wasted no time. Military training began the following morning after breakfast. Before we were allowed to eat, the whole company had to fall in on the parade ground, holding *The Little Red Book* high in the air in our right hands. The company commander shouted, 'First of all, let us wish, with the reddest sun in our hearts, an endless life to our great leader Chairman Mao! An endless life! An endless life! An endless life!'

We repeated the slogan at the tops of our voices, waving *The Little Red Book* above our heads. Then we had breakfast. We did the same every day without fail, irrespective of how hot or how cold it was. We were told that 'spiritual nourishment', which was everything concerning Chairman Mao, was more important than food. But it was hard to appreciate this in the pouring rain or under a burning sun.

It didn't end there. Chairman Mao was constantly with us. After breakfast, we had to study his writings in *The Little Red Book* for an hour. Then one of us was chosen to recite from memory, word perfect, the thoughts of Chairman Mao. Nobody could afford to make a mistake. The slightest error meant punishment, such as extensive drill, while reciting over and over again. Every evening, before going to bed, we had to stand in a row and loudly shout three times: 'Let us wish our dear deputy commander Lin Biao excellent health for ever and for ever and for ever!' because Lin Biao was then the Minister of National Defence. The three shouts in the morning were called 'Morning Consulting' and the three at night were 'Evening Report'.

Everyone had orders to supervise everyone else to make sure we all did our duty. As Morning Consulting took place before breakfast nobody could possibly forget it. But Evening Report was made in the hut by each soldier just before retiring, and at the beginning of our army life we often forgot to do it. After we had been reported and had been punished, we learned our lesson. Reporting to the leaders was commonplace because the reporter was highly praised, and the forgetter was punished.

We were also taught to sing: 'Father is dear, Mother is dear, but not as dear as Chairman Mao' and to dance the 'Loyalty Dance' as we sang. That didn't amount to much: we just moved our feet backwards and forwards while waving *The Little Red Book* in the air.

I found the ritual pointless, humiliating and monotonous, but of course I couldn't say so. Every girl, including me, tried her best to show her 'boundless' love for and loyalty to Chairman Mao. One girl even wrote a letter to her parents, in which she said, 'Dear Father and Mother, I love you very much, but I love Chairman Mao more. If I ever have to choose between you and Chairman Mao, I will always choose Chairman Mao.' She read it to us and posted it. I didn't think her parents would be happy to receive such a letter, but she was highly praised by our platoon leader. The army ensured that Chairman Mao was in our thoughts every second of our daily lives.

The excitement of joining the army soon waned, and I was worried at my lack of enthusiasm in idolizing Mao. I was under great pressure of my own making and constantly wary of giving myself away. It was not army life I objected to – I was beginning to enjoy it and was putting all my efforts into being a good soldier – it was having to pretend to worship Mao that gave me problems. I hated my duplicity and hypocrisy. However, anything was better than being sent to the countryside.

After an hour of political study, we always marched to the parade ground for drill. Loudmouth would march into our midst and shout horrible things into the faces of the frightened recruits. I will never forget the first time he did it to me. His squat nose came so close to mine that I could smell his stinking breath and rotting teeth as he shouted obscenities.

After a few days we were given real rifles, which we had to clean before being taught how to take them to pieces and to reassemble them. We repeated the exercise dozens of times until we could do it blindfold. Loudmouth had a wonderful time tormenting us until we got it right. We spent much of our free time cleaning our guns along with the rest of our kit. It was a hard life, made better by the friendships that developed between us girls.

Most of us supported each other to make our lives easier. If Loudmouth made someone feel worthless, the rest comforted her. Only the reporters, who were always trying to gain praise at our expense, were left to look after themselves. The comradeship we enjoyed was denied them.

After a week, we were given live bullets and taken to the butts to fire them. The first time I squeezed the trigger of my rifle, the explosion made my ears ring, and I felt a painful thump in my shoulder from the recoil. None of us could move our right arms that evening. But there was no sympathy from Loudmouth: he took us for grenade-throwing next morning.

At that time of year, it was either blisteringly hot or we got soaked in heavy rain, but because we had to become hardened to all weather conditions we were out every day drilling and training. We were repeatedly told that the US imperialists with their running dogs, including Chiang Kai-shek, might launch a surprise attack at any time and start the Third World War. We were members of the greatest army in the world and must be ready to take our place in it (although, according to Loudmouth, we were the dregs and had no business in uniform). At night we cleaned ourselves and our kit. We never had time to relax for a minute. If we had any spare time, we were called upon to recite Mao's

Old Three Articles. No complaints were allowed. We had to shut up and get on with it.

In addition to the training, we had to cope with emergency musters. These happened between three and five times a week at any time between midnight and four in the morning. Everyone had to wake up and get dressed in double-quick time as soon as we heard the whistle. Then we had to make up our bedrolls and sling them on to our backs before we ran outside to be numbered off. Everything must be done in complete darkness, because, according to Lin Biao's instructions, 'All modern wars are launched by surprise attack, therefore we must be prepared at all times.'

Speed was paramount. Usually, we could get outside within two minutes of the whistle sounding and the quickest in just over a minute. If we took longer, we were severely criticized and made to do more practice the next day, until we got it right. Then we would have another emergency muster the following night, which affected us all, so lateness was quickly eliminated.

In the early days of our training, we could not make up a tight bedroll. Many loosened and we lost some of our kit. A few girls tried to leave the bulk of their kit behind, only to be punished when their scheme was discovered. We had to take everything with us, and there were regular equipment inspections. In the beginning, a number of girls put their shoes on the wrong feet, which made the march uncomfortable. Some lost their shoes, and came back with bleeding feet, and others put their trousers on the wrong way round. Hair would be tousled if the weather was dry, heavy and lank if it was raining. With pride we noted that at least we all completed the night marches and made it back to camp.

Tired, sleepy, and often irritable, we would take a break until dawn, then force ourselves out to find our missing kit. It was easy to see where we had been: our route was littered with mugs, kettles, socks, underwear and other bits and pieces. One or two of the girls never found all of their equipment and were made to do self-criticism for misusing the 'properties given by the people'.

Many girls had not experienced the countryside as Little Ping, Tsao Lin and I had. They had been too young to be sent away before the start of the Cultural Revolution and the closing of the schools. After the first emergency muster, they cried bitterly: never before had they suffered such hardship as they struggled through the forced march in the dark, carrying the heavy bedrolls. They had had easy lives, spoilt by their high-ranking parents before joining the army. Our squad leader, who came from a labouring family in Yangzhou, showed them no pity: she had joined the army before the Cultural Revolution, when no children of high-ranking families had wanted to join, and she had had to pass a strict political and physical inspection before being accepted.

Before the Cultural Revolution, children of high officials wanted, and expected, an easy life: lazy schooldays followed by a good university and a soft job. Now things had changed, and the army was their best choice. What upset our squad leader more than anything was that they had joined so easily, with no health check, no political assessment, just a telephone call from a parent to a contact. She held us in contempt and scornfully told the crying girls: 'Shame on you for crying! Compared to the hardships suffered by your parents and those brave comrades who did the Long March, this is nothing! Chairman Mao expects his soldiers to fear neither hardship nor death. If you cannot bear such a small inconvenience, go home!' The crying stopped. No one wanted to be sent home and shipped off to the countryside.

Every Saturday, after lunch, we were taken by truck to an army bath unit to wash. We needed it badly: the constant training and night musters made us sweat a lot, and our barracks did not have the facilities for anything other than a wash of our exposed parts: hands, faces, forearms, lower legs and feet. We did our best, but the Saturday bath-run became the highlight of our week. The first time we were ordered into the trucks we did not know what to expect. It was rumoured (there were always rumours) that we were to be taken to a river for a swim. Imagine our delight when we saw the lines of hot showers and an enormous steaming tub, capable of holding at least fifty girls. The air was hot and steamy, and smelt of carbolic. I chose a shower, but many couldn't resist the tub. They looked like dumplings boiling in a big pot. Many of us had been given a nickname. One otherwise beautiful girl had a birthmark on her backside shaped like the map of China, so we called her, 'Map-arse'. One girl with dark skin and red lips was 'Black-rose'; another was 'Fluffy' because she was so feminine and scatter-brained. My nickname was 'Squinty' because all those hours of study had caught up with me and my sight was deteriorating.

All too soon the whistle sounded and we had to dry ourselves and leave the bath-house. Hundreds more women were waiting their turn. Before leaving, I took a last lingering look behind me. The tub was almost empty, and a platoon of near-naked women were cleaning up our mess.

By the end of May we were looking more like soldiers. My two friends and I kept together and supported each other through the more difficult tasks such as the obstacle course. We had great trouble when we first encountered a high brick wall, but we helped each other until we could climb over it with our rifles and bedrolls.

The night musters gradually became easier. My sight was better in darkness, and as my physical fitness improved I hardly got out of breath as we marched along. Our rifle shooting was getting better too, and our scores were checked after every session. Each target was set up 100 metres away from us as we lay on our tummies and took aim. It was shaped like the top half of an American soldier carrying a rifle, and five white circles were painted on the green chest. The outer circle had a score value of six, the next was seven, up to ten for the centre circle, which was about two and a half centimetres in diameter. A bullet through the head of the American imperialist scored five.

Little Ping was a great shot and always scored well, but I was hopeless. I was so short-sighted I could hardly see my target, never mind the circles. Little Ping and I hatched a plot: after the first batch of nine bullets, when she had got her marks, she shot half of her bullets into my circles, and I fired at hers. In this way, her scores kept up, and mine improved. Tsao Lin was a good shot, so all three of us passed at shooting.

Then came the day I had dreaded: the throwing of live hand-grenades. We had to toss the heavy metal object at least eighteen metres because a grenade might kill you if it exploded any closer to you. We knew that many girls would find it difficult to throw a grenade so far, but we didn't have to worry because we would be well protected. The company commander had ordered a pit to be dug, deep enough to hide a tall man standing upright. The thrower was told to stand on the edge of the pit, so that the instructor, in the pit, could hold her ankles. As soon as she pulled out the pin and threw the grenade, he yanked on her ankles so that she fell into the pit. The instructor then covered her body with his, ensuring her safety.

Despite all the preparation, many of us were frightened. I stood far behind the pit, dreading the time when my name would be called. When it was, I stepped forward slowly and stood on the edge, the hand-grenade in my sweaty palm. I could feel my heart pounding as I put my left index finger through the ring, ready to pull. '*Throw!*' I pulled the pin and threw it as far as I could. Yank . . . grunt . . . whoosh! The explosion, when it came, was hardly noticeable. All I heard was heavy breathing in my ear as a few lumps of earth fell into the pit.

I opened my eyes slowly, and saw blue sky. I was safe. As I climbed unsteadily out of the hole, I saw big smiles on the faces of Little Ping and Tsao Lin. 'Well done, Squinty!' shouted Little Ping. 'You got it over the line.' Through the clearing cloud of dust, I was pleased to see a marker showing that I had thrown it more than the required eighteen metres. I heaved a great big sigh of relief and sent a silent thank you to Zhang for teaching me long ago how to throw.

At that time there was war in Vietnam and China was pouring in troops and armaments to help the Vietnamese take on the might of the heavily armed US invaders. There were women doctors and nurses among the medical units, and we thought that some of us would be going too. When the company commander told us that none of us would be sent, we were much relieved. Instead, he told us, we would be divided into groups of ten and posted to different hospitals.

A week later, our training ended and we were real soldiers. We went on parade for the last time, dressed in our best uniforms to perform the drills we had been taught. Loudmouth looked smart in his parade uniform, and so did our company commander. I felt wonderful as we marched and wheeled and turned, doing our small-arms drill. The commanding general took the salute as we marched past and away to our futures. Loudmouth smiled widely and walked among us wishing us well. He was human, after all! Then he marched away with a wink, saying he had to meet the next group of no-hopers – and there they were: frightened, confused little girls, wondering what was in store for them. And, as I looked, I swear I saw my double.

The list of postings was pinned up and we crushed forward, anxious to know where we were going and who with. I was peering at the lists, trying to make sense of the words in the fog of bad sight when I heard: 'Squinty! We're together . . . here!' My eyes followed Tsao Lin's pointing finger. Little Ping, Tsao Lin and I were going to the same hospital: No. 695 Field Hospital, Jiangshan County, Zhejiang Province. Then came another surprise. We were told to fall in for pay! Our first wages as soldiers. I hadn't given money a thought throughout the weeks of training because I had had little use for it. Now we were paid all our salary at once, and each girl received six yuan and seventy-five fen (cents). Not much, but ours to spend as we liked. Food, clothes, lodging, laundry and everything else in the army was free – except toilet paper! No one knew why an important item like that had to be paid for.

On 31 May 1968, at 20:00 hours (we had been taught to use the twenty-four-hour clock) we ten girls climbed aboard our train. We lifted our bedrolls effortlessly on to the luggage racks and sat down. We were in high spirits, thinking we would soon be floating around the hospital doling out pills and sympathy, adored by our grateful patients. We would not have to do any more morning drills or military training. We sang our full repertoire of songs of Chairman Mao's quotations as the train click–clacked along, aware of the admiring glances coming our way from the other passengers.

Fourteen hours later, we alighted at Jiangshan County railway station. We had managed a few cat-naps on the train but it was now 10:00 hours, on 1 June, and our good-humour had evaporated like the steam from the engine. We were desperately tired, but we tried to stride like soldiers along the platform towards the exit. A powerfully built male soldier and a female officer were waiting for us. They introduced themselves before calling out our names and ticking us off on a list as we answered. The soldier was named Sun Yu-song, a medical orderly at the hospital, and the officer was Zhao, chief nurse. They led us to a huge truck and told us to climb up on to the open back. It was a bit high for some of us, so the soldier made a step with his hands. It was raining hard, so we put on our raincoats as our escorts got in the front with the driver.

The truck drove through the middle of nowhere for about half an hour before we saw anything remotely military. Then long lines of army huts went by, followed by a large training area, a tall flagpole with a drooping flag, then more huts before we turned left and stopped at a guarded gate. We looked around us with great interest. There seemed to be hundreds of huts, all looking exactly the same: olive green with eight windows along each side, and sloping tiled roofs. We saw a company of soldiers on the square, soaking wet, drilling in the rain. And we had thought we'd finished with all that. Then there were more huts, linked together by covered passages and grouped around a new brick building: the hospital.

The truck stopped outside it and we were told to get off. A young soldier ran out with a wooden box for us to use as a step, and we climbed down wearily, holding our bedrolls. The chief nurse divided us into two groups of five. 'There are two clinics here. You five will work in number one,' she pointed to the other group, 'and you others will work in number two. This comrade [the young soldier who brought us the box] will show you to your quarters. Get settled in, and report here at 08:00 hours tomorrow morning.' Sadly we three friends were split up. Tsao Lin and I were in number two with Fluffy and Little Ping was in number one, so she had to go with her group to another room.

Our squad leader entered and, as we had been taught, we sprang to our feet and stood to attention at the foot of our beds. 'There's no need for that,' she said. 'This is the real army. We have to work together and live together, so things are different here. My name is Xiao Yun. Just obey my orders, and every order you are given. Salute officers and you will get along just fine. My bed is in the other room with your two comrades.' We nodded and settled to our unpacking. I was glad she was next door: she seemed like a decent sort but I had learned that leaders are best kept as far away as possible.

The following morning we reported as ordered, and found out a little of what was expected of us. Each clinic spent six months on duty in the hospital and six months camping, training or on military exercises. At the time of our arrival, clinic one was on duty so Little Ping started work in the wards straight away, while Tsao Lin, Fluffy and I, in clinic two, began our new life as nurses doing military training and political study.

At our first political-education meeting, the commissar of the hospital tried to explain the complicated situation of class struggle in the area. Uniquely, he stressed, in the area around the hospital, the relationship between the army and the local people was not good. Apparently Jiang-shan County, on the border of Jiangxi and Fujian provinces, used to be a stronghold of the old Kuomintang government and many of the locals had relatives in Taiwan. Also, according to the commissar, 'The land is fertile and gives up to three good harvests every year, unlike less fertile provinces where the yields are poor. In such areas, the peasants are eager to join the PLA and leave all their worries and hardships behind them. Here, the people have plenty of food and no desire to join the army or have anything to do with it. They think the soldiers are crude and uncouth.' For these reasons, he said, 'this place is full of class enemies and we must be constantly on our guard against possible sabotage'. The meeting continued with further warnings. If we met a peasant, it was better not to talk to them because they might have a close relative living in exile in Taiwan.

He moved on to another subject. The hospital had been built in a basin, surrounded by tree-covered hills, on the other side of which were paddy-fields. Sadly the trees had almost all gone: they had been cut down to feed the furnaces during the Great Leap Forward. The few that remained had to be guarded to stop the peasants stealing them for fuel. A replanting scheme had not been successful and the few surviving pine trees had been ravaged by insects. As there were no birds, they too might die. Our duties would include: 1. Going on armed patrol around the hospital perimeters to protect the older trees. 2. Going to the hills to kill the insects that were attacking the young trees. 3. Patrolling the inner areas of the camp to stop the locals from cutting through the wire to damage the installations, or to steal equipment.

Later that day, after the afternoon session of political study, we were taught some basic first aid. I thought of Little Ping and the girls of clinic one becoming familiar with the routine of the hospital and being taught how to tend the patients. They were mainly soldiers from the various units based in Jiangshan County, plus some of those wounded on the battlefields of Vietnam. In clinic two we were keen to prove ourselves as nurses, but we had to be content for the time being with practising first aid. In early July we would be going camping for three months. We were told we must be prepared for a possible spell in Vietnam.

I was disappointed. I had expected to be given a proper job caring for patients, while learning how to become a good, useful nurse. I was saddened to find that the hospital was just another school of Mao Tse-tung thought. Of course, when December came and it was our turn to go into the wards, we would be more experienced, so I made up my mind to learn as much as I could. Then I was jolted out of my reverie.

'You, Comrade Gao. Take this rifle. You are on guard.' I looked wide-eyed at the sergeant, shocked to the core. 'There are four bullets in the magazine, but whatever you do, don't pull the trigger unless you really need to.' He told me to report to the guardroom by the main gate. 'And don't let us down,' he said.

I was troubled. With my poor eyesight, how could I patrol anything? I walked to my hut because my mouth felt dry and I needed a drink of water. Tsao Lin must have seen my face, and followed me. 'Don't worry, Squinty, there will be others there so just ask them what to do. You had better take your raincoat.' That was good advice, because it began to rain heavily just after I had reported to the guardroom. It was the start of the wet season, and we would be lucky to see one dry day for the next month. I put on my raincoat, under which was the rifle, and left the guardroom to begin my patrol as directed.

I had been given a torch, told to keep it in my pocket and hand it over to my relief. An old grizzled soldier grinned at me. 'Don't worry. All you have to do is to follow the path. It will take you round the hospital and back to this point in one hour. I will be here standing guard when you get back.'

I set off. The heavy rain was pounding down, and it wasn't long before my legs were soaked. Soon, my feet were squishing in my 'Liberation Shoes' (made from green canvas with a rubber sole) and rainwater was running down my neck and inside my tunic. I had never felt so alone and so miserable in my whole life as I trudged along. At first I tried to avoid the larger or deeper puddles, but soon I was so wet it didn't make any difference, so I splashed through the lot. It was also very warm and humid, and I began to sweat inside my coat. The perspiration ran down my body in rivulets until I was soaked inside and out.

I kept my eyes to the ground for most of the way, and cursed my short sight. The hours I had spent with my head in books were catching up with me. Far away, I could just hear the shouted commands of an instructor as soldiers drilled on the square, and I could smell faint cooking odours, which made me feel hungry. Then, suddenly, I heard something just behind me and whirled around. I almost fainted. I had been nervous around dogs since childhood and there, not far away, were about ten large, fierce-looking dogs heading straight towards me. At first I was rooted to the spot, then I turned and ran. The dogs barked. It was more like the baying of wolves, which made me run even faster until my breath was about gone from my body. I was slowing down, and the lead dog was almost up to me. I could hear his growls.

I thought of my rifle hanging inside my raincoat, but there was no time to free it. I took a quick look behind and saw the leader trying to take the loose folds of my raincoat into his mouth. I screamed, and the animal stopped. It was surprised by the unexpected noise, I suppose, which gave me a chance to open up a small gap between him and me, but not for long as I finally ran out of breath.

I was trying my best to extricate the rifle as the pack ran towards me. I was about to be torn to pieces. 'Help!' I yelled, but there was nobody to hear me. My feet were taking me backwards as I covered my face with my arms.

The lead dog must have jumped at me because I felt its paws push at my chest as its warm breath hit my face. I was flying, and I felt a sharp pain at the back of my head just as my body sank into cold water. A foul-tasting liquid filled my mouth as I struggled for breath. I coughed and spluttered, opened my eyes and struggled to a kneeling position. What had happened?

I discovered I had fallen into a pit at least two metres deep, and half full of foul-smelling water. The dogs were standing around the edge, staring down at me. They might jump at any minute. I'm finished, I thought, matter-of-factly, without a trace of panic. But they didn't jump. They just stood silently looking down at me. I gazed at the grey sky. 'Dear Mother, I'll be seeing you soon,' I murmured, and closed my eyes.

'Comrade Gao! Little Gao!' I knew that voice but I was too frightened to put a name to it. 'Where are you?' A face came into view. It was our sergeant. He knelt down and reached out to me. 'Come on, give me your hands.' I raised my arms to him and he pulled me up and out of the pit. 'How are you feeling?' he said, with a gentleness I would never have guessed he possessed.

'Fine,' I said, and collapsed in a heap. When I opened my eyes, I was being carried on a stretcher by two male ward orderlies. The sergeant was walking beside me, taking my pulse. When he saw I had come round, he smiled. 'You are in shock,' he said, 'but a few days in hospital should put you right.' He handed me over to the nurses, who had come to the main doors to meet us. 'Look after her,' he said. 'She has the makings of a good soldier.'

The following evening he came to see how I was getting on. Little Ping and Tsao Lin were sitting on chairs listening to my story when he entered the ward. 'Ah,' he said, with a chuckle, 'the Three Shadows. I will come back in a while. I have to take your report, Little Gao.' And from then we three friends were known as the Three Shadows by everyone, soldiers and officers alike.

When I had come to the end of my report and had signed the form, the sergeant asked me how long the episode had taken. I had to think. At the time, it had seemed like hours, but in reality it couldn't have lasted longer than a few minutes. I asked him how he had come to my rescue so quickly.

'The drill officer on the square heard the barking of the dogs followed by your scream. And a good thing he did. But how did you know that pit was there?'

'I didn't,' I replied. 'I fell into it. That was when I banged my head.'

I gently touched the bruised area at the base of my skull. 'I had to have three stitches,' I said almost proudly, 'and two injections.'

'Well, it's over now,' said the sergeant. 'But I'm surprised. The dogs don't normally attack the guards.' Then he told me that the hospital raised the dogs to be used by the medical staff to practise surgery. Few of the soldiers who came in required delicate operations. Most of the wounded were patched up before their arrival and just needed time to heal. Routine operations, like appendectomies, came in from time to time, but little else.

They also used the dogs to teach the nurses how to take care of the wounded under battlefield conditions. Sometimes they caught a dog and broke its legs with a hammer, then performed an emergency operation before putting the legs in splints. At other times they shot real bullets into a dog, then extracted them. After the operations, the dogs were treated like real patients and the doctors and nurses made notes of their recovery – or not.

They performed experiments on the animals, such as cutting off part of the liver, removing a kidney, or damaging the spleen to simulate a lienal rupture. Sometimes the doctors took out sections of the brain or performed heart surgery. Their findings were meticulously recorded and filed away for future reference. Of course, many dogs died, and if the body was clear of infection, it was sent to the kitchens and everyone had a nice piece of dog meat for dinner. The sergeant looked into my eyes as he told me that the delicious meal I had just eaten had been made from dog flesh.

'I thought it was rabbit!' I exclaimed.

Apparently, the patients thought of dog meat as a special treat and encouraged the nurses to neglect the dog 'patients' so that they died.

Dogs are not loved in China as they are in the West. In Mao's China, even before the Cultural Revolution, pets were considered a 'bourgeois decadence'. After it began, all household pets were banned, including goldfish and caged birds. Anyone caught with a pet animal would be, at least, severely criticized and, at worst, beaten to death as a class enemy.

Even today, only the army and the police can keep and train dogs – they use them for hunting criminals and undesirables – but even they must have the approval of the local Public Security Bureau. Those living in remote areas may ask permission to keep a dog for protection, but have to pay a high price each year for a licence. If anyone is caught raising a dog without a licence, they are fined heavily, the dog is destroyed and probably eaten by the authorities.

Normally, our dogs were kept locked away in a kennel, but that day a careless orderly had failed to shut the door properly and they had got out. Some of the animals were vicious, and were trained by the military police to patrol the fences and guard the camp against intruders. Those were the ones that had chased me. The sergeant told me that although they looked fierce, they had been trained to attack peasants, not soldiers. I thought about this, then said, 'The state I was in, I probably looked like a peasant!' We both laughed.

He stood up. 'Before I go, is there anything you want?'

'Yes, please,' I said. 'I have an urgent need for glasses. Is it possible for me to see an optician?'

He looked surprised. 'Of course. The army has some of the best eye specialists in China. I will arrange it for you.'

During my first few months in the army, I ate all kinds of things supplied by the kitchens, and never bothered to find out what they were. Although I had always been a little fussy about what I ate, I thought the food, in general, was very tasty and nourishing. We ate everything with great enjoyment – until one day, the chief cook carried in a large tray heaped with shredded meat, and began to dish it out. By this time, he and I knew each other quite well, and he sometimes gave me a little extra as I passed by. He did so on this occasion as I gave him one of my special 'I'm your best friend' smiles. I had found that the army could be a reasonably comfortable place for a female who smiled all the time, especially at the leaders!

I ate the meat, with the usual rice and vegetables, and it was delicious. It tasted like suckling pig cooked in soy sauce. After dinner, the cook winked at me and told me that I had just eaten rat. Apparently he set several traps in the grain store and almost every morning he collected a few. He believed rat meat was nutritious and good for people's health. I was stunned. I never touched meat again during the time I was in the army.

After three days I was discharged from hospital, still with a bandage around my head. I was told to return to have the stitches removed, but otherwise I had made a full recovery. However, the episode left one enduring legacy: I was never happy around dogs before it, but ever since I have been terrified of them.

★

In the training camp everything had been done to the whistle. After we arrived at our permanent camp, it was replaced by a bugle. Every morning at six o'clock, when the 'get-up' bugle sounded, we were expected to jump out of our beds and shout our 'Morning Consulting' to wish Chairman Mao an endless life. Then we had to dress and run out of the hut to join the doctors and other medical staff for physical exercise. Only after this could we wash and clean our teeth.

After breakfast, Little Ping and the others in clinic one went to work in the wards, whilst we in clinic two continued our training. Often we were taken to the drill square to practise first aid and how to move a wounded soldier out of danger. As I weighed the least, at around 40 kilos, I usually had to be the wounded soldier. I lay on the ground and waited while two of the others crawled up to me as if they were avoiding enemy fire to tend my wounds before dragging me out. I didn't like this because I always got bruised, and my clothes took a lot of punishment. When my rescuers reached me, I had to tell them what my wounds were – they had been whispered to me by the instructor before I flopped to the ground. The first thing they did was give me 'artificial respiration', which meant putting their hands on my chest and pressing down hard, then lifting them suddenly, causing my lungs to suck in air. I had to put up with this over and over again and the consequent bruising to my chest. When it was agreed that I was back with the living, they covered me with yards of bandage, pushed a long bamboo pole down inside my clothes, which often scratched me, and half dragged, half carried me to 'safety'. Usually I got some more bruises as they heaved me the ten or so metres to the feet of the instructor. I used to wonder how we would cope if we had to carry a large male soldier.

Eventually I got so fed up that I asked if I could be a rescuer some-times, and learn how to save a life. The next day, the instructor chose a big fat girl to be the victim, and another small girl and me as her saviours. It took all morning for us to get her to safety so I never asked again. I think I must have been the worst first-aid-trained nurse in the PLA and it was a blessing to our soldiers that I was never let loose on the battlefield.

Army discipline was strict. It was easy to get into trouble, and punish-ment was severe. Failure to keep our space or kit up to standard could result in public criticism at the morning meetings, or even a week or two in detention, depending on the frequency of the offence. We were allowed no excuses for slovenliness and spent much of our free time washing and cleaning ourselves and our kit. Our clothes, hands, faces, ears, necks and fingernails were checked daily. So, too, was our hair. We had to keep it shoulder-length or shorter, and clear of lice. Should we be caught with nits, or with hair of an unacceptable length, we were marched off to have it cut short and treated with an evil-smelling concoction.

Every afternoon our sergeant presided over political study. During meetings we had to sit to attention, backs ramrod straight, facing the front, feet together, our hands in our laps unless we were writing notes. When we stood, we didn't dare to slouch, or put our hands in our pockets, or lean against a convenient wall.

While life in the army flowed smoothly, violent factional fighting was still going on between the two Rebel groups in the nearby Jiangshan County town. Many were killed or injured, and the army had orders to support the struggles of both factions. The Rebels had access to unlimited supplies of arms and ammunition, which included mortars, hand-grenades and small cannon. After one big battle, there were so many wounded that the local hospitals could not cope, so a large number of injured Rebels were brought to our hospital for treatment. This meant that when my mates and I in clinic two were crawling about on a pretend battlefield, Little Ping and the rest of clinic one were busy with the real thing.

Every evening, Tsao Lin and I got together with Little Ping for the last half-hour before lights out to have a good gossip. She told us the two largest sections of the hospital were full to overflowing with Rebel wounded and the doctors were having all the practice they ever dreamed of. There were lots of bullets to be dug out, broken bodies to be reassembled, and fractured bones to set. There were eight Rebels to a room and the two factions were mixed together. As far as the medical staff were concerned, they were just patients and no attempt was made to separate them into their two groups. The patients with broken legs were kept together, and after their legs had been straightened and splinted, they were put into traction for up to six months for the bones to heal. Their beds had two tiers. The patients lay on the top tier, which had a big hole for the backside to fit into, and underneath, on the lower tier, stood a chamber-pot. The male patients had enamel kettles near to hand for urinating. Little Ping told us the first thing clinic one had to do when they reported for duty was to clean all the urine kettles and chamber-pots. She wrinkled her nose as she described the stench she walked into as she opened the door of each room. The first morning she had almost vomited.

The Rebels certainly couldn't fight in traction – but they could quarrel. And quarrel they did, for hour after hour. They were rude to the staff too, who still had to give them the best care they could, and to do it with a smile, because a reported complaint from a patient could get them into trouble and affect their promotion chances. Not that the Rebels cared: they had no feelings for anyone except Chairman Mao. All the medical staff had to wear white gowns when on duty, so they were called 'soldiers in white' and the hospital commandant gave the following order: 'All soldiers in white must serve the people heart and soul.'

One evening, after a particularly difficult day, Little Ping whispered, 'If those Rebels are real revolutionaries, I cannot see any good coming from the Cultural Revolution.' On hearing this, I froze: anybody who dared to criticize the Cultural Revolution was branded 'Anti-Chairman Mao', the worst label of all. Usually the offender was executed immediately.

We were of the same mind, but it was too dangerous to say anything: there were spies everywhere and one tiny slip of a tongue could easily end a life. However, Little Ping knew we were true friends and would never betray her, so she just smiled and shrugged her shoulders. I admired her bravery and her honesty, qualities that were rarely seen in those times of persecution and betrayal.

Little Ping continued to give the Rebels her best care and attention. Every day she washed their chamber-pots, cleaned their rooms and fetched and carried for them. She took temperatures, straightened beds, rubbed backs, treated bedsores and made sure every Rebel's needs were catered for. Her days were hard, and at the end of the year, I would be taking over. She was proving herself a good nurse, but I was not sure I wanted to look after those rowdy, ungrateful Rebels.

The rain kept falling all through June, but there were times when the sun shone for a while. Then groups of us were sent to the hills to kill insects. In the hills around the camp, young pines were being eaten away by black caterpillars. There were hundreds of the horrible things on every branch, and we were ordered to shake the trees to dislodge them, then stamp on them.

The first time we shook the trees, some girls screamed when the horrible things fell on to their hands and bare arms. I remembered the castor-oil-plant caterpillars and felt like screaming too. The sergeant came over. 'Revolutionary soldiers fear neither hardships nor death. So if you are not afraid of death, what else on earth can you possibly be afraid of?' He glared with mock irritation at the girls who were making a fuss. Poor Fluffy was almost hysterical, because she hated all creepy-crawlies and usually kept her distance from insects, but she would not let the sergeant see her fear, and performed her share of the killing with white-faced determination.

The sergeant never knew how terrible she felt. In fact, he was a kind man, and helped each group in turn. 'I'll shake the tree,' he said, 'and you only have to kill them as they fall to the ground.' Later, during a break, he told us he had a younger sister at home, and he understood how girls felt about insects. He never submitted bad reports to the clinic leader, only good ones. If a girl warranted a bad report, he gave her extra duties instead. We exterminated thousands of caterpillars, but that was only a tiny percentage of them and by the time we came back more had hatched and the numbers had increased again.

Two weeks after we arrived at the hospital we began anatomy lessons. The lectures were given by one or other of the hospital doctors on Wednesday and Friday afternoons after the daily dose of political study. At the beginning of the first lecture, the doctor hung a large drawing of a human skeleton on the wall. We learned that every human had 206 bones in their body, and that it was important for us to know their names and their exact location – it might mean the difference between life and death. As the lessons progressed, the doctors became more and more frustrated, until one could stand it no longer. 'I cannot teach you any more without the aid of a proper skeleton!' he bellowed.

The hospital leaders came up with the idea of enlisting the help of the local police to get hold of the dead body of a recently executed criminal. Of course, it had to be kept secret from the man's family because they had been forced to pay for the bullet used by the executioner and for his funeral. However, as the crematorium workers had joined the Rebels and were off marching the streets every day, there was nobody to burn the corpse, so the bereaved had to arrange for the body to be buried instead.

The shot 'criminal' was an 'Anti-Chairman Mao' counter-revolutionary, who was actually a hero in the eyes of the local people. He had not agreed with the slogan of 'Ten thousand years to Chairman Mao', saying it was against all of Karl Marx's teachings. He also disagreed with 'Endless life to Chairman Mao'. He said such calls were a form of absurd idealistic metaphysics, because nobody could live an endless life. 'And what is more,' he was reported to have said, 'it goes against Mao's own instructions that we must "seek truth from the facts" and such calls are blatantly not factual and therefore not truthful.'

If his death was intended to shame him and frighten others, it failed. The young man became a legend from the moment he was dragged through the gates of the prison and thrown on to a flat-bed truck. He was pulled upright, tied to a post and paraded through the town. His hands were bound behind his back and a big square of white cardboard hung round his neck. It bore his name, which had been crossed through with bright red paint. A dozen armed police were grouped around him on the truck as he stood there, head high, unafraid. In fact, he was so relaxed, he nodded to anyone he knew in the crowd. Almost the whole population of the town, plus many thousands from the surrounding countryside, lined the streets as he went by and all vehicles stopped.

The crowds became bigger as the truck approached his own neighbourhood, and when it passed his home, he shouted, 'I am sorry, Mother, I shall not be able to care for you when you grow old, but I will pray for you in the other world. Please forgive your unfilial son. Goodb–'

He didn't finish. A policeman expertly dislocated his jaw.

The truck followed a prepared route round the town and down every street. Throughout the long journey, the young man held his head high, his jaw swinging loose. It must have been painful, but his face gave no hint of it. Neither did he show fear. 'A real man!' people whispered to each other. 'Even during his last hour on this earth, he thinks only of his mother as a true filial son should!'

The day following the execution, bulletins were posted on every noticeboard throughout the town, and in many shop windows. They were poster size and gave an account of the man and his 'crimes'. A big red tick stretched right across the paper to confirm that he had been shot. Such bulletins are still put up today to tell the people of the punishments given to wrongdoers. A big red tick still denotes an execution, almost always by a single bullet into the back of the head. The family took away the man's body and buried it on a hill not far from our hospital. It was a good thing they never knew what had been planned by the leaders of the hospital and the police. If they had ever discovered the body had been stolen, they would have had the right to claim it back, because it was a terrible and unlucky thing for the superstitious Chinese to know that one of their family members had been dissected after death. We didn't hear about it until it was all over, and only after we had been sworn to secrecy.

Because of his exceptional strength, our sergeant was chosen to lead the mission to steal the body. Accompanied by a doctor and two policemen, he drove to the burial place in a jeep. When they arrived it was pitch dark, with a storm brewing.

When they found the grave and got out of the jeep, there was a sudden flash of lightning, quickly followed by a deafening crash of thunder, which caused the wolves to howl further up the hill. For the first time in his life, our brave sergeant was so scared his hair stood on end and his legs quaked.

He was not religious or superstitious but grave-robbing was wrong. Nevertheless his orders were clear. He took a shovel out of the jeep and joined the two policemen as they began to dig. Eventually a spade hit the thin wood of the coffin. The doctor was standing on the edge of the grave keeping watch and directing the operation. 'Here,' he said, 'use this to lift the lid,' and passed down a crowbar.

The face of the dead man appeared at the same time as another flash of lightning lit up the hole, followed by a thunderclap. The startled sergeant fell into the coffin with the dead man. A belch of evil-smelling gas came out of the mouth of the corpse, straight up the nose of the sergeant. The sergeant was off the body and out of the hole before he realized what he was doing. He bent over and vomited.

It was several minutes before the men could carry on. The sergeant jumped back into the grave, put his arms around the corpse and lifted it, until the others could drag it out. Then he shut the coffin lid and climbed out. The others carried the body to the jeep and sat it upright in the rear seat. Then they filled in the grave. The body was taken to the mortuary and immersed in formalin to sterilize and preserve it.

The next day, the sergeant told us his story during political study. 'So you see, comrades,' he concluded, 'there are many ways for us to give our support to our country and our great leader Chairman Mao.'

About two weeks later, the sergeant gathered clinic two together and said it was time to prepare our skeleton. I had just been given my spectacles. They were thick, black, horn-rimmed bifocals and, of course, my mates called me 'Four-eyes', 'Froggy' and 'Owl-face'. I didn't mind, though, because it was wonderful to see again.

The day chosen for the collection of the bones was warm and sunny, and I enjoyed the march up into the hills. We went about two kilometres away from the camp, accompanied by a platoon of male soldiers. They carried the body and the equipment we needed. The same doctor who had helped steal the body directed the soldiers to build a strong frame from the metal scaffold tubes we had brought with us, and we scoured the area for wood. Then we built an enormous fire under the frame. I was mindful of the wild dogs, and kept close to Tsao Lin and Fluffy.

When the fire was going well, we filled a huge cauldron with water from a nearby stream and hung it over the fire. Then the corpse was brought forward by the sergeant. Several girls shut their eyes. The sergeant looked pale as he slid the body into the water, then covered his embarrassment by shouting, 'Come on, get out and collect more wood!' We girls scattered again.

Soon, a powerful aroma of boiling meat spread over the area. The smell carried on the wind, and it wasn't long before about a hundred wild dogs and wolves appeared and began to circle our area. The soldiers were placed at intervals all around us to keep the animals at bay, but I was nervous when I heard the growling, barking and howling. The sergeant looked at me with concern in his eyes, then beckoned me to stand next to him. 'Don't worry, Little Gao, they won't come near us.'

The body was boiled for about two hours, then we put out the fire. An hour later, the human stew was cool enough to be moved, and we emptied the contents of the pot on to a large canvas sheet. We could easily part the bones from the flesh, and we collected every one, even the three tiny bones from each inner ear. It was perfect. The young man must have been in excellent condition because every tooth was in place and gleamed white. The only damage was the small jagged hole where the bullet had entered. By this time the dogs and wolves were going crazy and getting closer. The sergeant fired a shot from his revolver to scare them away.

It was really dark when we finished. The doctor and the sergeant carried the bones between them, followed by the soldiers with the equipment. We brought up the rear. I stumbled frequently. I was still getting used to my glasses, and had difficulty judging distances. I heard a commotion behind me and looked back nervously. The dogs and wolves were fighting over what was left of the flesh. In a few minutes there would be no trace of that brave young man. I consoled myself with the thought that he would continue to be of use by helping young nurses understand the human body, resulting in some of us saving lives.

Nevertheless, it was ironic that he would be serving the regime he had despised and which had abused him so cruelly.

We were given another unexpected anatomy lesson a few days later. A woman in an advanced state of pregnancy decided to travel all the way from north Jiangsu Province to Jiangshan County to be with her husband, a senior army officer. She wanted him beside her when she gave birth. The journey was long and hard. In those days the roads were not very good, and almost non-existent in country areas. She had to travel over rough cart-tracks in a dilapidated old bus for several hours to the nearest railway station, then take a fourteen-hour train ride.

Unfortunately the baby decided to make an appearance during the latter stages of the train journey, and was well on its way by the time her husband helped her off. He had travelled to the station in a jeep to meet his wife, so she had to sit in the back, bumping and swaying as the driver sped towards the hospital.

The baby was born during the last kilometre of the journey, in its mother's trousers, and drowned in blood and amniotic fluid. If the woman had taken off her trousers in the jeep, the baby might have survived, but she was a countrywoman and too shy to do so in front of the male army driver.

The infant was a fat, healthy baby boy, and a male child is important to all Chinese people, especially to the peasants who live in the country areas: only a boy can continue the family tree, and men are the main labour force in the fields. Both parents came from remote country areas, and they already had two girls, so the loss of their son was a heartbreaking blow. They were too distraught to look at the body, so clinic two was ordered to bury it up in the hills.

The clinic leader led this expedition. He was not a nice man. He was a devout follower of Mao and very politically motivated. Our squad leader carried the baby's wrapped body carefully in her arms. She was obviously moved by his sad story, as were we. We had looked at his chubby little face, and felt sad for him and his parents. When we reached the hill, she laid the little body down on the grass. He looked like a doll with go-to-sleep eyes, and we gathered around, waiting, while a shallow grave was dug by two male soldiers who had come with us.

The clinic leader stepped forward. 'We will have an anatomy lesson.' He bent down and, with a scalpel, cut open the little body from the neck to the penis. The breastbone was in two halves and we could see everything inside. I could barely take in what was happening, and heard some sharp intakes of breath.

'Look attentively! Here are the lungs and this red, round thing is the heart. The brown bit, here,' the clinic leader pointed with the scalpel, 'is the liver and the green one is the gall bladder.' We saw all the different colours of the inside of a human being at close quarters. There were the white intestines neatly coiled in circles, and the dull grey stomach.

After our initial shock, we all leaned forward to get a better view, and some girls even knelt down and poked with their fingers. The clinic leader said to us, 'This is an order. Nobody is allowed to utter one word about our anatomy lesson today. We can never let his parents know about this, because it would be too big a blow to them. What I have done today is to help you to learn, and it may help you in your future medical studies.'

With these words, he put the baby in the hole and nodded to the men to cover it up. Then he stamped the earth down with his feet. Several wild dogs had already gathered nearby, and as soon as we moved away from the little grave, they began to scratch at the ground. We had walked perhaps twenty metres when we turned to look back. One dog was eating a tiny foot, and as we watched, the whole body disappeared.

It was one of the saddest moments of my life and I felt ashamed to have been there. It was not difficult to keep this horrible scene a secret.

One afternoon, a seriously wounded young peasant woman was brought in for emergency surgery. She had carried two heavy baskets filled with peaches, one at each end of a long shoulder pole, several kilometres to the centre of the town in the hope of earning some badly needed cash. As she was crossing some railway tracks, she did not see the train bearing down on her at high speed. She was almost across when it hit her, severing her legs. When she arrived at our hospital, the stretcher brought in three pieces: two legs and a torso. There was blood everywhere, and the woman should have been dead, but she was still breathing.

This was a real emergency, and all of the nurses in clinic one were busy elsewhere in the hospital, so I was called in to help. This was my medical baptism and I was thankful that all we had to do was follow the orders of the chief nurse. I was impressed with her competence and speed around the operating table, and I wanted to be just like her.

The injured woman was immediately put on a drip and given blood. About ten minutes later, her eyes opened. The senior doctor asked her her name and address, and she replied in a faint, but clear voice. She spoke a local dialect, which was incomprehensible to me, but the doctor seemed to understand. She was twenty-one and lived in a village some ten kilometres away from the hospital. The doctor wasted no time in arranging for a jeep to be sent to the woman's home to bring her family. Sadly, she died before they arrived, and her body was sent to the mortuary.

Two hours later, the sergeant came to me. 'Little Gao, would you mind helping me dress the dead woman? Her father and brother are here. They know she has died and they want to take her home, so I have been asked by the chief nurse to try to make her look better.' How could I refuse? First, I liked this strong, gentle, sensitive man but, second, I had to obey an order without question. However, the sergeant had not given me an order, and if I had been reluctant, I am sure he would have found someone else – but I would have risked losing something good that was building between us. By now, I had even given him a nickname. If we were alone, I called him . . . the nearest English word is 'Guv'.

We collected some bits and pieces of old uniform from the bedding and clothing warehouseman and hurried to the reposing room. The three bloody pieces of the woman were lying on a wooden board. I felt a little squeamish. She had been a pretty girl when she had opened her eyes that morning, probably looking forward to her trip to town. I wondered if she had planned what to buy with the money she had expected to earn from the sale of the peaches.

'Come on, Little Gao, let's get on with it,' said Guv, as he lifted an arm and inserted it into one sleeve of the uniform jacket. Then he beckoned me to help him turn the body over so it was lying face down. He tried to put her left arm into the other sleeve, but he couldn't. It was too stiff and straight, with the fingers clenched into a fist. 'She must have died in great pain to have made a fist like that,' he said. 'Here, hold this.' He handed me the empty sleeve then he forced open each finger in turn. 'I'm sorry, little lady,' he said to the corpse, 'I have to break your arm.' And with a swift chop with the edge of his open hand, he released the elbow. *Crack!* The sharp snapping sound echoed in the empty room, and he slipped the arm into the hole. 'Put your hand into the sleeve at your end and pull the arm through,' he said to me. 'I'll pull the front part of the jacket.'

I did as I was told, and pushed my hand into the empty sleeve until my outstretched hand met the cold dead fingers. 'Oh!' I burst out. 'It's like shaking hands with a ghost!' I shivered and pulled the hand through the sleeve. My tummy lurched, and I had goose-bumps all over my body. Even my feet felt cold, and I stamped up and down.

Guv looked at me with a sympathetic smile. 'The same thing happened to me the first time I touched a dead body,' he said. 'Don't worry, it will pass.'

I buttoned up the jacket, then helped Guv as he put the three body parts together and sewed the legs to the torso. Then we slipped on the trousers, and when we stood back to check our work, the woman didn't look too bad. We could tell where, under the uniform, the three bits of her had been sewn together, but I didn't think the father and the brother would notice.

I didn't say anything to my friends. The experience had left me feeling sick, and sad. I missed dinner that evening and went straight to bed, but I couldn't sleep much. Nightmare images of the dead woman kept coming back to me, mixed up with the baby, a boiling man and ferocious wild dogs.

My first months in the army flew by. In the short time I had been at the hospital, I had learned more about life and death than I had in the previous ten years. The rain stopped as summer came, which meant the time had come for the reserve doctors, nurses, and we medical orderlies of clinic two to leave camp with half of the garrison for three months of military manoeuvres. We had a long way to go, and every day we marched about forty kilometres under the hot sun with our bedrolls on our backs.

We girls enjoyed the occasional respite from the tedium when we were ordered to form ourselves into 'Propaganda Teams of Mao Tse-tung Thought'. As the army marched on, we were driven to the outskirts of a nearby village with a doctor and a few soldiers for protection. Our task was 'to take the words of our great leader Chairman Mao to the masses'. First we would rest awhile just outside the village while the local leaders gathered the villagers in the village square. Then we marched in, to be welcomed by our loyal supporters, some waving our national flag and others offering freshly made green tea from their best china pots with their best cups to drink it from. 'Salute our brave comrades from the People's Liberation Army!' they would shout in welcome, and as we waved our cups in the air we shouted back, 'Learn from you poor and lower-middle-class peasants!' Then we read passages from *The Little Red Book* and shouted slogans. But that was not the end of it. We girls had to sing and dance for the villagers while our doctor gave free medical advice and treatment.

If we were delayed in a village, we took over the local school or community centre for the night. It was the summer vacation, but the schools had been closed for several years anyway. The villagers would bring us food, which always consisted of many delicious dishes cooked in the traditional ways of the area. In return, we danced and sang to them again before bed.

The following morning, after a good breakfast, again provided by the villagers, we would set out to catch up with the main force. We looked like we were marching away, and the villagers came out to wave us off, but they knew that we were only going to march to our truck and ride back to the main force. Sometimes, as I lay down to sleep, I thought of my mother. She had done much the same kind of thing all those years ago, when she went on her recruitment and propaganda missions.

It took almost a month of hard marching to reach Xiakou County, the place where we would make camp. It was a remote region of Zhejiang Province and also one of the most beautiful. The mountains were thickly covered with many species of tall trees, some over a thousand years old. As we climbed the hills, following the well-worn paths of long-dead soldiers, we felt part of the natural order of things. There were no wild dogs or wolves here, just a few bears, which kept well away from us.

We settled down to weeks under canvas. Poor Fluffy searched every centimetre of her sleeping area for bugs. Her phobia about creepy-crawlies was worse than mine about dogs. At least I expected to sleep at night, but she didn't. She was already exhausted from the march and ready to break down, but not a word of complaint came from her to the ears of any officer, except our squad leader, and we had already sworn her to secrecy.

I was having a good sleep that first night when the whistle woke us up at midnight, just as it had during our training. Fluffy was up and out first because she had not been asleep. The rest of us dragged ourselves on parade as best we could, and off we went, marching in the dark for an hour. The night-time exercises disturbed our sleep all the time we were there, and soon we all looked as drawn and haggard as Fluffy. I heard an English word in a film recently that adequately described what we looked like: zombies.

Fluffy had become friends with Little Ping, Tsao Lin and me, and we were being called the 'Four Shadows' now. She was a bright, intelligent, funny girl, who made us laugh. Everyone had to practise shooting and now I had my glasses I was a reasonable shot even without the help of Little Ping. The doctors used pistols, and the army men fired their automatic rifles. The mornings always ended in a cacophony of bangs and bursts of machine-gun fire as we practised the art of killing other human beings.

The afternoons were better. For three hours we had to go to the river outside the village to learn to swim, or improve our stamina by swimming longer and longer distances. I was a swimmer, so I was told to lead clinic two into the water. It looked cold but it was warm, which suited me because I disliked cold-water swimming. 'Come on in, it's wonderful!' I called, and the rest of the girls waded out to where I was standing. Suddenly I noticed I was surrounded by hundreds of brightly coloured fish. 'Look.' I pointed downwards, hardly daring to breathe in case I frightened them away.

'I have some too!' squealed Fluffy.

It was magical. The little fish, about eight centimetres long, hung motionless in the water. As it flowed, their colours flashed and we each had a delightful display of ever-changing glisters of colour.

Those afternoons were the happiest hours I spent in the army. All of us enjoyed ourselves. I learned to dive to the bottom and to stand on my hands. Sometimes I would bring up a smooth pebble and marvel at its intricate patterns. The river became our main source of recreation. In the evenings, as the sun set, we returned to the water to wash our hair and clothes. Sometimes it was nice to sit on the bank, writing letters home, or just alone with our thoughts. I often sat day-dreaming of my dear Hui, and it was during those long warm summer evenings that I missed him most.

Our three months camping passed quickly. We got back to the hospital in mid-October, tanned, refreshed and happy. We all had stories to tell those who had been left behind. At the first opportunity I went looking for Guv, and found him bandaging a boy's arm. 'There,' he said, when he had finished. 'That will keep it clean, but don't go falling on any more glass!' I admired his hands as they worked. I was not in love with Guv, but I liked and respected him as my best male friend.

He turned, and saw me. 'Hello, Little Gao,' he said, with obvious pleasure.

'Hello, Guv, I've missed you,' I said.

An hour later, I stopped talking, and he laughed. 'My word, Little Gao, you can talk when you want to,' he said, looking directly into my eyes. 'It's nice to have you back.' His meaning could not have been more plain, and I blushed with pleasure.

There were still several weeks to go before we took over from clinic one, and our main duty until then was political study. We also had lessons on how to use acupuncture needles to treat many different disorders and diseases, and we were encouraged to practise on ourselves and each other. It was strange to feel the movement of the needles in the various points and experience their effects. Muscles could be made to move and nerves to irritate. Afterwards we felt sore, and sometimes bloated or numb. It was a painful way to learn, but our leaders said it was the best treatment for almost all diseases, and much better than western medicine, which relied too heavily on man-made drugs. We had to master this art because we would be using it on almost all our patients when we began our medical work.

We also had to go to the nearby People's Communes to help the peasants gather in the last harvest of the year. It was just as unpleasant as it had always been, but now I was fitter and stronger from my life in the army. For ten days we used hand sickles to cut the rice, then we gathered the stalks into bundles and carried them on our backs to the storage sheds. There they separated the rice grains from the stalks and carefully filled hundreds of sacks. Then each sack was weighed and tagged before being stored. Most of the rice was destined for Nanjing, with precious little given to the hard-working peasants.

During the last few days of October, I heard from the radio that the Nanjing Yangtze River Bridge was finished. Construction had stopped in October 1966, and restarted at the beginning of 1968 on the instruction of Premier Zhou. The newsreader reported proudly that on the day the bridge was officially opened the first vehicles to cross had been a hundred trucks crowded with students of middle-school age. They were being sent to settle in the countryside. They were among the first batch to be sent to various parts of China, including the border areas, and during the next few weeks, millions more followed them. The mass movement of young boys and girls went on for several years, until tens of millions of families lost one, sometimes two, and even three children aged between fourteen and twenty-one. Many were never seen or heard from again, and even when the families managed to keep in touch, it was years before they were reunited. The next day I saw photographs in the *People's Daily* of the trucks full of students on their way to nothing and remembered I could have been with them. I felt lucky to have escaped.

But we had not got off as lightly as I had thought. In one of his editorials, Chairman Mao stated, 'The PLA must support the workers, the peasants and the revolutionary leftist Rebels.' Our commanding general decided to have us taken to the worst of the nearby People's Communes to 'support the peasants'. For two weeks we marched there in the mornings and returned to camp in the evenings.

The locals were not friendly, and when we took off our shoes, rolled up our trouser legs, and stepped into the water-filled paddy-fields (this commune did not drain them before collecting the harvest), they stood by with folded arms, laughing at us. 'Hah! Look at the PLA! They are all comrades of Lei Feng, serving the people heart and soul!'

We felt insulted, but as we had been warned by our leaders not to utter a word of complaint, we went to work, fuming inside. We were supposed to win the hearts of the local peasants with our hard work and good deeds, but all they did was make fools of us.

While the male soldiers cut the crops, we girls were told to spread manure in the fields from which the rice had already been harvested. It was made up of animal and human shit, and it stank. Surrounded by millions of flies, we stood in water that came half-way up our legs and trampled the muck down into the mud with our feet. It was dirty, stinking and slippery, and I hated marching on the spot, feeling the manure squelching between my toes and over my ankles. What was even worse was discovering the first leech. When I raised my leg, a dozen of the disgusting things were clinging to me.

The girl next to me screamed a split second before I did. Then I heard Fluffy yell in terror. Nothing could have prepared us for such a shock. Every one of us was having the blood sucked out of us by dozens of the black, slug-like creatures. Usually, three or four were stuck to one point. They climbed up to the tops of my legs, and more and more joined in as I churned up the muddy bottom. Like all the girls I was frightened, but I dared not stop working. I gritted my teeth, fought back my tears, and trod up and down, up and down, up and down.

During a break, Guv came among us. 'Pat the skin beside the leeches and they will drop off.' We slapped our legs as we trampled the manure into the mud, and the leeches indeed fell off, only to return almost at once. We had to bend and pat ourselves constantly, but we could not get rid of all the leeches. Slowly our skin became red from the patting, and holed and bleeding where the leeches had bitten into it. I worried that I would contract a deadly infection.

The strange thing was, the leeches never attacked the men while we girls were there. The men grinned at us, and said the leeches only liked delicate skin, which made us feel worse.

Every evening, after we finished our work and stepped on to dry land, there were always a dozen or more leeches hanging on to each leg. We stamped our feet and patted our legs until they fell off and then we stamped on them. It was not nice to see our own blood spread over the ground. Sometimes they hung on resolutely to their blood-hole, but we couldn't pull them off with our hands. We had learned that if we did they left their suckers under our skin, which resulted in the wound becoming infected. When the last leech had gone our legs were running with blood: they secreted a kind of saliva that stopped it clotting, so the bleeding went on for quite a long time.

We marched back to camp in our bare feet, looking forward to a shower. The manure seemed to penetrate every pore, and was deep under our toenails and in every cut and leech-hole. We had to wash and rinse, wash and rinse, over and over, while blood turned the water red, but none of us felt really clean even when we put on our socks and shoes to go to dinner.

When the two weeks of 'supporting the peasants' were over, we cheered silently to know the terror of the leeches was over. Every day had seemed a week, and the two weeks had seemed a year. We returned to the daily meetings of political study with relief, something I would never have thought possible.

At last the time came for clinic two to change places with clinic one. We took over the care of the patients with enthusiasm. It was hard, tiring work. I learned to give injections, and practised on myself until I could do it without inflicting too much discomfort. I soothed horrible bedsores, and tended wounds. My days were busy, satisfying and flew by.

One day, after I had been on the wards for a few weeks, Guv motioned for me to come into the office. 'We have had a number of good reports from the patients about you,' he said. 'Here, take a look at this.'

He handed me a sheet of paper. I took it from him, full of curiosity. It was a letter from one of the patients praising me for the way I looked after him. When I came to the end and read the signature, I did a double-take. 'It's from Comrade Ching!' I burst out. 'He's the most awkward man I've had to care for. Fancy him writing a letter like this!' What an honour!

'And we have others like it,' said Guv. 'Well done.'

A few weeks later it was time for all the troops in China to choose their 'Five Good' soldiers. The 'Five Goods' were: good study of Chairman Mao's works, good thoughts, good virtue, good military training and good unity with other comrades. Only about forty per cent of soldiers ever received the award, but Fluffy, Little Ping, Tsao Lin and I all had Five Good Soldier certificates. In addition I was honoured as a Fear Neither Hardships Nor Death Soldier, and my photograph and an article about me appeared in the local PLA newspaper. Comrade Ching had been interviewed, and had given me a glowing report.

At last I belonged somewhere. For all of my life since the death of my father, I had felt that something was missing from my life. Even my mother had been unable to fill that gap inside me. In the army I felt more secure and fulfilled than ever before, and my future seemed rosy when those who had been awarded the Five Good Soldier certificate were assembled together. 'You soldiers have proved yourselves worthy of being considered among the best soldiers in the PLA. If you want to progress, be promoted and earn glory, you should apply to join the Communist Party,' we were told. The four of us wrote out our applications and handed them in.

12. The Hidden Arrow

Throughout my time in the army, I kept in touch with the important people in my life by regular letters. In return I received a flow of news from Andong, the odd letter from Wei-guo, regular letters from Hui and, as usual, nothing from Pei-gen.

Nanjing was still in the grip of the Cultural Revolution. The army was now in control and occupied all the leadership positions. The old civilian government officials, from the highest to the lowest, had been sent to 'cadre schools' in the countryside to do manual labour. They had sprung up all over China as a way of getting rid of those who were of no further use to Mao.

By January 1969 every educational establishment was governed by Workers' Propaganda Teams, who had been selected and appointed by Maoist Rebels. The students of my old middle school who had not been able to join the army, along with half of the teachers, had been sent to the countryside. Large numbers of university students had been allocated jobs, most of which were on collective farms far away in the border areas. Some luckier ones were given positions in distant cities and towns, where they sat and did nothing. Only a fortunate few were employed in their home cities, where they too had little to occupy them because the factories were closed.

By this time, Andong had married her Zhan, and was about to accompany him to Huhehot in Inner Mongolia, where he had been assigned to work in a boiler factory. I received a long letter from her, pleading with me to try to return to Nanjing for a visit before she left, because Huhehot was 2,000 kilometres away and she knew we might never see each other again. I felt awful. I loved Andong. She had always been more than a sister to me: she was my closest friend too, and I was about to lose her, perhaps for ever, so I applied for leave and was given a week.

Andong and I met and hugged each other in the compound of the Nanjing Municipality. She was staying with a girlfriend because Zhan had left for Huhehot a week previously. Andong told me in a low voice that he had been branded a counter-revolutionary by the Workers'

Propaganda Team because he did not agree with them. He was lucky to get away with his life. Now she was under strong pressure to end the marriage. But she was a fighter: she had refused and been denounced as a counter-revolutionary sympathizer. Luckily, because of her background, the case against her was dropped. Bullies the world over behave in the same way: because they were not sure of her connections, they dared go no further.

During my short stay with Andong, she was surrounded several times by rowdies, but all she would say was, 'I don't care if you brand me a counter-revolutionary, too, as long as I can be with my husband. Come on, do your worst, and be sorry for it!'

I had to admire her bluff. She knew nobody would come to her aid, but the bullies didn't, and eventually they slunk off, muttering among themselves. I also admired my brave sister for her loyalty. I knew her goodness, but I had never realized how strong-willed she could be. She was ready to go to the furthest corner of China, or the earth, to be with her husband. Nothing would ever make her betray him.

She told me Zhan had been taken into detention for the three months before he had been exiled, and she had tried every day to visit him but was stopped by workers standing guard outside his prison. They instructed a number of students to write some big-character posters criticizing her, and had them draped over the railings of the building. But still she went, day after day, to try to visit Zhan. At night, people stood outside her bedroom window and shouted slogans against her, but she never gave in. I felt so proud of her.

Such things went on all over China, and usually a spouse was forced to comply with demands to denounce their husband or wife, causing countless innocent people to be imprisoned. Eventually, because the Workers' Propaganda Team could not prove Zhan was a counter-revolutionary, due to Andong's refusal to testify against him, he was set free. But they had their revenge by assigning him to the worst job they had available.

The day after my arrival in Nanjing, I had to stay in bed with flu. Andong came in at intervals to bring me soup and hot chrysanthemum tea, a proven remedy against colds and influenza. In the late afternoon when she appeared I could see she had been crying. 'What's the matter?' I croaked.

'This is not fair!' she sobbed. 'To be with my husband, I have to say farewell to my family. What is wrong with this country? Is there no one who cares about ordinary people any more?' There was no answer to that so I just held her tight.

I had never seen her so distressed. The past months must have been hell for her, but not a word of her troubles had gone into her letters to me. She never wrote anything that might cause trouble for me with the army authorities. She knew that the slightest hint to the censor that I had a possible counter-revolutionary in my family might bring down trouble upon my head, so she had given no clue to how sad she was.

I felt so angry with those who could do this to her. Neither Andong nor her husband deserved such treatment because they disagreed with the Workers' Propaganda Team. But there was nothing I or anybody else could do to change things.

The next day, Wei-guo came to say goodbye to Andong, and as it was our last few hours together, we went to a studio to have our photograph taken. As we walked along, I knew something was different. At first, I couldn't work out what. Then, in a flash, it came to me. 'Of course!' I exclaimed. 'There are no schoolkids!' Andong and Wei-guo were astonished, and I had to explain. Not one young person aged between fourteen and twenty-one was to be seen. They had all been sent to the countryside. Wei-guo and I were the only people of that age walking along the street. Mao had plucked the young flowers of Nanjing and sent them off to wilt and die.

I gave my address to the studio receptionist as we paid for the pictures and the girl promised to send them on to me. Then it was time for us to go to the station where we waved to Andong until the train disappeared.

When the photographs arrived, a letter of apology told me that the one of me with Andong had not come out. It was ten years before I saw her again.

I had been looking forward to spending some time with Hui, but I couldn't find him. Then a friend told me he had been sent to a cadre school in north Jiangsu Province just a few days before my arrival in Nanjing. I was disappointed, and felt acutely alone after Andong had left, so I decided to go to my old home in Orchid Garden and visit my grandparents. But their rooms were now occupied by strangers. They told me that my grandfather had died and Grandmother had moved away to live with her youngest son. Uncle Jiang had also died after being persecuted by the Red Guards, and Auntie Zhu had been moved out to an unknown address. No one I knew was living in Orchid Garden any more, and I was the stranger. All my dear ones had disappeared.

I was upset, so I went to the cemetery to have a talk with my parents and, to my delight, I discovered that the grave of Uncle Jiang was just five metres away from theirs. I learned later that he had not been beaten or hounded as badly as many others, and he escaped being called a class enemy because he had retired long before the Cultural Revolution had begun. But he had been heartbroken to see so many of his close comrades-in-arms branded 'capitalist roaders' and tortured to death. He died, suddenly, of a stroke. Auntie Zhu buried his ashes as close to my mother and father as she could, so that he would not be lonely in the next world.

Another of our neighbours, Uncle Zhuang Cun, who had arranged Mother's funeral, died at the hands of the Rebels. His grieving widow had buried his ashes in a quiet corner of Orchid Garden before she was forced to move away. Several years later, after his good name was restored, she retrieved them and reburied them beside Uncle Jiang. Slowly, through the passing years, many other urns, containing the ashes of the real heroes of China, have been recovered and reburied with honour in the same area. Thus, my parents, their two old friends, and many more are comrades in death, as they were in life. As I write this, so many thousands of miles away from my mother and father, I am comforted by the knowledge that they are not alone.

After my leave, I was assigned to work in the outpatient department of the hospital. One day, a peasant carried in his five-year-old daughter. The day before, she had complained of a bad tummy-ache. Then, in the early hours, she had screamed loudly, jumped out of bed and fainted. The man had carried her many kilometres to the hospital, where she was found to have a serious intestinal obstruction and needed an operation without delay. She needed a transfusion, so the doctor asked the father for permission to take some of his blood to give to his daughter. To our astonishment, he refused. He told us that he was the main labour force in his family, and if he gave blood it would reduce his strength, making him unable to earn work-points to feed his family.

When the doctor told him that any delay in carrying out the operation might result in the death of the girl, the father shrugged his shoulders and said, 'If she dies, it is her fate.'

The clinic leader spoke sharply to the peasant but still failed to persuade him, so, as a last resort, he offered to buy the blood from him. The peasant agreed, but the child died on the operating table.

It was easy to judge the father but, to him, his reasons for refusing to help his daughter were valid. Later that day the mother arrived. She was six months pregnant with her seventh child. She was only twenty-nine – although she looked at least fifty – and she had given birth to six girls. During the Cultural Revolution there was no birth control, so the peasants continued to have children until they got a son. Even then they were not satisfied, and wanted more and more sons. No child was killed in those days because everyone, even newborn babies, were entitled to grain rations.

At the end of the Cultural Revolution family planning was introduced and a one-child-per-family policy was strictly enforced by the Party – this law is still in effect today. If anyone violated it, the punishment was often severe. A Party member, no matter how important he or she might be, could be thrown out of the Party, dismissed from their post and fined a huge amount of money.

Second births did take place, but extra children were – and are – hidden away and not registered. They have become part of the growing 'underground population'. Children without proper registration have no rights: they cannot go to school or be employed by the State when they grow up. Neither can they get married and have a lawful child of their own. This policy has caused enormous social problems in China, resulting in a marked increase in homelessness, begging and crime.

In country areas, sons mean labour and labour means wealth and security, but daughters mean nothing. Millions of newborn baby girls have been killed by their mothers, and pregnant women now travel hundreds of miles to a hospital with a scanner, to determine the sex of their unborn child. If the scan shows a girl, the woman has an abortion. In many areas, only boys survive, so in the future millions of men will be unable to find a wife and whole family blood-lines will die out.

I was kept busy in the outpatient department. A steady stream of people came through our doors with all sorts of injuries and ailments. If I had ever wanted to do a crash course in nursing, this was the place to be. Everything possible that can happen to a human body came my way over the next few months, and I absorbed an enormous amount of knowledge.

We saw an increasing number of distressed school-age girls and boys, who had been transported to the countryside to settle down in communes near the hospital. Generally there was nothing wrong with them, they just wanted us to issue a certificate saying they had contracted a disease such as hepatitis. Then they would be allowed to return to their home city. A recent law had been passed to allow them to return home if they had TB, hepatitis, poliomyelitis or epilepsy.

The young people who came to us all told the same story. The boys were subjected to brutal treatment by the peasant officials, and the girls were raped repeatedly by the production brigade leaders. If they resisted, they were given the worst jobs with the lowest work-points. There was no joy in their lives, only terror, pain and ill-treatment. Sadly we could do nothing to help the majority of them – we did not dare issue false certificates, because there would be more tests when they returned home. Some, mostly girls, got a false certificate by giving their bodies and money to those who had power over them. But all too often the leaders took the money and continued to rape them, with no intention of ever letting them go.

Many young people of both sexes committed suicide, often by drowning. Others fell on sharpened sticks or hanged themselves. Of those who returned home, many were in poor health and out of their minds. Some never recovered.

During my time at the hospital, all the girls had visits from home except me. Every week a few of my friends were looking forward to seeing their parents or other relatives. While the other Shadows were with their visitors, I felt sadness envelop me. Of course, they tried to persuade me to join them, but after a quick 'hello' I left them to catch up on their own private lives. I usually used the time to write my letters.

After my return from Nanjing, I had written more to Hui and less to Pei-gen. Then one weekend, for something to do, I wrote a long letter to her. After all, she was still my sister, and although she had never shown me any warmth, I should write to her because she was a true revolutionary soldier. It was my duty as a member of the PLA to be friends with as many revolutionary comrades as possible. Then I wrote to her every week, even though I knew I was unlikely to receive a reply.

But I was wrong. A few weeks later, to my great surprise, I had a letter from her – with kind words. I was so happy to hear from her that I wrote back the same day. In her letter, she told me she had been assigned to work in a Xinjiang petroleum field, where the average salary was three times higher than that in Shanghai. She had been given the job in recognition of her good work as a Rebel and because she was a daughter of two revolutionary martyrs. It seemed I was not the only child who had benefited from my parents' status.

Although I didn't know it, my revived letter-writing to Pei-gen heralded the beginning of the end of my safe, secure life in the army. A few days after I sent her my letter a new intake of girls and a woman sergeant arrived. The next morning, half of clinics one and two, with Guv, were told to pack their kit because they were leaving for Vietnam. I was not affected, nor was Little Ping, but Fluffy and Tsao Lin were driven to the railway station. About three weeks later, news filtered through that both girls and Guv were dead, killed trying to save the lives of their comrades. Little Ping and I cried for hours.

A second letter arrived from Pei-gen. It was full of warmth and sisterly concern for me. How was I? How did I find army life? Did I like my work? I was so happy to hear from her. My heart had felt as heavy as lead since my friends had been taken away to Vietnam so I unburdened myself to her. I told her about the two weeks we had spent with the leeches in the paddy-fields, how much I hated it and how I disliked the attitude of the peasants. Of course I told her about the good things too, such as my Five Good Soldier award, and that I was about to join the Communist Party. In my next letter, I told her about the patrols, and how I had been chased by the dogs. Her letters kept coming, and she said she was worrying about my health. 'You should take a good rest after the night patrols and all your hard work in the hospital,' she wrote.

I was moved, and I began to trust her as I trusted Andong. Slowly but surely I told her everything I dared not say in public. The bad behaviour of the Rebels, the ill-treatment of the boys and girls and other sensitive things. 'Politics is ruining everything in China. It has totally spoiled the lives of Andong and her husband, and all of our friends. I *hate* politics!' I wrote. I felt I had a real eldest sister at last.

My leaders became cold to me during the second half of 1969, but I wasn't bothered. I was still working hard and doing everything the army asked of me to the best of my ability so I had nothing to fear. I thought they were busy preparing for the big move. In October, Lin Biao had issued a general order that all army units had to relocate and everyone in our hospital had been ordered to move to Yixin County in Jiangsu Province. We were to be replaced by a hospital unit transferring from the north. I was glad to move, because the new location was much nearer to Nanjing. We were told the move was necessary because war was imminent. Everybody was ordered to remove the red cloth badges from the collars of our uniform, print our name, blood type and permanent address on the back, then replace them. We were assured that full-scale war could break out at any time against Russia, Chiang Kai-shek or the USA and we might be sent without warning to the battlefields. The badge was our identification if we were lucky enough to sacrifice our lives for the revolution. It would also be helpful in saving the lives of the wounded, because a blood transfusion could be quickly arranged – a contradiction in terms if ever there was one.

We did as we were told, and we were very alert: we expected one or other of our enemies to attack us soon. It was even rumoured that they might join forces and China would be attacked by all three. It was a tense time, and before we left, most of the girls wrote what they thought was a 'last letter' to their families before dedicating their lives to China and our great and glorious leader Chairman Mao. Our final act was to assist the patients to the transport. They were being sent home or back to their original army units. When we left, the hospital was empty.

All of the hospital personnel left in one long convoy at noon on 25 October 1969. As our huge trucks lurched towards the new camp, we passed a seemingly never-ending convoy of army trucks going in the opposite direction. At a crossroads, hundreds more were lined up waiting for our convoy to pass. The thick clouds of choking dust raised by thousands of wheels made us think that war had started, and we looked like clay statues when we arrived at Yixin County twenty-four hours later.

Our new hospital was almost an exact replica of the one we had left, so life carried on as if we had never moved. I was again in the outpatient department. At the end of 1969, I was again nominated for the Five Good Soldier award – but, to my shock, the honour was not approved by the hospital leadership. Something must have happened. A huge hammer was poised, ready to drop on my head. What had I done wrong? I was still praised by the patients. They wrote a collective letter and gave it to our new woman sergeant, and she let me read it before passing it to the clinic leader. I was flattered by what I read, but too worried to take any real pleasure from the kind words.

Then the hammer fell. The clinic leader told me to accompany him to the office of the hospital leader. When I was before him, the hospital leader told me calmly that he had decided to demobilize me and send me back to Nanjing. It was just about the worst punishment a female medical soldier could be given. I stood to attention in his office and heard his words, unable to breathe. I felt the blood leave my face, and I knew I was about to faint. But, with a huge act of will, I stayed upright. Somehow, I had committed a grave mistake, but I had no idea what it was. My dismay turned to anger. All I could think of was the waste of almost two years of hard work, just as I was about to be enrolled into the Party, and I burst into tears of frustration. If I had not had the discipline of the army, I honestly believe I would have struck the man before me. 'Please, can you tell me what it is I have done wrong?' I cried.

'I will let you know,' he said.

After dinner that evening, clinics one and two were told to assemble in the meeting hall. The clinic leader was holding some papers in his hand as he said, 'Comrade Gao wants an explanation for her being discharged from the army.' There were gasps of astonishment from those around me. I had been too shaken and ashamed to tell anyone, not even my good friend Little Ping. 'I have some letters,' the leader continued, 'sent to us by her sister. I shall read them aloud, and you will all know why.' Then he read, in a slow, clear voice, what my eldest sister Pei-gen had written:

Dear Leaders of Clinic Two,

Being the eldest sister of Gao Anhua, I feel I have the responsibility to tell you the truth, so that you will not have a false impression of her. Gao Anhua has been a two-faced person since her childhood, and she is very good at cheating and lying to her leaders. She can behave very well in public but she is really very bad inside. She is a real bourgeois decadent, but pretends to be a true revolutionary. If you trust her, then you have been fooled by her. If you want to recruit her into the Party, then you are about to make a big mistake. I enclose some of her letters to me to prove my words, and to let you get to know my worthless sister a little better.

The clinic leader then read out the letters I had written to Pei-gen. The assembly heard about my dislike of politics and of some of the activities we had been forced to endure in the army. I was looking straight in front of me, eyes pinned on a dirty mark on the far wall. Things I would never dare to say in public, even to my best friend, shot like bullets from the mouth of the clinic leader straight into my heart.

Naturally my words had given great offence to the leaders, and were conclusive proof of the truth of Pei-gen's accusations against me. It was clear to everyone that I was a hidden bad element, and it was right for them to get rid of me. 'And in conclusion,' said the clinic leader, 'we have put a full report into her file, which will follow her for the rest of her life.' This meant I would never be trusted again. When he finished talking, the leader thrust the letters into my hand, then turned and left the hall.

I was dying. I could feel myself curling up inside. Then the wall slowly disappeared as a blackness blotted it out. Vaguely I felt a hand grip my arm, and that stopped me from collapsing to the floor. I had at least one loyal friend, and I silently turned my head to show my gratitude. It was Little Ping, of course. The hand pushed, and I went meekly where it guided, until I was back in my room, where it allowed me to fall on to my bed. The initial shock was wearing off, and my brain started working again, but all I could see behind my closed eyelids was the leering, sneering face of my . . . I could no longer think of her as my sister. In China we have a saying, 'It is easy to dodge a spear in the open, but hard to guard against an arrow shot from behind', and I had been hit by the hidden arrow.

Slowly everything closed down, and for days I seemed to float in a big ocean, tossed hither and thither by the waves. Little Ping spent as much time as she could with me, sitting on my bed, holding my hand. And one by one the rest of the girls found courage to come and say how sorry they were. They all understood what the blow meant to me. 'Was she born to your mother?' they asked. Many girls had half-brothers and sisters, because it was not uncommon for high-ranking army officers and Party members to divorce their wives and marry someone younger. Little Ping had four younger half-siblings. Her father had divorced her mother and married an actress. Usually, half-siblings born to different mothers resented each other, which is why the girls thought Pei-gen might be my half-sister.

I was at rock bottom. This was one blow too many. Nothing could help me, not even Little Ping. All I wanted was to be gone, away from this place, the scene of my downfall. And after a week I had my wish. The hospital leaders summoned me to confirm my punishment. Five of them were sitting in a straight line at a long trestle table. They each had a file of papers, a pen and a mug of tea before them as I was marched in, to stand stiffly to attention between two tall army policemen.

I had been expecting this and dreading it, but it wasn't so bad: the leaders were looking at me with sympathy. The senior officer said, 'We have spent a long time considering your case because there are so many contradictions and confusing facts. There is no doubt that you did write those bad things to your sister, and for that reason alone you must be discharged. However, we also had to consider the dozens of good reports we have had about your work as a medical soldier. Also, we have obtained reports from all your leaders from the squad leader upwards, and they all give glowing reports of your attitude to army life. Even the doctors have submitted a request that we deal with you in a sympathetic manner. On the other hand, we have to accept the fact that your sister knows you better than anyone, so her words must be given precedence. However, none of us around this table can think of you as a truly bad element. We have all seen you tending to your patients and doing your work, always with a warm smile for everyone, and that is what we will remember about you after you have gone. Therefore, we have decided to dismiss you from the army because of ill-health. You will have a clean file when you leave here. The report made by your clinic leader containing a full account of your stupidity has been removed, so that the Demobilized Soldiers Office in Nanjing can help you to find a good job. We were helped in our deliberations by the fact that you are the daughter of not one but two revolutionary martyrs. All we ask, Comrade Gao, is that you do not let us down by doing anything so stupid again.'

I was thunderstruck. I had been expecting the worst but I had been let off! I think I staggered slightly as I turned and marched out. 'Please wait here,' said one of my escorts, before marching away.

The senior officer came out of the room. 'Comrade Gao, I have to tell you that I knew your parents, and I remember them as two very fine soldiers and comrades who treated me with kindness when I was a young recruit. You seemed to be following in their footsteps until this happened.' He sighed as he looked at me. 'We tried to find a way of keeping you here, but you made it impossible for us.' He held out his hand, and I shook it. 'Good luck, Little Gao,' he said, and strode away. So, he too knew me as Little Gao. Thoughts of Guv flooded back, and I burst into tears.

13. Back to the Class Struggle

On 27 January 1970, after receiving my last payment from the army, I removed the red star from my cap and the red cloth insignias from my collars. I was a soldier no longer. I was allowed to take everything the army had issued to me, including my uniforms, underwear, quilt, bed-sheet, satchel, mug and water-bottle. I packed everything into the quilt, made a bedroll, and was ready to go. I took one long last look around the room. All my friends and comrades were out working or training, so I was alone. How I wished I hadn't been so naïve.

As I reread the letters Pei-gen had sent to my leader, I began to understand. She was jealous of the progress I had been making in the army, and my impending acceptance into the Party. She had not been asked to join, even though she was a high-ranking Rebel. Also, as a Party member, I would have been given more responsibility and she hated the idea of me being promoted more quickly than her. In her letter to my leader, she had shamelessly requested him to write to her leader and inform him that she had placed righteousness above family loyalty, for the good of the revolution.

I walked out of the hut with the bedroll strapped to my back and climbed on to the truck that would take me to the railway station. The female sergeant was waiting to give me my ticket to Nanjing. Suddenly, the whole of clinic two burst out of the hospital doors to bid me farewell. 'Go well, Squinty, we'll miss you!' shouted one, and others nodded and waved. I looked for Little Ping, but she wasn't there.

Then, 'Squinty! See, she has come!' and there she was, running towards me, arms outstretched. As she got nearer, I could see she was carrying something in her right hand and crying. I climbed down, and we fell into each other's arms. After a few seconds Little Ping pulled away and said, 'I haven't got anything good to give you, so please take this new pair of shoes as a little gift.' She thrust the little parcel into my hands. 'Goodbye, Squinty, I hope you find some good luck soon.'

'Goodbye, my good friend, I will write,' I replied, before getting back up on to the truck.

The truck started forward and picked up speed. My friend waved until her figure was a tiny black dot, and finally vanished. I sat down and opened her present: a pair of new black cloth shoes. Little Ping is still my friend and her shoes are safely tucked away in the old camphorwood trunk.

It was dark when I arrived in Nanjing. I had nowhere to go. I had left the city in high spirits, filled with dreams of my wonderful future, and now I was back, sad and lonely. My file was clean but I was not looking forward to meeting my old acquaintances and trying to explain why I was no longer in the army. I was going to lose face, that was for sure.

For my first night back in Nanjing the sergeant had given me the address of an army hostel. Early the next morning, I reported to the Demobilized Soldiers Office of the Nanjing Revolutionary Committee. A Rebel official took me into his office and I gave him my papers. He read them with care, then looked at me more closely. 'I can see you are in poor health,' he said. And he was right, I was not feeling well. 'You had better sit down before you fall down,' he continued, and I sat on an old wooden chair standing against the rear wall.

The Rebel picked up the telephone and talked to somebody. 'There,' he said, triumphantly. 'That is settled. You have a nice easy job in the Nanjing Radio Factory.'

I was impressed. It was all so easy – but only because I had not been branded a hidden bad element. I stood up and stuck out my hand. 'Thank you so very much,' I gushed, giving him my best smile. 'I am most grateful to you.' I saw his chest expand and he seemed to grow two inches taller.

The Nanjing Radio Factory was a huge military establishment employing over six thousand people, producing transmitters for every fighting unit of the PLA. It also manufactured walkie-talkies for use in Vietnam. It had, and still has, an army designation: No. 714 Factory. Every military factory has a number and these numbers have a special significance. For example, the number of a factory producing radio parts has 7 as the first digit, and the other numbers also have hidden meanings. So factory No. 720 produced radar equipment and No. 734 made electronic tubes. Because of the top-secret nature of the products, the workers were paid higher salaries than those employed in non-military establishments. However, I was not aware of my luck when, with my bedroll strapped to my back, I wearily climbed on to a bus heading towards my new employment.

The factory was a fair distance from the city centre and I had to stand for most of the way until the bus emptied. By now I was feeling really ill and I hadn't eaten properly for ten days, during which I had learned a lot – such as the simple truth that every action, good or bad, will result in a reaction that might affect the lives of those who follow us, perhaps for generations to come. The terrible things that had happened to Pei-gen when she was a child were the direct cause of her bitterness and her hatred of all humankind, and of me in particular.

The bus stopped and I got off. At the factory's main gate I was stopped by a security guard. He looked at me curiously because of my ex-army uniform and the bedroll on my back. After I showed him my letter of introduction, he pointed to a four-storey building covered with big-character posters. I took little notice of them as I went through the main entrance and climbed the stairs to the personnel department.

A woman cadre read my file and said, 'You have been assigned to the Research Institute. Since you were given only a small promotion in the army, I can only offer you the position of an assembly worker, making prototypes of newly designed pieces of equipment. The Research Institute is a place where about two hundred Stinking Old Number Nines [intellectuals] are gathered together, so you must increase your vigilance against their subversive bad influence, and follow the dictates of the centralized leadership of the Party at all times.'

My mind drifted as she droned on about the dangers of the intellectuals, the glory of the revolution and all the usual jargon of Mao's China. '. . . and now, Comrade Gao [my attention jumped back to her], you must always remember that being a worker is a great honour, because the workers are the leading class in China. The class struggle is still very fierce, and as we must make use of the technological skills of the Stinking Old Number Nines, people like you are the key link. We have recently received orders from the Central Leading Group of the Cultural Revolution in Beijing to restore some of the production because the electronics industry has become a most important part of modern warfare. You will be taught all you need to know as you go along. Have you any questions?'

I said no, so she asked me some more about my family and became less autocratic when she learned I was alone in Nanjing. She telephoned the caretaker of the female workers' dormitory to make sure I had a bed. 'You will be sharing with three other girls,' she informed me. I thanked her and went on my way. The same guard at the gate gave me directions to the dormitory, which turned out to be three kilometres away in a sparsely populated area of Nanjing, near the imposing Zhongshan Gate set into the ancient city wall.

I walked into a huge compound, flanked by many three-storeyed buildings, which housed and serviced the workers of the factory. The area looked cheerful enough, with lots of trees and shrubs. My spirits rose slightly. I was surprised by the quiet: this was home to thousands of people and yet the place was empty, with the exception of an old lady gatekeeper who showed me the way to my dormitory. 'Tomorrow is the Spring Festival, so everyone has gone home,' she told me. The Spring Festival! I had not heard those words for years. So the people of Nanjing were celebrating it again. Good. It was the most important holiday of the year and was intended to honour the unity of the family. Then I remembered that to me it was meaningless. I had no family here.

A sudden sadness hit me and my eyes filled with tears. We trudged up the stairs. We were both breathing hard when we reached the top. Two long corridors ran at right angles from where we stood, one to the left, and one to the right, with about forty doors in each. The floors were made of concrete, and the walls had recently been lime-washed.

The old lady did not seem to notice my misery as she said, 'The toilets are at the end of each corridor, and the public bathrooms are down in the courtyard behind the dining hall. They are always open. The dining hall feeds over a thousand people at a time and is open all day. Here is your room.' She opened a door and I followed her inside. 'Of course,' she went on, 'everything is closed until after the holiday, so the best thing you can do is put your things away and go home. Your family must be missing you.'

I watched her shuffle away. This was my home now. I looked around the empty room and let my bedroll drop to the floor. I felt too weak to do anything more than unwrap my quilt and climb into bed.

Sleep was impossible. The happenings of the last few weeks flowed backwards and forwards through my brain and I fell into a world of feverish imaginings, a world of sadness, betrayal, misery and pain. Then, quite suddenly, I was wide awake, crazy with thirst. The room was as black as pitch, so I knew it was night, but what time was it? What day? Why was I alone? I swung my legs out of bed, slipped my feet into my shoes and stood up. My brain whirled and I fell to the floor, banging my cheek and forehead against something. I lay there, puzzled and confused, for a while.

I had to find some water. I got up and staggered around in the dark, bumping into things until I found the door. I was leaning against it as I turned the handle, causing it to fly open, so that I fell through and crashed into the far wall of the corridor. Pain shot through my neck and left shoulder. I edged my way along the corridor in the direction of the stairs, expecting to find the stair-rail. Instead I went down head first.

The pain was terrible. My head, shoulder, back, left arm and wrist were telling me I needed help. But where from? I couldn't answer this, so I just stayed where I was. It was so peaceful. I curled up and drifted off to where I could see my mother smiling at me. 'Come, Little Flower,' she was saying, as she waved me forward.

'Mother! I am coming to you at last!' I said to her, happiness flooding through me just before blackness smothered everything.

'Hello,' said a soft voice, as I opened my eyes. It belonged to a woman dressed in a white medical gown.

'Little Ping!' I shouted, thinking I was still in the army.

'I'm sorry, but you will have to make do with me,' said the woman. 'My name is Li Ming, and I'm a doctor. What's yours?'

'Gao . . . Gao Anhua,' I replied. 'What time is it? Where am I?' I tried, unsuccessfully, to sit up.

'Don't move,' ordered Li Ming. 'You have a number of nasty injuries, and you are in the factory sick bay.' I looked around and saw I was on a drip. 'Liquid and food,' said the doctor. 'You were seriously short of body fluids, and very undernourished. How did you get into such a state? Here, take a look at yourself.' She held out a mirror.

I saw a stranger. She was thin, pale and haggard, with dark rings under her eyes. Her lips were cracked and sore, there was dried blood in her hair and a bandage wound around her head. 'Is that me?' I asked. I tried to lift my arm higher. 'Oh!' I squealed. 'What's happened to me?'

'A broken collarbone, I'm afraid,' said Dr Li. 'And if you look at your left wrist, you will find it in splints. You have broken that too.'

'I am surprised to find a doctor here,' I said. 'Apart from the army doctors and a few others, we heard that all the doctors had been imprisoned as "Bourgeois Academic Authorities".'

'That is true,' she said sadly. 'My own husband is in a cowshed outside the city.' I saw the beginning of tears before she forced a brittle smile. 'Just think yourself fortunate. The Rebels let me stay because of my job here.'

Almost all doctors, dentists, opticians, writers, artists, top athletes and even the model workers who had done a good job in their workplace had been victimized. Many had died and the rest were either in detention or forced to work long hours, seven days a week, in manual jobs.

I had been lucky. Apparently I was found curled up on the landing, unconscious, by a worker who had returned to the dormitory to collect a present for her mother. When she found me it was already mid-morning, and I was suffering from hypothermia along with everything else. Fortunately the doctor was still in the compound so I was given immediate medical attention. As well as the broken wrist and collarbone, I had two big cuts on my head, a badly bruised shoulder, and was running a high fever.

'What day is it?' I asked.

'The day after the Spring Festival. You have been unconscious for about forty hours.'

'Can I get up now? I feel fine,' I said. I thought it would look bad if I missed my first shift at work the day after next.

'No, you are very sick. How old are you?'

'Twenty years and ten months,' I said. The doctor looked at me. 'You've had a bad time and it is my job to get you better, so no getting out of bed for a few days, and I want you to eat and drink as much as you can.' She smiled and left.

I closed my eyes and slept until I was woken by the doctor bringing me a bowl piled high with rice, another of vegetables, plus a huge jug of boiled water. 'The more you eat and drink,' said Dr Li, 'the happier I will be, and the quicker I will let you out of here.' She spoke in a mock scolding voice and held a cup of water to my lips. 'I want it all gone before I return.'

I drank a little, picked at the food and sipped some more water, then put the dish aside. My head throbbed, my body was stiff and sore and my broken bones ached. I lay back and closed my eyes. It was quiet but for the ticking of a clock and the gentle sough of the wind passing through the trees outside.

The doctor came back to ask me if there was anyone she could contact for me. At first, thinking only of my family, I shook my head. Then, I remembered that there was someone, if he was in the city. Thanks to Dr Li, Hui came to see me the next day. After he was settled in a chair beside my bed, I told him what had happened to me and asked him to go to my room and fetch my letters to Pei-gen and the one she had written. It wouldn't do for them to be read by strangers. When he returned I allowed him to read them because I thought he had a right to know everything about me. I was not sure how he would respond.

'Rubbish!' He threw the letters on to the bed. 'How could she possibly do that sort of thing? Her heart must have been eaten by a dog!'

Hui came to see me every day, each time bringing me a little surprise. With his support I improved steadily. One morning a strange man struggled into the clinic, carrying my camphorwood trunk, followed by Hui. 'I thought you might like to have this nearby,' he said.

'Oh, yes!' I was touched by his thoughtfulness. 'But I cannot keep it here, it must go to my dormitory.'

'Yes,' he replied, 'but I wanted you to know it was safe. It has never been opened since you left it with me.' I watched as he helped the man carry it away. Another day he returned with my bicycle. Such simple things helped me to gather together the broken pieces of my life. A new beginning was emerging from the ashes of the past.

By this time, everybody was back at work. Outside the clinic, the whole place hummed with noise and movement. My new room-mates called in and introduced themselves, and assured me my belongings would be kept safe until I was better. The leaders of the Research Institute and my immediate boss came to see me too, bringing some delicious home-cooked food.

I thought I was going to like working in this factory: everyone was so kind and considerate. With a huge feeling of relief, I realized that no one knew anything about my recent past, and simply accepted my presence in the clinic as confirmation of the reason that I had given for my discharge from the army.

As day followed day, I grew stronger, physically and mentally, but it was many months before I could look at my mental scrapbook without tears. Time heals but I have never stopped missing the dear friends killed in Vietnam. From her letters, Little Ping feels the same. She too has had her fair share of good and bad luck. True happiness was rare in China during those turbulent years of Mao's Cultural Revolution.

As my fever subsided, my strength slowly returned. I was still eating and drinking little, despite Dr Li's efforts. I was content to lie in bed staring at nothing, doing nothing. Eventually Dr Li decided I might be better off in the company of my new room-mates and moved me to the dormitory, where she visited me twice a day.

After a few more days, I felt strong enough to talk to Hui about our future together. His time in Nanjing was almost up. He was due to return to the cadre school. I wanted to surprise him so I got up, dressed and made myself as attractive as I could. I had lost a lot of weight so most of my clothes were much too big, but I resurrected a few items from my camphorwood trunk and looked reasonable. I walked nervously out of the compound and caught a bus to town, then walked the short distance to Hui's dormitory.

He was out, but his unlocked door told me he would be back soon, so I decided to wait. I went in and immediately noticed an enlarged framed photograph of Fang, the eldest of the Five Golden Flowers. My tummy lurched. Several more were hanging on the walls. At first I was stunned. It didn't take much to work out that during my absence they had become lovers.

When Hui came in, I looked at him in silence. His face showed surprise, then pleasure, then guilt, and he looked away. I continued to look at him until he was forced to say something. 'How are you feeling?' he asked.

I don't know what showed in my eyes but the hurt was clear in my voice: 'Please be straightforward with me, Hui. I need you to tell me the truth.'

He sat on the side of his bed. 'I'm sorry, Anhua,' he said, his eyes on his shoes. 'It was not intended. I was so lonely after you joined the army. Fang gave me companionship and looked after me when I was ill. You can understand my need for company at that time, and neither of us, you nor me, knew that Fang had loved me for a long time. She had kept silent about her feelings. Only after you had gone and I was ill did she tell me. At first I told her it was impossible for me to respond to her because I already had you.'

He looked at me, searching for a reaction, but I could only stare back. Inside, I felt like a jellyfish. He continued: 'You know well enough what you need most when you are ill and alone. As time went by our friendship developed until my heart responded to hers. I learned to like everything about her, and then to love her.' He paused to light a cigarette.

At last I found my voice. 'Why didn't you tell me sooner?' I asked, determined not to cry.

'I wanted to, but the right words never came. When I wrote to you, I tried to put everything down on paper, but couldn't. Then, when you returned to Nanjing, you were too ill for me to tell you the truth. I'm glad you have found out,' he said, relief in his voice.

'Why her?' I asked. 'What has she got to give you that I haven't? How is she different from me?'

Hui thought for a few moments. I hoped he was about to change his mind and take me into his arms with words of love. At last he said, 'She is healthy and she has more passion.' I felt a whirl of dizziness, and my face must have shown my distress because Hui stood up and held out his hands to hold me.

'Passion?' I spat, pulling away, angry at last. 'More passion? How could I know passion? I am still a virgin! Was Fang a virgin when she showed her passion? I bet she wasn't! She is second-hand goods –' I broke down.

'I'm sorry, Little Flower. I did not look for this to happen between Fang and me. I just couldn't stop it and then I did not want it to stop.' He was pacing the room. 'Both of us think highly of you, Anhua. We want to be your good friends, and regard you as our sister.'

I don't know how I got to my room. I do remember vomiting several times in the street. I had to shield my eyes from the light. Every time I let my hand drop my head spun and I vomited again. I remember lying down on my bed, eyes closed, motionless. The slightest movement of my head or the dimmest light brought on another bout of sickness. One of my room-mates went for help.

Dr Li came as quickly as she could. She examined me and said she thought I might have vertigo. She wanted another doctor to take a look at me.

The next day an important-looking man bustled in with her. 'Hello, young lady, I hear you've got problems,' he said, not wasting any time.

Once again I was subjected to an examination. This one was very thorough, and his questions were searching. I described the strange floating sensation and the dizziness, all without opening my eyes. I also recalled how I had suffered the same symptoms after the death of my mother.

'Everything you say points to just one thing – Menière's disease. I must do some more tests before I can be sure,' he said.

It was confirmed as Menière's disease, which can attack without warning at any time. The sufferer suddenly feels dizzy and as if their head is filled with rushing water. Then comes the vomiting. Once you develop it, you will probably have it for life.

I lay in bed for two days, as motionless as possible with my eyes tightly shut. By the third day, the attack had eased and I was able to get up.

However, every few weeks I had another attack and was forced to stay in bed until it went away again.

When I was better, I reported for my first day in the factory. I had my photograph taken and was issued with my ID card. Everyone had to wear their card at all times inside the factory grounds and have it checked every time they went in or out of the gate. To get from my work in the Research Institute to the main gate, I had to walk more than a kilometre, then two more kilometres around the high perimeter wall to get to the dormitory. Later my room-mates showed me a back gate, which meant it was less than a kilometre to my bed.

I didn't like using the main gate very much, because of the constantly blaring loudspeakers and the big-character posters, which were stuck up everywhere: on the front of the office buildings, the perimeter wall and tree trunks. It was the way the factory Rebels debated their favourite causes. At least it was better than having them kill each other, I supposed.

I had not heard many loudspeakers or seen any big-character posters during my time in the army, but in Nanjing they were a constant reminder to me to be careful of what I said and did. I hated the streets: they seemed full of violence and hatred. However, I thought it prudent to stop and read some of the posters, just in case I was being spied on. There were many unseen eyes on the lookout for any supposed breach of revolutionary behaviour.

The factory was kept as clean and orderly as any army camp. French plane trees lined both sides of the roads between the various buildings and workshops, giving us plenty of shade in high summer. The grassy areas were neatly trimmed all the year round and flowers grew everywhere from March to October. Inside most of the buildings, efficient air-conditioning systems kept the workers and machinery cool and comfortable.

My production group was located on the second floor, together with the designers' offices. Cleanliness was strictly enforced. Everyone had to take off their street shoes and change into freshly laundered cloth slippers each time they entered the building. On my first day, as I ambled into the building without changing, I was pulled so roughly back by my arm I had bruises. The security guard apologized as he told me that if he hadn't stopped me, we would have been severely punished. He handed me a new pair of white cloth slippers and a white laboratory coat. Even though there was no production, we still had to wear them, hands had to be scrubbed and women had to cover their hair. There was a strict no-smoking rule, too.

Political pressure was as strong as ever. The old leaders of the factory had been swept away and replaced by the Revolutionary Committee. The current top man was a high-ranking PLA officer. He strutted around the factory like an all-conquering invader. One of his first orders to his subordinate leaders was to reorganize the factory along army lines. The workshops were renamed companies and the director of each workshop was given the title company commander. The Party secretary for the company became the political instructor. My production group leader became a squad leader.

There were twenty workshops plus the Research Institute. As most of the Stinking Old Number Nines worked in the Institute, the top man gave it the name Company Number Eleven so that it had ten workshops above and ten below, to remind the intellectuals to strive for re-education from the workers on both sides of them. Exactly what they were supposed to learn was never explained. All the workers, even the Stinking Old Number Nines, were in the militia, a sort of watered-down Rebel unit, so from my first day I became a militia-girl, although due to my poor health I was never called upon to take part in any of its activities.

I learned that the factory, which had been built by the Kuomintang government in 1936, had been designated a highest-level Red Banner factory by the old Nanjing People's Government, with the best engineers, technicians and skilled workers employed there.

The ravages and chaos of the Cultural Revolution had been kept away from the factory. Of course, people had been arrested and imprisoned or killed, but even during the worst of the factional fighting, the area had been heavily guarded, with the result that no equipment had been damaged. At the time I reported for work, nothing was being made. Instead, we had hours and hours of political study or meetings to denounce class enemies. Our company commander told me that my most important duty was to get involved in the class struggle.

The current class enemy in our Research Institute was a good-looking young man named Qian Shou-shan. He was a university graduate, so he was 100 per cent Stinking Old Number Nine. I was told he had been taken into detention in 1969 while I was in the army. The top man gave orders for the female toilet on the second floor to be converted into a cell. A bed, a table and a chair were put inside for the prisoner. Nothing else was allowed, and he was guarded twenty-four hours a day.

My squad leader was the woman who had visited me in the clinic. Her name was Wu, so we called her Master Worker Wu, and she told me that the young man had been caught during militia shooting practice firing at a target on whose reverse side had been chalked the name of Chairman Mao. Of course he was taken into detention and branded a counter-revolutionary. From then on, he was forced to attend his own denouncing meetings at regular intervals.

The first denouncing meeting I attended was in early April 1970. It was held in a big workshop, which had been converted into a meeting hall on the first floor of the Institute. Before Qian Shou-shan was brought in, we sang revolutionary songs and shouted revolutionary slogans. Then a speech was given telling us how vicious and cowardly Qian was to shoot secretly at Chairman Mao. Following more shouted slogans, Qian was pushed into the room by two militiamen. He was filthy, with long lank hair and a scruffy beard. He looked ill and he had the marks of past beatings on his face.

His guards forced him to bow low in front of us. One guard forced his head down by yanking at his hair, and the other held his arms straight out and to the rear, almost forcing them out of the shoulder sockets, in the painful 'aeroplane' position.

'Confess your crime!' shouted the political instructor.

'CONFESS YOUR CRIME!' chorused the rest of us, including a reluctant me.

'Why did you shoot at our beloved Chairman Mao?'

'WHY DID YOU SHOOT AT OUR BELOVED CHAIRMAN MAO?'

Silence.

'Speak!'

'SPEAK!'

A weak voice came from the bowed head. 'I have nothing to confess. I did not see what was on the other side of the target when I shot.' To me, those words sounded as though they had been ground out through gritted teeth, and I couldn't help admiring the man. He had been locked up for over a year yet he still protested his innocence. I could see the political instructor becoming angry and, red-faced, he shouted, 'If Qian Shou-shan does not confess his crime, smash in his dog's head!'

'SMASH IN THE DOG'S HEAD . . . SMASH IN THE DOG'S HEAD . . . SMASH IN THE DOG'S HEAD!' shouted the crowd, raising their right arms towards the ceiling with fists clenching *The Little Red Book*,

23 In 1963, at the age of fourteen, I was chosen to be the model student in Shanghai during the campaign of 'Learn from Comrade Lei Feng'. Mending socks was to show my plain living. This photo appeared in the newspaper *Liberation Daily* with extracts from my diary

24 In front of my parents' grave, November 1967

25 As a Red Guard in Tiananmen Square, Beijing, September 1966

26 My Red Guard friends Old Pei (centre), Ya-dong (first from right), Yan-wen (second from right) in Yan'an, October 1966

27 Mao Tse-tung at a Red Guard rally in 1966

28 Red Guards, holding *The Little Red Book* and cheering for Mao at a rally. I attended the third great rally

29 On patrol at the army hospital,
December 1968

30 Three army friends: Tsao Lin (left), me
(centre) and Fluffy (right), 1968

31 Little Ping (left), my best friend in the army, and me, 1968

32 My sister Andong in January 1969 before she went to Inner Mongolia

33 My brother and me in January 1969 after seeing Andong off to her
husband in Inner Mongolia

34 Wearing my summer army uniform, 1969

35 At the Plum Flower Hill in the eastern suburb of Nanjing in spring 1975

36 My wedding photo, 1974

37 My baby daughter Yan, 1976

38 My father's handwriting on a column in the eastern suburb of Nanjing. The four Chinese characters mean: Deep Pine Trees in Lingu Valley. He wrote and carved this lettering in 1952 and it is still clear today

39 Little Yan and me in a park at Suzhou, two years after my husband died, July 1985

40 The judge (front) on a mission, *c.* 1980. He worked at the court as a policeman at the time

41 The judge (front) leading criminals out of prison to the execution ground to be shot in the mid-1980s

42 The judge (holding revolver) carrying out his orders

43 The first photo I sent to Harry

44 Harry visiting me in China in 1994, when he and I toured my high school

feet stamping in time with the words. I raised my arm and shouted with the others. Because it was a must.

When the noise died down, each group among the crowd sent one representative to the front in turn to denounce the prisoner. They each gave him a hard kick in the body or a punch in the face. Soon, blood was dripping on to the floor and spreading around the feet of the captive and his guards.

When the representatives had finished, another man came out and stood beside Qian and shouted, 'Qian Shou-shan! You must make a clean breast of your crimes. Whoever hates Chairman Mao hates us all. And we working class hate him back. Here, listen with your dog-ears how your girlfriend has behaved better. She has written a letter to you to declare her true class standpoint and she is determined to draw a clear line between her and you, and stop the relationship with you from today onwards. Here is the letter.' He thrust the paper under the dripping face of his victim. 'Read it aloud, so we can all hear it.'

I could see the effect the letter had on Qian. His body trembled and sagged when he recognized the handwriting. But he did not read it out. A man from somewhere in the audience shouted, 'How dare you refuse the revolutionary masses? Crime plus crime! We demand that you read the letter!' He went forward and gave Qian a heavy kick between the legs and a hard upward punch in the face. I heard the crunch of bone against bone.

The political instructor took the letter and used the back of Qian's shirt to wipe the blood off it. Then he read it out. I could see the misery in Qian's eyes when one of the guards pulled his hair to force his head back to allow someone else, a woman, to punch him. By this time, I was feeling sick but I dared not leave the room, or even look away. Qian's face was a mess of blood and broken flesh.

The meeting lasted about two hours, then Qian was taken away. He had confessed nothing, so he was going back to his cell to wait for his tormentors to drag him to another meeting like this one. Then suddenly, before we could leave the room to return to our own workplaces, we heard a commotion from the corridor upstairs. One of Qian's guards ran back into the room. Panic and fear showed on his face. 'He . . . he . . . he has jumped out of the window!'

As Qian was being taken back to his cell, he had seen the open window at the end of the corridor and had pulled away from his captors. He ran to the window and dived through, head first, to the concrete below and died instantly. He was twenty-four and had barely begun his journey through life when he ended it. But there was no pity in Mao's political China. A new denouncing meeting was immediately held in the same room as before because the political instructor said, 'Even death does not expiate his crime.'

Ten years later, Qian Shou-shan was rehabilitated as a 'good comrade' and a formal funeral was held in his honour. His girlfriend spoke at the funeral. Tearfully she said she was unable to forgive herself for having written that letter. She had been forced to do it. It had been the final crushing blow, extinguishing Qian's last good reason for living. Brave and defiant to the end, he had killed himself rather than submit to his tormentors.

14. Ping-pong Diplomacy

The next few weeks dragged by. I missed Andong and even my brother, so I wrote my first letters to them since my dismissal from the army, and explained the reasons for it. I made copies of the letters Pei-gen had sent to my army leaders and enclosed them to prove my words. Soon I received their replies. Andong was angry. 'Too brazen and shameless!' she wrote to me. 'How could she betray her own little sister? Thank goodness our parents are dead, because she would have denounced them as capitalist roaders.' Her words made me feel better and, though we were far apart, our hearts were together.

My good mood was crushed when Wei-guo's reply came. I tore open the envelope and unfolded the thin page of paper. 'You are a bad bourgeois decadent,' he wrote, 'and I support Pei-gen. As your brother, I have a duty to try to extinguish your traitorously bourgeois thoughts with my proletarian bullets.' My hands trembled. 'Pei-gen did the right thing to safeguard the glory of Mao Tse-tung's thought by placing righteousness above family loyalty. You are a disgrace to this family. We are the children of two revolutionary martyrs, who faithfully followed our great leader Chairman Mao to victory over the Japanese, the Kuomintang and every other enemy of China, and you have let them down . . .' I had to stop reading to catch my breath. 'Three feet of ice cannot be frozen in one day just as your stubborn bourgeois thought has taken years to be formed. If you do not reform yourself with Chairman Mao's thought, you can only be a dog's turd!'

I screwed the paper into a ball. He was denouncing me in exactly the same way as the Rebels denounced the capitalist roaders. He made it clear that he believed I was about to bring political shame crashing down upon his head and he wanted nothing more to do with me. I was stunned. I knew I was not a true supporter of Mao Tse-tung and the Cultural Revolution, and I hated all politics for the unhappiness I saw every day, but I did not think I deserved the hatred of two of my siblings. Not for the first time I began to wonder if I should feel ashamed of my lack of enthusiasm for all that Mao Tse-tung stood for.

I remembered the adoration I had felt for Mao on the day I had marched with the other ten-year-olds and wondered where my devotion to him and my unqualified support for Communism had gone. And gone it certainly had.

One thing was glaringly obvious: I could never place my trust in anyone ever again with the exception of Andong. She continued to support me. We understood each other to feel the same way about life in Mao's China, but our letters contained little of how we really felt. It was well known that mail was intercepted and scrutinized so we developed a sort of code to enable us to correspond without others understanding the real meaning behind our words. In one letter Andong wrote that Pei-gen had sent our brother a lot of money, thus buying his support. I was not surprised because at that time in China people were hungry for personal gain, capable of selling their souls without a second thought. Family members ruthlessly betrayed each other just to have it noted on their personal files that they put Party loyalty above even the safety of their own families.

I lived in a kind of emotional vacuum for a long time. Many months passed as I went to work, attended political meetings and chatted with my workmates. I ate, bathed, slept, endured regular attacks of Menière's, and went about my normal business just like everybody else. But inside I was as cold and detached from life as it was possible to be. I took no interest in anything – not even when a workmate killed herself, or another was sent to a cowshed. I stayed behind my emotional barricade, living everything but feeling nothing.

I don't know how long I would have continued like this if Jia Chen had not come into my life. One morning as I was on my way to work, I had an unusually sudden and severe attack of Menière's: one moment I was walking along, immersed in my thoughts, and the next I was vomiting and sinking to the ground as the world spun crazily before my eyes. That is how Jia Chen and I met.

Later I found out she had been walking behind me when I collapsed. As the crowd gathered, she was one of the few who showed concern for me. I vaguely remember a gentle hand wiping my face and a soft, soothing voice. It was she who enlisted the help of two strong men to support me back to my room before she hurried off to fetch Dr Li. As I recovered my composure, I was surprised to see her sitting calmly by my bedside.

She smiled as I opened my eyes a little and stared at her through my eyelashes. I didn't know her, but her radiant smile found a way straight into my heart. 'Hello,' she said, her voice like a tinkling bell. 'How are you feeling?' I closed my eyes and raised a hand to shield them from the light. I think I groaned a response, because the bell came again. 'My name is Jia Chen.' And that was the beginning of our friendship.

Jia Chen was exactly the person I needed. She was a cheery girl of twenty-three, the same age as Andong, and two years older than I. Her father was the chairman of the revolutionary committee in another large military factory in Nanjing, so she was considered trustworthy by all levels of leadership in our factory. She was always happy, with a sweet face and dimples when she smiled. She could joke with everybody without causing offence and laugh heartily, as if she had never known what misery was, without having to worry about being branded bourgeois. She met me when I was at my worst, yet she stayed by my side until I was on my way to recovery. She asked Dr Li what was wrong with me, and as soon as she understood, she made sure my room was kept dark. My room-mates were very considerate: they were used to my attacks and knew what I needed. As soon as I was over the worst, Jia Chen brought me food from her home, which she had cooked especially for me, and sat and talked to me while I ate it. Her voice charmed me into feeling better. And it wasn't long before I could almost feel the protective wall I had built around my inner self crumbling away, allowing me emotionally to open up like a flower at dawn.

Jia Chen was a Red Five and, like my sister Andong, she had fallen in love with an intellectual. He was a twenty-nine-year-old Stinking Old Number Nine university graduate named Mei. She admired his academic prowess and thought his spectacles were very smart. It wasn't long before their friendship was reported to the leaders by one of the many 'unseen eyes' in the factory, and Jia Chen was warned that a spouse from an undesirable family background would ruin her future. She took no notice: she was determined to marry the man she loved and her attitude reminded me of my sister Andong, making me feel very close to her. She soon became my best friend in Nanjing.

There were eight working grades in the factory. I was a grade-one worker with the lowest monthly salary of 33 yuan (about £2.50), which was one grade up from an apprentice who had no salary but was given a 14-yuan food allowance. Jia Chen was a grade-two worker so she earned a bit more – 39 yuan (£3.00) a month. After a year I was promoted to grade two, with the same salary as her. However, during the Cultural Revolution it was normal policy for the wages of grade-two workers to be frozen. So from 1971 my salary as a grade-two worker remained unchanged for a decade.

Jia Chen lived with her parents in a nice house only a few hundred metres away from my dormitory, so we met most mornings and evenings and walked together to and from the factory. She told me many things about it that I had not heard before. From the end of 1966 to early 1970, there had been no production at all in many factories. People appeared at their workplace at eight a.m. to clock in then went home. Thus they guaranteed their wages each month. Many of the young workers got married and took advantage of all the free time to look after their homes and babies on full pay, and had no need of the State-controlled nurseries, which had been closed down anyway.

By early 1970, things were beginning to change. Jia Chen told me that when I was assigned to work in the factory the authorities had begun to insist that all workers stay at their workplaces full time, even though there was no production. We filled our hours with endless political study and the denouncing meetings. Once a month the whole workforce had to gather together in the games area to denounce as many as twenty 'typical class enemies' selected from the workers of each company (workshop).

At those mass rallies, our leaders invited denouncing teams from other factories to attend and to denounce their class enemies along with ours. In return, we sent denouncing teams to other factories. This was known as 'the exchange of experiences of class struggle'. If the weather was bad, the mass rally was held in the auditorium with a representative body from each company in attendance. The rest of us were told to return to our workplaces and listen to the proceedings on the factory loudspeaker system.

The most active and enthusiastic workers at the denouncing meetings became members of the factory denouncing teams and were absorbed into the Communist Party. They felt proud of themselves for inflicting so much misery on others and my hatred for everything connected with politics intensified.

The following year, 1971, was an important one in Chinese history because it was the year Mao Tse-tung began to consider resuming normal diplomatic relations with the Americans. President Nixon was keen for this to happen. The two leaders were uneasy about the increasing military strength of the USSR and wanted to show a united front against it. But it wasn't that simple. The USA had always been demonized by Mao as the enemy of the Chinese people, and the whole world knew that the United States was the number-one enemy of all Communist regimes and of China in particular. How could Mao find an excuse to begin talks without losing face?

The solution came by accident. Table-tennis is the most popular sport in China, even though the game was invented by the British and brought to China by the British invaders. From 1966, when the Cultural Revolution began, all the best players had been persecuted after the chairman of the National Athletics Committee, Marshal He Long, was declared a capitalist roader. With all the outstanding athletes branded as members of the Black Gang or some other label, China did not attend any international sporting events for several years. However, in 1971, the 31st World Ping-pong Championships were to be held in Tokyo and Mao thought it a good opportunity to make contact with people from the West. He ordered that China send the best table-tennis players to compete in the tournament. The ex-world champion Zhuang Ze-dong was chosen to lead the men. Though he was out of practice and nowhere near match-fit, he beat almost all of the best players of other countries and was the main force of the Chinese men's team.

An unexpected incident during the Tokyo tournament led directly to the thawing of Sino-US diplomatic relations. An American player called Kern overslept and missed his team bus one morning. In a panic, he jumped on the only bus left in the athletes' village heading for the tournament. It was the Chinese bus. China and the USA were enemies and in China it was inconceivable for anyone to communicate with a 'Yankee devil'. He was stunned to find himself alone in a bus full of Chinese, and the Chinese were astonished to see him there. They knew that if they threw him off it he would miss his chance to compete that day in the singles event. However, it might be a major political mistake for the Chinese team to take him with them.

Zhuang, the team captain, looked thoughtfully at the American for a few seconds, then he smiled. 'You are welcome to our bus,' he said, in faltering English, before turning to explain to his team that the young man was only an ordinary American person and not a member of the American government, so therefore they should not treat him as an enemy.

Kern was grateful for the ride, but he probably did not realize the danger in which this simple act of kindness had placed Zhuang. However, in the world of sport, there is a natural comradeship, respect and understanding that transcends political differences, and so it was between these two men. The bus stopped outside the tournament building and the door swung open. As the young American turned to leave, he took off his jacket emblazoned with the logo of the United States table-tennis team and held it out to Zhuang.

Behind the two men, a hundred serious eyes were staring, their owners too frightened to make any move. Zhuang saw how sincere the American player was and could not refuse to take the jacket. In return he took out a silk-embroidered neckerchief and handed it to him. 'Good luck in your tournament,' he said quietly. Then East shook hands with West, probably for the first time since 1949. 'Thanks,' replied the American, and left the bus. 'Ping-pong Diplomacy' was born.

The Party secretary of the Chinese team thought that Zhuang had committed a serious political offence and reported the matter to his superiors. He wrote: 'I consider that Zhuang Ze-dong has committed a lofty crime by communicating with the American. Even worse, they exchanged gifts and shook hands with each other.'

A long telegram was dispatched from Tokyo to Premier Zhou En-lai asking for instructions on how to deal with the Chinese team captain. They fully expected to be given instructions to place Zhuang under open arrest until he could be dealt with on his return to China. But, to their surprise, Premier Zhou sent back a telegram praising Zhuang because Chairman Mao had said it was a good opportunity to break the thick ice between the two countries. 'The normalization of diplomatic relations can only start from such a simple exchange of gifts as a token of friendship between two ordinary people.' Zhuang breathed a long sigh of relief.

Mao decided to invite the American table-tennis team to visit China as the first step along the road to opening full diplomatic relations with the old enemy, and suggested that Kern be a member of the American team. He became known world-wide as the 'ping-pong diplomat' when Mao said, 'This is to use a small ball [ping-pong] to push a big ball [the earth].' Kern became an overnight celebrity.

Zhuang was promoted to chairman of the National Athletics Commit-tee. Unfortunately he came to favour during the Cultural Revolution. After Mao's death in 1976 and the subsequent downfall of his Gang of Four, Zhuang again became a victim of politics. As a so-called 'follower of the Gang of Four', he was deprived of any chance of another govern-ment-sponsored job and thrown into prison. Five years later he was exiled to the north-west of China. His wife divorced him and he was reduced to the lowest-paid worker in a factory. He used his spare time to write a manual of ping-pong entitled *Practice and Creation*. With more than a hundred photographs and dozens of sketches, the book became the Bible of every table-tennis player. A few years later he was transferred to Beijing and assigned, under strict supervision, as coach to the Chinese national junior ping-pong team for children up to thirteen.

But that is not the end of his story. A beautiful Japanese woman named Sasaki had admired Zhuang since she saw him play in Tokyo. She had been a teenager then, but her love had never diminished, and when she was sent to Beijing as a representative of a Japanese company in 1980 she was determined to meet her idol. It didn't matter to her that he was no longer a man of importance: it was him, not his fame, that she loved.

During her first year in Beijing, Sasaki spent her leisure hours improving her Chinese before going to the table-tennis coaching school. At first, she was not allowed through the gate but she turned up day after day until the gatekeeper relented sufficiently to send a message to Zhuang to come out. When she told him of her feelings for him Zhuang was stunned. He rejected her advances at first. However, she continued to visit him every day and finally he fell in love with her.

A year after their first meeting, he asked his leader to approve their marriage. Of course his request was ruthlessly turned down – he was a political criminal and she was from imperialist Japan. But the lovers did not give up. Their constant application for permission to be married came to the notice of Deng Xiao-ping, the highest leader of the Communist Party, and he said it was a good thing for true lovers to be together. Permission was granted and now they are married and very happy.

In late September 1971, the whole population of China was stunned to hear the news that Lin Biao, the Minister of National Defence, had betrayed Mao. He and his followers had planned to assassinate Mao but the plot had been discovered. Then he had tried to flee to the Soviet Union in a Trident aeroplane but it had crashed.

We were dumbfounded. How could we believe this when Lin Biao had been Mao's closest comrade-in-arms from the beginning of the Cultural Revolution? Indeed, Lin Biao had been chosen by Mao himself as his successor.

As a result, around 20,000 largely innocent people were arrested, and China, already overflowing with those detained as class enemies, became the biggest prison in the world.

15. Digging Out the 5.16 Elements

In February 1972 my good friend Jia Chen married Mei during the Spring Festival holiday. Once again I celebrated alone, but this time, thanks to her, I could enjoy my solitude. When she returned to work she brought me a big bag of 'double happiness' sweets. 'Double happiness' is a phrase used exclusively at weddings, and her smiling face was glowing.

Life in China had settled down somewhat. We were all beginning to live normally and the shops were slowly filling with essential foodstuffs and other goods. In February 1972, the Central Authority of the Cultural Revolution issued instructions that as the electronics industry had become the most important sector of manufacturing in the modern world, our factory must make some of the parts to be used in the new satellite programme. At long last I learned how to assemble transistors, diodes, resistors, coils and capacitors. As there had been no production until now, I knew nothing of electronics, and had to begin my training by learning what each thing did. At the same time, I was shown how to solder bits and pieces on to the hard brown plastic circuitry boards. I went about my work with enthusiasm because I was happy to be learning something useful.

It didn't last long. On 20 March, Mao gave his latest instruction. He said there was a nationwide secret counter-revolutionary organization called the '5.16 Conspiracy Clique', which had taken its name from Mao's 16 May 1966 instruction that had officially launched the Cultural Revolution. The aim of this clique, Mao told us, was to overthrow the government by opposing everything connected with the Cultural Revolution. Its members were hidden within every section of society. Not even parents, wives, husbands or children knew their identities. Mao told us, through the media, to dig deep to expose these traitors so that they could be wiped out.

So began the years of the most horrible of all Mao's political campaigns. It became an integral part of the Cultural Revolution and in accordance with his 20 March instructions, '3.20 Groups' (3 for the month and 20 for the day) were set up in factories, shops, offices and every other area of life to carry the campaign forward. Jiangsu Province, of which Nanjing is the capital city, became Mao's model example of how the campaign was to be conducted.

Our factory revolutionary committee hastened to form a leading 3.20 Group in its headquarters and a subordinate 3.20 Group in every company. The old class enemies who had been or were currently in detention were the first to be branded 5.16 Elements. They were forced, by the worst possible methods, to 'confess' and to name as many people as possible. It wasn't enough for them to name a few: the list had to be a long one. At first nobody confessed, so the 3.20 Group took turns to interrogate their prisoners twenty-four hours a day. If a prisoner dozed off, the interrogator dropped eucalyptus oil into his or her eyes. The terrible pain ensured that the victim did not fall asleep again. Punching, kicking and worse were inflicted on the prisoners constantly until they were prepared to confess to anything. The tormentors triumphantly displayed the false confessions, with each group trying to outdo the rest in the number extracted. Those named in the confessions were taken into detention and the campaign snowballed. In less than a month, several hundred 5.16 Elements were dug out in our factory. The same thing was going on all over China.

Human dignity was non-existent. If prisoners complained of being hungry, they were made to eat sewage. It was rumoured that when they asked for water, their nostrils were sliced open and urine was poured into their lungs. When they coughed up blood, the only thing they heard was laughter. It was easy to believe such stories as we watched the bundles of wretched bloodstained humanity being paraded before us at the meetings. We heard daily of those who had died in detention.

Production halted again in our factory. Every day we had meetings or mass rallies to listen to the latest confessions. After a while a strange thing happened: those taken in for questioning began to name the members of the 3.20 Groups themselves! And so in seconds their status changed from victimizer to victim. Nobody was safe and we all went about our daily lives in fear. Nobody knew what would happen to them from one hour to the next. It was the time when the 'Red Terror' spread over China.

One morning in early April, I saw Jia Chen walking ahead of me and ran to catch up with her. She was crying bitterly and my heart sank. Her eyes were red and swollen and her voice was hoarse. I realized that there could be only one reason for her unhappiness. I took her in my arms as she was racked with sobs.

A voice whispered in my ear, 'Her father was dug out as the main force behind the 5.16 Clique in Nanjing and has been taken into detention.' It was a young girl from the factory. 'She has been called to give evidence tomorrow morning, and to be asked if she, too, has joined the counter-revolutionary clique.'

My spine turned to ice. I stood there, motionless and silent, like a puppet. Another worker found Jia Chen's husband to accompany her home and she left me with a last sad glance, as if to bid me a silent goodbye.

At eight thirty the next morning we all filed into the big meeting room. It was time to listen to Jia Chen confess her crimes, but she was not there. The Party secretary was angry with her for being late and told two workers to go and get her. 'Bring her here even if you have to drag her by her hair!' he yelled after them.

It was more than half an hour before the workers returned, panting for breath. They had knocked at her door and tried to open it, but it was locked. One had clambered on to the shoulders of the other to scramble through the transom window – only to fall backwards with a loud cry because he could see the head of someone hanging from a rope attached to a hook on the other side. The two workers had forced open the door and found her body. Later, we found out that she had been expecting a baby. Her suicide had ended two lives.

That morning she had asked Mei to leave first, explaining that she wanted to make a special effort with her appearance. She said she wanted to look her best before the meeting. As he was a Stinking Old Number Nine, he dared not be late so he had gone to work not knowing that his beautiful young wife was planning to kill herself.

When our Party secretary heard the news, he immediately contacted the workshop company where Mei was employed and had him taken into detention. He was branded a 5.16 Element and was locked away for over two years without knowing what had happened to Jia Chen – the 3.20 Group thought that if he knew his wife had killed herself he would shift all his own crimes on to her. As a dead person cannot confess, they would never be able to prove his guilt.

Only when he was released, looking twenty years older than his real age, did he find out what had happened to his wife and child. When he went back to his house he found her note. In it, Jia Chen had asked for his forgiveness and explained that she could not face bringing a child into such a cruel world as China had become. Poor Mei died not long afterwards of a broken heart.

In those dark days, suicide was widespread. There wasn't a day that went by without us hearing stories of people killing themselves. Often, they killed their children first to save them from a life of misery. If there was a way to die, then someone somewhere had tried it. The most common method was jumping from the long bridge into the Yangtze River. Others were poisoning, hanging, wrist or throat slitting, and jumping from the tall Lingu Pagoda, upon which my father had left some of his beautiful handwriting.

Over the next two years, more than two thousand people out of a total workforce of six thousand in our factory were branded 5.16 Elements. How I managed to keep clear of it all I don't know. Perhaps a quiet, sickly thing like me represented little glory to a would-be accuser. All I know is that I was one of the lucky ones.

At the end of April 1972, there was a city-wide denouncing rally. It was held in the big sports stadium where 100,000 people could be accommodated in the stands and on the field. Those people of Nanjing who were not there had to listen to the rally on the loudspeaker system, which covered every corner of the city. Before it began, our Party secretary told us that this particular meeting was important because the campaign had achieved a notable victory over the 5.16 Elements. The number-one leader of the clique in Jiangsu Province had been dug out, and he was to confess.

None of our company had been invited to attend, so we assembled in the big meeting room of the Institute. We faced the gaping mouth of a powerful loudspeaker hanging on a wall high above our heads. This was the first time such a meeting had been arranged and we sat in rows, waiting for something to happen. And at exactly two o'clock something did.

The loudspeaker crackled into life and the denouncing rally began. To my astonishment and gut-twisting fear, the number-one 5.16 Element of the whole province turned out to be Uncle Wang Ye-xiang, the man who had sponsored my father into the Communist Party all those years ago in Yan'an. His wife Auntie Shi, whom Andong had helped to write her self-criticism at the beginning of the Cultural Revolution, was also branded a 'Backbone Force of the 5.16 Conspiracy Clique'.

I heard Uncle Wang's familiar voice as he confessed to being the biggest 5.16 Element in the whole of Jiangsu Province and that he was deserving of being killed in the worst possible way ten thousand times over for his activities. Then he said that despite his lofty crimes against the great Cultural Revolution the benevolent Communist Party had shown him the error of his ways and had guided him back on to the true path of revolution. The Party was going to treat him with leniency. They had given him a chance to begin his life anew after he confessed his crimes while in detention and now publicly for all to hear.

My first thought was that Uncle Wang might have given his inquisitors some names, including mine. I can still remember the terror that ate away at my entrails. I was trembling from head to foot. My next thoughts were of ways to kill myself that wouldn't cause me too much pain. The result was that I did not hear the remainder of the rally.

For the next few days I waited fearfully for my name to be called, unable to think of anything else, but as day followed day I relaxed as I realized I was in no danger. Later I found out that Uncle Wang had not named anyone. Apparently he had said that as he was one of the top men in the Clique, he had a secretary to keep his records for him, including the name list. Because the secretary had destroyed all his files before committing suicide shortly after Mao had launched the 5.16 Elements campaign, the name list had been lost. He had been able to avoid naming names because he 'couldn't remember'.

Of course, I knew that his confession had been one big lie from beginning to end. I admired his bravery. He had branded himself a counter-revolutionary without giving his captors the opportunity to accuse anyone else. Auntie Shi had done the same. During the following weeks a recording of the rally was played over and over again through the loudspeakers, and I listened with a heavy heart. If any two people had been true supporters of Communism and were loyal Chinese, it was Uncle Wang and Auntie Shi. How low our country had sunk.

About five years later, after the death of Mao, both Uncle and Auntie were pardoned. Deng Xiao-ping, the new leader of the Chinese Communist Party, said in 1980 that there never had been any such counter-revolutionary clique called 5.16 and not a single 5.16 Element had ever existed. But that made no difference to the millions throughout China who died because of the campaign. Not to mention the destruction of hundreds of thousands of families.

16. A Book Worm

The ten years of the Cultural Revolution were a waste of our lives. Our country achieved nothing and suffered almost irreparable damage. Factories lay idle and children learned little except how to read and write political slogans. They became known as 'the lost generation' and today can get only the lowest-paid jobs.

While young people in other countries were given a good education to equip them for their journey through life, our young were taught to hate and fight. Their prime emotion was fear and their education was in how to worship Mao.

During my employment in 714 Factory, my spare time was dull. There were no books, no cinema, no television, and the radio gave out nothing but political jargon. Games such as chess and cards were banned. Everything that might enrich the spirit or improve the mind was considered 'bourgeois' and disallowed. Sundays dragged by, and although work was a terrible place to be it was almost a relief to return there every Monday morning.

As I ate in the factory dining room I did not have to cook, so the only thing left was to gossip with my room-mates, but we had nothing interesting to talk about and soon got fed up. Even my letters to Andong were short and uninteresting. The less I did, the less I wanted to do, and even the chore of washing myself and my clothes became too much of a burden. Like everyone around me, I sank into a spiral of apathy brought on by mental deprivation.

One lunchtime I did something I had not done for a long time: I wandered into the factory library in the hope of finding something interesting to read. I was disappointed, of course, because the only books on show were by Mao, Marx, Engels and Lenin. I saw a row of technical papers about radio but I had no interest in them so I left. With nothing to do for a while, I ambled into the technical-information office and it was then that my lethargy left me. My head swivelled and my eyes popped out as I saw a young man reading what looked like an English magazine!

Dumbfounded, I walked over to the table where he was sitting and just stood there, unable to believe my eyes. 'RACAL SHOW THEIR LATEST WINNER!' I could read the headlines with ease, even though I didn't know what they meant.

The young man looked up. 'Hello,' he said, with a friendly smile.

'Won't you get yourself into trouble reading that?' I croaked.

I was in two minds: my first impulse was to run away in case I was accused of reading the magazine, the second was to stay and read it!

Luckily the young man was a decent, friendly fellow, and after we had introduced ourselves he told me why he was there. His name was Wang Wen-yu and he was a Stinking Old Number Nine. He had graduated from Beijing Foreign Language Institute with a degree in English just before the Cultural Revolution and had been assigned to the information office in our factory. His main job was to translate into Chinese all the English-language trade and technical journals published by western countries. In this way, other intellectuals could read them and keep up with the latest western advances.

I told Wang that I had been recommended by the old leaders of Nanjing to enter the same institute to study English just before the Cultural Revolution was announced, and I was still interested in improving my skills. We chatted on until, with a start, I realized the time and had to go, but not before we had promised to meet again the next day.

I felt alive again! It was wonderful to be free of the mental vacuum I had lived in for so long, even for just that little while, and I looked forward to our next meeting. So too, apparently, did Wang: his face was one huge smile when I entered the room, and he stood up and placed a chair for me next to his. He was delighted to know that at this time of political movement, when everybody was expected to stick to the revolutionary road, someone was still eager to study.

I was a little distrustful of him at first, and he was wary of me. He was, after all, a Stinking Old Number Nine and I was a Red Five. Thankfully it wasn't long before the wall of doubt crumbled beneath our mutual honesty. I told Wang how dull my life was without books and he invited me to his home after work where he had a small collection of novels. He said I was welcome to borrow them, a few at a time. I was overjoyed.

We met at the factory gates after work that evening, and he took me to his home. His wife welcomed me warmly. Apparently Wang had told her of our encounter the previous day and, as she, too, was a scholar, she understood our pleasure at finding each other. They had met at the Foreign Language Institute and she was now an English teacher at a middle school in Nanjing. But as no teaching was going on, she spent most of her time caring for her husband and their toddler son.

'I'm in paradise,' I said, as Wang moved aside a huge dresser to reveal the books hidden behind it. I was keenly sensitive to his trust and anxiety, and turned to them both. 'Don't worry, your secret is safe with me,' I said.

I couldn't believe my luck as Wang pulled out book after book by authors such as Charles Dickens and Victor Hugo. As we flipped the pages, I saw that some were in a simplified English to help students make progress in the language, but many others had been printed exactly as the authors had written them. 'Oh!' I said, hugging *A Tale of Two Cities* to my chest. 'May I borrow this?' My brain had burst into life again as I consumed the words on the last page. 'It is a far, far better thing that I do . . .' I could read no more because of my tears of joy.

My new-found friend allowed me to borrow that one, *The Gadfly* by Voynech, *The Quadroon* by Thackeray and a small dictionary. He told me I must return *A Tale of Two Cities* within two weeks because it wasn't his. The other books I could keep longer. It was then that I realized Mao was right: there was indeed a secret society! However, the aim of this society was not the destruction of Communism but the improvement of the mind. Looking back, perhaps it came to the same thing.

Before he agreed to let me have the books, Wang gave me a little test. He began to speak in English. To his surprise and my delight, I answered him without hesitation. I had not touched an English book or uttered an English word since May 1966, more than six years previously.

The next day was a Sunday so I was able to begin *A Tale of Two Cities*. With a sense of awe and excitement, I opened the book and turned to the first page. To begin with, when I came across a new word, I looked it up in the dictionary, but it wasn't long before I was so involved in the story that I couldn't stop reading. When I didn't understand a word I guessed the meaning without bothering to consult the dictionary. I had to devour this book as fast as I could, like a starving man shoving food into himself. I began the book lying on my bed at about eight in the morning and finished it under a dim light at eleven that night. I had only a short break for lunch and forgot to eat anything in the evening.

As I read the last chapter, I was deeply moved by Mr Carton condemning himself to the guillotine in place of the husband of the woman he loved. My heart was beating fast, and I had to read the last page again and again. How I would treasure the love of a man like that!

During the next few days I flipped open the pages at random and read the words of this great book. I wanted to keep it for ever, but how could I? I had promised to return it in about ten days. I decided to copy out the whole book by hand. It was not an easy job. First I went to the city and purchased ten notebooks, a pen and a bottle of black ink. Then I spent every second of my spare time writing it out, word by word. Every evening I worked into the small hours under the inadequate light in the dormitory, writing those beautiful English words until my body ached all over. Sometimes there was a power-cut and I had to light a candle to continue. The dim light damaged my eyes but I didn't care: I would have my own copy of this wonderful story. I finished with just hours to spare. As I wrote those marvellous lines, 'It is a far, far better thing that I do, than I have ever done; it is a far, far better rest that I go to, than I have ever known', I felt my spine tingle. I knew I had just completed one of the best things *I* would ever do.

I returned the book on time, and during the following weeks I also read and copied *The Gadfly* and *The Quadroon* at a more leisurely pace. By the time I had finished, I had written down the words of three master storytellers, and in this way I absorbed many new English words and expressions. Several years later, I managed to get hold of a battered old English typewriter and taught myself to use it by typing up my old handwritten copies. It was not until 1995, in an English bookshop, that I was able to purchase my own printed edition of *A Tale of Two Cities*. But I still keep my handwritten copies stored away in the old camphorwood trunk with my other treasures. They will always remind me and my descendants of those dark, dreadful days of the Cultural Revolution.

In the autumn of 1973, Mao decided to reopen some of the universities to workers, peasants and soldiers. The prospective students, because of their lack of education, were not expected to sit an entrance examination. Their acceptance depended upon a recommendation from their leaders, based only on political behaviour. A paper test was held and used only as a teaching reference by the lecturers.

One applicant named Zhang Tie-sheng could not answer any of the questions and handed in a completely blank paper. He had written on the back of it that because of his devotion to the causes of Chairman Mao he had used all of his time in furthering the revolution. He had settled in the countryside and worked in the fields, so he had

had no time for lessons. Otherwise he might have achieved full marks.

His comments came to the notice of Mao's wife Jiang Qing, who had the story printed in all the newspapers and broadcast over the radio. Zhang became an overnight hero. He was admitted to the best university and joined the Communist Party. Such strange things happened all the time during the Cultural Revolution.

In our factory, every company was allotted one university place to fill. All of those who wished to enter could apply. After such a long time without education, the Chinese people wanted to learn again and there was great interest in the scheme. As the worker-peasant-soldier students were not to be thought of as Stinking Old Number Nines, many people applied, including me. As usual, there was no fair play. Some children of high-ranking army officers in our factory were not approved by their fellow workers but got in through the 'back door'. It seemed nothing had changed. Though they were resented by most of their fellow workers because of their arrogance and 'I'm better than you' attitude, their applications were approved anyway, for the factory leaders were fearful of upsetting the fathers. The abuse of power caused a huge upsurge of indignation in our factory.

By the time the universities began to enrol students my parents had been dead for many years, and most of their old friends had either retired or were being held in 'cowsheds', so there was no one to whom I could turn for help in getting into a university. I went to see the chairman of the revolutionary committee in our factory and told him I had a good understanding of written and spoken English and would be a good student if I could have the chance. But he couldn't help. Yes, he realized a knowledge of English was desirable in China. Yes, he thought I would make an excellent student. Yes, he felt sorry for me. But there was nothing he could do because all the vacancies had been given to people with powerful, living parents. I returned sadly to my workplace. Now I knew my mother's dream would not come true, and that night my pillow was wet with tears of disappointment.

And yet it is strange how small fragments link together, like pieces of a jigsaw puzzle, to make a difference to our lives. My newly revived enthusiasm for learning was kept alive by a steady stream of books from Wang. A few weeks after I had finished copying *A Tale of Two Cities*, another piece fell into place.

The educational department in our factory decided to hold English-language evening classes. English was no longer denounced as a capitalist pursuit because, as Mao said, 'The great master of socialist thought Karl Marx once said a foreign language is a weapon in the struggle of life. We are Marxists, so we should learn foreign languages.' Naturally my new friend Wang was appointed the English teacher. His students were the scientists and engineers employed in the factory. They had orders to improve their English-language skills so that they could follow the western technical papers that would assist them in their work. Mao was at this time very mindful of the technological gap that existed between China and the West and he wanted us to catch up. So he was keen to get these English classes started.

Two months later Wang was ordered by the Foreign Ministry to go to Beijing. He was to interpret for a month during some high-level diplomatic talks. As the English classes had to continue, he suggested that I should take his place during his absence. It was important that the English courses were not interrupted, he said. And that was how, with no qualifications, I became the teacher to a roomful of Stinking Old Number Nines with more degrees than I could count.

I had never taught before, so I used my middle-school English tutor's methods to teach my students. I wrote with white chalk on the blackboard and explained the intricacies of English grammar to the best of my knowledge. Soon the sound of clicking tongues settled my nerves. We Chinese show approval by a quick movement of the tongue, which makes a peculiar and distinctive sound. I spoke clearly and this attracted more Stinking Old Number Nines to join the class on my second evening. In fact, so many turned up that there weren't enough chairs.

It wasn't long before the top man in the factory got to hear about me and he came one evening to see for himself. He must have been impressed because he instructed the educational department to contact Nanjing University to allow me to attend English classes in the foreign-language department. However, nothing had ever come easily to me and this was no exception: there had been only ten vacancies there and they were already filled by the sons and daughters of much more powerful people than the head man in our factory. Fortunately the wife of the leader of our educational department worked at Nanjing University and was in charge of all the training courses, so she arranged for me to attend as a 'sit-in-class' student in the English faculty. This meant that I was not considered a proper student but an observer and, as such, I would not be given a diploma even if I got good marks at the end of the course. But I didn't care. I was happy to be going into a classroom again. The factory agreed to pay my tuition fees and I was released on full pay. On 20 September 1973, seven years after my last middle-school lesson, I jumped on my bicycle and pedalled to my first session in a real university.

I was impressed by the campus of Nanjing University. There were tall trees lining both sides of the roads, which would have been a wonderful sight in the old days. Unfortunately they were spoiled by the hundreds of big-character posters hanging from every branch. Many more were fixed to the walls of the once-beautiful buildings. Most of the windows had no glass and the buildings bore the marks of the fierce fighting that had taken place between the Rebel factions.

I found my seat at the back of the classroom. It was a condition of my acceptance that I must keep silent so I was never given the opportunity to speak any English there. Of course, we students used some English during the breaks but I spoke it mostly in the solitary confines of my bed. I asked myself questions, then answered them, and recited everything I learned in class. It wasn't long before my notebooks were full of a mixture of Chinese characters and English words and phrases.

One day a student came up to me and looked over my shoulder as I was reading them. 'Chinglish,' she said, laughing.

'What?' I said, a little irritated at being disturbed.

'Chinglish!' she repeated. She pointed a finger at the open page. 'Look, Chinese and English, Chinglish!' And we both laughed.

The classes were not difficult. Most of the other students' English was a long way behind mine, and a large part of every lesson was taken up with the translation into English of our well-known political slogans.

We should have had our final examinations in July 1975 after completing two years' study. However, the classes were cut when instructions came from Beijing that all worker-peasant-soldier students must report to the nearest army base to receive a military training for three months. Worse was to follow. After that they were going to the countryside to be 're-educated' by the poor peasants for another three months. Only then could they graduate and receive their diplomas. I felt better about being an observer because, as far as I was concerned, no diploma was worth spending three days in the countryside for, never mind three months.

On my return to work, I was disappointed to learn that the English-language classes in our factory had been stopped. Instead Mao had issued instructions on 21 July 1974 that all factories should run a Workers' University to ensure that the workers had control of their own educational establishments. If a factory was too small to operate a university, several factories had to join together. It wasn't long before there were 7.21 Workers' Universities everywhere in China. Disappointingly for me, English was no longer taught and mathematics became the main course.

I had hoped to continue teaching but instead I was obliged to return to the same old round of political meetings. The 5.16 Campaign was still going strong, which meant that more and more people were paraded in front of us. Most of those we saw were so badly beaten and mutilated, they died. Those not yet accused lived with fear and a heavy heart.

By 1975 China was one huge torture chamber with thousands dying every week. In fact, we became so used to it that news of the death of someone we knew, perhaps even liked, caused little or no comment. There was nothing we could do to stop what was going on.

17. My Marriage

It was about this time that I began to correspond with Zhao Lin, a young soldier, the second son of my father's good friend Zhao Bi. May 1 is International Workers' Day, a national holiday. Everybody had gone home and I was alone in the dormitory. I took out my family photograph album and was browsing through it when I came across a picture of my father and Zhao Bi. I had heard that he had been branded a capitalist roader and thrown into a cowshed, but I thought he might have been 'liberated' by now. On impulse, I wrote a letter to the Party secretary of Suzhou Region asking for news of my old family friend, not knowing he had been persecuted to death by the Rebels six years earlier during the summer of 1967. His wife, Feng Bin, had gone off with the Rebels to show her loyalty to Mao. She, too, had been in danger of being branded a capitalist roader, so she did her best to please the Rebels by supporting them in every way. She kept well away from her husband during his weeks of torture and death at the hands of the same Rebel group to which she belonged. Their four sons were away travelling in other parts of China when all of this was going on. Feng Bin was like Pei-gen in that she put her own needs before family loyalty – but she was in a no-win situation: loyalty and terrible death versus survival.

My letter was forwarded to Feng Bin, who targeted me as a possible wife for one of her sons. She urged her two elder sons to write to me, and one morning I received two letters, one from each of them. I replied to them both. In his second letter the eldest son told me that he had already fallen in love with a girl, so he would like to be my friend and brother but not my husband, and he suggested we stop corresponding. I continued to write to his younger brother, Zhao Lin.

Zhao Lin swamped me with letters full of pure poetry. He had a beautiful hand and his command of Chinese was excellent. There are over eight thousand characters so, with a clever use of them, a good writer is able to fill the mind of his reader with wonderful pictures. And Zhao Lin did that for me. He wrote eight to ten pages every day and brought me many moments of delight in an otherwise bleak world.

He recounted the last visit my mother had made to his house in 1960 when he was just a boy. He remembered how bitterly she was crying as she told his father about the last dreadful days of my father's life. He said he remembered me from those days as a tiny bundle of misery with the heart of a hero. My brave little smile, he said, had remained in his memory since those long-ago childhood days and his feelings had not changed. He wished he could hold me, care for me, and protect me. He said he understood my feelings of loss, because he, too, had suffered greatly when his beloved father had died. His letters warmed my heart and soon the hurt of losing Hui melted away.

As time passed, we both felt able to write words of love. Lin said he loved me so much that if any other boy dared show any interest in me he would fight him to the death. His love for me was consuming him like a fire. Never had anyone written such words to me, and because I was eager for love and wanted my own family, I accepted his proposal of marriage. From his photographs I knew he was not handsome; his face was too thin and bony. But that didn't matter, because what I needed in a husband more than anything else was a good heart. If he truly loved me I didn't care about his appearance and, anyway, I was not much of a catch myself.

Although Lin and I had known each other as children, we had not seen much of each other since then. His family had moved to Suzhou Region after his father was appointed Party secretary there. In 1973 we could not possibly have recognized each other without photographs. We had conducted our love affair by letter and had decided to marry before we met again as adults. He was a soldier and, because of his skill as a writer, he had been appointed the personal secretary of the commanding general. He had done well and had been accepted into the Party. By the time we were planning our marriage, though, he wanted to leave the army and try his luck elsewhere. He was demobilized with honour at the end of 1974.

When I first laid eyes on Lin, he was in his new army uniform, which suited his thin frame. There was no camouflaging his face, though: he had prominent cheekbones and his cheeks sank inwards like two pits in his sallow face. However, in my headlong rush towards happiness, I didn't care. His letters had convinced me that he loved me deeply. That was enough.

My marriage application was approved without question by my factory leaders because Zhao Lin was from a revolutionary family and a Party member. Although his father had died a capitalist roader, his mother was still a leader in Suzhou, so it was not held against him. He had a good record and so did his mother. After his demobilization, Lin came to Nanjing and got himself a decent job with the help of an old family friend.

We registered our marriage and moved into a small flat in the centre of the city at the end of 1974. There was no wedding ceremony because such frivolities were considered bourgeois. We had a 'revolutionary marriage', which meant the simpler the better. I bought some candies and cigarettes and distributed them among our friends to declare that our marriage had taken place but that was all. My wedding gown consisted of my old army uniform. Our furniture was simple: a double bed, a small dining table and a two-ring table-top gas cooker. We had no wardrobe, dressing-table or easy chairs – we sat on high-backed wooden dining chairs of which we had two. The walls were just rough concrete. My camphorwood trunk was the best piece of furniture in the flat, and I stored my clothes in it.

Today the Chinese spend huge amounts of money when they get married: a wedding may cost as much as 50,000 RMB yuan (about £4,000), which is a lot when you consider that the average monthly wage in China is only 500 RMB yuan (£40). A wedding is paid for by every adult member of both families of the happy couple – everyone makes a contribution and the parents put in their savings. They hire several black limousines covered with red double-happiness posters to carry the two families to a big expensive restaurant where hundreds of friends will already be gathered. It is not uncommon for as many as twenty-five tables, each seating a dozen people, to be filled at such gatherings. A sumptuous banquet, with as many as thirty exotic dishes, will be placed on every table, with rice-wine and beer. The happy couple will go to live in a nice flat, completely furnished with everything they need from the best table linen to a new washing-machine. Things have changed in China.

When I got married, my husband and I were lucky to have the flatlet to ourselves, and were the envy of many other young couples. Before our marriage, I had gone to the Nanjing People's Government for help. As luck would have it, the man who was in charge of the real estate department happened to have been in the same department as my mother, who had once been his leader. He remembered her with affection and that is why we were given our small flat.

It was difficult then to find decent accommodation in Nanjing. The political upheavals had left a severe housing shortage. There had been almost no houses or flats built during the previous ten years and many married couples lived with their families or were forced to live apart in the dormitories. Only during the holidays when the dormitories were empty could they spend time alone with each other. Many delayed having children, but I became pregnant quickly. I had a difficult pregnancy – I could only keep down boiled water and a porridgy mush called Xi-Fan – but I didn't care about the discomfort. I had my own home, my man and my coming baby. I looked to a future full of happiness.

I stopped eating in the factory dining room, and Lin and I cooked our meals on the little gas stove, which was also our only source of heating. We were happy as all newlyweds are. Every evening we boiled water in a big tin kettle, poured it into the thick earthenware sink and washed ourselves all over despite the extreme cold of winter. We huddled together under our two quilts when we weren't washing, cooking, cleaning or working.

I wrote to Andong, who was still with her husband in Huhehot, Inner Mongolia. I told her about my marriage to Lin and sent her a photograph.

She replied right away. Unfortunately Lin read her letter first. His factory was only three minutes' walk away from home, so every day he got back before me. He saw the envelope lying on the floor, picked it up, opened it and read it. In it, Andong said I should have waited to marry because I could have easily found a better-looking man.

When I arrived home and saw Lin's face, I knew something was wrong. He silently handed me the letter and watched as I read it. I realized he had been deeply hurt by Andong's comments and I tried to make him feel better by saying that it didn't matter to me how he looked. 'After all, Lin, it was you I chose.' My words made no difference: from that day on, Lin hated Andong.

As time went by, I learned that my husband was a narrow-minded person. He felt inferior because of his appearance and became a lifelong enemy of anyone who dared to suggest he was not my match, even if they were joking. He became jealous and possessive and, apart from my work, he never allowed me to leave the flat. It was he who did the shopping, he who controlled the money and he who had friends. All I was allowed to do was the household chores.

Sometimes we had visitors, usually his workmates, and every now and then mine. But if he ever saw me talking to a man he would scold me in front of my visitors. It wasn't long before my friends stopped calling at my home. If I remonstrated with him about his conduct, he flew into a rage and slapped me across the face with such force that I spun helplessly into a wall or to the floor and feared for my baby. After the shock of the first slap, my happiness ended and misery began.

I began to hate Lin, but I could not change things: divorce was out of the question in those days, because no matter how unhappy the marriage might be, divorce was considered dishonourable for a wife. It was one of the quickest ways of losing face, and a divorced woman was gossiped about by everyone who knew her. I could not face that, so I pretended to everyone that I was still the happy young bride.

Marriage to Lin was awful. I had lost all my freedom. He even viewed my love of books and study with suspicion. He wanted me to think only of him and to devote my entire life to his needs.

Sometimes I reminded Lin of the days before we were married and how he had changed. I recited passages from his love letters to me, but he laughed in my face. 'Those were only empty words written on paper, you simpleton. Now we are married and I expect you to obey me.' He also said, 'You should know who is the boss in this house. You are my wife and you cannot escape. Not now, not ever.'

I had no privacy. When I washed or went to the toilet, I had to leave the door open so that he could keep an eye on me. He opened and read all my incoming letters and insisted on reading every letter I wrote before it was posted. Not that such behaviour is unusual in China: we believe that there should be no secrets between husband and wife. Spouses may open each other's letters, and parents their children's, especially when the children are in their teens. Usually Chinese parents insist on their right to approve any teenage friendship, particularly when it is between a boy and a girl, so that they can help their child to avoid making a mistake when choosing a friend. Teenagers are not allowed to date, and teachers co-operate with parents to control the love affairs of the young. If a schoolgirl is found to have a secret boyfriend, she will be severely criticized and gain a reputation for being a 'bad girl', which could affect her whole life.

The Chinese take a more relaxed attitude towards boys. If a boy is found to be involved in a love affair, it usually passes without comment. In my marriage, I was under constant scrutiny. Lin had his own life and mine too.

In China, people are still strongly influenced by the old ideas that men are superior to women. Before Communism, a man could have as many concubines as he wished, but a woman gave herself to just one man. Even if her husband died when she was still young, she was expected to remain a widow to show her continued loyalty to her dead husband. If she remarried, she was despised by everyone, even her children. A widower could remarry at any time after the death of his wife, and remarry as many times as he wished.

Chastity has been demanded of women by Chinese society for thousands of years, and even today, in some remote areas, if a wife or a widow is found guilty of an affair, she may be put to death. In such cases, it is usual for the villagers, led by the women, to throw her into a river, stone her or burn her at the stake. She will be branded a 'fox-demon', able to seduce men from their families. So what Lin said to me was true. As his wife, I could never escape him.

One warm evening in May 1975, just as it was getting dark, I was sitting by the open window trying to finish an article in the local newspaper before the light faded when I heard my name shouted from somewhere down below in the courtyard. 'Gao Anhua!' I put down my paper and leaned out of the window. 'Who is it?'

'It's me! Greg!' In the gloom I could see the dim figure of a soldier. As soon as he saw me, he came to attention, clicked his heels and saluted. I was overjoyed to see him. We had not met for over seven years.

'How did you find me?' I asked, full of curiosity. But Greg didn't answer. He just gave me a crafty grin. He had been the cleverest boy in my class and I had often wondered about him. I thought he had probably forgotten me. I ushered him in and gave him the customary Chinese greeting: 'Have you eaten?'

He had, so I made some green tea and we settled down for a good gossip. We talked about anything, everything and nothing. As I looked at his handsome face, a thought flashed across my conscious mind: I wonder if he was ever interested in me? If only he had said something at school. If only he had become my husband! I felt flustered and a little ashamed of myself. Greg was still talking, unaware of my feelings. And I was unaware of how my husband was reacting.

Greg spent a little over an hour at my home and then he left. From then on, Lin used Greg's visit as a reason to hit and bully me. What upset me most was his apparent disregard for the safety of his unborn child. I hated him for that.

Later I found out that he was urged on in his violence by his mother,

Feng Bin. Now she had the chance to vent on me all the hatred and jealousy she had once felt for my mother. She had harboured her jealousies from the days when they were in the New Fourth Army together. She had never forgiven my mother for being promoted above her and now she had me at her mercy.

'Your mother was nothing but a worn-out shoe!' my husband would shout at me when he was angry. His mother said it too. They knew the things they said were not true and so did I, but their words cut through me like knives. Even though I knew how much they enjoyed hurting me by saying them, I was still outraged whenever they insulted my mother, so a quarrel always followed. It usually ended with a good beating for me from Lin.

My only haven was my time at work. For those few hours I could escape the torment Lin put me through. Nothing was right. My cooking was too salty, not salty enough, too spicy or too bland. The house was spotless, but not to him. He found filth everywhere, even in a sparkling clean rice bowl. He scolded me until I felt I could take no more. He and his mother made my life a total misery, which was their way of feeling superior to me. As for me, I think that had it not been for my growing baby they would have driven me to suicide.

My only defence was to feign indifference to the cruel words, but even that prompted another beating. I suffered in silence for fear of losing face with our neighbours. The block had been built of poor materials, and every noise could be heard by someone, so I had to endure his thrashings without making a sound.

Early one morning, in the middle of a beating, my waters broke, which frightened Lin. He put me in a chair and asked our neighbour to help me. That was the end of his participation in the birth of his child. He said he had to go to work, and he left me to make my way to the hospital. Fortunately the neighbour, with whom I had become quite friendly, helped me down the steep concrete stairs of the block. Then she braved the wrath of her leader by being late for work as she supported me the two kilometres to the hospital.

I was put in a ward with seven other women who were waiting, like me, for their babies to be born. As I was the only one without a husband beside her, I felt sad. Two nurses helped me change into the hospital gown and I saw them look silently at each other when they uncovered the new red weals and old blue bruises on every part of my body. Later they gave me extra attention when they realized my husband wasn't going to come. But even their kindness didn't stop me from feeling very alone as the day progressed.

One by one, the other women were wheeled away on trolleys, their men walking beside them. Others took their places in the beds until all the originals had gone, and even some of the replacements, while I was still waiting. I began to panic. What if Lin had hurt the baby and it couldn't come out? But, of course, I could say nothing about my fears.

At last it was my turn to be taken to the delivery room. By now it was after six the next morning and my contractions were coming so fast I could barely take a breath between them. Eventually my baby jumped out of me at 8.34 on the morning of 17 October 1975. A nurse said, 'A nice little girl.' But where was the crying? I was panic-stricken.

I watched, horrified, as the nurses worked on the little blood-spattered body. One held my daughter while another put a rubber hose into her tiny mouth and I heard a small sucking sound. Then a nurse lifted up the little mite by her feet and smacked her bottom. There was no panic – they had done all this thousands of times before. But not to my precious baby! I was reaching out to stop them hurting her when I heard it: an intake of breath, then a strong yell. I fell back as relief flooded through me.

A nurse placed the tiny body in my arms and I gazed at the face of my daughter. Her eyes were closed. She had a pink face and a mass of black hair. Her little rosebud mouth was trembling. She was the most beautiful thing I had ever seen. I checked her tiny hands and feet. She was perfect. Her deep, black eyes opened and looked at me as if to say, 'Hello!'

My daughter came into this world twenty days ahead of schedule. She weighed just five pounds. For the first two days she was not able to suck milk, so she was put into an incubator. On the third day she managed a little glucose water, but the doctors decided to keep her in the warm incubator for another twelve days. I was allowed to stay to help the nurses care for her.

As I gazed at her through the glass, overwhelming love filled me and for the first time I could understand how my mother must have felt when she had me. I gazed down at my baby's tiny face for hours on end, full of wonder. How had Lin and I made such a beautiful child as this? I felt the greatest happiness and contentment I was ever to experience.

I arrived home two weeks after my daughter had been born. It was the first day of November and unseasonably cold. An icy north wind was blowing across Nanjing and the freezing temperature was well below normal, and it cut through my thin autumn clothes as I sat shivering in the pedicab, cuddling my precious parcel.

My husband had been disappointed when he heard I had given birth to a girl. He had been expecting a boy, and he showed his disapproval by not visiting us in the hospital. But when he laid eyes on his baby daughter and saw the little image of himself, he loved her immediately. He named her Yan, which means 'Three Revolutionary Fires' after her three dead grandparents, his father, my father and mother, which pleased me because, despite everything he had said about my mother, he had honoured her when naming our daughter.

Baby Yan looked very much like him, not only in her face but also in her body shape, her legs, her hands and her fingers. Even her eyelids were like his – he did not have a distinct fold along the edges and neither did she. This was her great sadness as she grew up. She wanted folded eyelids to make her eyes look bigger, and she often used to say to me, 'Mummy, I wish I had your eyes instead of Daddy's.' Then, to our delight, it happened. Just like magic at the age of eleven. Something of me had appeared at last.

I was given the customary fifty-six days' maternity leave with full pay. I expected to be fully recovered from the birth by the time I had to return to work, but had to stay at home for several more weeks without pay on the orders of Dr Li. I did not stop bleeding and I had trouble with feeding. At first I used a glass sucker to express my milk but I ended up giving her fresh cows' milk mixed with rice juice. There was no baby-milk powder in China then. The usual thing for women who experienced feeding problems was to hire a wet-nurse, but we couldn't afford one.

Lin couldn't take any time off work to help me because his salary would have been stopped too, making things difficult for us, so, although I was weak from loss of blood I had to make the best of it. In China, the first month after her confinement is considered important to the mother. She is expected to remain in bed for at least a month without even having a bath for fear of catching a cold. It is customary for a grandmother to come and help with the household chores and the washing.

Such a luxury was not for me. My mother was long gone and my mother-in-law refused to help. All she did was write a letter scolding me for producing a girl. She would not even come to look at her first grandchild, never mind help me recover from the birth. There were no labour-saving gadgets in Mao's China: cleaning was done the hard way, on hands and knees, and I had to wash the baby's clothes and nappies in cold water. I had never even heard of washing-machines, while a vacuum cleaner was a longed-for luxury that was far out of reach.

Life was difficult and I was exhausted. On top of everything the Menière's got worse after Yan was born. However, whenever I looked into her deep black eyes, or when she lay sleeping in my arms, the pain in my back and my head-reeling tiredness were, for a moment, forgotten.

We didn't have a cradle so Yan slept beside me in the big bed. I was constantly fearful that she would wake Lin, who would blame me for his disturbed sleep. I had to get up at least three times every night to feed and change her, instantly alert to her first whimper. Fortunately, my little baby was sensitive, and as soon as I touched her she stopped crying.

When she was two months old, if I kissed her she would give me a tiny smile, which filled me with joy. But in the end the tiredness won. I was too exhausted to care for myself. I lost my appetite and for days on end I drank only small sips of warm water and ate nothing. Eventually one morning, as I was trying to change Yan's nappy, the room spun and I fainted.

I opened my eyes to find myself tucked up in bed. Lin and Dr Li were standing on each side of the bed, looking down at me. The doctor said I shouldn't have worked so hard after having my baby. The most important thing for me, she said, was to have a good rest. Lin was shamed into agreeing to care for Yan at night so that I could sleep. But the moment the doctor left, his face told me he was not happy with that, so we compromised by taking turns.

Of course I still had the house to run, but at least I could sleep soundly for one night in two. It wasn't long before my appetite returned and, with it, my strength. The bleeding finally stopped, and I was pronounced fit to return to work. We registered Yan's birth at the local police station, and she was officially named Zhao Yan. But everyone we knew, ourselves included, called her Little Yan. Lin was good with his daughter: he treated her with the utmost care, patience, gentleness and love. And to see him with her, one would never have guessed that he had such a cruel streak. He reserved that for me – and he had begun again to beat me. He had got over his fright when my waters broke.

Children below the age of three are not accepted by any nursery or kindergarten, so we found an old lady who lived nearby to care for Little Yan when we were both at work. She had three babies in her charge. Their families supplied the milk, sugar (when you could get it) and any special foods their child required. We did the same. Each family paid the old lady 12 yuan a month, which added up to the salary of a second-grade worker. In this way everybody was satisfied.

18. Farewell, Premier Zhou

On 8 January 1976, a couple of weeks before I was due to go back to work, I got up early to answer Yan's cry. I turned on the radio as usual to listen to the morning news, but what came out was funeral music. When the music ended, a voice said, 'Our beloved premier Zhou En-lai passed away in the early hours of this morning after failing to respond to all medical treatment. He was aged seventy-eight. According to his last wishes, he will be cremated and his ashes will be scattered over the soils and waters of his beloved Motherland.' The funeral music began again.

They say that everyone in the West knows where they were when President Kennedy was assassinated, and if you ask any Chinese, you will get a similar response for when they heard the news about Premier Zhou. I remember the weather, which suited the sadness of the day: it was cold, windy and grey, with thick black clouds scudding across the sky. I remember feeling my insides lurch with fear, my knees felt weak and I had to sit down. At that moment I could see no future for China. Premier Zhou had been the last barrier between we ordinary Chinese and the excesses of Mao's wife and her thugs. I felt that even more horrific political persecution was about to descend upon us, and I feared for the life of my baby.

History will show how great a man Premier Zhou really was. Already we know that he understood Mao so well that he left nothing behind for Mao to despoil. Not even a grave. In the open, Zhou had been Mao's constant loyal companion and supporter. In private he had used his power to save many people from death. Naturally, he had to protect himself first before he could help others, and this he did with the utmost skill and ingenuity, proving himself a brilliant politician. He was also a skilful diplomat, who earned the respect of politicians the world over. If there had been no Zhou En-lai, the Chinese economy would have collapsed within a year of the start of the Cultural Revolution.

I felt a terrible loss when I heard the news, almost as if Premier Zhou had been a close member of my family, and my first thought was to get three black armbands, one for Lin, one for Little Yan and one for myself. When I went out, I found that everyone was already wearing them.

Many people had pinned small white flowers above the black, and some were wearing full mourning clothes, so that the streets seemed filled with widows, widowers and orphans. Everyone had tears in their eyes.

The shop assistants were polite that day, their voices low, as though they were frightened to speak normally in case they disturbed *his* sleep. There were no more black bands to be found, so one shop manager produced a huge roll of black material from the storeroom and the counter staff cut it into strips to hand to everyone free of charge. I tied one to my left upper arm straight away.

On my way home I saw our national flag at half mast on all the government buildings, and the next morning, the radio announcer informed us that the UN flag was also at half mast, and that every representative of the United Nations Assembly had stood in silence for one minute in memory of Premier Zhou En-lai. He had been respected by everyone, even his enemies.

The radio should have been silent for the week before the premier's memorial meeting: the Zhou En-lai Memorial Committee had decided no music should be played anywhere in China. On the fourth day, though, Mao's wife Jiang Qing and her gang instructed the Central Radio Station to broadcast songs of the quotations of Chairman Mao and other revolutionary tunes, followed by a series of denouncing articles. This caused great indignation among all the people of China, and everywhere I went, I heard people curse Jiang Qing.

To our relief, Deng Xiao-ping was allowed to speak at Zhou's memorial meeting. He praised our hero and gave a glowing account of his life. After the meeting, the body was taken out of Beijing to the Babaoshan (Eight Treasure Hill) Cemetery in the western suburbs to be cremated. That day the weather was dry and very cold. But that didn't stop the people from turning out to pay their respects. In the freezing wind, with temperatures well below zero, over a million people lined the route. There were tiny babies, white-haired centenarians and people of every age in between. They stood grief-stricken, as the cortège travelled the ten kilometres from the centre of Beijing to the crematorium. Most cried as the cars passed by, and even when there was nothing more to see, no one went home. In fact, the numbers swelled to almost two million and the people stood for hours waiting for the return of the car carrying Zhou's ashes. When it had passed them, they quietly followed behind as the ashes were taken to the Great Hall of the People and carried reverently inside. Only then did they leave for home. The next day the ashes were taken up in a special aeroplane and scattered over as large an area of China as possible.

Mao was no fool. He was well aware of the love the Chinese people felt for Premier Zhou and how angry they were with his wife and her collaborators, so he did not appoint Jianq Qing, or anyone connected with her gang, to take over the responsibility of premier in the State Council. Mao trusted none who showed themselves to be as ambitious as him, but he was always happy to use them to persecute anyone who might endanger his hold on absolute power. It was not unusual to see a Mao trusty replaced by an ambitious upstart. Therefore it came as no surprise to hear that his choice of premier was an unknown provincial official, Hua Guo-feng.

When the Sweeping Tomb Festival arrived on 5 April, more than a million Beijing residents went, completely independently, to the Monument of the People's Heroes in Tiananmen Square carrying wreaths. Many pledged their life to protect the memory of Premier Zhou. Others read out remembrance poems. As one group, thousands strong, left the area, another moved forward to take its place. Everything was calm, peaceful and dignified.

In Nanjing, from early morning on the day of the festival, more than half a million people, headed by the workers from the military factories, marched towards Yuhuatai cemetery carrying wreaths. Many had been idle for a long time, so they used their wasted skills to produce wonderfully ornate wreaths as an expression of their love for Premier Zhou. The biggest was six metres across and was so heavy it took ten people to carry it.

The mood of the marchers was not hostile, but after nearly ten years of suppression, their feelings were about to erupt. As they marched through the city, they were joined by vast numbers of others until the streets were blocked by a human tidal wave flooding towards and into the cemetery. A new people's revolution was brewing.

The workers of our factory also went to Yuhuatai – except the Stinking Old Number Nines who, as intellectuals, were considered unfit to be involved. However, a new breed had evolved from the army-officer families. Many had been given a good education before the onset of the Cultural Revolution and most were Party members, so could not be considered 'Blacks'. These hybrids had become known as 'Red Intellectuals' or 'Revolutionary Intellectuals' and one of their leaders, Wang Zhan-zhan, formed a committee and wrote a huge slogan denouncing Jiang Qing and her gang by name, a risky thing to do.

Wang had become a good friend of mine through the secret book society, so when I heard the news, I left my own group and ran upstairs to see what he was doing. On entering the room, I saw another intellectual from a Red family, writing something with an enormous brush. Each Chinese character filled a piece of paper at least a metre square. I stopped in the doorway, unable to believe my eyes. Wang was there too, making sure the slogan was correctly written. When the two men saw me, they grinned.

'Is is true you're planning to write a huge slogan naming names?' I asked.

'Two,' they said. 'One to go on the wall to the left of the factory gate, and one on the right.'

And they did. On the left wall they hung 'Down with Jiang Qing and Zhang Chun-qiao!' and on the right wall was 'Dig out the real Khrushchev of China!' The giant-character slogans were the bravest I had ever seen. They reflected the secret thoughts of so many people who had never dared put them into words. As soon as I understood what they planned to do I declared my full support. Nine of us were involved, eight intellectuals and me.

Of course, we were nervous as we stuck up the huge white squares of paper with the black characters painted on them. It was a big moment for me: never before had I openly shown my disapproval of any leader. And yet, on that day, I felt justified in helping to criticize the second most powerful person in China. We all knew that anything could happen to us later, but we wanted to air our grievances. We did not think much about the danger. We knew the majority of factory people supported us, and we understood why they dared not join in. As we worked, we were aware of many faces watching us from the windows of the factory buildings.

Wang used a big sorghum broom to brush the paste on the wall. Others slid the paper squares into position, and the rest of us patted them down. As the characters began to spell out the words, we attracted a crowd of passers-by, who began to clap and cheer. Many people shouted, 'Well done! Salute to the 714 Factory!'

A middle-aged woman standing near me said, 'This slogan represents the desire of the whole Chinese people!'

News of our protest travelled fast. In less than ten minutes the leaders of the factory Revolutionary Committee hurried out and asked us to take down the slogans. They had already received a telephone call from someone representing the Nanjing Revolutionary Committee, who had instructed them to stop us. But we did not move. Then the police arrived in a military-style jeep and swaggered across, confident that they could take care of this minor event. They began by tearing down the slogans as we and the ever-growing crowds looked on. Then we were taken into detention.

Fortunately, because there was so much unrest in the city, the police were having a busy night. As soon as they had escorted us to an empty cowshed in the Research Institute and locked us in, they were happy to leave the factory leaders to deal with us. I have trouble in describing exactly how I felt – I think I was more fearful of how my husband would react than anything else. I was confident that he would care for Little Yan because, whatever his failings as a husband, he was a good father. I knew that now, though, I had given him the perfect reason to beat me. Also, once his mother found out about my activities, she would be certain to encourage him in his violence. But I felt good too. For once in my life I had hit back. And I had enjoyed every minute of it. And, of course, I was apprehensive about what might be in store for me the following day.

That night none of us slept much. The room was bare, so we sat on the cold concrete floor with our backs against a wall. We talked in whispers until we dozed off. No one came near us until early the next morning when we were herded into the office of one of the factory leaders. He looked like thunder and scowled at us as we lined up in front of his desk. 'You stupid fools!' he shouted. 'You have done it now!'

After he had gone on for a while, it became clear that principally he was angry with us for bringing his regime into disrepute. Our so-called crime seemed of little consequence against his loss of face. 'You have disgraced us all!' he ended, waving us away.

We were taken back to the cowshed. A guard handed a pencil stub and a pile of paper to each of us and ordered us to do self-criticism. Our leader, Wang Zhan-zhan, refused. 'I am not wrong!' he shouted. 'I could stand by no longer and see our People's Republic ruined by this group. Too many people have died for China to allow such high-handed acts against the will of the people to go unchallenged. The slogans we put up only reflected the true wishes of the people. We were right to do it.' The rest of us followed his lead and refused to do self-criticism too.

The chairman of our factory Revolutionary Committee was a veteran army officer and his deputy, Feng, had been the pre-Cultural Revolution factory director. They both loathed Jiang Qing and her gang, and when they talked to us, it became clear that they were on our side. They didn't want to punish us, they said, but they would have to do something to satisfy their leaders.

Once again we were told to do self-criticism but we kept silent and wrote nothing. At nine o'clock Feng came to see us. 'If you do not write your self-criticism, we cannot help you,' he said sadly.

During the previous evening my husband had come to look for me. It was the first time I had not gone home after work to have dinner with him and he had been anxious. When he heard about the slogans and my involvement, he left in case the leaders dragged him into it. To save his own face, he returned the next day and asked to see me. When I was brought before him, he scolded me in a voice loud enough to be heard by my captors, which, he hoped, was sufficient proof of his own innocence.

Despite my predicament, I reasoned that I had several things in my favour. I was the only worker in the group and a worker was considered a proletarian. Moreover I came from a Red family and I thought I was guilty of nothing. I had merely been following the mood of the majority, so I asked to see the leaders. 'I would like to go home with my husband,' I said. 'I have done nothing wrong. What I did was out of my love for Premier Zhou, and I have a baby to look after.' For some strange reason, I was not scared – and it must have shown, because my request was granted immediately. The rest of the group were kept in the cowshed for another night.

When I got up the next morning, the seven o'clock news gave an account of what had happened in Tiananmen Square. The announcer said there had been a counter-revolutionary event. One million people had been whipped up by a few plotting conspirators to demonstrate against the central Party leadership headed by Chairman Mao. They had burned police cars and shouted reactionary slogans. A man with closely cropped hair – which implied that he was a criminal – had led the people in preventing the police from taking away the piles of Zhou En-lai's wreaths. He had then led a riot. Hundreds were arrested and it was hinted that Deng Xiao-ping had backed them. Deng was dismissed from all of his posts and moved out of his office – for the third time in his career.

As I prepared for work my heart was heavy. I went to the factory after breakfast as usual and arrived in time to find a crowd of people gazing up at the top window. Wang Zhan-zhan's body hung out of it. His kicking legs were up in the air and his waist was held tightly by a pair of arms belonging to someone inside. I was shocked and my breath stuck in my chest. From the same window, six years before, Qian Shou-shan had jumped to his death. Now Wang was trying to do the same. Perhaps because this was the quickest way to die. Instantly. That was the way we all wanted to go if we had to. But Wang was dragged back into the building.

We soon learned that he had been branded a plotting counter-revolutionary and he was taken into detention. All the corridors inside the building were suddenly full of big-character posters denouncing him. Wang knew exactly what all the fuss meant and he did not want to suffer the torment. So at the first opportunity, he had shouted, 'Long live the People', run up the stairs and dived head first out of the window.

His fall was halted by an ex-soldier worker named Lang. Wang had pushed past him in his rush to the window, but just as he dived, Lang leaped forward and grabbed him around the waist. Wang, completely outside the window, struggled to get free while Lang hung on, with his knees pressed up against the wall and his arms around Wang's roly-poly belly. And there they remained for several seconds, Lang inside, grasping Wang, trying to save his life, and Wang outside, cursing his saviour, wanting to die.

When help came, they pulled the furious Wang back into the building. Poor Lang. It was he who had suffered most: his trousers were torn and his knees grazed by the rough wall. He had pulled his back muscles and dislocated a shoulder. All the thanks he got was a tirade of abuse from Wang as he was led away.

I saw Lang a few minutes later. He was being helped by two comrades towards the clinic. I gave a thumbs-up and shouted, 'Great, Lang! You were wonderful!' He nodded, without speaking.

The rest of the slogan group were released from the cowshed and told to report to the political instructor. So was I. He demanded to know the truth. What kind of counter-revolutionary influence had we received from Wang? We might as well tell him, because he already knew the truth anyway. Each of us was taken to a separate room to be interrogated. This, they said, was to prevent us from colluding with one another to make our statements tally. Wang was in detention but the rest of us were allowed to go home at the end of every day when we had completed a satisfactory amount of self-confession and criticism.

The political instructor warned me that if I didn't make a good confession and self-criticism, my future would be affected, but his words had no effect on me. It is hard to remember why I felt no fear. The 5.16 Campaign was still going strong and many innocent people were being tortured and persecuted.

'I went to help Wang because I considered he was acting from true revolutionary motives,' I said to the political instructor. 'He did what he did out of love for Premier Zhou. So did I, and we did nothing wrong.' I reminded him that he himself had declared his love and admiration for Premier Zhou and therefore if I was wrong, how could he be right?

I could see my words going home, and the man's sudden realization that he, too, might be taken into detention and questioned. I could almost see his brain counting up the times he had praised our premier recently, and fear showed in his eyes. We both knew he could threaten me no longer. He left the room, saying I should think over my situation. I was left there alone until five in the afternoon when I was allowed to go home. I did not confess a word. Every morning, I was escorted to that room and told to write my confession and self-criticism on paper they left for me. I didn't. Every evening I went home to cook and clean. My husband was not a supporter of Jiang Qing so he kept silent. This went on for seventeen days. During that brief time I was ice-cold calm and at peace with myself in a way I had never been before.

Without my confession, they could do nothing to me. The end, when it came, was an anti-climax. One morning there was no escort waiting for me, just the political instructor. He took me into his office and asked me to sit down. I knew I was no longer in trouble. He explained that I was not the same as the intellectuals. I was not politically mature and I had been used by them because I was young and naïve. By now I was twenty-seven and married with a young baby, so I felt flattered that they thought of me as 'young'. In fact, the factory leaders were going through a face-saving exercise and this was their way out of a difficult situation, which they hoped would be accepted by their city bosses. I was told to report back to my work unit. I heard later that the others had all written confessions and were kept in detention. It was several months before they were released and sent back to work. None was condemned except Wang Zhan-zhan.

In July 1976, I learned that Jiangsu Foreign Trade Bureau was looking for people who understood English. Along with every other important academic subject, English had been banned from middle-school education for so many years that there were few who spoke it. Those who had been taught English prior to the Cultural Revolution had been dispersed in the countryside, or had escaped to the army. There were few like me who could read and write it with any confidence.

There were fifty vacancies and the Foreign Trade Bureau sent recruiters out and about in the country areas looking for former middle-school students to fill them. Whenever they tested a promising candidate, they found that, after years of hard labour without academic stimulation, he or she had forgotten almost everything they had been taught. The recruiters saw thousands, but found only forty-two who were anywhere near the required standard. By now, the Old Three Grades were about my age or older: late twenties to early thirties. All had remained single because the policy was that once they were married they would lose all chance of getting back to the cities or entering university. The forty-two lucky recruits were sent on an English-language refresher course before they were assigned to work in one of the many burgeoning State-owned import-export companies.

By the time I heard about it, there were still eight vacancies, so I decided to try my luck. The name of the Bureau leader was Xie Jin-sheng, and I wrote to him. After he had checked and approved my political background, he arranged to test me.

I was called away from my workplace and told to report to a Zhang Zhi-wei. He asked me to sit at a desk and then he handed me an English business letter written by a customer in London. 'Please read this out in English for me, Comrade Gao,' he said. I did, with a few hesitations over the unfamiliar names of some chemicals. Then he asked me to tell him the meaning of what I had just read, which I did.

'Can you analyse the grammar?' he asked, in English. His nodding head told me how well I did. 'Why do you want to join the Foreign Trade Bureau?' he asked.

'Our country needs proletarian foreign-language interpreters if we are to be successful in world trade,' I improvised. 'I am a true proletarian member of the working class and I feel I can make a bigger contribution to the prosperity of China and the needs of the Cultural Revolution than I am doing in my present place of work . . .' On and on I went, spouting all the usual platitudes.

Eventually Zhang smiled. 'I know exactly what you mean!' he said, with a chuckle. We chatted for a while longer until my interview came to a natural conclusion. We had said not one politically dangerous word but understood each other perfectly.

That evening, unable to wait any longer, I telephoned the Bureau to ask how I had got on. I was told that my test result was very good and that Zhang had said in his report that I more than fulfilled the criteria required. The personnel department had been asked to try to arrange for me to be transferred to Jiangsu Foreign Trade.

However, another problem arose. I was a worker, not an intellectual. And, according to the peculiar system of different areas of work in China, all workers belonged to the labour-force department and all intellectuals were run by the cadre department. Nobody was allowed to cross between the two.

At that time, I was a lowly grade-two worker, and usually it was impossible for a worker to become a cadre, unless he or she had a special skill. Therefore, when Mao said the working class was the leading class, he deliberately misled them to keep them happy: in fact, the workers could never occupy leading positions. A worker was, and still is, kept in the lowest social and financial status in China.

I tried talking to the personnel bureau of Jiangsu Province about my possible transfer, but they refused even to discuss it and dismissed me rudely. The Chinese people had become ever more suspicious of strangers during the Mao years. Kindness and courtesy had been replaced by aggression and hostility. And government employees behaved nothing like civil servants: they were rude, arrogant and unhelpful to anyone they thought they could bully. I was intimidated and made to feel small before I left.

For several days I felt sick at heart. Then, one morning, my trivial problem was brought into sharp perspective, and I realized just how lucky I really was.

On the 28 July 1976 early-morning news, the announcer blurted out the terrible news of one of the strongest earthquakes to hit China. It read 8.3 on the Richter scale and in a few seconds Tangshan City in Hebei Province had been demolished. Suddenly 240,000 people had died, more than 400,000 were badly injured and thousands of homes had gone. Over a million more people died under the rubble or were never accounted for.

A few days later, the first of thousands of broken people from the stricken area began to arrive in every big city, including Nanjing. The army had already erected enormous tents in the grounds of all the hospitals, each of which could accommodate up to three hundred people. Those arriving had endured days of rough travelling and many had died on the way. Many more were to die during the next week or so, but also thousands of lives were saved. The most pitiful sight was the hundreds of tiny babies who had survived the earthquake and were now orphaned. They ended up in orphanages throughout China, never knowing who their parents were.

On the day of the earthquake, my workshop boss had just had an operation for gallstones, and because he had always been good to me, especially during my 'slogan' period, I visited him in hospital. I found him in one of the big tents with some of the casualties from Tangshan. All the patients had been moved from the main building because the authorities feared an earthquake in Nanjing too. He was in a noisy, hot, uncomfortable section. It was high summer, and that day the temperature rose to 38 degrees centigrade. No air-conditioning, of course, so the tent was like a food steamer. It stank of urine, faeces and medicine. Healthy people found it unbearable and left after a short while, but the sick just had to put up with it.

We heard a rumour that the International Red Cross had offered to send an experienced investigation team to help with the search for survivors, plus doctors, nurses and badly needed medical equipment, but Mao's wife, Jiang Qing, said, 'No! We will not allow any imperialist to see our ruined city. We don't want capitalist charity!' So no foreigner was allowed into China to help the people of Tangshan, which resulted in tens of thousands of unnecessary deaths due to lack of suitable equipment and medical attention.

In Tangshan the corpses piled up. The army collected the dead and buried them in huge bulldozed pits, but hundreds of thousands of people were trapped under the rubble. Tangshan became one huge rotting, stinking pesthole under the hot sun, which caused even more deaths from disease.

Jiang Qing's attitude proved to me, and probably to millions like me, that in the eyes of our rulers, the lives of the people were of no interest. During August and all through September, most of the population of China slept out in the open. In Nanjing, every park, playground, side-street and courtyard filled up at dusk with people carrying their bedding, emergency supplies and, if they had it, plastic sheeting to make a simple tent. People even found their way into the underground tunnels that had been dug in readiness for the 'Third World War'. Although I witnessed the nightly exodus from our block, I slept inside, because I remembered a geography teacher telling us at middle school that Nanjing was not situated in an earthquake area.

I had stopped cursing my bad luck at not being able to change my job, because I now knew thousands of people were far worse off than me, but I never stopped trying to think of ways to make it happen. It became clear that the only way was for me to go through the back door. I contacted Liu Lin, who had once been a friend of our family. He had been a fellow comrade-in-arms during the 1940s and 1950s. By 1976 he had survived a long period of cowshed victimization before being released to take up his present position of second Party secretary of Jiangsu Province.

Liu Lin had aged considerably since I had last seen him, but his bright, twinkling eyes were just the same. I had grown from a little girl to a woman, yet he greeted me with as much warmth as if we had parted just the day before. He had always been kind to us children: in those days he told us enchanting stories whenever he visited our home, and we had liked him. I told him some of what had happened to me, carefully relating only the official version of why I had left the army, and what had happened since. Then I got to the reason for my visit: my desire to work in foreign trade so that I could use my English. I said I wanted to make a more positive contribution to my country at a time when China needed interpreters of good family origin. I told him of my difficulties in making the transfer from worker to cadre. Liu nodded and said he would talk to the personnel bureau.

Two weeks later a formal notice of my transfer arrived. The Jiangsu Provincial Personnel Bureau had accepted me at Liu's suggestion because some worker Rebels were now employed in government offices, under the title 'using a worker instead of a cadre'. Apparently it was a 'new socialist emerging thing', or so it said in the transfer notice. In other words they had found a way round the rules – not that I cared on the day I reported for work at 50 Zhonghua Road, Nanjing. I was assigned to work as an English interpreter in the chemicals and pharmaceutical department of Sinochem of Jiangsu Province. Unfortunately I was going to do the work of a cadre while only getting my grade-two worker salary. It didn't seem fair.

19. Foreign Trade

Sinochem occupied half of the second floor of a fairly new four-storey building, and my desk was near a window overlooking a busy thorough-fare. When I had little to do, or if I was ever searching for inspiration, I liked to look out of the window at the stuttering movements of the traffic and the tangled paths of the people.

I was met by the same Zhang Zhi-wei who had given me my English test. We shook hands, a very civilized thing to do, but it was not yet common practice in China for a man to greet a woman in that way. Usually it was just a nod and perhaps a smile. However, Sinochem did business with foreigners, who shook hands with men and women, so it had become the custom in the Sinochem offices too. 'Welcome, welcome,' he said, smiling warmly. 'Come, let me introduce you to everyone here.'

First there was the section chief, Xu, a fat man with a smiling face and a keen eye for business. He greeted me by lifting a big coffee jar filled with green tea and drinking from it. The shape of the jar showed that it was a foreign one, and it looked luxurious to me. At that time foreign goods were rare in China, so a simple thing like this coffee jar was a real status symbol. I had never seen anything like it before. As a section chief, Xu spent a lot of his time with visiting foreign business people and he must have been given the jar, full of coffee, as a gift. Compared to the green tea we normally drank, coffee was expensive and not widely available until the late 1980s. Xu was the only person in the whole building at that time to own a foreign coffee jar, so everyone admired him. Most of us used Chinese pickle jars.

Office work was comfortable, relaxed and congenial. Because foreign trade with China was still in its infancy, most of our working time was spent drinking tea, chatting or reading a newspaper. Sometimes we even went shopping during office hours. The lunch hour was, more often than not, two hours, and three in high summer. We played Chinese chess and cards during our breaks.

Home was where I worked hard. After the slogan episode, my husband did nothing to help me and had started to beat me again. Yet he was proud of my success, because that gave him good face.

I went to work from Monday to Saturday, stopping on my way home only to do some shopping. Sundays were always busy. I had to do the weekly pile of laundry by hand, clean the flat while the clothes were drying, then do the ironing with an old-fashioned flat-iron, which I heated on the gas ring. Add cooking, Little Yan, a good beating followed by near rape, and you can imagine exactly what my Sundays were like. Fortunately I had six days to get over one, and prepare for the next.

Two weeks after I started working for Sinochem, I was told I must go to Guangzhou, in the south-east of the country. I was to join up with a group of other employees being sent there for six weeks to help make ready the huge exhibition building for the official opening of the Chinese Export Commodities Fair on 15 October. Then I would attend the fair for a month.

I was excited at the prospect. I would miss Little Yan, but I would be away from my husband for ten weeks, I would come face to face for the first time with foreigners ('big-noses', we called them) and talk to them in English. My husband hated the idea of me being out of his control for such a long time. With foreigners no less!

There were no passenger aircraft flying from Nanjing to Guangzhou in those days, so I bade Little Yan goodbye and set off by train via Shanghai. It took six hours to travel from Nanjing to Shanghai, and another forty hours from Shanghai to Guangzhou. Sleeping cars were reserved for foreign-trade employees at the time of the fair, which was China's principal window to the outside world, so I felt very superior as I boarded the train and found my compartment. If I had been like all the ordinary passengers, I would have had to sit on a hard wooden seat – or, worse, stand – for almost two days to get to my destination.

I arrived in Guangzhou on 28 August 1976 and met the other Sinochem staff. Every morning we twelve, with about a hundred others from different companies, gathered in front of the fair building. It was guarded all year round and the ordinary people were never allowed in. Only foreigners and pass-holding Chinese working in foreign trade could enter.

The entrance hall of the main building was wide and cavernous. Directly in front of us was the Great Hall exhibiting the works of Marx, Engels, Lenin, Stalin and Mao. The rest of the ground floor and three upper floors housed the stands of all the different chemical and pharmaceutical delegations. There were six more buildings, all four floors high and just as big as ours, which housed hundreds more stands to be used by other exporters of engineering, textiles, fancy goods, mining and goodness-knows-what-else. The seven buildings were linked together by covered walkways, and the whole complex, including the surrounding car-parks and gardens, must have covered at least a square kilometre.

I gasped with astonishment the first time I walked into one of the halls. I felt like an ant in a shoebox. The sun was streaming in through the almost wall-to-wall windows, and the gaily decorated stalls waited in long rows.

Everywhere arrows pointed in all directions with words written in Chinese and English: Chemicals, Foodstuffs, Ceramics, Textiles, Machinery, Light Industry, Native Produce, Minerals, Arts and Crafts, Birds and Flowers, Fancy Goods . . . this way, that way, up, down. There were restaurants, a splendid cinema, with bright red carpet, meeting rooms, an enormous shopping centre, studios for radio and television interviews and a photographic studio. I was overawed, and felt a surge of patriotism – something I hadn't experienced for many years. Everything at the fair exuded luxury, compared with the drabness of normal daily life.

It took us the whole morning to visit every hall and I was glad of a rest during lunch because my feet ached. I realized that if I was going to be at the fair for ten weeks, I had to get a pair of comfortable shoes. We started work in the afternoon. I was surprised at how much there was to do, and understood now why we had been sent ahead so far in advance of the opening date. Slowly our hall began to take shape. The job was scheduled to be finished in a month, and it seemed as if it would take us all of that time to complete our task. We threw away the old samples from a previous exhibition, except for the fish-liver-oil capsules, the vitamin tablets and the tubs of royal jelly: they had been on the shelves for six months but that didn't stop us distributing them among ourselves. Each of us got a large bag for nothing.

On the afternoon of the twelfth day, we were told to tune in the radio at three o'clock for an important broadcast. We all stopped work, and crowded nervously around the radio with the faint hope we would hear some cheerful news. Instead we heard some sad, frightening, wonderful, terrible, glorious, disastrous news. At one o'clock on the morning of 9 September, our great leader Chairman Mao Tse-tung had died at the age of eighty-three. After the announcement, a eulogy was read then funeral music played. For one and a half hours, we listened to the same broadcast, repeated continually. As the minutes ticked away, I felt elation rise up in me, coupled with acute anxiety at the thought that Mao's monster of a wife might take his place.

Mao's state funeral and memorial meeting were held on 15 September. The principal meeting place was Tiananmen Square, but other meetings were held in every city, town and village across China. They began promptly at three o'clock but the Chairman Mao Funeral and Memorial Meeting Committee ordered that everyone must be in their appointed place before noon that day.

In Guangzhou, the leaders decided to use the local sports stadium. September is usually very hot, and that day the noon temperature in Beijing reached about 35 degrees centigrade. In Guangzhou, it was even hotter, 39 degrees. Nothing unusual for that time of year, just a bad day to hold a state funeral. Further north and west of Beijing it was hot, humid and wet. All over China people had to stand for hours under the burning sun or in pouring rain. We heard later that thousands of mourners collapsed because of the unbearable strain of standing motionless to attention for such a long time. Sunstroke affected thousands more, who vomited where they stood. I say 'mourners', but unlike the day when Premier Zhou was cremated, most of those attending the Mao meetings were not there by choice: they had been ordered to go. It was a great political task, and anyone who failed to attend would have been punished severely.

I was lucky because everyone working in the fair building was ordered to gather in the cinema. It was much better than standing outside. We were herded in long before noon and told to stand bare-headed and stiffly to attention. After about half an hour, I began to feel dizzy. Ten minutes later I wanted to sit down and rest, but it was not allowed. I could feel the edge of a seat pressing into the back of my legs, but I dared not sit down. I could only put my hands on the back of the chair in front of me and take some of my weight on my arms, which helped a little. Time seemed to have stopped and soon I ached all over. Other people experienced the same pain, as they said later. Several old men and women fainted and were dragged out by their feet.

I was about at the end of my strength and ready to sink to the floor when the voice of Wang Hong-wen boomed out of the loudspeakers. He had been the leader of the Shanghai January Storm Rebel Faction in 1967, and had been the first Rebel to wrest power from the local-government leaders, to be followed by Rebels all over China. Chairman Mao had made Wang his deputy, so now he was presiding over the state funeral. I can't remember what he said. I spent my time praying for the meeting to be over but it went on and on. As soon as I got back to the hotel I fell into bed. The next day I had an attack of Menière's disease, and spent the next few days in darkness.

The preparations for the 1976 Autumn Guangzhou Fair were finished several days ahead of schedule, so the Sinochem group were taken sightseeing. We went by minibus to the city of Zhaoqin, some two hundred kilometres away. We wanted to see the beautiful mountains and lakes there. Everybody had been in high spirits since the death of Mao and gasped at the sight of the famous Seven Star Rock reflected in the waters of the lake. It was like my idea of fairyland.

That day was magical. We climbed the hills, rowed boats on the lake and gazed down into the clear depths, seeing big fish swimming far below us. We sat in the shade of the tall trees on a carpet of wild flowers and enjoyed a picnic. Tourists were there from Hong Kong and other parts of China too, and the air was filled with the sound of laughter. There was no sign of sadness at the loss of Mao. We came back refreshed and happy.

While we were waiting for the fair to open we heard that Mao's wife and the Gang of Four had been arrested on 6 October. The good news spread far and wide. The whole country buzzed with jubilation. The shops sold out of wine in no time as people celebrated her downfall. The Chinese people felt as if they had been liberated for a second time from the old society. China was one big party as the people celebrated by laughing, singing, dancing and crying tears of joy. Because now they had hope. Everyone who had been thrown into prison by the gang could be released. Those who had been unjustly branded counter-revolutionaries could be pardoned. Life would be good again! Nasty stories started circulating about Jiang Qing. 'Jiang Qing has slept with more than fifty men.' 'She wears a French wig and has a false hip.' 'She wet her knickers when her hands were put into handcuffs.' The more exaggerated the tales, the more the ordinary people enjoyed them.

The Autumn Fair was due to open on 15 October, but it was put back a day because the city leaders decided to hold a celebration parade. By this time, most of the foreign businessmen had already arrived in Guangzhou and were told that the official opening of the fair had been delayed. Firecrackers exploded everywhere. Ten long strings of about a thousand export-quality ones were hanging from the roofs of each of the fair buildings. As we marched by, they were set off, one building at a time, to coincide with the passing of the parade. The noise was deafening, and the sparks dazzled my eyes. A stranger might have thought that China had been liberated from a foreign invader instead of just five Chinese people. Because, no matter what the leaders said, we thought of the Gang of Four as really a Gang of Five, headed by Mao.

When the Autumn Fair opened I had my first opportunity to speak to a foreigner. Before that could happen, though, our pricing priorities were spelled out to us. Pakistan was to be given the most favourable terms because the Pakistani government had held Chairman Mao in such high esteem. Last on the list were the British and the Americans.

At exactly nine a.m. the marching tune of 'Five Star Red Flag' blared out from the loudspeakers and the doors opened. I was wearing my best clothes: a new navy-blue worsted army-style uniform jacket, made especially for attending the fair, and my best khaki trousers. For more than six years since leaving the army I had worn my old uniforms. Due to our tiny wages, my husband had never allowed me to spend anything on new clothes for myself although he spent a big chunk of our joint income on cigarettes and alcohol. My attendance at the Guangzhou Fair would give him big face – but not if I had to wear my usual shabby clothes. He gave me the money to buy the material and have the jacket made by a local tailor. I wore these clothes every day, washing them every Saturday evening, paying particular attention to the jacket.

I bought myself a pair of second-hand flat leather shoes with my travel subsidy from Sinochem. Like all the other Chinese women attending the fair, I had my hair cut to ear level to look 'revolutionary'. No makeup, of course: at that time women never gave a thought to such things as lipstick and powder. Any female caught trying to improve her looks or showing the slightest vanity would be accused of being under bourgeois influence and criticized. I had no idea then that, within a few years, it would become fashionable for women to look feminine again.

We stood in lines in the huge entrance hall, waiting to greet our guests. I stared at these strange-looking men in their western-style dark business suits, white shirts and colourful ties. They had funny-shaped faces with round eyes. And they really did have big noses! They had come from all over the world, and yet, apart from their different-coloured complexions, they looked the same to me. I nudged Zhang, who was standing beside me. 'How can we tell the difference between the Americans, the British, the French or the Germans?'

He smiled and whispered, 'Don't worry, you will soon recognize the differences.'

Every visitor was given an English version of *The Little Red Book* and through an interpreter each person was asked to read a few paragraphs from the book before being allowed to enter the discussion rooms. The Japanese were the most cunning: some carried as many as four volumes of the *Selected Works* of Chairman Mao under their arm, pretending that they were the most friendly towards China. In this way, they hoped to get the best prices. And they did – because our leaders had been told that if any of these foreign visitors showed respect and friendship to China by praising Chairman Mao, we should sell our goods to them at low prices. Even if we didn't cover our own costs, we had to show our friendship in return.

A girl working at the Dong Fang (East) Hotel, where many of the foreign visitors stayed, told me that 90 per cent of the businessmen threw *The Little Red Book* into the wastebin before they checked out. But others were smarter. One Englishman I got to know during my first Guangzhou Fair returned year in, year out, carrying the same copy he had been given in 1976. He told me it looked so well used that the Chinese were convinced he continually read from it. In this way, he always managed to get the best prices from his Chinese suppliers.

I met people of all nationalities and in time could tell the difference between them. At first it seemed strange to be face to face with these US imperialists and their running dogs, whom we had condemned as the 'rubbish we Chinese must sweep into the dustbin of history'. Now I was doing business with them, and they had become our distinguished guests and the saviours of China! But they were not trusted. I was told later that every one of the foreigners was followed by our secret police everywhere they went, twenty-four hours a day.

Everybody, whatever country they were from, was requested to speak English, so for the month I was at the fair I was surrounded by the capitalist culture. I seemed to fit comfortably into it. Honesty was not required by our leaders in doing business. If we had to lie and cheat to get an order, then that was what was expected of us. Finding excuses for delayed delivery dates, poor quality and broken promises was part of the game. Whoever did the best cheating was usually praised for their good negotiating skills.

Our section chief Xu was considered one of the best negotiators because his brain was quick and he could always find an immediate answer to hide our shortcomings on previous orders. As he was fat and had a big belly, our foreign clients assumed that he was a big boss and went to him to complain rather than to our real leader. Many things were listed in our export catalogue that were not available and the most commonly used excuse for the shortage was the big earthquake that had happened just three months previously in Tangshan. Other items were deliberately shown as being in short supply. This helped to keep the prices up and give the buyer a sense of importance when Xu winked and said he could lay his hands on whatever was wanted.

Things went well for us at the fair and we exceeded our sales target. We were to make substantial profits at each fair over the next four years. However, over 80 per cent of the profits had to be handed over to the State. Without that Shanghai would have become a rich city and Jiangsu Province would have been a nice place to live, but any spare cash went to Beijing. Everything was controlled by the Central Party Committee.

In October 1978, when Little Yan was three, I sent her to a boarding nursery. I delivered her there every Monday morning before work, and collected her on Saturday evenings on my way home. I was also able to get my husband Lin transferred from his factory to foreign trade. Thus, he too became a 'worker doing a cadre's job' like me, and life became easier for us.

Up to 1980, my salary as a grade-two worker remained the same, until news came from Beijing that the salaries of 40 per cent of the workers in China would be increased as they were to be promoted to the next grade. To qualify, each person must have a work record of more than ten years. As I had joined the PLA in 1968 and had worked for the country ever since, I qualified with over twelve years of proven work record, which meant I could be promoted to grade three. I was still not a cadre but at least my salary would be increased by 2.5 yuan a month (about 20p). Not a lot, but as I had not had a salary increase for ten years, it was welcome. Lin was in the same position, so we looked forward to a small improvement in our lifestyle.

But it was not quite as simple as that. A list of names was printed of everybody in our company and we were all given a copy. Each of us was asked to tick the names of those we thought deserving of a wage increase. After the first round, about half the names disappeared from the list. Most of the early losers didn't qualify, so there was no damage done, but then we had to tick again to get rid of another 10 per cent. There were still too many people on the list. A check was made to see if all the remaining names qualified for the increase. They did, and my name was there. It was a big problem, and the final decision was left to the company managers. Of course, they could omit those whom they disliked most. For them it was a good chance to take their revenge.

In China, the relationship with your boss was, and still is, the most important factor in your working life. No matter how capable and good at your job you might be, if you have offended your boss at some time, even unintentionally, he can make your working life a misery – for ever, if he so wishes. We call it 'forcing people to wear small shoes', which means he can stop you making progress in the company. On the other hand, if you are a favourite, no matter how bad your work you can get everything: the best job and quick promotion is yours. The company was electric with tension. Everyone on the list had their supporters, and we all waited anxiously to see if we would be omitted.

There were two men and a woman in our company who had graduated together and had exactly the same qualifications for a pay increase. Two of the three were scratched off the list to comply with the 40 per cent rule. Their male manager liked the girl, so he 'persuaded' the two men to agree to have their names deleted. Then the same manager omitted another man he disliked, which made the numbers right. So I got my increase. Naturally, the men who had lost their chance had to keep quiet in case they were given 'smaller shoes'.

Things did not go smoothly in other companies. We heard quite a few stories about people coming to violent blows over the 40 per cent. In some factories many of the women workers cried all day long, insisting that they qualified. When the final list was released, quite a number committed suicide when their names weren't on it. They could not face another ten years without a pay-rise. The 40 per cent rule was bad: it resulted in hatred and jealousies among the workers, which never went away.

20. The English Language Centre

Early in 1980 the Chinese government, with Deng Xiao-ping in control, decided to speed up the economic recovery of China by inviting foreign investment. Joint-venture enterprises, funded by foreign money and run by a partnership of foreign and Chinese management, were considered the best way forward. Many high-level business negotiations began in Beijing and other big cities but progress was slow due to an acute shortage of English interpreters.

As the ordinary Chinese people got to know more about life in the West (or their concept of it), they began to worship everything western. After so many political upheavals, they were beginning to realize just how gullible they had been. They had allowed Mao, through his never-ending campaigns and the Cultural Revolution, to trick them into fighting, killing and persecuting each other. Now the truth was clear: China was not the Utopia they had been led to believe it was. The workers in the West had not been exploited by their governments in the way we had been exploited by ours. We now knew we had been told one big lie. The West was decades ahead of China technologically and its economies were far more affluent. The average Chinese thought of all western foreigners as millionaires.

It is easy to understand how such a misconception came about. A foreigner in China could not speak our language or work out the money, so it was easier for him to offer large-denomination banknotes to pay for things rather than to figure out the actual price. It wouldn't be long before he had a wodge of small-value notes and a pocketful of coins, which gave the impression to the Chinese that every foreigner had unlimited amounts of money. Also, a westerner always exuded an air of confidence. He or she was better dressed and groomed than even the highest Chinese leader, so it was no wonder that every big-nose was thought wealthy. Many Chinese, old and young, tried every possible way to get out of China to any western country, with the USA as the favourite.

In May 1980, to help China train good English interpreters, the United Nations sent a team of American teachers to open an English language centre in Beijing. It planned to recruit two hundred people from all over China and from every stratum of society. They were looking for those with a degree in English or more than three years' experience in using the language. This was a wonderful opportunity. The enrolment-requirement bulletin was put on the wall of our office building. I thought I fulfilled all the requirements, so I applied to take the entrance examination. If I can't go abroad, let abroad come to me, I reasoned. A foreign education would earn me more respect and open up opportunities for promotion. It would change my life for ever, so I was delighted to be told that my name had been included in the list of fifty applicants from Jiangsu Foreign Trade. These were sent to the Ministry of Foreign Trade in Beijing to be checked, and fifteen names were deleted from the list. They were middle-school graduates and were not qualified to take the entrance examination. Apparently I was the only worker applicant and, as I had no degree, my name was in danger of being deleted too. Luckily, my good work in Guangzhou was taken into consideration and I was allowed to take the entrance examination.

The exam was held in the ten biggest cities on the same day, 5 August 1980. In Nanjing, about one hundred and fifty of us trooped into the examination hall. Two invigilators had already checked our pockets and bags for anything that might help us. I was amazed at how many bits and pieces were confiscated.

The examination papers had been carried by two special couriers from Los Angeles to Beijing and sent out to the various cities in the official mail, which nobody dared tamper with. They had been put into one big envelope, then in another and sealed finally with red sealing wax, to ensure that the papers were kept secret until they were opened in front of us and handed out. I took mine and looked at the front page. It was blank. No help there. When we had all settled, with pens ready, at exactly nine o'clock in the morning, we were told to begin. I settled down to do my best.

One month later I received a letter. My hands were shaking and my tummy fluttered as I tore open the envelope. When I had read the contents, I flopped down on a stool, drained of all strength. 'I'm in!' I squeaked. 'I passed the exam!'

The whole section was overjoyed for me. Only twenty-two of the hundred and fifty Nanjing applicants had been accepted, and I was the only one without a degree. I had come third with a score of 559. I was asked to pay a 200-yuan tuition fee – five months' salary, which I could not possibly afford, and a huge lump of disappointment filled my throat. However, Xu had been given great face for having had the foresight to employ me in the first place, so he suggested to the company that as I had been the only one from Sinochem Jiangsu to pass the examination, they should pay it. And that is what happened. Not only did Xu do that for me, he also arranged for a banquet in my honour to be held in the Xuanwu Lake Park Restaurant, one of the best in Nanjing, the day before I boarded the train for Beijing on 10 September 1980.

Three days later, the two hundred lucky students from all over China came together for the first time at the language centre. It was located in the western suburb of Beijing, in an old cadre school. To me it looked like an army camp. The huts were the same, and so were the dining halls. We were divided into three levels according to our entrance examination scores. I was in Level C and shared a hut with eleven other girls. Directly opposite our hut was the school, and just to the right stood the dining hall we students used. We had been issued with food coupons to cover all our meals. There was plenty of hot water to bath or shower every day if we wished, so we wanted for nothing. The American teachers always had lunch with us. They loved Chinese food, they said, and it was so incredibly cheap!

Mr Taylor and his colleagues were excellent teachers, and I enjoyed all the classes. From Mr Taylor we learned the complex political structure in America, and how the country had developed from the first settlers to the present day. He gave us an in-depth understanding of its finance, religion and education. He was honest about his country's shortcomings, telling us about the depression and America's race problems. Our homework was to write a diary every day, comparing the cultural differences between China and the USA.

The Americans brought some of their western habits with them – for example, they only worked five days a week, from nine in the morning to four thirty p.m. Mondays to Fridays. In China we normally worked six days, so we students enjoyed an extra day off. The Americans arrived and left in a luxurious coach and hated to walk anywhere. Sometimes they invited a few of us to dinner and took us to their hotel in a coach. There, we would have dinner in one of the hotel restaurants, paid for by our hosts. They explained that for them the cost of such a dinner was only a fraction of what the same thing would cost in America. Now not only did I dream of one day going to Britain, I also wanted to visit the USA.

In October, I heard that an international trade fair was being held in the Beijing Exhibition Hall, so one Saturday I decided to go and have a look. It was similar to the Guangzhou fair but on a smaller scale. I paused at many stalls: Japan, France, Germany, Holland. I then spied the British flag, which looks exactly like the Chinese character for 'rice', and headed towards it.

At first I saw nothing unusual in the pictures hanging around the walls, until I came to a familiar face looking out of a framed photograph. I couldn't remember exactly where I had seen those eyes before. Then, with a jolt, the memory hit me. 'Sofia!'

There was no doubting it. The lady was older, but just as beautiful as she had been in the photograph Sofia had given me all those years ago when we had said goodbye in Shanghai. It all seemed such a long time ago, yet it could have happened yesterday. This film star seemed just as graceful, kind and sincere to me in 1980 as she had in 1963. My only regret was that I had forgotten to remove her picture from my wardrobe before returning it to the government warehouse in Nanjing. I leaned forward to read the words beneath the photograph: 'Her Majesty Queen Elizabeth II'. I was stunned.

'Can I help you?' From behind me, a cultured English voice interrupted my reverie. Flustered, I shook my head and gathered up a handful of literature before hurrying away. Later, on the train, I shivered at the thought of what could have happened to me if I had been discovered hiding a picture of the Queen of Britain – monarch of the number-one running dog of the US imperialists!

On 20 November, historic events claimed our attention. Every student was instructed to watch the evening television news, which contained a full report on the first day of the public trial of the Lin Biao Clique and the Gang of Four, headed by Jiang Qing. The trial was held before a special supreme court. The Chinese leaders were very clever to combine the two groups in one trial; in this way, they hoped to keep the name of Mao Tse-tung out of the proceedings.

Most of the defendants pleaded guilty to the charges of falsely imprisoning Party leaders, persecuting large numbers of people, plotting to assassinate Mao and plotting armed rebellions. All except Jiang Qing and Zhang Chun-qiao asked for leniency. Jiang Qing shouted revolutionary slogans and claimed that she had only been implementing Mao's policies and following his orders. Zhang Chun-qiao remained silent. Whenever the name of Mao came up, the proceedings were halted to allow the prosecutors time to change the direction of the hearings. Eventually the court ruled that many of the Gang's crimes had been committed without Mao's knowledge: the most vicious criminal of all was exonerated.

Two months later, the television showed the Gang being sentenced. We expected justice to be done and to see them being taken out that same day and shot. We were disappointed. Jiang Qing and Zhang Chun-qiao were sentenced to death with a two-year probation period, which effectively meant that they would never be shot. The rest received long prison sentences.

We were indignant: there had been not a single ordinary person in China who had escaped suffering during the Cultural Revolution, and we were watching those responsible getting away with it. The law in China was, and is, perfectly clear: if a person is found guilty of just one murder, the punishment is death by shooting. Jiang Qing had been responsible for the murder of millions yet she was spared. We wanted the whole lot of them dead and gone, but it wasn't to be. In the end, the Party had saved itself from destruction by looking after its own.

We students of Level C completed the course at the end of November, and everybody received a report and a certificate. Mr Taylor told us five scholarships were to be awarded to attend a top university in the USA but he had no idea who would get them. Unfortunately they were controlled by the Beijing authorities, so no matter how well we had done in the language centre, we had no chance of winning one. They would be reserved for back-door children, whether they were good at English or not.

I had enjoyed my time with the American teachers and before I left to return to my husband and daughter in Nanjing I went to each in turn and thanked them for everything they had done for me. Mr Taylor and his wife gave me a tin of biscuits for my daughter. But the real gift from the Americans was the doors they opened for me: after seeing my certificate, the personnel bureau of Jiangsu Province promoted me. A written notice with an official government stamp on it was sent to Sinochem confirming my promotion to a grade twenty-three cadre. With it were instructions that I was to be treated as if I was a college graduate. At last I had managed to go part of the way towards fulfilling my mother's dream for me.

That was the good news. The bad was that my home life became worse than ever. My husband was even more of a tyrant. Looking back, it is obvious to me now that he was jealous of my success. He constantly lost his temper and beat me unmercifully for up to half an hour at a time with anything he could lay his hands on. My body was constantly black and blue with the marks of shoes, sticks, his umbrella and cooking implements.

I could not think of divorce, because my mother-in-law was a leader and would persuade the authorities to blame me for the breakdown of the marriage. In fact, she once told me she would say I was a bad, disobedient wife, even an adulteress. Life was a mixture of good at work and bad at home. But even at home there was my beacon of happiness: Little Yan. I had her transferred from the boarding nursery to a daily kindergarten so that she and I could spend more time together. Every morning, from Monday to Saturday, we went out hand in hand, she to her kindergarten and me to work. Every evening we walked back again, having fun as we shopped for our supper.

In April 1981 I received a telegram from Andong to say she would be arriving in Nanjing the following Sunday, and would I meet her at the railway station. I was so excited; eleven years had passed since we said goodbye when she left for Inner Mongolia. Also, I had been worried about her. She had always written, regularly as clockwork, one letter a week, all through the years, until the last few months, when sometimes there would be no letter for two or three weeks, or I received several at once. Her writing was strange too. Sometimes a letter arrived full of crazy ramblings, but the next few would seem perfectly normal.

My husband forbade me to go and meet her. He had never forgotten the letter in which Andong had said he was not suitable to be my husband. (How right she had been!) This time, I was not prepared to obey his orders.

It was a lovely sunny spring morning the day Andong was due to arrive in Nanjing. I told Lin I must go to meet her and bring her home, otherwise she would never find her way. He roared at me and pushed me into the bedroom. But the moment his back was turned I fled from the flat. I ran through the front door, down the stairs and headed for the bus stop. Lin ran after me and gave me a couple of hard punches to my chest, one on each breast. I stood my ground and, with the help of a woman who had seen everything, I got on the bus and away to the railway station.

I arrived early and had to wait half an hour for the train to chug along the platform and roll slowly to a stop. I peered over the barrier, anxious for my first glimpse of Andong. And suddenly there she was, hurrying along the crowded platform, holding the hand of her nine-year-old daughter. I waved wildly and she waved back. In a minute we were embracing. I turned to my niece and gave her a huge hug too. The three of us walked happily out of the station towards the bus stop.

Andong looked much older, and her exile had not gone well with her. I could see the hard life she had lived in every line on her face. Happily, her smile was the same, and her love for me still shone out of her beautiful eyes, just as I remembered. She told me she had returned to try to contact some of our parents' old friends. Most of those who had survived the Cultural Revolution had now been released from detention, cleared of all accusations, and reinstated in their old government positions. She was hoping to find someone who could help have her family transferred back to Nanjing.

On our way home, she said she was looking forward to meeting my husband and hoped that she and Zhao Lin could at last be friends. She also admitted that she felt guilty at having written such a bad letter about Lin without first meeting him. I kept silent, although I badly wanted to tell her that her instincts had been right.

Andong told me that she had suffered a great deal in Huhehot. At first she had had no job and her husband was paid a low salary. She did her best not to be a burden to him, because he was a good man and he deserved a good wife. She did all kinds of hard labouring jobs that nobody else wanted, such as pushing a heavy cartload of coal twenty kilometres, which earned her two yuan (about 15p). Zhan, her husband, begged her not to do such things but she would not listen and lost their first child. She became pregnant again three months later. This time she took better care of herself and delivered a daughter without any problems. They named her Zhao-zhao, which means Bright Sunshine.

Eventually, because of her educated background, Andong became a primary-school teacher – some schools in Inner Mongolia remained open during the Cultural Revolution – but both she and her husband missed Nanjing.

When we got home, Andong greeted Lin with a smile, but he said rudely, 'If you want to stay here, you must pay ten yuan per day for your keep.' Immediately Andong pulled her purse from her pocket and took out ten yuan.

Before she could offer it, I put my hand over hers. 'No!' I almost shouted. 'She is my sister, they can stay for as long as they want for nothing.' Lin scowled, and I saw his fists clench. I glared at him defiantly. Then, without thinking, I spat out a scornful 'Pah!' This was just too much for Lin, who lifted his hand and hit me so hard across my face that my ears rang. Then came another blow, and another. He kept hitting me until I fell to the ground. 'Don't you dare disobey me!' he roared, and kicked me.

Little Yan was crying and Zhao-zhao had backed away into a corner. Andong lost her temper. She walked over and stood in front of Lin. 'Who gave you the right to beat up my little sister? Even our mother and father never laid one finger on us children. How dare you do such a thing? You are just a woman-beating bully!'

'You have no say here,' retorted Lin, still angry. 'This is my home and I can do whatever I want in it!'

Andong stood before Lin and poked him in the chest with a stiff finger. 'This is also the home of my sister and my niece, so I do have a say.' Her finger stabbed with each word, forcing Lin to give way. 'You are not a real man! Real men have no need to beat their defenceless wives, and you had better stop *right now!*'

Andong was no match physically for my husband, but where he was a coward, she was brave. She stood there, face to face with him, and they argued until our neighbours came in and got between them. The two girls and I were still huddled together in a corner. Then Andong said to Lin, in front of the neighbours, losing him much face: 'I cannot stay here with a monster like you. I shall go to one of my old classmates where I know I shall be made welcome.' When she left with her daughter, Little Yan and I went with her.

Andong and Zhao-zhao were indeed made welcome by her old classmate called Ming. So were Little Yan and I. We were given a room with one huge bed in it where all four of us could sleep. That evening, as I was washing, Andong saw the hundreds of bruises on my body, including my breasts. At first she was so upset, she cried for me, and insisted on gently rubbing in some balm. 'I cannot ignore this, Little Flower,' she said. 'He must be reported to his company leaders.' I was reluctant because I thought it could only lead to even worse behaviour from him. 'Please don't say anything, Andong. I have grown used to it, and now I hardly notice the pain, except when he hits me here.' I pointed to my swollen blue breasts. I explained that divorce was impossible. Not only would I lose face and the hard-won respect of everyone I knew, I would probably lose Yan too.

Andong wouldn't listen. 'You must have justice,' she whispered sharply, in the quiet of our bedroom. 'And I will get it for you.'

The next morning Andong made me go with her to see Mr Choo, the manager of Lin's company. She showed him some of my bruises, and insisted that my husband be punished. To my astonishment, Mr Choo agreed. 'I cannot abide wife-beaters,' he said, 'but I must admit that I am very surprised to learn this, because your husband seems to be such a nice, quiet man and a good worker too.' Andong reminded Mr Choo that, as Lin was a Party member, he violated the disciplinary code of the Party every time he beat me. Mr Choo nodded. 'Leave this matter in my hands,' he said. 'I will deal with it today.'

He was as good as his word. Lin was ordered first to report to his immediate boss for a reprimand. Then he had to face a much sterner lecture from the company Party secretary. Finally, Mr Choo gave him a severe talking-to. Lin was also ordered to write his self-criticism. All this resulted in him behaving a little better towards me for a while. By this time I loathed everything about him. I dearly wanted to leave him and only stayed for the sake of Little Yan.

After we had seen Mr Choo, I stayed with Andong at her friend's home for another night. We thought it prudent to keep away from Lin. The next morning, Andong told me she had decided to return home to Inner Mongolia. 'I cannot stay here any longer,' she said. 'Though my friends have said I can stay as long as I like, they are very poor and they refuse to take any money. I cannot let them spend any more on Zhao-zhao and me, it wouldn't be fair. I already feel guilty. Your husband has made it impossible for me to stay with you. And I cannot afford a hotel.'

Andong and Zhao-zhao left Nanjing the following day. As she had used all her savings to come, she left with a heavy heart and little hope of coming back. I tried to persuade her to stay longer until something could be done about her transfer, but she refused. We wept together as the bus carried us to the railway station. As I watched the train leaving, I vowed that I would do everything to help her.

21. Changes in My Life

After Andong left I hardly ever spoke to Lin. Every evening after dinner I washed Little Yan and myself and went to bed with her. Lin was writing a novel and was convinced he would be hailed as a great author. He didn't allow any sound to disturb him when he was writing, so he shut the door to the bedroom where Little Yan and I were sleeping and stayed in the other room. Only when he wanted sex did he come and shake me awake. Sleep was impossible for me for the remainder of those nights. So I used to lie awake, planning my escape, but in reality there was nothing I could do. This was the traditional Chinese way, just as the old proverb said: 'A good woman should follow her husband, no matter what his lot in life. Even if he is a chicken or a dog.'

The winter of 1982–3 was hard and cold, and Lin would light a gas fire in the room where he sat writing. On the evening of 19 January, he lit it as usual after Yan and I had gone to bed.

I woke up at about four o'clock needing a pee but decided not to go in case I disturbed Lin. Eventually, an hour or so later, I had to get up. The moment I opened the bedroom door I smelt gas. I ran into the kitchen and opened a window and the flat door, then went into the toilet. Afterwards I switched on the light, which was a stupid thing to do, but I was not thinking properly.

Lin was asleep in his bed, and the gas was coming from the heater. The flames were out, but it hadn't been turned off properly and gas had been leaking into the room for hours. I was coughing now, so I closed the bedroom door to protect Yan from the gas, and went over to Lin. I tried to shake him awake. 'Zhao Lin, wake up. Wake up!' I was frightened. He wouldn't wake up. He couldn't wake up. He was dead.

It was still dark outside as I knocked at the five other doors on our landing, screaming at our neighbours for help. They got up quickly and hurried into our flat. The man who had intervened when Andong and Lin had been quarrelling felt Lin's wrist for a pulse, and then hurried away to telephone the nearest hospital. Nobody answered his call. It was over three hours later, at about eight thirty in the morning, before medical help came. But, of course, Lin was beyond help.

His body was taken to Gulou Hospital, where a doctor confirmed him dead and ordered an immediate post-mortem. I sat on a bench in the long corridor with Little Yan and a couple of women neighbours, to wait for the result. It was as we had expected: Lin had died from carbon-monoxide poisoning. The report said that had he been found half an hour earlier he might have survived. This was a shock: I realized that I could have saved him when I had first woken, if I hadn't been frightened of disturbing him and getting a beating.

I felt a mixture of emotions, which ranged from guilt to anxiety about the future. I regretted all the hours I had spent thinking up ways to get rid of my husband. Perhaps I had even willed his death. I burst into tears. What was I going to do now? I was a widow at the age of thirty-three, and I could see nothing in front of me except years and years of empty struggle and loneliness. Thank goodness for Little Yan. Poor Lin, he had been very young, only thirty-four. And Yan had lost her father. He had been a good father. Suddenly his behaviour towards me seemed unimportant. He had never looked at other women, and Mr Choo said he was a good worker. At one time he had been quite a nice man. His mother was to blame. She had brought him up to be the way he was. I cried harder.

At the age of seven, Yan did not really understand what being dead was, and that her father had gone for ever. She knew something bad had happened, so she cried along with me. We looked like a pair of wet rags when we arrived home, but there was no opportunity for us to wash and change. The leaders of both our companies and many of our friends and my colleagues were waiting to pay their respects and express their condolences. I agreed with great relief to let Lin's leaders organize and pay for the funeral.

Two days later, the memorial meeting for Zhao Lin was held at the crematorium in the southern suburbs of Nanjing. It was hard to bear. Memories of my parents' memorial meetings flooded back. I seemed always to be attending the funerals of people close to me.

After the meeting, Lin was cremated and I was given a small brown carved wooden box containing his ashes. To the side of the crematorium there was a big room with shelves lining the walls from floor to ceiling where the relatives of the dead could pay to leave the box in the care of the crematorium, which I did.

For several months I couldn't face the reality that Lin was gone. I was riddled with guilt at my initial reaction: Bloody good! had been my first thought. How horrible I had been. Now he was gone. And I missed him.

People kept coming to see me. My old classmate Greg turned up again. He had left the army in 1978, was happily married and working in the foreign affairs office of Nanjing University in charge of the increasing number of foreign students. He and his wife invited Little Yan and me to go to Xuanwu Lake Park with them.

Somehow Greg understood how I was feeling. 'Don't blame yourself like this,' he said gently. 'Zhao Lin was entirely to blame. He left the gas on, not you. And he was a bad husband to you.' He lifted a hand at my protestations. 'Yes, he was. I remember him well. Come, give yourself a chance to live again.'

Hui, too, came to see me one evening, with his wife and son. He said he had never forgotten me and often wondered how I was getting on. He had wanted to come before but had not dared, for fear that I would be upset. Then he had heard the news of the death of my husband and he hoped we could be friends again. He regretted his love affair with my friend Fang; they had parted after a particularly bad row. He was married to a gentle primary-school teacher, and was happy.

I was pleased to see him. He had supported me all through the darkest days of the Cultural Revolution and when I was ill after being demobilized. Now, he was offering his support once more. We parted as friends.

When Andong heard the news she wrote, 'It is a good thing for you because from now on you can take control of your own life and nobody will be able to bully you again like he did. The son of a bitch-dog! This is God's will that he should die long before you. Now you must get on with your life. You have nothing to reproach yourself for. Put such thoughts out of your mind. You don't want to let his ghost haunt you for ever, do you?'

After that, I began to get things into perspective. It took a few months but at last I drew the curtains on my dead husband and the past, and opened up the door to my future.

My new life as a widow meant change, and one of the first things I wanted to do was to change the name of Little Yan from Zhao to Gao. I expected to encounter some resistance from the authorities, but they agreed without argument. Also I could not go to the fairs at Guangzhou any more because I had to stay at home to look after my daughter. I had no regrets: she was a constant source of joy and wonder to me. I enjoyed helping her with her homework, and just watching her, remembering myself at the same age.

My biggest worry was money because Lin's salary stopped on the day he died. Then Mr Choo came to my rescue: he arranged for his company to pay me twenty yuan a month to help with Yan's upbringing. I would receive the allowance until she reached her eighteenth birthday. Also, every year I was to get a forty-yuan one-child bonus, to which I was entitled according to the policies laid down by the Party as part of their new family-planning laws. So, although money was always going to be tight, I could manage.

By the end of 1984 imports of electronic goods to China had increased dramatically, especially of colour television sets and tape-recorders. The Chinese people were demanding more and more sophisticated equipment, but as we did not have the technology to manufacture such things as colour-TV tubes, we had to import them. I heard a rumour that the Electronics Import and Export Corporation of Jiangsu Province badly needed English interpreters. I contacted the company, who said they would love to have me there. However, the leaders of my own company at first would not let me go. Then the personnel department of the Electronics Corporation wrote to them: 'Such a move can only carry forward the Communist spirit by giving us exactly the right person to help increase the size of our business. All is for our country. Nothing is for ourselves.' This was almost a form of blackmail – and they caved in.

Sinochem put forward a plan to allow Electronics to borrow me for six months at an agreed 'rental' payable to Sinochem monthly on the understanding that I would return to my old job as soon as the six months were up. The general manager of Electronics thought he could have me officially transferred to his company before then, so he accepted the terms and signed the 'borrowing agreement'. This is the Chinese way: everyone was a winner without anyone losing face. Sinochem made a profit, Electronics had a badly needed interpreter, and I changed my job with an increase of salary.

And what a change! I reported for my first day in my new job on 1 March 1985. From the beginning I was given a lot of responsibility. Because my English was good, I was soon trusted to meet with foreign business people from all over the world. Every day I saw someone new and interesting. I was very busy and happy.

Towards the end of June 1985 I spent several days translating at a

conference in which thirty-five Chinese and Japanese negotiators and
their staff hammered out a huge deal. The technical director of the factory
that had won the contract was a tall thin man. He looked middle-aged
to me because he always had a pair of glasses perched on the end of his
nose, which he peered over when he talked. He was almost bald, and
what hair he had left was grey, but his eyes twinkled with good humour.

On the third day of the conference, during a break, I was gossiping
with the Japanese woman interpreter and mentioned the name of my
old school. The voice of the technical director came from behind me:
'Did I hear you say you studied at the school attached to Nanjing Normal
University?'

I turned round and looked into the twinkling eyes. 'Yes,' I replied.

'When?' he asked.

'1965 to 1967,' I said.

'So did I!' he exclaimed.

We looked at each other quizzically. I was certain I didn't know this
man but I asked, 'Did you know my classmate Greg?'

'He was my classmate too! What's your name?'

'Gao Anhua.'

'Ahhh, Little Gao! Do you know who I am?'

I looked at him carefully, then shook my head. I did not recognize
this face. Eighteen years had passed since I had left my classmates behind
to go to my glorious future in the army.

'I am Old Tian!' he said. 'Tian Zhi-min.'

I remembered the name, but surely this couldn't be him.

He continued, 'Little Gao, surely you remember. We were in the
same Youth League branch with Greg. Have I changed so much that
you cannot recognize me at all?'

His eyes jogged my memory. 'Of course it's you!' I said. 'Oh, Tian,
of course I recognize you now! But you didn't recognize me! Have I
changed so much too?'

We stretched out our hands at the same time and clasped them tightly.
'You look splendid,' Tian said. 'You are so young-looking still, but you
didn't wear those glasses at school.'

'And you are thin!' I replied. 'And you had lots of hair in those days!'

He insisted that he would treat me to a dinner in a hotel restaurant
near his home to celebrate our meeting again. I knew it would cost him
about two weeks' salary, so I tried to refuse, but he wouldn't take no for
an answer. I learned that he, like Greg, had joined the Communist Party

while in the army. Then, with the help of his father, he had managed to get into Nanjing University as a worker-peasant-soldier student and gain his degree. After graduation, he married a young university teacher and they had had a daughter. He was a happy man. Others, however, had not been so fortunate: murder, betrayal, suicide and misery had stalked their lives during the years of chaos.

Shortly after this meeting, Tian was transferred to a new company as a manager, and Greg went to the United States as a visiting scholar. He had seen political problems in China and wanted to know why these had occurred. He thought he might find answers in the West. He knew he could not change it, but at least he might understand it better from a wider perspective. The day before he flew to the other side of the Pacific Ocean he came to say goodbye. We three have remained friends to this day.

A month after Greg left for America, I was arrested and accused of being an 'enemy agent and a foreign-paid spy'.

22. In Gaol

My arrest took me by surprise. On 10 September 1985, after lunch in the company dining room, I returned to my office and put several chairs together to make a bed. Then as usual I had a nap. In hot weather we had a three-hour lunch break, and many people went home for a rest but a few of us stayed behind, including me. At two thirty I was shaken awake by the company Party secretary. He asked me to go with him to his office for a chat.

We walked down a long corridor, past the open doors of all the other departments, went in and he closed the door, which was unusual: in hot weather everyone kept their doors open. He motioned me to a chair and poured me a cup of tea before asking me about my family in a friendly way. I answered his questions, thinking he was just checking that my home life was settling down after the death of my husband, and waited to be told why he wanted to see me.

We had been talking for about ten minutes when the office door was kicked open and five policemen and one policewoman rushed in. I was dragged to my feet by my hair. The woman grabbed my left wrist and removed my wristwatch, which I never saw again, twisted my arms behind my back and handcuffed me.

'What's going on?' I cried out in alarm. 'Why are you doing this?' The Party secretary glanced at me and turned away.

'Shut up, you bitch! You know why,' shouted one policeman, and slapped me. I was dragged out of the office with my arms pushed up towards my shoulder-blades.

By this time, everyone in the building had been roused from their naps and was standing watching in astonishment. I was devastated. They would think I had committed some big crime, but I had no idea what it was.

The police pushed me into the back seat of a jeep parked directly outside the main entrance of the building, where hundreds of people had gathered as if by magic. I was sandwiched between two policemen, and each held a pistol aimed at me. The jeep rushed away, sirens blaring, and came to a stop fifteen minutes later outside the building where I lived. I was pulled out of the jeep and manhandled up the stairs. My wrists were painful from the handcuffs and I asked to be allowed to walk at my own pace but this only encouraged my captors to go faster, dragging me behind them.

'Keep up, you filthy bitch turd!' shouted the woman, as she gave a painful yank on my arms. I was searched until my flat keys appeared. The door was opened and I was shoved violently into the kitchen. Four of the men began to search the rooms. They pulled out all my clothes from the wardrobe, and when they had checked them, they dropped them on the floor and walked on them. My makeup was smashed. Every drawer was pulled out and the contents rummaged through. Nothing was missed. My old camphorwood trunk was turned upside down and the contents searched. My suitcases were broken open and everything tipped out.

From time to time I heard a grunt of satisfaction as a foreign newspaper was found, or the copies of my handwritten books were discovered. Soon there was a pile of bits and pieces to be used as evidence against me. It didn't take long for these professionals to turn my neat flat into a disaster area.

'Search carefully for any written material,' growled the oldest policeman, who had yellow teeth and one of the ugliest faces I had ever seen. Meanwhile, because it was his duty by law to inform the local police whenever they took action against a citizen, he had sent for the policeman responsible for my neighbourhood. The local police must take part in the search and arrest. Only then did I learn that my captors were not from the Public Security Bureau (the normal police), but from the recently established State Security Bureau (SSB).

I now knew this was serious. The SSB had been set up to deal with all real or suspected espionage. The Party had put great emphasis on anti-espionage recently to combat the activities of enemy agents from the Soviet Union, the USA and Taiwan. It was said that quite a number of Soviet and US spies had been captured by the SSB in Beijing since 1984. The Chinese SSB was, and still is, regarded as the equivalent of the Soviet KGB. The SSB's ranks were hand-picked by the Party from among the most trusted of its members and, as such, considered themselves above the law. They kow-towed to nobody, and even high-ranking officers, government officials and the judiciary were frightened of them. They were feared and hated throughout China.

My local district police refused to come to my home to help with the search. Apparently the SSB had not informed them in advance of the raid, which was a procedural breach. I heard later that the police had no wish to persecute me as I had gained a reputation as a good wife, mother, widow, comrade and neighbour. Moreover, I was the only person in the area both of whose parents had been revolutionary martyrs, which was considered an honour for the district. Above all, they did not want to get involved with the SSB. Nobody did.

The lack of co-operation by the local police increased the fury of the searchers, who flew into a rage, cursed them in the foulest language and began systematically to wreck everything of value in my home. I had saved hard to buy a new electronic keyboard for my daughter. It was smashed to bits. So, too, were the frames containing my family photos. They reduced my few items of furniture to matchwood, kicked in the tube of my old black and white television set and threw my radio against a wall. By now tears were running down my face as I watched my home destroyed by these brutes.

When they had finished, only the old camphorwood trunk was intact. It had ended up in a corner of the room with my bed quilt thrown over it. And there it stayed, unnoticed, except by me. It gave me a thrill of victory to know they had missed my most prized possession, and in some strange way it gave me courage. My tears stopped and defiance overrode my desolation. I was still in custody, and fearful. I knew I was in for a bad time once I was in prison and under the control of these bastards.

They went into my kitchen, made themselves tea and ate whatever they found in my cupboards. Then they used my towels to wash the filth from their hands and faces, which was the height of bad manners in China. I protested, but they roared at me exactly like the worst bandits I had seen in films. It is strange what motivates people. I had seen my home ruined, and I had been slapped, punched and shouted at in the most humiliating way, yet it was their behaviour in my kitchen that angered me most. How dare they! I thought furiously. And from that moment, although they didn't know it, I was fighting back.

After their rest, they sifted through the pile of my bits and pieces. Nothing interested them. They read every one of about forty letters I had kept in a drawer. They were from Andong and friends inside China, except two which were from Hong Kong. They put all the letters in a pile and placed the two from Hong Kong on top. Yellow-teeth produced a camera and began photographing the pile to give the impression that the whole lot were from outside China. I protested, and the woman slapped me hard across the face. Little did she know that I had endured years of such treatment, so her puny effort meant nothing to me.

Yellow-teeth was getting impatient. He knew they had found no evidence to support whatever it was I was accused of. He pushed his face close to mine. 'Hand over your bank book!' he yelled at me. 'Hand it over, or else I will beat you to a pulp, you dog-shit!'

'You have all my money,' I said quietly. And they had. I had seen them pocket twenty-two yuan, which they had taken from my purse. 'There is nothing else.'

Yellow-teeth turned away in disgust. Then his eyes fell on something, and he leaped forward with a satisfied grunt. He picked up, out of the wreckage, my handwritten copy of *A Tale of Two Cities*. Now he had some 'evidence'.

'What language is this?' he yelled.

'English.'

'Why do you have this book? Is this your handwriting?'

'Yes. I copied it from a proper book years ago, when –'

'So you have been operating for a long time.'

'Will you tell me what I am accused of?' I asked.

Yellow-teeth stared at me with his piggy eyes. I returned his hard gaze with my own cool one.

'You know very well. A spy! A filthy enemy agent! And I have the proof,' he shouted, waving the book under my nose.

'No! I am not a spy!' I shouted back angrily. 'Do you see with your own eyes what is on the wall? See! Over there.' Yellow-teeth followed my gaze to the two certificates of my parents. When he looked back at me, he looked less sure of himself. I continued, 'I am the daughter of two revolutionary martyrs. I have no reason to be an enemy agent. Why should I? I am only an English interpreter. So where is your evidence against me?'

Everything in the room was still. I would guess that nobody had ever spoken to Yellow-teeth like that before. Normally his victims would have been cowed into submission, but I had gone through too much to be put down by these brutes.

Yellow-teeth pondered for a moment. Then he again waved the book under my nose. 'This is my evidence,' he said. 'You use this as a code book to send messages to other agents. Tell me where you have hidden the invisible ink you use to write your messages.'

I couldn't help it. The whole thing was too ludicrous. I laughed, and got a punch in the mouth for my impudence. My glasses flew off. I knew my lip was split from the blood running down my front. I spat. Another punch broke my nose. More of my blood spattered down. My nose has a bump in it now, and I have a scar on my lip.

They prepared to leave. The only 'evidence' they had was the photographs of my piled-up letters, my handwritten copy of *A Tale of Two Cities* and some foreign newspapers and magazines. They did not take my letters as 'evidence' because they contained nothing incriminating, so their haul was pitifully small. Yellow-teeth told me to point out some spare clothes and underwear, which the woman picked up. I was pushed outside my flat and the door was locked. One of the men sealed the door with a criss-crossing of white paper strips with an official government stamp printed on it. I asked if I could leave a note for my daughter, who was still at school, but my request was refused. I was not to know what happened to her until I was released.

Whatever it was I was accused of, I knew it was false. I also knew I was already guilty in the eyes of the Party. From long experience, like all Chinese people, I knew that it mattered not whether I was innocent or guilty. If the Party said I was guilty, that must be the truth. Even if they are wrong, they are always right.

I was taken to the harmless-sounding Wawaqiao (Infant Bridge) prison, which had been built by the Japanese in the 1930s. Then it had become the main prison of the Kuomintang to torture and kill Communist Party members after the Japanese had been driven out. Since 1949 the Communists have used it to interrogate their prisoners. It was, and still is, a place of evil.

The part of the prison I was taken to was for prisoners awaiting trial. It was guarded by soldiers armed with rifles topped by fixed bayonets. Two stood at the tall iron gates between high brick walls with rolls of barbed wire running along the top. One of the soldiers checked our jeep, then slowly pushed open the heavy gates to let us drive in. Once inside we faced another, more modern gate, guarded by two more armed soldiers, this time carrying sub-machine-guns. We stopped and waited for the outside iron gates to close, then we were let into the inner compound. We drove across an open space and drew up beside a dirty green-painted door set into an ugly brown-brick building.

By now my nerves were jangling, my tummy was filled with gnawing rats and my legs felt like jelly. All my earlier defiance had deserted me.

I had heard many stories about how people were tortured and tormented in this place. Never had I thought I would end up here myself.

I was hustled out of the jeep and bundled through the door. We went down a long, echoing corridor and into a white-tiled room that stank of disinfectant. The handcuffs were removed and I was ordered to strip to my underwear. Two women gaolers moved forward and searched me and my few belongings. They put their hands inside my brassière, down my knickers and inside me. Then they removed every button, zipper and metal catch from my clothes. The iron nails were taken out of the heels of my leather shoes. All this was done in silence.

Then I was told to stand against a wall. A square of white cardboard with my name on it was hung round my neck. My near-nakedness embarrassed me in front of Yellow-teeth and his pals. I tried to hide myself behind my arms, but was told to stand up straight with my arms at my sides. My glasses were handed to me, and I gratefully put them on. Their weight hurt my broken nose, but I felt better with them on. My 'criminal photograph' was taken. Then I was led to a table where my open hands were guided first into a plate of black ink and then on to a big piece of white paper. One of the women took a look at my damaged lip, but said nothing.

I was told to dress. The black ink from my hands dirtied my clothes, but I was much more dismayed to see how much blood was congealing on them. I dressed as quickly and carefully as I could, trying to avoid my own blood. I was handed a piece of cloth, about ten centimetres square, which had numbers printed on it, and was told to pin it to my blouse. One of the women said, 'From now on, you are number 1720. We shall never use your name here, nor can you use it. Remember, you are nothing here, just a number. That is you.'

Suddenly a flash of memory of the episode describing the Bastille in *A Tale of Two Cities* came to me. I remembered how Dr Manette was persecuted and incarcerated in that horrible place. He was called 'One Hundred and Five, North Tower' during his long imprisonment. Now I was treated the same way by the Communist Party. I was 'One Thousand Seven Hundred and Twenty, Infant Bridge'.

The other woman came up to me and whispered in my ear, 'You will not be handcuffed. But if you do not behave yourself you will be punished, much worse than you can ever imagine.' I felt a strong sense of injustice and I wanted to strike out at my captors, but I dared not. I began to realize how the capitalist roaders must have felt when they had been victimized. The woman continued, 'You are not allowed to give your name to any other prisoner, nor are you allowed to ask for theirs. In here you are nothing, lower than dog-shit!'

When all was done, it was already late in the evening and dark outside. All the time, since leaving home, worry about Little Yan had gnawed at me. Where was she? She was not allowed to take down the paper criss-crossing the door to our flat so she was as good as homeless. She had no money and nothing except the clothes on her back. Anger filled me. This was no way to treat people. Even if I was found guilty of something, she was just an innocent child. Why punish her? Was she such a danger to the State that they had to deny her a place to sleep? How low China had sunk. I didn't care what happened to me, my life had never been much more than a series of sorrows, betrayals, disappointments, humiliation and pain. Now Little Yan was on the way down the same path.

I left Yellow-teeth behind when the gaolers led me down to the cells. One unlocked a big padlock and pulled open a thick metal door, the other pushed me inside. With a loud bang they shut the door behind me. The sound struck directly into my heart, and I broke down in tears.

A woman rose up from the floor, put an arm around me and guided me to a corner. 'There, there,' she said. 'Let it all come out. We have all been through it. Come, cry on me.' Never was such tenderness so welcome. We sank to the floor and I buried my head in her shoulder, soaking her chest with my tears. That was the only time I cried during my time in gaol.

When I had recovered, I was introduced to my three cell-mates, two middle-aged and one very old. It had been she who had held me. She was number 1701 and she was accused of hiding her son, who was wanted for murder. The two middle-aged women were number 180, accused of theft, and 453, who was branded as politically corrupt. I introduced myself. 'I am number 1720 and I don't know why I am here, except that they called me an enemy agent.'

Eyes looked at me in astonishment. This was big stuff! 'Wow!' said one, 'and I thought I had troubles.'

The old lady, number 1701, told me supper had just finished so there was nothing for me to eat that night. I was welcome to share what little water they had. I thanked them for their kindness, sat down on the cement floor and leaned against a wall. I noticed a small barred window high up in the outside wall, through which I could see a single star. I thought again of Little Yan.

Our cell measured about three metres by three metres. There was a bright electric light bulb hanging from the ceiling, but no furniture. We had to sit and sleep on the concrete floor. The small window was so high that none of us could reach it, but at least we could tell when day and night changed places.

In one corner, beside the door, there was a pit. A pipe jutted through the wall with a cold water tap attached to it. This was our toilet and washing area. The pit emptied into a huge open sewer pipe. Every time someone further up the corridor used theirs the smell came up through our hole. It reminded me of the bucket we had used as a toilet in the countryside. I haven't made much progress, I thought.

It was mid-September and the weather was exceptionally hot and humid – we called it 'The Autumn Tiger'. Our cell was filled with mosquitoes. 'You will have to learn to endure everything here,' said 180. 'Nobody will take any notice of your complaints about the bad conditions. Your protests can only be added to your list of crimes.'

'Yes,' interrupted 1701, 'those in uniform here are all heartless bastards. One woman was sentenced to ten years. She was cold and asked for a quilt the night before she was due to be sent to do hard labour. She never got her quilt, but her sentence was increased to fourteen years the next day. So you had better keep quiet or it can only be the worse for you.'

I was greatly disturbed by all that had happened to me that day, and I couldn't sleep. Fortunately my cell-mates needed to talk to me. They asked for all my news about the outside, and I tried to bring them up to date. We talked in whispers, but not quietly enough, because a small sliding peephole opened in the door and a pair of eyes appeared. They stared at us for a few seconds, then a male voice shouted, 'Go to sleep! Don't talk!' The peephole closed and we heard him walking away.

The cell was so small, we had to huddle together on the floor. I looked around, trying to find the light switch. 'No, you won't find it,' whispered 180. 'The light stays on night and day, every day, because even during the daytime it is quite dark in here and the gaolers need to keep watch on us all the time.' She paused, then continued, 'I bet they've taken all the metal things off your shoes and clothes.' I nodded and 180 came closer. 'We heard that some prisoners had attempted suicide by swallowing everything metallic they could find, and they don't like suicide. They like to keep prisoners alive so that they can get confessions from them to satisfy the charges that have been brought against them.'

There was quiet for a while, then 180 spoke again. 'Did you say you don't know what you have been accused of?'

'Yes,' I whispered back.

'Your case must be a serious one,' she said, 'because big numbers from 1700 upwards are all serious cases. You see her?' She pointed at number 1701. 'Her case is connected with a murder, so she was given a big number. And you are 1720, so it is no small matter. I assume you are an intellectual and probably your case is a political one.'

'But I haven't done anything wrong to our country!' I protested angrily.

'Don't be silly,' she said. 'Don't you understand that no case is decided according to the facts? The evidence is made to fit the accusation. Most of the prisoners here have little or no education. They don't know anything, not even how to defend themselves when they are wrongly accused. See 453? She came from the countryside to join a group of workers to take up jobs repairing houses. Her job was whitewashing the walls. They were paid by their clients and they divided the money among themselves without handing over a percentage to the local leaders. The whole group was arrested and charged with being politically and financially corrupt. They are accused of taking an illegal income. Number 453 was separated from her group to stop them forming a "defensive alliance". She can't read or write, and her signature is her thumbprint. The police wrote her confession for her, and she put her thumbprint at the bottom of the paper. She cried all day long for the first month because she missed her husband and child. The gaolers used to pull her hair and bang her head against the wall whenever she began to cry. Now she has become used to prison life. She even said it was not too bad in here as she has free food.'

Number 180 was accused of theft. She and two of her friends lived off what they could find in the garbage boxes of the city. They picked out waste-paper, glass bottles and scrap metal, which they sold to a recycling plant for just enough money to survive. One day they came across a pile of waste metal outside a factory wall and sold it for enough to live on for at least two weeks. However, the manager of the recycling plant reported the matter to the police because he suspected that the metal he had just bought had been stolen from inside the factory. The three friends were arrested.

Naïvely, 180 believed the police inquisitors when they said she would go free if she confessed, so she did. She was not given her freedom but, because of her 'correct attitude', she was moved to our cell as cell leader. She had to submit a report every day on the behaviour of her cell-mates, in which she was expected to reveal if any of us complained or said anything that might help the police prove their cases.

'I bet you are one of the highest educated here,' she said to me. 'I was moved to this small cell to be with you only today. I am very happy because there will be no fighting here. Intellectuals use their brains and don't fight. In the other cells the women are always quarrelling and fighting, usually over nothing. Sometimes there are fights over food and water. The rations are small so they grab rice from other bowls and drink water not belonging to them. They are uneducated labouring people who behaved badly before they ended up here. Such people are usually the cell bullies and I hated to be in the same cell as them. But now I am with you, 1720, I'm sure I shall not be bullied.'

Her words slowed to a faint mutter. Then her steady breathing told me she was fast asleep. The bulb above my head was so bright it seemed to penetrate my closed eyelids. The mosquitoes made their irritating noise around my ears and their bites kept me scratching. If 180 was right, I was in serious trouble. But why? I lay awake the whole night, thinking of all the possibilities, trying to come up with a reason for my arrest. Event after event, conversation after conversation, face after face floated around in my head. Nothing came to me . . . until, through the little window, night began to turn to day. And in my mind a gleam of light also appeared.

It must be, I thought. I had been doing business with a Hong Kong company. My contact there was a Wei Dai, who had changed his name to the English David Wei.

Two months previously, in mid-July, the young businessman visited our company. He hoped that we would use his company as a regular supplier of tape-recorders. He was about twenty-five and I received him in our company discussion room. As this was our first meeting, we spent about an hour discussing ideas without getting down to hard business and we got on well. At the end of our meeting, we shook hands and he left.

At about four o'clock that same afternoon, I received a telephone call from the Jinling Hotel. It was David Wei. Would I meet him for dinner that evening? He was so charming and sincere, I couldn't refuse, so I took my daughter with me and we had an excellent meal with him in the hotel restaurant. After dinner, David and I talked about general things, as well as touching on business. Little Yan spent the time sucking a soft drink through a straw and looking over the balcony at the Chinese and foreign-looking people coming and going below in the foyer.

David told me he had only been in Hong Kong for about a year. His parents had been Party officials in Beijing and he had served in the PLA for four years. Whilst in the army he had joined the Communist Party. His mother had been sent by the Party to work in Hong Kong and he had left the army to go with her. She had found him a good position in the company she was going to manage. He was still a member of the Party because it considered the Hong Kong company to be a window for Beijing to look out to the West.

He said, 'I have little business experience. I need your help and I assure you of my best co-operation. This is my first business trip to China since going to Hong Kong and my very first visit to Nanjing. I have the impression that you are experienced in business, and that you are honest. I feel that I can trust you, and be your friend.' He reminded me of my dear long-dead Guv.

He returned to Hong Kong, and over the next few days we negotiated prices for tape-recorders. On 27 July, David again came to Nanjing and we signed a contract. I thought I had just done a nice little bit of business, but unfortunately my actions upset my general manager. He had been planning to give this business to a Hong Kong woman who had quoted a higher price but who had a good relationship with him. When he asked me to move the business to her, I refused as the contract had been signed, and anyway, I had got the better price. He had looked upset as he walked away.

Three days later, on 30 July, the company held a full staff meeting at which we were told that the import policy on electronic goods into our country had been changed: all imports needed an import licence and had to be approved at a higher level. This meant that the contract David and I had signed had to be cancelled.

After the meeting, I wrote to David explaining the change in our import regulations, and asked him to agree to the cancellation of our contract. In my letter I told him it was not I who didn't want to honour it, it was outside my control, but I hoped we could still do some other business. As a token of our continued friendship, I referred him to an old friend of my parents, Xu Jia-tun. He was at that time the chairman of the Xinhua News Agency and the number-one leader of the Communist Party in Hong Kong. I told David that I would write a letter of introduction to Xu in the hope that David would find more opportunities to do business with China. I put the letter in the tray for the post-room to deal with and thought no more about it. I was soon to discover the interpretation that had been put upon it.

At six a.m. a loud whistle sounded and we got up. Each of us was given a small cup of boiled water. Tap water in China cannot be drunk without being boiled first. This tiny amount of water was all we were given until the same time the following day: 180 advised me to save half of it for the afternoon, otherwise I would have nothing to drink. She told me many women gulped it all down as they got it. Later they became so thirsty, they couldn't resist drinking from the tap. She didn't have to tell me the rest. We all knew unboiled tap water caused severe tummy upsets. This meant many visits to the pit and a constantly stinking cell.

Other discomforts were huge centipedes, at least ten centimetres long. We never found out where they came from. Whenever we spotted one we had to kill it: they gave a very nasty bite, which almost always turned septic. Slugs climbed the walls, which was bad enough, but one particularly nasty-looking species was bright red and about twelve centimetres long. I was assured that they were harmless, but I hadn't the courage to touch them. As 180 didn't like them either, 1701 picked them off the walls and dropped them down the hole. As each one was pulled off, it made a low sucking sound. I felt sick at first but, as with everything else in that horrible place, I got used to it.

I had my first breakfast in Wawaqiao Prison. It was a mush of mouldy rice with a few dried-up salty radishes, which we called 'pickles'. 180 told me the food was the same all the year around. I was strongly reminded of the swill we used to feed to the pigs.

At eight thirty the cell door opened and a voice shouted, 'Number 1720, come out!'

I was taken into a gloomy room. Two men from the SSB were already there, sitting behind a desk. One was fat and the other was small and skinny. No chair for me.

'How many leaders at provincial level have you contacted recently?' Fatty asked.

'Only one. That is Liu, the second secretary of the Party Committee of Jiangsu Province. He has known me since I was a little girl. He often invites me and my daughter to his home to have dinner, almost once a week.' Then I added, 'What about my daughter? She has nobody to look after her now.' I had decided before entering this room that I would ask about Little Yan as soon as I could.

Shorty spoke for the first time. 'Don't you worry about her. She is being taken care of by someone we appointed. It is your own situation you should be worrying about.' He had a voice to go with his appearance. It was high and squeaky.

The fat one came back at me. 'Why did you deny your guilt of being an enemy agent?'

I remained calm. I was not frightened of these men, only of their power over me. 'Because I am innocent.'

'We have the proof. Listen to the words of your own general manager.' He opened a file and, with puffed-up self-importance, began to read: 'The class enemy outside China can use the information to analyse our economic policy and this letter will only supply the needs of a foreign spy.'

So, there it was. I had been accused of being a spy for a foreign power!

'It is ridiculous!' I cried. 'I was raised by the Party and the People's Government. I have no reason to harm my country!'

Fatty: 'Why did you tell this man David about the change in our import policies?'

Me: 'Why shouldn't I? I must be honest in doing business. All business representatives do the same in their negotiations with foreign businessmen. If I was wrong to tell the truth, that means everybody in our company is wrong.'

Fatty: 'We know a lot of your colleagues do the same as you, but we haven't got evidence about them. We have evidence about you! You should not tell anybody outside China. The change to our import policy is a State secret.'

Me: 'I didn't know. Nobody said anything about that. All I know is, the new policy was published in the newspapers one week after we heard it at the meeting. Is anything in the newspapers a secret?'

Fatty: 'It was a secret before it was printed in the newspapers. It was a secret during that week when you wrote your letter to David Wei. And it was against the law to tell the Hong Kong people about it.'

Me: 'Nobody has ever said such a thing to me. Moreover, David Wei is the son of a trusted Party member, and he is also a Party member himself. Why was it wrong of me, a non-Party member, to tell such a thing to a Party member?'

Fatty and Shorty together: '*What?*'

Me: 'David Wei is a full, current Chinese Communist Party member. So where does this charge of being involved with a foreign power come in?'

The two men were stunned. It was obvious they had never considered that a man with a name like David could possibly be a Communist Party member. I watched their faces as they realized their case had collapsed. For several minutes neither of them said a word. Fatty sat forward, hunched over the desk, smoking furiously and drumming his fingers. Shorty had turned sideways in his chair, his right leg over his left, staring at the far wall. He, too, took deep sucks on his cigarette.

Suddenly Fatty shouted: 'You are lying!'

'Of course I'm not! If you don't believe me, just make a telephone call to Beijing and you will find out. And another thing. What has all of this got to do with my book *A Tale of Two Cities* that your people confiscated?'

Fatty: 'Shut up! Even if he is a Party member, he is still from Hong Kong, and the news should not have been leaked out to there. Hong Kong is a dangerous capitalist place. This is a serious political question. Your general manager and the Party leadership here cannot be wrong!' He was up on his feet and roaring at me like a crazy man. His face was red and his eyes bulged. I thought he was about to have a heart-attack.

As he started to bend over, ready to sit down, I leaned forward and quietly said, 'A mistake has been made here. You should admit it, and let me go.' I looked directly into his eyes, forcing him to look away.

Finally he said, 'We cannot be wrong – ever!'

'So you won't let me go, even though you have no case,' I said accusingly.

'Never!' he barked. He gestured to the gaoler to take me back to my cell. My first interrogation was at an end. In fact, I never had a second one. They never explained to me what they had found in the book, presumably because there was nothing to find.

Every day 1701 was taken for questioning in the morning and again in the afternoon. 453 was also taken away several times a week, but 180 and I were left alone. We were almost never allowed out of the cell, and we both said a nice session of interrogation would be a welcome relief from the boredom. But we didn't really mean it. And then there came a day when the cell door was opened and my number was called: '1720, come out!'

This time I was taken to a much brighter room. A nicely dressed man was sitting at a table, and there was a chair for me. The man smiled and stood up, gesturing with his hand. 'Come, please sit down,' he said, holding the back of the chair for me. I was suspicious. Was this an SSB trick?

'My name is Chen Bo. I am a lawyer. I am here to defend you.'

'Oh,' was all I could say. It was a total surprise.

'Yes, the Party secretary in your company instructed me. He feels very sorry for you, so he arranged for me to be your lawyer. Don't worry about my fee. I am being paid by the Electronics Corporation. So let's get down to business.'

I was puzzled. I said, 'Have I understood you? The general manager of the Electronics Corporation is my accuser, the Party secretary has arranged for you to defend me, and your fee is being paid by the same company?'

The lawyer nodded and smiled. 'I must confess to never having heard of such a thing before. That is exactly what has happened.'

Chen was about thirty. He told me he had graduated from the East China Law and Politics Institute, and he seemed to know his job. He had already found out that my case had been passed on to the People's Court for a verdict. The judge who had been assigned to my case had argued with the SSB for bringing a false accusation and had refused to give a guilty verdict. 'As a guilty verdict would mean a long term of imprisonment, or even the death penalty, the judge was not happy with the evidence in your case,' said Chen. However, the SSB were determined to prove they were right and had gone to the next higher level of the judiciary in an attempt to force the People's Court to pronounce me guilty.

Throughout the whole proceedings I was never asked to confess to my crimes like other prisoners – not that I would ever have admitted to being an enemy agent. My case turned into a power struggle within the Party between the People's Court and the SSB. I was just a pawn. The SSB did not think they needed my confession. If they said I was a spy, that, in their opinion, was sufficient for me to be found guilty. They knew that I was not a spy: they only wanted a guilty verdict to save their faces. Once they had that, the People's Court could give me whatever sentence they liked. However, for once, the court wanted to see justice done.

At first the judge was put under tremendous pressure to give a guilty verdict. Then the bullying tactics of the SSB annoyed others within the judiciary, and soon he was under equal pressure from his colleagues not to do so.

I was told by my lawyer that a so-called clique of enemy spies had been unearthed by the SSB in Beijing during the previous April. That group had been formed, said the SSB, by a group of children of some of the old high-ranking Party officials who had suffered during the Cultural Revolution and whose positions had still not been restored to them. The SSB had made a number of arrests, and because the two cities often echoed each other in important political events, they believed there must be a similar clique of enemy agents in Nanjing. When the general manager of my company contacted them, they thought they had a clue, and hoped to open up the Nanjing clique when they arrested me.

The SSB had followed me secretly for more than a month without discovering anything unusual except my visits to Liu. These were innocent meetings between two old friends but to the SSB I was guilty. They were convinced that I only went there to read whatever documents I could so that I could pass the information I gathered to a foreign power. They realized their mistake after my first and only interrogation but they demanded a guilty verdict because, as Fatty had said, the Party was never wrong.

On three occasions the SSB sent officers to 'negotiate' with the judge – or, in fact, to threaten him. The judge simply refused to co-operate.

I was so angry at what the SSB was doing, I cried out: 'They don't mind victimizing me just to save their own faces! It is definitely not the policy of our Party to sacrifice an innocent person like me.'

'We all know very well,' said the lawyer, 'that if either of your parents was alive, they would not have dared to lay a finger on you because your parents were senior Party officials.'

I became even more angry. 'What has this to do with my parents? Why should my situation change totally if my parents had lived? Is there any law in this country? Is there any justice?' Sadly, I already knew the answer.

The lawyer looked at me understandingly. He leaned forward so there was no possibility of being overheard. 'You know very well the words of the leaders are the law. Your case is quite special. We have one leader in your company accusing you, and another leader of equal rank arranging for your defence. We have a judge who says you are innocent, and the SSB saying you must be guilty. I have never known the courts to refuse to convict before, but these are unusual circumstances. You have a great ally in the judge. Your case is no longer criminal. It is now political.'

I looked at him. I knew that the judge, whoever he was, had placed himself in danger by helping me but all I could think of as I sat facing my lawyer was my own predicament. 'Does this mean I must stay here for an unknown time while the power struggle is taking place?' He nodded. 'And who do you think will win?' I asked.

Chen thought for a moment before replying. 'I really don't know. The judge, I think. He seems to be the strongest-willed of them all.'

I felt a surge of gratitude to this stranger who was fighting so hard for me. I wanted to meet him but Chen thought it unlikely that I would, or at least not before I was taken to court to face my accusers. 'And that may never happen,' he said, as he bade me goodbye.

The women prisoners who caused no trouble were given some knitting work. The gaolers received the wool from the factories, and the best-behaved prisoners were allowed to knit long scarves or square shawls. They never got any money for their work: the factories paid the gaolers, who divided the money between them. However, the prisoner who knitted the best quality together with the highest quantity was given a very good report for her behaviour.

In Wawaqiao, 180 and I were offered the chance to knit, and we said yes. It helped to break the mind-numbing monotony. Nothing else was allowed: no newspapers, no books, nothing. We would not even have known the date if we had not made marks on the wall with toothpaste. In fact, we had lost track of time until one day we heard fireworks. Then we knew it was 1 October, the day when Communists celebrate their victory over the Kuomintang government. It is our National Day and a holiday. In prison it meant nothing, except that we could begin to keep track of the days.

In due time, 180 and I learned to like and trust each other. We began by telling each other about ourselves, our backgrounds, our hopes and our dreams. She was the first person I told about my dream to travel to the country on the edge of the sky and meet their queen. She had smaller dreams, like a nice house where she could live happily with her loving husband and a beautiful baby son.

She told me that, during her daily reporting, she informed the gaolers she had found out that I had many important family and personal friends in the governments of Nanjing and Beijing. That way, she hoped I would be treated with more respect. And it seemed to work. One day she and I crossed the line to total trust. She secretly whispered her name to me: Xiao Xue, which means Little Snow. A beautiful name, which suited her very well, because I soon realized she was a truly beautiful person. In return, I told her mine: Anhua, Tranquil Flower.

During my first few days in prison, I had been so disturbed by my arrest that I had buried myself in my own thoughts and had not paid much attention to the appearance of my cell-mates. Now I looked at Little Snow more carefully and saw a natural beauty. Although the food was poor, she still had a little rosy colour in her flawless skin, as if she used some light rouge, while we other prisoners looked unhealthily pallid. She had big round eyes, which seemed to shine from within, strong white teeth, and her black hair was thick and lustrous with a hint of curl. She was taller than me, and her figure was full and round but slim. It was easy to imagine how beautiful she must have been under normal conditions.

Later when we were given knitting, Little Snow used some loose pink wool to braid herself a bracelet for her left wrist and some rings for her fingers. She said her dream had always been to be decked out in shining bright jewellery, and a dream it remained. When she finished decorating her hand, she raised it to show me how beautiful it looked with the wool ornaments.

Most prisoners became very depressed, but not Little Snow. Every day she tried to look her best, because she hoped that one day, when she was released, she could look beautiful for her family. Her inner strength was a great inspiration to me and helped me to get through the dreadfulness of every day.

One night we were awakened by a series of piercing screams. A woman was crying out, obviously in great pain. 'What's that?' I whispered in alarm. Little Snow leaned up on one arm and said, 'It sounds like someone is being given the Tiger treatment.' By now, all four of us were wide awake. 1701 said she had heard of it, but didn't know what it was, and 453 had never heard of it. Neither had I. 'Well, it is instruments of torture,' said Little Snow. 'I saw it twice in my old cell.' She told us her story.

'I have been in this prison for over a year now. In the early days, beating prisoners was part of the daily life of a gaoler. There were all kinds of beating, whipping and torture going on all the time, and the prison was full of the screams of people in agony. Slapping and punching was not counted as beating. Whipping was used the most, and it was usually enough to make prisoners confess. The tougher prisoners who refused to confess, even when they were whipped repeatedly, were given worse and worse treatment until they either confessed or they died.

'Sharpened bamboo sticks or iron needles were pushed under fingernails. If that didn't work, then each finger in turn had nails hammered through it and into the wood underneath. Nobody could stand such pain and most prisoners fainted several times before their tormentors could finish nailing down all eight fingers and two thumbs. And every time they passed out, the torturers poured hot chilli water into their nostrils to wake them. Sometimes they put salt on their wounds.

'They wanted confessions because most of the cases had no evidence to support the charges. Most were imaginary accusations, so only a confession could be used as proof of guilt. They did this all the time, and every confession proved that their methods of arrest were correct. Many of the prisoners confessed on the threat of being harmed, and often confessed to much more than their original charges. Many of these people were ignorant peasants and they did not understand what was going on. They believed the interrogators when they promised freedom on confession.

'In fact, it was stupid to confess to anything that was not true. The more crimes they confessed to, the more guilty they appeared. "Confession earns lenient treatment" was just a trick to get prisoners to provide their own evidence to meet the charges made against them. But to resist was to be branded an "anti-Party person" which was a great crime and severe punishment naturally followed. In other words, once someone was in here, they had no chance of ever getting out with a clean name. They were guilty, guilty, guilty! Never innocent. Because the Party is always right.

'The Tiger treatment begins with handcuffs. There are handcuffs used in here where part of the metal that touches the flesh has been sharpened. The cuffs are put on very tight, so that the sharpened metal cuts into the flesh to the bone. Often the cuffs cut through tendons, making the hand useless, which seems awful, but compared to the rest of the treatment, it is not so bad.'

Little Snow paused, and looked at me. 'The worst torture was the Tiger Bench. Have you ever heard of it?'

'Yes,' I nodded. 'I read about it in some books, which described how cruelly the Japanese and the Kuomintang tortured the Communists. It said they tied a prisoner in a sitting position by binding the legs to a bench and the arms to a pole behind the back. Then they put bricks and wooden wedges under the heels to force the feet and lower legs upwards until they broke. Usually at the knees.'

'Exactly like that!' agreed Little Snow. 'The Communists condemned their enemies for such barbarity and banned the use of the Tiger treatment in the 1950s. Then all forms of torture were restored by Mao after the start of the Cultural Revolution. The Communists began carrying out exactly the same tortures as the Japanese and the Kuomintang had done. But this time it was the ordinary people who were victimized, especially in the custody houses of the rural areas. Such tortures were also very widely used in the cowsheds during the 5.16 Campaign.

'Fortunately, in this prison, things have improved since Deng Xiao-ping said all forms of torture must be banned. The gaolers here still use torture, but now they call it punishment for bad behaviour. And as a refusal to confess can be considered bad behaviour, torture is still used when the SSB or police want a confession badly enough.' I shivered. I was glad they had never wanted me to confess.

'The gaolers here have invented a new punishment called a Tiger Jacket,' Little Snow continued. 'Although it can bring enormous agony, they can use it at any time because the Party does not consider it to be a method of torture. It is used here a lot to punish those who dare to resist. I have seen this twice in my old cell. A woman who constantly complained was given the Tiger Jacket treatment.

'It is a very heavy thing made of iron, and it looks like the chest part of ancient armour. But it is very small and tight. The gaolers first bound the arms of the woman behind her back. Then the Tiger Jacket was put on to her. They squeezed her upper body into it so that she couldn't move any part of her torso from the neck down to her hips. It was so tight, she could hardly breathe. The minimum time for having the Tiger Jacket on was forty-eight hours. If the prisoner complained, the time was prolonged.

'With her arms bound behind her inside the jacket, the woman could do nothing for herself, and we were not allowed to help. So she wet and messed herself. And she was unable to eat or drink because she couldn't bend from the waist. Secretly, during the night, some of us did our best to feed and clean her, but we could do little for fear of being punished by being put into a Tiger Jacket too.

'At first the woman shouted at the gaolers. Then, as time dragged by, the pain became worse and worse. As her blood circulation almost stopped, her arms, shoulders and back swelled up, making the pain even more unbearable. And breathing was agony. In the end she was crying bitterly for help, but the gaolers only laughed at her and watched her suffering with great pleasure. They shouted, "You asked for trouble and now you have got it!"

'The woman was supposed to be an example to frighten us into submission, but all I could think of was that no human being deserved such treatment.' Little Snow paused. 'She could not sit comfortably, could not lie down and could not sleep. The gaolers watched her increasing agony as hour followed hour, gloating over her worsening health. It is said that one week in a Tiger Jacket will kill a young healthy male, a woman in five or six days. The woman I am talking about was in it for only two days and it almost killed her. When at last she was released, she could not move. The bones and muscles in her arms were so severely affected by the lack of blood and having been stuck in one position for so long that the smallest movement caused her great pain. And she had to endure the agony when her blood began to flow again through her veins.

'She said afterwards that the pain she suffered after the jacket was taken off was much worse than when it was on. It took us over six hours to bring her arms to her sides and another two hours to get them across her chest. For hours we took it in turns to rub them and her stiff, cold fingers. Even when we had got her arms in front of her, she still felt that they were not hers. For over a week after the jacket was removed, she was unable to use her arms and hands. The woman said the feeling was indeed as if her arms had been bitten off by a real tiger. Such is the Tiger Jacket.'

I was so upset that when I spoke I forgot to whisper: 'It is cruel and inhuman. How can the gaolers be allowed to use such things, even after the downfall of the Gang of Four?'

'They just are,' said Little Snow. 'They are all cruel, sadistic devils.'

Suddenly the peephole opened. 'Stop talking and go to sleep!' yelled a female voice. We were quiet, but throughout the night, the cries of agony could be heard. We couldn't sleep much, and at dawn we heard footsteps. The noise stopped, and Little Snow guessed that the prisoner had been moved somewhere else, or had died. During my imprisonment, the same kind of night screams happened several times a month.

One morning, after 453 and 1701 had been taken away to be interrogated yet again, Little Snow and I got out our knitting. 'It was a lucky day for me when they put me in this cell,' said Little Snow. 'They are afraid of you and they dare not treat us badly. We don't have to write self-criticism every day in this cell, but all of us had to do it in the other cell before I was moved here.'

'Why?' I was surprised to hear this.

'Well, you remember when I told them that you had some important family and friends?'

I nodded.

'Well, I hear things when I go to make my report. It seems that there are all sorts of rumours going around about you.'

I looked up from my needles and, curious, I asked, 'Rumours about me?' I was mildly flattered and amused.

'Well, it seems they are now convinced that you are very important, and that you will soon be released. You are so important, they say, you have your own lawyer. They are also saying that the SSB people are afraid of you, and so, too, is the judge. He will not find you guilty.'

'How stupid!' I spluttered. 'I am as important as that beetle over there.' I pointed to a big black thing climbing a wall.

'Perhaps,' replied Little Snow. 'But that is what the rumours say. And it is working. We do get better treatment in this cell. The gaolers are saying that the SSB are so worried about you they don't want to interrogate you. It is unheard-of for a prisoner only to be interrogated once and for such a short time. So the gaolers are worried too, in case you make a report about the happenings inside here after you are out. So I have really benefited from being put in here with you.'

At that moment there was a knock on the wall from the next cell. We acknowledged, and gave a gentle bang on the opposite wall. A gaoler was coming. We stopped talking and began to knit furiously. The peephole opened. We knew it without lifting our heads.

The prisoners had their own way of dealing with life. One was the signal system. When a gaoler was on the way, an inmate of every cell knocked on the wall between them and the next cell to give a warning. I had found out such things on my first day. I had returned after my interrogation, and 180 and I were talking quietly. Suddenly she said, 'Hush! A gaoler is coming!' And she was right. The peephole opened and closed.

'How did you know?' I asked. That was when 180 told me about the secret codes used by the prisoners.

'Although most of the prisoners haven't had much schooling, they are not stupid. The SSB, the police and the gaolers treat them as though they are, but most of them are quite intelligent. Many compose wonderful poems, which they recite but cannot write down. When I was in the big cell, someone told me about the signals invented by prisoners long ago, just as we saw in the films about when the Communists were in the Kuomintang gaols. The Communist prisoners passed messages to each other by knocking on the walls and pipes. They sent messages such as "Go on hunger strike against the ill-treatment."

'We just learned from them. We make friends inside here, then lose them because prisoners are constantly moved from one cell to another. The authorities are afraid that we will organize ourselves into gangs if they keep the same people together for too long. When we are split up, we don't want to lose touch with our friends, and we want to exchange news of our cases. So those prisoners of long ago invented the knock-on-the-wall information codes. Usually it is done by relay. A message can be passed from cell to cell until it is delivered to the right person.

'There are lots of codes, and you will learn them if you are here long enough. For now, just learn that one knock means: "Attention! Here comes the gaoler." Two knocks mean "There will be a trial tomorrow." Three mean "Someone has been sentenced and will be sent to a labour camp." And four knocks tell us "Someone is to be shot." And to add to the knocks, whenever we can, we make use of any time we are together, such as when I go to make my morning report, or the rare time when we are allowed outside for exercise. We use facial expressions, body language and a finger code to pass messages. I will tell you how to communicate the next time we are let out on exercise.'

For the first time in gaol, I smiled broadly. I looked at 180 and thought how clever and loyal the prisoners were. Almost all of them had been betrayed by people on the outside, yet they still tried to help each other inside. Many squabbled with their cell-mates, but that didn't stop them uniting against the common enemy: the gaolers.

In 1985 winter came much earlier than usual. The first snows fell in mid-November. I sat on the cold floor with both feet wrapped in my newly issued quilt, knitting furiously. I couldn't get warm. I felt chilled to the bone from the terrible cold and the damp. The temperature in our cell must have been almost the same as outside. I had all my clothes on. Every stitch I had been allowed to bring with me was on my body.

Unfortunately, when I had been arrested it was hot, so my clothes were meant to be worn in warm weather, not in winter. 1701, who had even thinner clothes than me, was already suffering from frostbite on her hands and feet.

Sometimes, Little Snow sang in a low voice while she knitted, always the same song.

> In a small village far away,
> Lives my old mother in a small hut.
> She leans on the door every day,
> Looking into the distance and
> Calling me with her heart.
> 'My child you have left home for over a year,
> When can you come back to me?'
> Oh! The love of my mother and the kiss of her,
> Makes me homesick and heartbroken.

Tears always flowed when she sang. Before my eyes I saw my Little Yan, leaning against the door of our home, waiting for me to return. Big tears dropped from my eyes and wet my knitting.

There was no news about my case. Every day we heard through the prison communication system news about this person on trial, or that person being sentenced, or somebody else going off to labour camp. We never heard of anyone being set free. Why didn't they get on with it and find me guilty? At least I would know my fate. The waiting was hard to bear.

By now, my last shred of faith in the Communist Party had died. How could I believe in Communism after all I had witnessed? And if a political party could persecute a widow with a young child, then that party is corrupt and worthless.

I made a request to the gaolers to see my lawyer. It was granted and a few days later I was ushered into the same bright room. After the usual preliminaries, I asked him how my case was progressing. 'Now it is not your case that is the problem. The situation has gone much further, which has resulted in it remaining static until a breakthrough comes. At the moment the stalemate still exists. The whole of the judiciary, from the top man in Jiangsu Province downwards, is in conflict with the SSB. Both refuse to budge. You will have to wait patiently.'

'Wait until when?' I asked.

'Nobody knows. I know it is hard for you, but at least you have hope of being released. Things could have gone against you a long time ago and you could be in a labour camp now. Please be patient, Anhua. A lot of people out there are fighting for you, people you have never met and probably never will meet. The only thing they ask of you is that you continue to behave well and get good reports.'

'So it is the quarrel between the SSB and the People's Court that is prolonging my time in gaol?' I said.

Chen nodded and pointed out that if there hadn't been a quarrel, I would have been found guilty and sentenced to many years' hard labour. 'Think positively,' he said. 'You have been lucky so far. Let's hope your luck holds.'

A few days later, I began to bleed. I knew why: before I had been arrested, hospital tests had revealed the presence of a big tumour in my uterus. The report had recommended an immediate operation. However, as the weather was so hot and humid, the doctors had decided to operate in early October. No operation for me now. My usual Menière's attacks continued in prison and my cell-mates had to put up with my sudden vomiting followed by a few days trying to get better under the bright light. There was never any sign of a doctor, so an operation was out of the question.

The bleeding got worse and my health declined rapidly. Little Snow said she had reported my condition but the gaolers took little notice.

Around this time, I was disturbed by the surprise appearance of three female and two male gaolers. The cell door opened without warning just as I was naked from the waist down, trying to clean myself. I was standing over the hole, and fortunately I had a towel in my hands, which was just big enough to cover me. They came in and began ransacking our belongings. Our clothes were searched, then flung on the floor and walked on. Our bedding was checked and thrown about. The knitting was pulled from the needles and unravelled. They were in the cell for about five minutes: we had so little, it didn't take them long to ruin it all. Then they left.

My trial came at last, on 30 November 1985. When the woman gaoler came to take me out, I nearly fell down as I stepped out of my cell. She stretched out her arm and dragged me up. I felt so weak, I staggered like a drunken woman, and she had to support me with her arm around my waist. She helped me into the jeep waiting to take me to the court. It was good to be out, and I breathed in a deep lungful of fresh air.

I looked at everything as the jeep was driven fast to the court. The leaves had left the trees: they filled the gutters and whirled around in the wind. People were wearing heavy winter clothes, with gloves, scarves and hats. I suddenly saw myself in the driver's rear-view mirror. I hadn't seen my face since the day of my arrest, and I was horrified at the change. My hair hung limp and lifeless. My hands were handcuffed in front this time, so I poked at the dry strands with my fingers, wishing I could wash it. I removed my glasses. My eyes looked huge in my pale, much thinner face. I looked old and sick. I saw my broken nose and the scar above my lip.

Ten minutes later, we arrived at the People's Court and I was taken to a big room, which had a huge national emblem on the wall. Under the emblem was a long table with several chairs behind it. There were more chairs lined up in rows on the other side, facing the table. The room was empty except for me and my escort. There was to be no audience allowed in to listen to my case.

As I later learned, trials at that time usually resembled mass denouncing meetings, with representatives from all walks of life attending, together with the press, radio and television. But my judge had made sure nobody was allowed to attend my trial by saying my case concerned 'State secrets'. In fact, he had done that to make me feel less humiliated.

When the judge appeared, he was in uniform. He was tall, slim and handsome. He was about forty-five, and he had piercing bright eyes. He walked into the trial court from a side door, followed by his two assistants. Then, from the rear of the court, my lawyer and the public procurator walked in. The five men sat down behind the long table with the judge in the middle. I was motioned to sit on one of the chairs, directly in front of the judge. I was not put into a wooden cage like other prisoners. This made me feel optimistic. I began to hope for release after the trial.

The proceedings began at nine o'clock in the morning. The judge started by asking me some questions. To my surprise, he spoke gently. He asked my name, address, occupation and so on. Once he had finished, the public procurator stood up and read out a statement of charges. He said I had committed the crime of telling people State secrets. I was not, I noticed, branded an enemy agent or a spy, as had been the case when the SSB had first arrested me. He opened a file and pulled out the letter I had written to David.

The only testimony was by the general manager of my office. He was not in the courtroom; instead his written statement was read out. His final paragraph said: 'With this letter addressed to David Wei, people outside China might guess our foreign-trade policy and it might bring harm to our socialist economic order.' To be fair, the public procurator did slightly emphasize 'might', which put a more favourable perspective on my supposed crime. 'Might' is not 'can' or 'will', and cast doubt upon my possible guilt.

My lawyer stood up to speak for me. He read out a letter signed by all the staff members, except the general manager. 'Comrade Gao Anhua has always worked very hard and efficiently since she came to our company. She has a good command of English and high skills in doing import and export business. She has made friends with everybody and earned the respect of us all. Nevertheless, she has shortcomings like everybody else. For instance, she uses makeup and wears fresh clothes every day to make herself look attractive, which is considered bourgeois, but, in view of her job, it is not surprising. We wish to let it be known that Comrade Gao has always worked hard for China despite her poor health, and we appeal to the People's Court to be lenient with her.'

Fair enough, I thought. The lawyer showed the letter to the judge and to me as well. I felt warmth run through my heart. It was good to know all my colleagues were sympathetic and supportive. That was the end of the prosecution and the defence.

I was grateful for the lawyer. Not many defendants had lawyers, although they were entitled to one if they could afford it. However, in those days, a defence lawyer was mostly to make the public think the accused had rights and was given a fair trial. Was it my imagination or was my case an exception? Certainly the judge and the procurator seemed to agree with my lawyer. They both spoke to me in friendly tones. The procurator looked at me as he told the judge that the photographs taken in my home by the SSB had not been admitted, because there was nothing in them to support their accusation that I was an enemy agent.

The judge said directly to me, 'My name is Lu Wei, and these are my assistants. Don't worry too much about your case.' He paused, and I thought I would be released. However, when he spoke again, my hopes were dashed. 'You will be taken back to prison to await the final verdict. It may be some time before you hear anything because we have to report to the leaders. If you have any questions or want to talk to me, you can ask your gaolers to send for me.'

The trial I had waited so long for had lasted just twenty minutes, and then I was on my way back to prison.

Little Snow listened carefully as I recounted everything I could remember. Then she said confidently, 'Well, from what I know about trials, you will probably be acquitted. I have never heard of the judge being so kind to a prisoner. Usually they are cold and businesslike. I would think you will hear the result within one week, according to the rules.'

Her words cheered me. I sang while knitting, and I worked harder to knit more each day. I began to feel better in myself too. Little Snow suggested that we keep in touch. But how? Prisoners were not allowed to contact each other, even after release, and writing materials were not allowed, so we couldn't write down our addresses anyway. Every day we repeated our addresses until we were sure we would never forget them. And I never have forgotten Little Snow's.

1701 and 453 also asked me to memorize their addresses, which I did.

One week passed, and then another. No news came. I began counting the days. I woke up each morning full of optimism and went to sleep at night in despair. Every hour seemed like a day, and the days passed slowly. Still no verdict came. I began to think I would be locked away for ever. The gaolers ignored my request to see the judge. I started to lose heart and the bleeding worsened again.

At about one o'clock in the afternoon of 18 December 1985, just as we had finished our lunch, the door of our cell opened. '1720! Get your belongings ready and follow me. Leave your knitting with 180 and 453. Check the needles before leaving.' I hastened to do as I was told. Little Snow stopped knitting and looked at me. She dared not make a sound because the gaoler was beside me, but I understood the message of farewell in her eyes. I left my towel with her as a small parting gift, and stepped out of the cell.

I wasn't handcuffed for the journey to the court this time. It was a fine day, cold, crisp and sunny. I had been used to the light of the electric bulb in our cell for twenty-four hours a day, so the bright sunlight hurt my eyes and I had to put a hand up to shield them. I stepped into the jeep and was whisked away. Inside the court building, I followed the gaoler into a small room where my judge and his two assistants were sitting behind a desk. There was no chair for me.

'Now, listen carefully, here is the verdict,' said the judge. He began reading from a paper with the official red stamp of the People's Court. 'Defendant Gao Anhua, female, aged thirty-six, is accused of committing the crime of divulging State secrets. Due to the fact that the case is not serious and the accused has constantly adopted a good attitude while in custody, the Nanjing People's Court has decided to release Gao Anhua on probation for one year, the date of the probation to begin from the day of her arrest.' Then the judge looked at me. 'Do you understand the verdict?'

I understood. Oh, yes, I understood. The verdict meant that I was still guilty but I had been given a suspended sentence. The verdict would go into my file and follow me for the rest of my life, which meant that a dark political shadow would be over my head for ever. I looked at the judge, puzzled.

He nodded understandingly, and said quietly, 'This is the best I could do. You will not be sent to do hard labour and, according to the law, with a probationary sentence you will not lose your job. Your company has no right to dismiss you.'

'But I'm innocent!' I burst out. 'You know I am!'

The judge did not answer. He looked at me silently for a moment, then turned and walked away, followed by his assistants. I saw compassion in his eyes when he turned briefly to give me a last look. Then he was gone.

It was not a just verdict and I was resentful at the time. But from the safety of the passing years, I recognize that it was a monumental decision. In a land empty of justice that tiny bias towards a semblance of a fair trial was a huge and dangerous step for the judge to take. And it proved beyond a shadow of doubt that, despite all the years without a shred of human rights, bravery and decency were not dead in China.

23. The Judge

The procurator took me home in his car. I clutched my few belongings to my chest, anxious now to get behind my own front door. My first thought was to find Little Yan. When we reached my flat, the door was still sealed. The date of my arrest was clearly written on the paper alongside a red stamp. The procurator handed me my key, which he had got back from the SSB. He tore the paper and pushed it to one side. I unlocked the door. With a polite 'good luck', the procurator spun on his heel and left me alone.

My flat was a stinking, ruined shambles. I stepped gingerly into the kitchen. There was rotten food everywhere. Plates and cups sat covered in green mould. Flies buzzed, angry at being disturbed. I waved my arms, trying to frighten them away. 'Get out!' I cried, on the verge of tears. 'You have had three months of freedom here. Now it is mine again.' But it wasn't mine. Never again. I lived in that flat for another nine years, but from the day I returned, it was a place to live in, not my home.

My bedroom looked like a garbage dump. My shoes and clothes were lying everywhere, covered in dirty footprints. My bed was lying at an angle because one of the legs was broken. The mattress was ripped in several places and the stuffing pulled out. My pillow lay in a corner, spewing out feathers. Everything was smashed. Bits of furniture lay about among the other debris, which included my makeup, letters and books. 'Filthy, rotten, cowardly, dog-shit bastards!' I spat. My language had improved during my time in prison.

I had no money, no food and nothing left worth selling. The electronic keyboard was smashed. So, too, was my old English typewriter, my television and my radio. Most of my crockery was in small pieces on the kitchen floor. Even the electric light bulbs had been broken. It was at that exact moment, when I first noticed the remains of the light bulbs hanging sadly from their sockets, that I vowed I would get out of China, no matter how long it took me. I had had enough.

I was told by my next-door neighbours that Little Yan had been sent to live with my husband's brother in Suzhou and put under the direct supervision of my mother-in-law, Feng Bin. My neighbours were the only people to speak to me, and only that one time, to tell me what had happened to my daughter. The others living nearby dared not acknowledge me for fear of being implicated in my crimes.

They didn't know the truth about me. It was sufficient for them to know I had been arrested. They avoided me as if I was a plague carrier. Nobody wanted to be associated with me. Many looked at me with contempt when they saw me in the streets. As I passed, I could hear people whispering, and see them pointing at me. I was totally isolated. No words can describe how much it hurt. I had returned to a world of insult, unable to fight back.

With no money, I needed to return to work as quickly as possible. The verdict said I still had a job with my original company but when I contacted both the Electronics Corporation and Sinochem, I found it impossible to start work with either, due to a quarrel between the two companies. Neither wanted me. The Electronics Corporation said they had only borrowed me for six months, and as I had been with them for much longer than that I should go back to Sinochem. Sinochem retorted, 'She was no problem before she was loaned to you. Now that she has been found guilty of a big political mistake while in your employ, you should be responsible for her.'

They kicked the ball back and forth for nearly a year after I was released. During that time I was not given one yuan of salary by either company. Eventually the People's Court forced them to come to an agreement: the Electronics Corporation must pay my back salary for a full year, and Sinochem must accept me back as a staff member.

But for now, I had no money so I could buy nothing. Fortunately I had found a little rice in the kitchen and a few candles. I spent all the daylight hours cleaning. It was hard, heart-breaking work and, even after two days, I still had a long way to go. Then during the early evening of my third day out of gaol, I heard a knock on the door. I sprang up, panic-stricken. My first thought was that I was about to be rearrested by the SSB on another false charge.

When I opened the door, there in the darkness stood Little Zhu, who was my best friend at Sinochem. She was with another girl from the office named Shao. They brought with them some fruit, a few small cakes and a little money. Little Zhu said, 'We had to come and see you secretly because everyone in Sinochem was called to a meeting and told that nobody working for the company was allowed to visit you. Don't tell anybody we have been here.'

These two brave women had come, at great risk to themselves, to see me. I was moved by their courage. Their visit was a ray of sunshine, which lit a tiny ember of hope. Although the Gang of Four had been in prison for over nine years, anyone showing friendship to a political offender was still not tolerated. I had had many friends before my arrest, but only now, when I was at rock bottom, would I find out who were my real friends.

The next day I contacted Sinochem again to claim my right to work there. I was refused once again. The reason given to me was the same: 'It is the responsibility of the Electronics Corporation. You should go there.' Of course, I had no better response from the other company. I felt indignant: I had earned much foreign exchange for both companies. Now they regarded me as an 'unreliable bad element'. Such humiliation was beyond my endurance. The spark of hope that Little Zhu and Shao had just lit died out again. I decided to see the judge.

Before going to the People's Court, I sent a letter to each of the families of my three ex-cell-mates as promised. After postage, I had five cents left, about the value of an old English farthing. Not enough, even, for one small bowl of rice.

As I walked towards the office of the judge, I stared at the wheels of the buses as they hurried to their next stop. My thoughts were grim. Yes, I could do what so many political victims had done in the past and kill myself. It would be so easy to step into the path of a speeding bus. And I was tempted. The idea of eternal peace seemed attractive: I could be with my mother and father in another world, where there was no pain, no torture and no injustice. At last I understood why so many people killed themselves every day in China. The biggest protest anyone could make against the unfair regime was to take their own life.

But there was Little Yan to think of. She did not deserve to be an orphan. I would never be able to rest easy in my other world if I left her to face an uncertain future alone in this one. I must carry on. But how? Perhaps the judge would know.

I wasn't even certain he would see me. So many people had let me down, why not him? But he didn't fail me. He came to the reception area of the People's Court within a couple of minutes of knowing I was there. Suddenly I went to pieces. I felt foolish asking this handsome stranger for help. I managed to find my voice, and gabbled, 'Comrade Judge Lu, I have come to you because I have no one else to turn to. I remembered your kindness to me during my trial and I hoped that you could help me. I know I shouldn't have come, and I apologize for disturbing you –' He stopped my disjointed flow with a gesture of his hand and a kind smile.

I calmed down and told him everything from the beginning. He had not known that my flat had been wrecked by the SSB or that they had stolen my money. He nodded when I told him how Yellow-teeth had twice punched me in the face. I reminded him how, during my interrogation, I had proved beyond a shadow of doubt that I had committed no offence. Not even a small political mistake. But the SSB seemed determined to make me suffer. I thanked him for his efforts on my behalf. I knew he had been forced to withstand great pressure to convict me of being an enemy agent, and I wanted him to know how grateful I was. My present difficulties were not of his doing, it was the fault of my general manager and the SSB. I just wanted someone in authority to know I was having a hard time – not least because of the attitude of Sinochem and the Electronics Corporation. I needed money to live, but I was not being allowed to work. If it was not for my daughter, I would kill myself.

The judge didn't interrupt as I unloaded all my troubles. His face showed his concern for me until I spoke of killing myself. Then he said, 'How can you think of such a thing? I must be wrong about you. I thought you were a strong-willed person.' He continued, 'All I have done for you will be in vain if you kill yourself. Come, pull yourself together! Life is hard for you now, but it will get better. Killing yourself will achieve nothing, except bringing down scorn from everybody who knows you. Think how lucky you are. You could be in a labour camp now, being slowly worked to death.' His words jolted me. Nobody had ever spoken to me like this but I knew he was right and I felt ashamed of myself.

When he spoke again, his voice was gentler. 'I know how it is for you, and I sympathize, but you must begin to rebuild your life, if only for the sake of your daughter. And I know you do not want to let your parents down. Or me. You can and you will stand up and fight for justice. Your justice. The worst is over, now you have a chance to begin again. Please take it.'

I nodded, unable to speak. I shook hands with him and bowed my thanks. I felt hot tears of shame, and quickly brushed them away. 'You are right,' I forced myself to say. 'Please forgive me for my weakness. Life is difficult for me just now, and this is not the first or the second time it has knocked me down. But this time it is much harder to start again. My will-power to get up and fight back has almost gone. Please say I can come back and let you know how I am getting on.' The judge looked pleased and relieved. 'Of course you can,' he said quietly. 'I insist upon it.'

When I reached home, there was a letter in my mail-box. I opened it and found a fifty-yuan banknote inside a folded sheet of bamboo note-paper – fifty yuan was about the average monthly salary of a worker in Nanjing at that time. I read the note. 'Comrade Gao, I hope you will overcome your present circumstances and make a new start in life. I will do my best to help you out of your difficulties. The money enclosed is not much, but it will help. When you are on your way, you may return it to me if you so wish.' The signature was unknown to me: 'Fish and Sun'. It was a puzzle.

In Chinese, many characters are made up of two or three different characters, very similar to the way an English word is made up from different letters. The character 'fish' plus the character 'sun' makes the character 'Lu'. The judge. His family name was Lu. A lump came to my throat. He had known all the time I was complaining to him, and talking about killing myself, that his money was waiting for me at home. I felt gratitude, shame, relief and happiness. It was too much. I sat down and bawled my eyes out.

The next morning I rose early, had a quick breakfast, and set off for the People's Court. I wasn't sure if I should use his money, much as I needed it. Surely he had a family to support? My prime need was to thank him. I felt he was a man sent by the gods to protect me. I knew the court opened at eight o'clock. I arrived, as planned, at seven thirty and waited near the main entrance.

It was freezing cold and very windy. The temperature was about zero, but it felt much colder. It wasn't long before I was frozen to the bone, despite being wrapped in warm clothes, including a woollen shawl and gloves. I stood motionless about twenty metres from the gate, my feet feeling like blocks of ice. But I had no intention of leaving until I had spoken to the judge. People began to trickle into the building. After a while they flowed through the gates like a river.

Then I saw my judge riding a bicycle towards the entrance. I moved forward a few steps and called, 'Judge Lu, was it you who wrote to me?'

He didn't answer immediately. His eyes made a quick survey of the immediate area. When he was sure nobody was listening, he asked, 'Do you have a telephone at home?' I nodded. 'Quickly. Tell me your number.' I did so. Then he muttered, 'It is not convenient to talk here. Please go home and wait for my call.' He gave me a nod of farewell. I watched him park his bicycle and head for the entrance. He was swallowed up in the throng and lost to my sight in seconds.

The local government had allocated me the telephone. I was considered a priority case because of my Menière's disease. Actually, like most things in China, it had been a fiddle. I asked an old family friend to help me get it and it had been fitted a month before I was arrested. At six o'clock in the evening of the day I had seen the judge, the telephone rang. He didn't waste time on pleasantries. 'Please go to the bus station on the East Beijing Road and wait there. Look out for me. I will be wearing simple plain clothes. A blue Chinese-style jacket and a peaked cap.' Before I could ask any questions, the telephone went dead. Surprised, I stared at it for several seconds, in two minds whether to go or not. It was such a strange request. But I owed this man a great deal and, anyway, my insatiable curiosity would not be denied. I put on my warmest clothes and went out into the dark street.

The same strong north wind was blowing into my face as I headed towards my destination. Crowds of people filled the pavement as they hurried home from their workplaces. In the road, thousands of bicycles flowed in both directions. The air was filled with important-sounding bicycle bells. At this time of day it was always difficult to cross the road. There were not many cars in 1985 but the roads were already busy and crowded.

I hurried along, huddled up against the wind. It took me almost half an hour to get to the bus station. There was no sign of the judge, so I found a convenient doorway from where I could see the buses pulling in and disgorging their passengers. During the next hour a steady stream came and went. I was frozen to the bone and on the verge of leaving for home when, at last, I spotted him. I stepped forward and called, 'Judge Lu!'

He didn't answer. Nor did he look at me. He buried his cheeks in the turned-up collar of his coat and walked straight past me. I was nonplussed. What was I supposed to do? Then, when he was about five metres past my doorway, he beckoned me to follow him with a hand gesture so slight that only I noticed it.

I followed him in silence, about ten metres behind. We walked a little way then turned into a small lane. He stopped and looked around. Under the dim street-lights the lane seemed empty. I caught up with him, and he whispered, 'Take me to your home. Don't talk. I will follow you.'

I felt like the spy I had been accused of being. I was reminded of the films I had seen, where the underground Communists went about their secret business during the time of the Kuomintang regime. I knew he was somewhere behind me, but I didn't look back. Twenty minutes later, I entered the block of flats where I lived.

By the time I had found my key and unlocked the door to my flat, he was with me. I held open the door and he went past me into the dark kitchen. I showed him into the living room, and switched on the light. I had bought the new bulbs only that day from the money he had sent me. He put his briefcase on the floor and sat down. I stood, waiting. 'Why are you standing?' he said, smiling. 'Please sit down. You are not a prisoner now. We are equal.' I sat down opposite him. I was very nervous. What did he want with me? I hoped he wasn't just looking for a cheap affair!

He looked at me apologetically. 'I'm sorry,' he said, 'I have to be very careful. As a judge, I am not supposed to have any contact with any litigant except inside the court building.'

'I understand,' I replied. 'I did not realize how dangerous it must be for you to be here.' He looked at me with respect, which set me at my ease, then said, 'Please don't hate me. I was unable to say you were innocent, and I was forced to give you the probation. I researched your case carefully. I visited your working units and your middle school to find out all about you. I even checked up on your family history. From what I found, I knew you were being wronged by the SSB, and I wanted to release you as not guilty. But the Provincial SSB head office sent people to discuss your case with me and the chairman of the People's Court on three separate occasions. And they telephoned many times. The local SSB also made it plain to me how upset they were with my attitude. I was followed everywhere, around the clock, for weeks.'

I gasped. This was pressure indeed, and I had to admire his strength of character. He then asked, 'Why didn't I give in to them? We had never met, so you meant nothing to me.' His look made me think he was calculating how much he could trust me.

I returned his gaze. Then I said, 'You don't have to worry. I will never betray you.'

He said, with a chuckle. 'You are very clever. You keep guessing correctly what is in my mind – in the court, in my letter and just now.'

He lit a cigarette and I passed him an ashtray. He continued, 'The SSB badly wanted to have you convicted of a crime, even though it was obvious to everybody that you had done nothing wrong. They thought when they arrested you that they could dig out some enemy agents through you. They suspected David Wei. They were convinced that he was a Hong Kong spy, until they knew he was a Party member. They expected to catch a big fish after arresting you, but they soon found out how wrong they were. You were not even a small tiddler and David was above suspicion.' He laughed as he recounted how the SSB had lost face when the truth was revealed to the judiciary. His eyes were sparkling with humour as he said, 'You can imagine how stupid they looked.'

I made us some green tea. The judge lit another cigarette, and when he spoke again, the humour had gone. He was very serious. 'You know, of course, our Party will always find a scapegoat to take the blame for any mistake. The SSB do the same just to save their own faces. They contacted me saying that the image of the Party must never be tarnished, therefore Gao Anhua must be sacrificed.' He stopped to drink. 'I regret to say I have knowingly judged innocent people to be guilty in the past, simply because it was demanded of me by the Party. But your case was so blatantly unfair, that I hesitated. I needed time to think. In my heart I knew it was wrong to convict you. When the SSB tried to bully me into giving a guilty verdict, that made up my mind. I resented their threatening attitude and decided not to do as they demanded. I have seen enough futures destroyed for no good reason.

'Sometimes I have been involved in making such things happen. And every time I felt very bad afterwards, unable to eat and sleep for days on end. Evil is evil, no matter how justified it can be made to appear. So it was not only you who was on trial . . . I put myself on trial too.'

The poor man was now agitated and unhappy. When he blew out some cigarette smoke, I clearly heard a tremor in his breathing. He needed to unburden himself and I was his willing listener.

'The sentence I gave you was the outcome of a compromise proposal put forward by the chairman of the People's Court. He is not a bad person and he did not agree with the demands of the SSB that you be sent to do hard labour. On the other hand, he is understandably afraid of the power of the SSB. So he said you must be convicted of "divulging a State secret" and given probation. And I was ordered to give you the verdict.

'I said it was my verdict, but it wasn't. It was the compromise verdict decided upon by him. I'm sorry. Although you are free, you will never have a clean file. You will not be trusted by your company and it will affect your career all the way through to the end. I hate what has been done to you. But at least you are here talking to me instead of suffering the harsh conditions of a labour camp.'

I stayed silent. What could I say? I felt close to this stranger. He had trusted me with his thoughts which, if the SSB ever got to know of them, would be enough to have him shot. I made some fresh tea. The judge drained his mug in one gulp and stood up. He looked me straight in the eyes and said, most sincerely, 'If you can find any of your old family friends who are still in power to reverse your verdict, I shall be very happy to comply. I won't mind being blamed by them for giving you the wrong verdict.'

He picked up his briefcase, opened it and pulled out a parcel, which he placed on the table. He reached in again for a sheet of paper and a pencil. He handed them to me, saying, 'Write down these names. They are the people who have been involved in your case.' He reeled off a dozen. Then he told me to write down the dates and places of the meetings. 'Your case was probably the smallest one in the history of our People's Court since 1949. But it alarmed the provincial leader Shen very much. He is responsible for the judiciary, and because he has a good relationship with the SSB, he backs them. You should not contact him. You must find other leaders to support you. In fact, your little case became a big quarrel of differing opinions within the Party. It ended up as a struggle for power, which had nothing at all to do with the rights and wrongs of your case. You were only a victim, and so was I.'

He let out a long sigh. He seemed happier. 'The souls of your mother and father must find it difficult to rest as they see the changes to our Party, and now they have witnessed how the Party has treated you and left such a bleak future for you and your daughter. As a man, I have never wept. But I did after I had given my verdict to you. I feel guilty to see you so persecuted. You can use any of the information I have given you to get your good name back.'

He opened the parcel. Inside were two sizeable carp, which he laid on the table. 'I bought these for you. The New Year's Day is near, cook yourself a good meal.' He walked towards the door. 'I must be leaving now. Please forgive me. Take care. And please, Comrade Gao, don't mention my name to anyone.'

I nodded. But I couldn't leave it at that. This decent man deserved something more from me. I spoke to his back: 'Judge Lu, please wait. I want to thank you.' He turned and looked at me expectantly. I continued, 'I know how hard it must have been for you. You are an exceptional man, and I thank you from the bottom of my heart for helping me. And for taking the time to explain things so clearly. I hope that one day we can be friends.' He smiled and left.

At first, all I could think of was the judge. He had left a big impression on me as a man of goodness and integrity. As I mulled over everything he had said, a deep outrage at the deeds of the SSB engulfed me, and hatred burned deep in my belly. How could they get away with such behaviour? Even the chairman of the People's Court was scared of their power.

Although I knew it was dangerous I wanted revenge on the SSB and my good name back. My first action was to contact Liu, the second Party secretary of Jiangsu Province. He and my parents had worked together and been good friends. I found him at home. He seldom went to the office: though he was no longer labelled a capitalist roader and he had regained his position, he still had a lingering fear of Party authority, so he claimed he was in poor health and needed a rest. Thus, he could keep his powerful job and good salary. I remember hearing him say, when I was a little girl, 'More work more mistakes, less work less mistakes and no work, no mistakes.'

He listened to everything I had to say. Then he said, 'Although I am sympathetic, Little Flower, it is no good to struggle against the SSB. They are not people to be trifled with. You will stir up a nest of hornets who will turn their stings on you. I am old, I have had my share of hardships, and all I want now is a peaceful life. The less trouble the better. Please understand.' He reached out and held my hand in his. 'It is good you are out of gaol. Take care of yourself and your child. Come and visit me and have dinner with me every weekend as before. Please listen to this old man. I have good advice. Let bygones be bygones.'

'But what about my future? What about the future of my daughter?' I withdrew my hand. I knew he could help me if he wanted to. He had the power and the connections. I felt let down. I tried once more to change his mind. 'If it was your own child who had been treated so badly and disgraced by a bad file, you would surely do something. My parents are dead. I have nobody to do me justice, so I came to you. But your friendship with my parents and to me and my daughter is not strong enough. You would rather let us suffer under a lie for the rest of our lives than risk offending the SSB.' As I left his house I was crying with rage. I never went back.

Liu had done all sorts of things to protect his own children. His eldest son had once gone joyriding in a big truck after an argument with his driving instructor and crashed into a shop, causing thousands of yuans' worth of damage. Liu used his power to prevent his son being punished. And that was just one incident involving his children, who were spoilt and headstrong. But he wouldn't help to put right the wrong done to me. I was at a loss. I couldn't contact any other of my old family friends. They had either retired, moved away, died, or I had lost contact with them.

I didn't give up. Going to see Liu had been the most obvious and easiest route to justice, but it was not the only one. I wrote many letters to the departments concerned, as well as to the media. For several months I heard nothing, which didn't surprise me, but I was obsessed. I wrote dozens more letters. Among them was a long, detailed one to the Minister of State Security in Beijing. It contained all the information the judge had given me – and at last someone took notice.

That letter was passed around, and eventually came to the attention of the chief of the SSB in Beijing. He asked for my case to be reinvestigated. The outcome came as a pleasant surprise. I had expected the SSB and their supporters to be vindicated by the State, but they were severely criticized on the grounds that, as the enforcers of the law, they should have dealt with me fairly instead of vigorously opposing a fair verdict. Their behaviour, said the report, had resulted in a denial of justice.

Meanwhile, my appeal to reverse my conviction was accepted by the Nanjing People's Court. They, too, issued instructions that my case must be thoroughly checked and reinvestigated by the judiciary. All of this activity made the local SSB officers fly into a rage from shame. They knew that someone had leaked 'internal secrets' to me, otherwise I could not have accused them of acting illegally in dealing with my case. Their bullying tactics towards the senior members of the People's Court and the judge, which had resulted in me being found guilty, became common knowledge, causing an extreme loss of face for them, which they had not experienced before.

Yet again, though, they abused their power. Instead of offering to assist the investigators appointed by the People's Court, they opened their own investigation to uncover the person who had leaked the information to me. They suspected the judge, but they had to get conclusive evidence and they wanted my confession. This time, however, there could be no sudden arrest and internment. The local SSB would not be able to beat and torture a confession out of me.

The investigating group came to my home one morning in May 1986. They were polite, showed me their ID cards and asked me to accompany them to the Nanjing People's Court. They said they wanted me to 'speak clearly' about something that had happened after I was released. This time I was given time to dress behind a closed door before being escorted to a minibus. I guessed it concerned the judge and silently, as we headed towards the People's Court where he was working, I warned myself over and over, 'No matter what they do to me, I mustn't say anything about the judge. I will die first if necessary!'

I was seated in the middle of a room. The group of five sat down in a semi-circle in front of me. The main interrogator was a woman in her mid-fifties. She looked at me, I looked straight back at her. Our eyes locked. I waited for the shouting to begin. Instead, she smiled. 'Comrade Gao,' she began in an I-want-to-be-your-friend tone, 'please tell us who told you about the processing of your case.'

'I can't remember,' I said, matching her, stare for stare. I was a bit nervous, but not fearful. I had long since passed the point where I could be frightened by such people. I now knew that they were at least as fearful of their higher authorities as I was of them.

'Come, Comrade, we already know who it was. All we need is for you to confirm it.' I mentally said, 'Liar!' but remained silent. 'Please, Comrade Gao. It is not your fault. We will not victimize you if you tell.' I knew very well what their tricks were. They would never get me to admit to having got up that morning, never mind who told me about my case. In prison Little Snow had taught me well. Admit nothing.

The woman stood up and walked to my side. She put her hand gently on my shoulder as she asked, 'Tell me, who told you the names of these people?'

'I cannot remember.'

'Oh, come on. Of course you can.'

I opened my mouth to say, 'I can't remember,' again, but what came out was something different. 'Why do you want to know who told me?'

I said, glaring up at her. 'It doesn't matter who told me. If what was said to me was the truth, then you should be questioning the real criminals, not the one who told me. Just think – I have no money, no social status, no parents. I am at rock bottom. Nobody can get any benefit from telling me the truth. It can only come from someone with a conscience. We have all lived through the Cultural Revolution, and I am sure you don't like the idea of people plotting, fighting and accusing each other the way it was then. Why do you waste your time trying to dig out a good, decent person, when you should be investigating the really bad people?'

My eyes searched each face in turn and it seemed to me my words had gone home. Nobody spoke. Their eyes told me all I needed to know as they dropped under my gaze. However, their orders told them they must find out the name. So she began again. This time there was no smile. 'Has Judge Lu ever visited you at your home?'

'I beg your pardon?' I replied, giving myself time to think. The woman repeated her question. 'What would he do at my home?' I said. 'Are you insinuating that the judge and I are immoral?' She blushed. She was as red as a radish. There was silence in the room for about half a minute while she regained her composure. Then she said, 'I didn't mean that. I once instructed him to go and see you.' (Liar!) 'Don't be afraid of saying so. I asked him to go to your home, so if he did, he was only obeying my instructions. Tell me if he has ever called to see you.'

She wanted to trap me into making a confession. I looked her straight in the eyes as I said, 'I am sorry to say he did not obey your order. He has never called at my home.' So far I hadn't told a lie. I had *taken* the judge to my home. He hadn't *called* there. I continued, 'I first met him during the trial, and again when he gave me his verdict. I cannot clearly remember much about both those times.'

'But there must be someone who knows your case very well who told you all about it. Who is that person?'

'I can't rememb –'

Suddenly an unexpected male voice interrupted: 'This is a very serious matter. Please understand. It is a crime for any law executor to reveal such things to an offender. I must make this clear to you because you are running towards trouble for yourself by not telling us what we want to know.'

I looked at the speaker and said, 'Isn't it a bigger crime to fabricate a case against an innocent person like me? And we both know why. Just to save someone's face! So why are you not using your time to investigate the perpetrators of the real crime?' I was choosing my words as carefully as I could. I did not directly accuse the SSB of committing the crime, but everyone in the room knew what I meant.

The man raised his hand to stop me. 'Yes, we know all about that, but it is a different case. Now it is yours. You had better tell us the truth, otherwise –' He paused and looked at me threateningly.

I was determined to fight to the end. There was no chance of me ever admitting that the judge had been to my home. He had saved me from a short and terrible future, and had put his faith and trust in me. I couldn't let him down. Anyway, I hated them all and I hated the SSB most of all. How dare they smash up my home!

'Comrade Gao.' It was the woman. 'We have been easy on you because we know your case, but if you don't tell us the name, we cannot protect you for ever.' Ah! Here it comes, the threat of punishment. Well, who cares? I held out my hands in front of me as though in handcuffs.

'You can throw me back into prison, if you like. I have already been humiliated and disgraced, so it doesn't matter to me if I become a prisoner again. And when you have me powerless, you can have me beaten to death, because my answer will always be the same: I can't remember.' With these words, I closed my eyes. 'I'm tired.'

For the remainder of the morning they asked me the same question over and over while I hid behind my closed eyelids and stayed silent. I didn't care if my actions caused them to bring a charge of contempt of court against me. At lunchtime we broke for food. The woman took me to the dining room and bought me a simple lunch. 'Please think hard and tell us the truth this afternoon,' she said, as she handed me a bowl of rice.

I thought about things as I ate. The truth, I thought. They don't deserve the truth. I remembered what Little Snow had told me about how she had told a pack of lies to her inquisitors. Perhaps I should do the same. But what? How? When? I idly watched a woman walk into the dining room. She reminded me of someone. At first I couldn't remember who. Then, suddenly I had it. Mrs Ding. Yes! Mrs Ding, I thought. She will do nicely.

Mrs Ding was the current Party secretary of Sinochem, and a very unpleasant person she was too – much too full of her own importance. She behaved unkindly to me and to most of the other lower grades of staff at Sinochem. She was continually boasting about her important friends, including, she often said, many high-ranking officers in the SSB.

She wanted everyone to be impressed by how powerful she was, and be afraid of her. Her whole day was spent going around the company bullying people.

By the time my interrogation began again in the afternoon, I had worked out my plan. I could kill two birds with one stone: first, get these people to follow a false trail away from the judge and, second, give Mrs Ding something to worry about. I knew what I wanted to say, and in what order. I had to make my questioners believe my story. I also had to appear to break down under their constant questioning so that they thought they had beaten me. But first I had to continue to act exactly the same way as I had in the morning.

After the first question, I said to the man who had earlier tried to intimidate me, 'From your age, old Comrade, I can guess you joined the Communist Party before 1949. You are a veteran Party official, and you know what is right and what is wrong. It is wrong of you to try to dig out your own honest comrades from the People's Court just to satisfy the SSB. You know it is right that those who committed the original crime should be punished, not the innocent.' The man looked at me for a few seconds. Then I saw an almost imperceptible nod. I knew he agreed with me but he was too weak to admit it.

I resisted them for almost two more hours. Like a swordswoman thrusting and parrying, I alternately attacked them and defended myself. At the same time I made myself appear less and less resilient, until, in the end, I murmured, 'All right, you have won. I cannot fight you any more.' All five leaned forward expectantly, the gleam of victory in their eyes. I looked downcast, apparently beaten, and began to tell 'the truth'.

'Please understand that I wanted to tell you the truth from the beginning, but I have been threatened by Mrs Ding, the present Party secretary of Sinochem not to say anything or else I would be for ever her enemy.' I looked up. All five were listening attentively. I went on, 'It was actually the SSB themselves who revealed the details of my case. Someone in the SSB told everything to Mrs Ding and she told others. Now everybody in my company and many others know how the SSB dealt with my case. You can go to Sinochem and question each and every member of staff there, if you like. You will soon find out I am speaking the truth. I suggest you start with Mrs Ding. In this way you will find out which member of the SSB first leaked the information to her. As for me, so many people came to tell me, I can't remember who was the first.' I stopped talking and gave a big sigh.

I wasn't sure if my story would be accepted or if they would check up. I was gambling that the SSB would want to keep quiet about the whole thing. They had lost enough face already and they would know their smokescreen had not worked. At least it would give me time to think of something to explain how I had been mistaken. My overriding concern was to protect the judge. I heard the faint scribbling of a man taking notes. Then the scratching of his pen stopped and there was silence. I sat in front of the five people, as calm as a Buddha, and waited.

They looked at me, then at each other. They began whispering to each other. I was reminded of my schooldays when a bunch of children exchanged secrets in a corner, but much more was at stake here. I looked out through a window. It was a lovely sunny May day. A few white clouds drifted in a bright blue sky and the trees were covered in new green leaves. What a beautiful picture. I thought of Little Snow, still locked away in that dingy cell and thanked her. She would probably never know how much the judge and I were in her debt. I hope one day she will read this.

A basketball game was going on somewhere. The sounds of young men and women shouting, laughing and having fun drifted in to disturb the quiet. The five continued to whisper, and I wished they would hurry up. So far there had not been any mention of my verdict being reversed. And, with an unclean personal record, I would never live as happily or peacefully as normal people. Suddenly, the woman spoke: 'What else can you tell us?'

I withdrew my eyes from the window and looked at her. 'Nothing. I think I have told you everything.' There was another period of silence, which I broke with: 'Please can I go home now?'

'Yes, after doing this.' The woman came to me with the notes the young man had written. She handed them to me and asked me to read them. 'If you believe you have told the truth, and what you have said is accurately recorded here, put your thumbprint on the paper.'

I read the whole thing through. Their lies and my lies were written down, to be analysed and dissected by minds buried deep within this building. The young man had recorded everything honestly, so I dipped the thumb of my right hand into the red ink and pressed it on the paper. This meant I agreed that the notes were correct.

After that I was allowed to go. No ride home. No escort. I had served my purpose. I was of no further interest. I was glad to be free of them at last. That day had seemed like a month, and I was exhausted from so much questioning and lying. I walked from the court building and followed the sounds to where the basketball game was being played. About fifty young people were enjoying themselves. I stood and watched for a while. I hoped they would never have to live through such repression as I had survived.

Two weeks later the judge did call at my home. This time he wore his uniform and he came in broad daylight. On entering my flat, he politely took off his peaked cap and smiled broadly. 'Thank you, Little Sister. We have won!' The investigators' report had concluded that the SSB was to blame for revealing the judicial secrets concerning my case.

'Frankly,' he said, 'I was very worried about it all. That morning I saw you being escorted into the court building by the five investigators and I was very nervous. I knew you would not willingly betray me because you had given me your promise, but you are so naïve I thought you would fall into one of their traps. I was prepared for the worst possible result. I knew I would be dismissed from my post and put in prison. I have no regrets for doing what I did. I would do it again if I had to. I am proud of you, Anhua. You did not let me down.'

I made some green tea and asked the judge if he had eaten. He hadn't, so I cooked us a few simple dishes. When we were eating, he said to me, 'You have proved yourself a courageous and true friend. And your story, turning the tables on the SSB, was truly inspirational. The investigating group have a tacit understanding that it was me who told you, but they did not really want to dig me out. They said they were impressed with many of the things you said to them and the way you conducted yourself. At the end, when you finally gave in, they were glad to hear your story clearing me and implicating the very people who had brought the charges. The whole of the Chinese people hate the SSB. Not just you ordinary people but everyone, from the top downwards.'

He pulled a bottle of red wine out of his briefcase. 'Let's drink a toast to celebrate our victory.' I went to the kitchen and found two goblets the SSB hadn't broken. I placed them on the table and the judge filled them. Before we clinked glasses he said, 'I have a small heart problem, so my doctor has forbidden me to drink alcohol, but today is a special day. *Ganbei!*' (It means 'drink all' – the same as 'cheers' in England.) He tipped his goblet and emptied it.

We spent the rest of the afternoon drinking wine and green tea. I told him of my experiences in gaol, and how Little Snow had unknowingly come to our rescue. He told me he was married with two daughters. I enjoyed myself immensely in his company, and that day we sealed our lifelong friendship.

The following Sunday the judge arrived at my home in his official car. He had promised to take me to visit the graves of my mother and father. By this time we were comfortable with each other and talked a lot. As he was seven years older than me, I called him Big Brother. He told me he was a member of a large revolutionary family from Shandong Province, where the legendary swordsmen of 'Water Margin' fame made their blood pact and set up their base about nine hundred years ago during the Song Dynasty. They were a large band of outlaws who enjoyed the support of the people but were persecuted as criminals by the emperor. Experts at kung fu and all martial arts, the brothers came together to attack the rich and protect the poor – just like Robin Hood in Britain.

We walked the short distance from the car to the graves. He knew that my greatest inner support came from my parents, and I wanted to take him to meet them. Silently he read the account of their lives carved into the tombstones. Then, as naturally as if he was their son, he knelt and cleared the weeds from around the tombs. My breath caught in my throat as I watched his simple gesture of respect. When the weeds were gone, he stood in front of the tombs, took off his cap and bowed three times to my father and three times to my mother. With a firm, low voice he pledged to my parents: 'Respected Comrades Gao Yi-lin and Zhou Hong-bin, I swear to you, for as long as I live I will look after your daughter, Anhua, and her daughter, Yan. I promise to do my best for them always.'

The surrounding area was quiet and still, and I wept. My tears were not only of sadness, joy was there too. How lucky I felt to have this man as my friend. And it was a rare friendship too: I doubt if there was ever before such closeness between a judge and a convicted prisoner. I knew my mother and father would approve of him. I looked at the sky. Under such a vast heaven it seemed as if there were just the two of us on the earth.

I stood behind my friend, motionless, spellbound. I wanted the moment to last for ever but of course it couldn't. The judge turned eventually and asked me if I was ready to go. I nodded, and we walked back to the car. Not a word was needed. We understood each other from our hearts. I was relaxed and happy during the journey back to the city. On the way we talked about Little Yan, of how I missed her and wanted her back.

I had written several times asking for the return of my daughter. My mother-in-law had replied just once, to say she could not tolerate the idea of sending her granddaughter into the care of a 'bad element' mother. She had even told Little Yan to draw a clear line between her and me for ever. I had thought of going to Suzhou to get her back, but I knew I would be no match for that vicious woman and her family.

The judge listened attentively as he drove the car. After I had finished, he said, 'Don't worry. I will help. Your daughter will be with you soon. The law states clearly that a child must always be with the mother. Nobody should break such a law, no matter how high their position.'

He kept his word. In early July, as I was writing another letter to the Supreme Court of Jiangsu Province requesting a hearing to have my verdict reversed, there was a knock at the door. I opened it and there stood Little Yan. I opened my arms, and she ran into them. 'Mummy, Mummy, oh, Mummy!' After many kisses and hugs, I saw the judge watching us, joy written all over his face.

He had been working to get her back since that day in the car. He had been forced to wait until the school closed for the summer. Then, on the first day of the holidays, he had driven all the way to Suzhou in his uniform. In China the judicial uniform is a sign of importance and power in the eyes of the people, which nobody dares ignore. Even top officials make concessions if they are ever confronted by a person in such a uniform. So that was how Yan and I were reunited.

Little Yan hugged me and hugged me. To feel her arms around me and her face next to mine was wonderful. 'Mummy, I was unhappy in Suzhou. Every day they found fault with everything I did and blamed me for things I didn't do. I don't want to leave home again.'

'Of course not,' I said, between kisses.

'Grandma told me you are a bad mother, a criminal, because you were arrested by Uncle Policeman.' All children in China are taught to be afraid of policemen. 'Uncle Policeman' is widely used by parents as a warning to naughty children of impending punishment.

Little Yan went on, 'I didn't understand. Why would Uncle Policeman arrest you? Then Uncle Judge told me you are a good mother and it was all a big mistake. You haven't done anything to hurt our country.' I looked at the judge and mouthed, 'Thank you.' The words flooded out of Little Yan. She had a lot to say. 'Uncle Judge said you were honest in doing international business but some people thought that was a crime. Grandma was always saying you were dishonest and a traitor to China.

But Uncle Judge said you weren't. You're not a traitor, are you, Mummy?'

Before I could answer, she was off again: 'Uncle Judge said if I am not faithful to you, I won't be a filial child, and I won't have any friends when I grow up, but of course I will have friends because I am a filial child and I love you, Mummy.' A quick breath. 'Uncle Judge bought me an ice-cream and a big ice-lolly. He also gave me some pocket money to buy myself a big doll.' She yanked a ten-yuan note out of her pocket. 'I can keep this, can't I, Mummy, and buy a doll?'

I laughed. 'Of course you can keep it, my precious. And you must buy the best doll in the whole of Nanjing!'

I looked up at the judge through my tears. 'I don't know how I will ever repay you for your kindness,' I said.

He dismissed my words with a movement of his hand. 'No, no. It isn't worth mentioning. Take care of each other, and if you have any problems, just give me a call.'

Since then, he has been an integral part of our lives. He helped me financially during the year or so I wasn't working – I don't know how we would have managed without him. He took me under his wing and I felt safe there. Unlike my husband, Lin, the judge was gentle, kind, compassionate, honourable and decent. And it is to him I owe my life.

24. Fight for Survival

I had lost my so-called friends and was unable to make new ones. Many people avoided me as if I had a terrible disease. Out of pride I stopped trying to renew old acquaintances and kept myself to myself. I had written to my brother Wei-guo, who was still in the army, and told him everything that had happened to me but he never wrote back. A call from my uncle explained everything: Wei-guo had received my letter and was so frightened that my news might reach the ears of his superiors that he wrote to Uncle Wang Feng in Shanghai, 'Tell Anhua, from now on she is not allowed to write to me any more, because it might affect my promotion. She is the first person in this family to be imprisoned in a Communist gaol. I always knew she was a bad influence. I am ashamed of her.'

I had kept in touch with Uncle Wang Feng from the day I left his home at the age of sixteen. The last time I had visited him was in January 1969 when I had been given leave to see Andong before she left Nanjing for Inner Mongolia. On my way back to my unit, I had stayed a night in Shanghai with Uncle Wang Feng. Then he had told me how proud he was of me. That was our last meeting. After he had told me what my brother had written, he never contacted me again. He, too, was ashamed of me. Years later Andong told me he had died in 1992 of cirrhosis of the liver aged sixty-five; his wife sent notice of his death to all of his relatives except me.

The rest of my family broke off contact with me, too, except Andong. During my time in prison, I had been unable to write, and Andong had given me a severe telling-off for my lack of sisterly concern. But I didn't tell her the real reason for my silence. She was in poor health and I didn't want to worry her with my problems. She and her husband were still living in Huhehot, the capital of Inner Mongolia, a thousand miles away from Nanjing.

By now I was really worried about my sister. Far too many of her letters were full of confusion. She usually began them sensibly enough, but as they progressed, she would write herself into a fury over some trifling event, and finish with angry words directed at me, as though I was to blame for her torment. Often her poor husband was the target of her rage, and I had to read through pages of incomprehensible, vitriolic ramblings. I wanted to reassure myself that all was well with her, but there was nothing I could do.

But it was not all bad. When my old classmate Tian, now a long way from home in Hainan Island and a manager of an import-export company, heard I was in trouble, he sent me 300 yuan. Another old schoolmate, Chi, was then head of the foreign-affairs department in the Jiangsu Province Television Station. When he heard of my situation he gave me some English TV programme scripts to translate into Chinese, for which I earned some badly needed money. Old Pei and Ya-dong, the Red Guard friends I had made in Shanghai, came to Nanjing especially to see me. The genuine friendship and loyalty of these people warmed my heart and gave me the courage to face those who despised me. They proved that true friendship could transcend anything the Party had done to me.

In October 1986, a month after Little Yan had started her fifth year in primary school, my health problems became serious. During the previous year I had coped well enough without medical help and, anyway, I had been too busy trying to get justice to have something done. Now I was forced to seek help. I went to the Gulou Hospital for a check. It was the same hospital where, twenty-five years before, my mother had died.

An old woman doctor in the gynaecology department conducted a series of tests, including a scan of my tummy, and said, 'You need an operation. Now, without delay. You have a big tumour and it could be malignant, so you must have a hysterectomy. Please go home and tell your family that you must return here this afternoon.'

I didn't know what to do. I said, 'My young daughter is my only family, and she needs me there to care for her. If I have to stay in hospital, I don't have anyone to look after her.'

'Where is your husband?'

'Dead.'

'And your parents?'

'Dead too. I lost them both when I was little.'

'Hmmm, quite a problem.' She looked at me sympathetically. 'Poor girl,' she said. 'You should have had this operation a long time ago, and it cannot wait any longer. If you have a working unit, the trade union of your organization should do something for you.' I nodded. She was right, but I couldn't tell her that I wasn't sure whether the trade union in Sinochem would help. Although the company had been forced to accept me back as a staff member, they had not allowed me to return to work. The doctor handed me a form. 'Please fill this in and take it to the in-patient department to get your bed and ward number.' She turned away from me and shouted, 'Next!'

I didn't go back to the hospital that day. My only hope was Big Brother, the judge. I wanted to discuss everything with him first, but when I went to the court to see him, I was told he was out of the city investigating a murder. I left him a message and went home.

Early next morning I received a phone call from Sinochem. When the kind old doctor discovered that I had not returned to the hospital, she had been worried. She checked my file and found the telephone number of Sinochem. She told them I needed an operation urgently. Out of kindness, because he knew me well and had never believed I could ever be a criminal, the trade-union official decided to help me. I found out later that many people in Sinochem were full of compassion for me but the leaders had forced them to keep away from me in case they too got into trouble. Despite this, the trade-union man told two people to drive to my home in a company car to collect me and take me to the hospital. I had to go with them. I was too weak and ill to refuse – but before leaving, I asked my neighbours to look after Little Yan.

I was away from home for twenty-four days. I shared a ward with three other women. Two had ovarian tumours and the other had the same as me. The conditions in this hospital were quite good; it was clean and had air-conditioning; the hospital kitchens sent up good meals three times a day, after I had ordered from a menu the night before and paid for them. However, most patients had families who brought in meals from home. Only people without families, like me, ate hospital or restaurant food. Not that I minded; the food was plentiful and good.

When Little Yan came to visit me after school on my first day in hospital, I decided to order two portions of lunch and dinner every day so that she and I could eat together. She was only eleven, and had not yet learned to make proper meals. I had taught her how to cook simple things, such as noodles, but only under my supervision. I had to light the gas for her because she was frightened of matches. She ate a simple breakfast and came to visit me in the hospital twice a day for the rest of her food, no matter how bad the weather.

On my second day, the doctor took blood and urine samples, X-rays and an electrocardiograph. When all the results showed normal, my operation was scheduled for seven a.m. on 26 October 1986. Then, aged thirty-seven, I was trundled along on the trolley to the operating theatre. I remember thinking, Thank goodness for Little Yan, because I would never become a mother again. My emotions were mixed: I was glad and sad at the same time. Also I was quite frightened at the thought of something going wrong. But nothing did.

When I woke up, it was just after one o'clock and I was back in the ward. There was a terrible pain in my tummy, and it was wrapped in a big bandage. Later I was able to count twelve big stitches running like black spiders down my belly. Little Yan was sitting beside me. She told me the doctor had given instructions that I was not to eat food for two days, and to drink only boiled water.

I drifted off to sleep again for a while. When I awoke, Little Yan was still sitting beside me, holding my hand. She let me have a sip of water while she told me about her morning. That day the school had let her leave her class to be with me. She had waited outside the operating theatre with a woman cadre from Sinochem. About eleven o'clock, a nurse had come out of the theatre carrying a big bowl. She stopped and pointed out the tumour, which was the size of a big pear. The cadre ran off to vomit and couldn't eat anything at lunchtime. Little Yan has always been a small-boned, delicate-looking girl, with tiny hands and feet, but her appearance is deceptive and she is stronger than she looks. She didn't enjoy having my insides waved under her nose, but the sight didn't turn her stomach.

She put her hands on my arm beside the drip and rubbed my muscles gently but firmly. It felt good. Oh, how lovely to have a daughter. I wanted to hug her but I was hampered by all the tubes. My insides felt as if they were on fire, but I was not allowed any pain-killers. The nurse said they would slow the healing of my wound. I had to endure the pain while Yan did her best to help me through the worst.

The following day I knew I was on the mend. My tummy was painful, but I had got used to it. In the afternoon Big Brother came to visit. He sat for a while chatting about little things, then slid an envelope under my pillow before he stood up to leave. He told Little Yan to look after me. I said that I couldn't be in better hands. Later, I opened the envelope and found four 100-yuan notes inside it.

Over the days a stream of office friends came to visit, bearing gifts of home-cooked fish soup, lightly steamed vegetables, watermelon and good wishes from others. How they found out about me, I was never to know. And it was because of those lovely people, with Little Yan and the judge, that I began to feel more optimistic about my life.

Three weeks after the operation I was taken home in the same company car. It was nearing the end of November and the temperature had dropped dramatically as a cold wind blew down from the north. But I didn't care: I was ready for anything life had to offer. Although not yet up to full strength, I was feeling better than I had for almost two years.

My way back to a normal life began with cleaning the flat. Everything was covered in dust. Little Yan had spent all her spare time with me, so had done nothing, but now I was well, I was home and I was happy. Unfortunately I overdid it. I wasn't as strong as I felt. That evening, I ran a high fever. Every joint in my hands and feet was stiff, red, swollen and painful. The next morning, Little Yan helped me walk slowly to the nearest street clinic. The doctor there immediately had my blood tested, and discovered that I had an attack of acute arthritis, coupled with a high fever.

I had to go to the clinic twice a day for a month, to let the doctor inject me with a big dose of penicillin. My behind was black and blue, and it was agony to sit down. I was forbidden by the doctor to do any household chores with cold water. I obeyed his every instruction, and his treatment worked. After the Spring Festival in February 1987, the arthritis and fever had gone. As the probation period given to me by the court was over, I hoped I would be allowed to go back to work. Actually, I wanted to be able to tell the judge that the fifty yuan he gave me every month was no longer needed. I was grateful to him but I wanted to be able to stand on my own feet.

But I wasn't allowed to return to work. The boss of Sinochem said I was not healthy enough and needed more time to rest. One good thing came of it, however: I was given 50 per cent of my salary to live on. In fact, I think the Sinochem bosses were surprised to find me so fit and well. As far as they knew, I had had no money coming in for fourteen months, so Little Yan and I should have been dead of starvation – which would have solved their problem. And so we would have been, if it hadn't been for the judge.

It was no good. I just had to get my verdict reversed. Until I did, no help would be forthcoming from the company. I began writing letters again, and generally making a nuisance of myself, but nothing seemed to work. The judge warned me that the Party only corrected mistakes made by those who had died or lost power. The present officials would never allow such a correction because of loss of face.

Some people had visited Beijing over a hundred times for thirty years following their convictions, in the hope of persuading someone to listen to them and give them back their reputations. During those years, they lost their youth, their spouses divorced them, children and relatives disowned them, but they battled on alone. They sold all their possessions and borrowed money to travel to Beijing time and again without success. I knew why they did it, because I felt the same. Only the wrongly accused know the feeling: it is impossible to make others understand the intense burning of injustice that lies deep down in one's entrails. But it was unlikely that I would succeed in my campaign. Always at the back of my mind was the memory of the SSB interrogator who, even when he knew I was innocent of the charges brought against me, had said, when I asked him to admit the mistake and let me go, 'Never!' That memory haunted me, and after a while I began to wonder whether it was worth spending perhaps the rest of my life in a hopeless search for justice. Would it not be better to use my time on more practical things? I should be trying to earn some money to improve our living standards – if not for myself, then for the sake of my daughter. The judge said I should improve my life first, and then, if and when an appropriate time ever came, try again to have my verdict reversed. 'Remember the old saying,' he told me. '"The overturned cart ahead is a warning to the carts behind." Be warned. Under this unreasonable regime, there is no point in wasting your life. It will only result in constant failure and disappointment.' Of course he was right. So I took his advice.

I began my search for a job by contacting my old foreign clients who had offices in Nanjing. I had kept all their business cards at home, tucked away in an old playing card packet. Luckily the SSB had missed them when they searched my flat.

I wrote many letters and had replies from almost every one. They were all the same: the writer was sympathetic, but couldn't help. Two American company directors visited me to tell me personally that they could not employ me: they were doing good business in China and did not want to cause offence to the Chinese authorities by employing me. Now that my political profile had changed, they would rather give me money than a job. I understood their position, and we still correspond regularly as friends.

I didn't give up. On 12 May 1987, I read an advertisement in a national newspaper: a nuclear-power joint-venture company in Shenzhen was looking for English-speaking Chinese secretaries for their foreign bosses. The closing date for interview was 18 May. The salaries in Shenzhen were many times higher than those in Nanjing. My heart leaped. Shenzhen! The magical place of business. We ordinary Chinese thought of it as being half abroad. Perhaps I could change my life there.

Because of its location, close to Hong Kong, it enjoyed a flexible approach to both domestic and foreign investment, and attracted thousands of entrepreneurial people who invested in new enterprises. Before 1980 it had been a small fishing village but a modern city had sprung up there at great speed. People from every corner of China moved to this magical place to make money and realize their dreams. It was said that Shenzhen was the only place in China where you could follow a career according to your ability without being politically acceptable to the Party.

I decided to have a try. I had only six days to get my application in and Shenzhen was 1,500 kilometres away. I had to move fast. It was no good writing: letters took for ever to get from one place in China to another. Fax machines were few, so there was only one thing for it. I checked my available cash: 100 yuan (about £8). The cost of a single one-way rail ticket was fifty yuan, and I would need to stay somewhere. Sadly Little Yan must stay at home and she was still only eleven. I hesitated . . . then decided it was worth the chance. If I could get this job, it would change our lives for the better. The alternative was to do nothing, which would mean our poor position might never change and our suffering could go on for ever.

I had a heart-to-heart talk with Little Yan. I told her she had to live by herself for a while. I didn't know what was in store for me: maybe I could earn enough to return quickly, or I would not be able to return for her until I had settled down. I was worried about leaving her alone, but Yan said, 'Don't worry about me, Mummy. You go to Shenzhen and get us a good future. Then you can come back for me. I will look after myself. Didn't I look after myself very well while you were in hospital? I will be fine.'

I felt great pride in my daughter. She had a good spirit – we call it a 'golden heart'. I gave her forty yuan, leaving myself just ten after paying for the train ticket. I kept repeating my instructions: 'Never trust strangers.

Never take their food if they offer. Never bring them home. Never go to their homes – they could be child-kidnappers,' just as my mother lectured me when I was little. I told her to go to Sinochem every month and collect my salary. 'Always take notice of the judge,' I said. 'I will telephone him and ask him to keep a fatherly eye on you.'

Early the next morning I kissed my still sleeping little daughter and left for the station, carrying my few half-decent clothes in the least SSB-damaged suitcase. I took the first train for Shanghai. There I could change for Guangzhou, and at Guangzhou, for Shenzhen. I was in Shanghai by lunchtime, only to be told by the ticket office that all train tickets to Guangzhou were sold out for the next six days. I knew that a few tickets were always kept to one side in case anyone important suddenly decided to travel by train, so I tried explaining how urgent it was for me to get a ticket. All in vain, of course. My life or death was of no interest to them.

I was in despair, but then I remembered that one of my old Shanghai classmates was now an official in the railway police, based in Shanghai. Perhaps he could help. I asked for directions to the railway police building, where Pan was pleased to see me after so many years.

To my delight, he helped me immediately. He took me to the same ticket office and demanded a sleeper at a discounted price. The man who had refused me a short time previously now moved quickly to do as he was told. He handed me the ticket with a bow and a false smile. 'I'm sorry, Comrade. I didn't know you were a friend of Director Pan. Next time you need a ticket, please come to me.'

I was upset by his attitude but I didn't dwell on it. I had my ticket. That was what mattered. Pan escorted me to my berth on the train and then he found the head of the train crew and told him to look after me during the journey. He handed me two bottles of Coca-cola before saying goodbye.

It took forty-eight hours to get to Guangzhou. I hurried off the train and pushed through the crowds to the ticket office, only to be confronted by another obstacle. A notice on the wall beside the window said that all travellers must show a border area pass-card when buying a ticket to Shenzhen. I was dumbfounded. I had no such pass-card. What should I do? I had no friends to help me this time. If I failed to get to Shenzhen and find a job, I would have no money to return to Nanjing.

I asked the man standing next to me how I could get such a card. He told me I must go to the Public Security Bureau and apply for one, then my application must be approved by my leader. My heart sank. I hadn't told Sinochem I was leaving Nanjing, so there was no chance of them giving their approval. Then the man added, 'Of course, government employees at provincial level can buy a ticket. With it comes a sightseeing pass-card valid for three days. All you need is your identification.' It was music to my ears.

I searched my purse frantically, and there it was! I pulled out my Sinochem identification card. Sinochem was a large company with offices all over China, and my place of work was under the control of Jiangsu Provincial Government. As far as the ticket seller was concerned, I was a government employee at provincial level.

I went to the window and, as carelessly as I could, flashed my Sinochem ID card and asked for a rail ticket and pass-card to Shenzhen. The woman barely looked at it, or me, as she pushed the papers through the small opening in front of her. I boarded my train and arrived at my destination during the afternoon of 15 May. With my last few yuan I found a bed in a cheap hotel situated opposite the Guangdong Nuclear Power Joint Venture Company (GNPJVC) building.

The GNPJVC was then the largest joint-venture company in China and it was contracted to sell 75 per cent of the generated electricity to Hong Kong. The director of the contract construction department was an Englishman named Ashmore and he needed a secretary. More than a hundred applicants from different parts of China had applied for the job, including me.

My interview was during the morning following my arrival, and I and the other applicants were given a written examination paper to complete. It was a translation of a big contract from English into Chinese, then back again from Chinese into English. I had been doing such work for years and found it easy. The papers were marked straight away and I got the highest scores.

Then those who had done best in the examination were taken to the eighth floor to be interviewed by Mr Ashmore. When my turn came, I was ushered into his office and invited to sit down in front of him. He was a tall, stout man, with a quick laugh and an acute sense of humour. He quickly put me at my ease and we had a relaxed chat. He wanted to be sure I would have no trouble understanding his spoken English, and I didn't. Not once did I have to ask him to repeat himself. It wasn't long before he had me laughing at his jokes. I liked him very much, and when he said I was the one for him, I was overjoyed.

Once he had made up his mind, he signed his approval on my
application form and passed it to me. We had a few more minutes of
conversation until a girl came to take me away. Before leaving he put
out his big hand and wrapped it around my little one. 'Welcome, Anhua.
May I call you Annie?' he asked. 'It is much easier for me to remember.'
I nodded. And ever since I have been known as Annie by all westerners.

So, now I was a secretary working for an Englishman. I was on three
months' probation and after that, if I proved satisfactory, the job would
be permanently mine. My photograph was taken, and I was given a
company ID card. There was no political check and no sign of political
interference. From the day I was employed, the company paid for my
hostel. I was also given a proper border pass-card, valid for twelve months,
which proved that my stay in Shenzhen was legal. After a year I could
apply for Shenzhen registration. I was delighted, and determined to work
hard to keep the job. In just a year I could become a resident of Shenzhen
and leave all my political shadows behind me in Nanjing. The future
seemed bright and I could look forward to living a decent life with my
daughter in Shenzhen. She would learn more about the world without
any political brainwashing. And I could regain my self-respect.

I was to work a five-day week and my monthly salary during the
probationary period was 180 yuan – four times higher than in Nanjing.
Once I was accepted as a permanent employee, it would increase to 300
yuan. Riches indeed! My only worry was Little Yan. I could not go back
to Nanjing and bring her to Shenzhen until my probationary period was
up – the journey was too long to do over a weekend. Long-distance
direct dialling had just been introduced in China but it was possible only
in five-star hotels and high-level government departments. I had to go
to the local post office and make my calls through the telephone operator,
and the charges were high. Fortunately Mr Ashmore had a direct-dial
telephone installed in his office, and his deputy allowed me to call home
every evening when Mr Ashmore had left for the day. In this way, at no
cost to myself, I was able to talk to my brave Little Yan most evenings
and make sure she was safe at home.

Two months passed. Then one morning, at the end of July, I received
a call from Nanjing. A friend named Wu had gone to see Little Yan and
found her thin and pale. To save money, she had only been eating plain
rice and instant noodles. She never bought herself any meat or vegetables.
Wu had decided to take her to a restaurant and give her a good meal.

Before the dishes were placed on the table by the waiter, Little Yan fainted. Wu took her to hospital where it was discovered she was suffering from hypoglycaemia caused by malnutrition. The doctors were angry: every eleven-year-old child needed good food to develop properly, and they extracted a promise from Wu that Little Yan would be properly cared for. Wu bought some meat-filled buns as she took Little Yan home. Then she telephoned to tell me to come back right away to care for my child.

My heart was broken. I blamed myself for being a bad mother. I went to the personnel department, explained my situation and said tearfully that I would have to resign my position. They were sympathetic but said there was little they could do for me because I was still only a probationer. If I went home they would have to terminate my employment. However, they would reserve my post for four weeks. If I returned within that time, I could have it back, although the probationary period would begin again. I accepted, and with my two months' savings tucked in my purse, I headed for Nanjing.

Even though it was much more expensive, I flew home – I wanted to be with Little Yan as quickly as possible. I got to Guangzhou airport that afternoon, an hour before the plane was scheduled to take off for Nanjing, only to be told that all the tickets were sold. For the first time in my life, I tried bribery – and it worked! I gave the female ticket clerk thirty yuan extra and got my seat. After that, my purse was empty.

When I got home I hugged Little Yan tightly. She was very thin in her summer dress, almost bony. I wanted to scold her for not telling me she was ill but I could not. I had left her with forty yuan and now, after two months, she handed me sixty yuan! It was too much for me. I burst into tears. She had gone to Sinochem to collect my salary on both pay days and had spent as little as possible so that she could help towards making our future.

In the past year and a half, she had endured much. It wasn't easy to be the child of a convicted political criminal. The playground is an unforgiving and cruel place. She had never complained, and as far as she was concerned, she and I stood shoulder to shoulder against the world. She was mature for an eleven-year-old. In China we say, 'Children from poor families manage household affairs earlier.'

During my absence Little Yan had not contacted the judge. She said that as long as she could manage she did not want to trouble him because she knew how busy he was. He had telephoned her several times and she had always said she was getting along all right. It was then that I decided to take her back with me to Shenzhen at the end of August.

And that is what I did. Before leaving, I handed the judge the keys to my flat and asked him to keep an eye on it. I was not about to make the same mistake as I had when I gave up my flat before joining the army. I told him that Shenzhen offered the best chance for Little Yan and me to make a new start and we must take it. He understood and agreed to look after my flat, until, as he said, 'You come back one day with good fortune'.

The next day he came with two air tickets in his hand. He had paid for them out of his own pocket. Never will I find a friend like him again. As children under the age of twelve did not need a border pass-card, we had no trouble getting to Shenzhen and the office kept its promise and gave me my job back.

The company trade union helped me to enrol Little Yan at school. As we were not officially registered to live in the city, I had to buy her a place. It cost me an extra eighty yuan above the usual tuition fees. The personnel department was kind, saying that as I was employed by the company my air fares would be refunded. (I didn't tell them about the bribe!)

Now Little Yan and I were happy together. Shenzhen was a wonderful place to live, and we felt as if a great load had been lifted off us. I was told that when I became a permanent employee we would be moved out of the hostel into a flat supplied by the company. That was something else to look forward to. And once all that had taken place, I could resign officially from Sinochem.

Little Yan settled in at school and soon began to get good marks. She made new friends and now her playground was a friendly place. A few weeks after arriving in Shenzhen, I was astonished to find her playing with her new classmates and talking perfect Cantonese. It was amazing how quickly she had learned this local language – it was too difficult for me.

In mid-November, ten days before my probationary period was due to end, I was offered a long-term contract of employment. My heart leaped. Then they said that they needed my personal file to be transferred from Sinochem. As this joint venture was under the authority of the Chinese, there would have to be a full political check and a proper transfer, just like everywhere else in China. On hearing this I almost collapsed. I had kept my imprisonment a secret from my new employers, believing that here in Shenzhen there was no need of a personal file. I had been wrong. I would never leave my past behind. It was to be with me like a shadow for the rest of my life. Like the Monkey King who can never jump off the open hand of the Buddha, I was under the control of the Party.

I had to return to Nanjing. In reply to the enquiry letter from my office, Sinochem Jiangsu wrote very clearly, with the company red stamp making it official, saying I was not suitable to do any job where I would be in contact with foreign nationals. Furthermore, as I had made a serious political mistake in the past, I could no longer be trusted. They did not say what kind of 'mistake' I had made, so the affair appeared mysterious and therefore serious. As I could not convince GNPJVC that I had merely been honest in my dealings with a customer, that was the end of that. Mr Ashmore was sad to see me go, he said, but as he did not understand how the Chinese justice system worked, he had no choice.

However, the office said, 'Get your verdict reversed quickly and you can come back.' They were kind enough to pay me an extra month's salary, and they bought our aeroplane tickets back to Nanjing. But I was bitter: I knew I would not be able to return. On 30 November 1987 Little Yan and I left Shenzhen and flew back to Nanjing. The judge was waiting for us at the airport with his car.

The leaders of Sinochem were annoyed to discover that I had found a job in Shenzhen – and even more angry that I had worked for a foreign boss. I had been deprived of the right to work in the Nanjing office of Sinochem and now they would not allow me to work in Shenzhen.

On my return, Sinochem told me to report for work the following morning, and I did. I was assigned a job in the stationery warehouse, my salary was cut to three grades lower than before, and there was nothing for me to do. I had simply been put out of sight and out of mind.

The humiliation was beyond words. It was explained to me that my new job equalled 'reform through labour' without hard labour. The tedium of doing nothing day after day was difficult to bear. I cried a lot, mostly from rage and humiliation. It seemed my punishment was never going to end. The leaders had no pity: they knew very well I needed a fair salary to survive, and I had hoped that my past and possible future achievements might allow for a little leniency, but it was not to be. They were intent on making my life a misery through political discrimination. And it worked, because Little Yan and I were very unhappy.

At about the same time it became a fad to have foreign magazines prominently displayed around the offices of the larger companies. Sino-chem followed the fashion and subscribed to a few. One was a BBC magazine from Britain. As most of the magazines were written in English, nobody was interested in or able to read them. At the end of each month they were thrown away. However, one day the company dispatcher handed them to me and said, 'You can read these. They'll help you to pass the time.'

I was grateful; it was nice to know that not everybody was against me. I thanked him profusely. He continued, 'You can keep them if you like, since nobody wants them. We can't understand them anyway.'

A year went by. Little Yan and I lived as frugally as possible on my tiny salary. She and the judge had become almost like father and daughter. Whenever he called to see us, she almost always had a few questions for him, and sometimes she telephoned him to ask his advice. I knew it was difficult for her at school and in the streets but she never uttered a word of complaint and was soon among the top pupils in her year again. Sometimes she wished she was back in Shenzhen, but so did I.

At work nothing changed. I read the magazines from cover to cover, and reread them. The boredom was driving me crazy. Then one day in November 1988, in a BBC magazine, I noticed an advertisement. The Churchill House Language School, situated in Ramsgate in Britain, said that students from all over the world were welcome to study English. Where on earth was Ramsgate? My heart beat fast in my chest.

Going abroad was a big thing in China in 1988. The Black Fives and Stinking Old Number Nines of the Cultural Revolution had the best chance to do so: they had a good education to offer other countries and many had relatives abroad. With their help thousands of Chinese had gone abroad at their own expense. Most chose a university or a language school and enrolled before they left China.

I wrote in English to Churchill House School, explaining my position. I was excited because I was about to post my first private letter to the Land on the Edge of the Sky. When I came to write the address on the envelope, I wondered again about Ramsgate. It seemed such an unusual name. I checked my English–Chinese dictionary and found that a ram was a male sheep and a gate was an entrance, so Ramsgate meant 'a male sheep's entrance'. British places do have funny names.

About three weeks later, their reply arrived. With a pounding heart, I read it. Would they accept me? They would. What did I have to do?

Complete the enclosed form and return it with my enrolment fee of £30. So much! I was shaken at first by the cost: a whole month's salary just to enrol! But after my shock I knew I had to dip into my savings.

I had talked everything over with the judge. He said he would support me financially as far as he could, and his understanding and encouragement urged me on. I was determined that, once I was out of China, I would never come back – better to wander the world like a nomad. As I posted the letter with the enrolment form, I had a pang of anxiety. Suppose it was just a trick to get my money? Then I let go of the envelope and it disappeared.

It wasn't a trick. Twenty days later I received my enrolment certificate and a receipt for the money from Churchill House School. They also wrote a nice letter welcoming me to Britain and saying they had already chosen a host family with whom I could stay. If I wished I could write to them before I arrived, which I did.

It wasn't long before my host, Gerald Sibthorp, wrote back. His letter was so friendly and welcoming that I felt a warm glow surround me. I replied immediately – and established a friendship. I applied to my leaders for a passport to study abroad. In fact, four of us applied about the same time. The other three applications were approved. Mine was refused.

But by now my mind was made up. I would find a way out.

My chance came in May 1989. By that time, joint-venture companies were springing up everywhere. The new economic policies put forward by Deng Xiao-ping, with foreign money, resulted in a rapid expansion of the Chinese manufacturing base – and with it more openings for those who spoke a foreign language, particularly English. The bonus was that the new breed of foreign-company bosses, unlike those who ran earlier joint ventures, paid scant attention to the political attitude or backgrounds of their employees. They wanted the best, and employed people strictly according to ability.

During my enforced idleness, I had kept myself as busy as possible by teaching myself Japanese and, although I was not as fluent in Japanese as I was in English, I knew enough to make conversation. Thus my command of the two languages became my greatest weapon in my fight back.

I began to tour the city, calling on joint-venture companies. It was a time of unrest, and thousands of students were on the march, shouting,

'Get rid of the corrupt Party officials!' and 'We want democracy!' As they marched, their numbers doubled then doubled again as people from all walks of life joined them, forcing the city traffic to grind to a standstill. It seemed to me, as I pushed my way along, that everyone supported the students in their quest for a fairer society.

I hoped it meant the beginning of the end of Communism in China. Sometimes, after dinner, I took Little Yan, who was now a bright and beautiful fourteen-year-old, to Gulou Square to look at the crowds before it got dark. Everywhere there were thousands of big-character posters, the like of which we hadn't seen since the end of the Cultural Revolution. In the days of Mao, the posters were always in support of the government. The new ones criticized the high level of corruption in the present government. The students had erected platforms from which they made speech after speech, their voices ringing tinnily from loudspeakers.

One evening after dinner, as Little Yan and I were heading for Gulou Square, someone called me. I turned round and saw a colleague from the Electronics Import and Export Corporation named Big Wang. He came up to me and said, 'Little Gao, I want to let you know we have taken revenge for you!' Then he told me that the general manager who had caused my arrest had been strongly opposed by all members of the company when the truth about my misfortune had become known. 'If what you did was sufficient for you to be accused of divulging State secrets,' said Big Wang, 'then the general manager himself should have been put in prison a hundred times over. He was found on many occasions to have divulged State secrets to Hong Kong people by showing them the secret printed documents with the red heading issued by the Central Party Committee. So when the campaign of "Rectifying the Style of Work within the Party" started in 1988, the only one of the Party members working in the company not to pass was the general manager. He was criticized by everyone, including most of the Party members. And some sent letters to his next higher leadership accusing him of abusing his public power by retaliating against a personal enemy. The result was that he was given an administrative punishment and dismissed from his position.'

I thanked Big Wang, and asked him to say thank you for me to everyone in the company. Of course the news made me happy. The general manager threw the stone and hit his own feet, I thought. However, his disgrace did not save me. The SSB still would not admit their mistake.

They were too powerful. But at least I now knew the true feelings of my workmates.

With a lighter heart, I watched the development of the movement for democracy. I did not join the students, although I secretly supported them, because I did not want to get into more political trouble. For many days the top Chinese leaders tried to ignore what was going on around the country, particularly in Tiananmen Square in Beijing where thousands of students began to fast. Every day we saw on the television the enormous expanse of the square filled with young people lying on the ground, too weak to move, yet refusing food.

Finally the government was forced into action. At first, towards the end of May, it seemed as if the students were winning. The government recognized the movement as 'a revolutionary event' and issued a bulletin that said: 'The students' feelings are understandable and their intentions are good.' Premier Li Peng said to them, 'I support your revolutionary action, and we will consider your reasonable requests.'

The day he said that, I submitted my resignation to Sinochem. It was accepted without argument because of the unrest and turmoil, when the fate of the Party was in the balance. I had been offered a job by the newly established Tai-wen Toy Company, with a huge increase in salary. The company had been founded jointly by a State-owned toy factory in Taizhou (a city about a hundred kilometres north of Nanjing) and an organization in Hong Kong. At last I could throw away my 'iron bowl', which was what we called a job with a State-owned company, where a lifetime of employment was guaranteed. After my resignation, I had a 'mud bowl', which meant I had no job guarantees. There was no political interference either, and I could do import and export business with foreign countries again.

I will never forget the moment I walked out through the doors of Sinochem, where I had begun a seemingly bright career thirteen years before. Despite their power, I had beaten them in the end by taking control of my life and resigning. *I was free!*

When I turned the corner into my street, I saw Little Snow standing in front of my door, holding a big box of bananas and apples. She was out of prison and had come to thank me for sending the letter to her family. I hastened to lead her upstairs and into my room. She put the fruit on the table as a special gift for me. She had been set free about a year after me and because of my letter to her family, there had been a joyful reunion. As she could not find a job because of her imprisonment, she was opening a little clothes shop and had already applied for her business licence. 'I have learned a good lesson and I know how to fight back,' she said resolutely. She also told me that 453 had been sentenced to four years in a labour camp. However, 1701 was still kept in Wawaqiao because her case became complicated: her son had been kept in the male wing of the same prison and both of them refused to confess their crimes. Nobody knew what would happen to them.

Little Snow stayed at my home for two hours. Then I accompanied her to the bus station. As I watched her disappear inside the bus, I felt that those people with the lowest status in Chinese society were the most loyal in the world. I kept in touch with Little Snow and I am pleased that her little business grew and grew. She is now quite a wealthy woman.

25. My Bridge to Happiness

The head office of Tai-wen Toys was a factory in north Jiangsu Province. It was a huge place employing about a thousand people. The office in Nanjing, where I was based, took care of the import–export side of the business and dealt with the overseas clients. Strictly speaking, I didn't work in an office. The company rented a suite of rooms on the ground floor of the three-star Dingshan Hotel, which was air-conditioned, clean, bright and cheerful.

As it was a new joint venture, all of us working there began with a clean sheet. I don't know if any of my workmates had a cloudy political past like me because we never discussed such things. We were happy to have left it all behind us. Even so, I didn't make the same mistake twice. I had learned from my experiences in Shenzhen so I made sure my new bosses knew all about my past, but all they wanted to know was if I could do the job. I could. As I was the only foreign-language speaker out of a staff of twelve, I enjoyed great face among my colleagues. It felt good to be working without worrying about my past spoiling things for me.

When I started there, the student movement was at its height. Hundreds of thousands of students and their worker supporters filled the streets from dawn to well after dusk. I had to push my way through the crowds every day to get to the office. The roads were full of demonstrators who blocked the traffic, and it took me over an hour to get in and to come home again at night. But I did it gladly.

During my first day in my new job, I saw plenty of messages spew out from the office fax machine. Many were sent from Hong Kong by our investors, showing cuttings from the newspapers about how our Hong Kong cousins supported the students. It was an exciting time. Rebellion was in the air, not the artificial kind, as happened during the Cultural Revolution, but real rebellion, stemming from deep convictions. Much help and encouragement were sent to the tens of thousands of students camping in Tiananmen Square. Their supporters from around the world sent money, food and warm clothing via Hong Kong.

For days we talked of little else in our new office except the latest news. Our few foreign clients withdrew their orders because we had been forced to admit that shipments could not be guaranteed. The railways, the Yangtze River Bridge and the main highways were filled with demonstrators. Everybody was watching and waiting, hoping against hope that the government would accept the aims of the students, and change their style of leadership.

Right up to 3 June, all we could hear from the radio was the same statement: 'The student movement is a revolutionary one with a good intention to help the Party.' Our faxes gave us the impression that the Chinese government was on the verge of collapse.

Then suddenly, the next day, we in Nanjing watched thousands of policemen in the streets rounding up and arresting the demonstrators. It wasn't long before traffic moved, the shops opened and the city returned to near normal. The police were armed with their favourite toy: the electric prod. One touch sent such a fierce bolt of electricity through a trouble-maker that it rendered them temporarily helpless, making it easy to arrest them. The police used their batons with enthusiasm too. We also heard many gun-shots, including automatic fire.

That same day we learned from the radio that the unarmed students in Tiananmen Square had been suppressed by the army, using tanks and machine-guns. Rumour said that thousands of young lives had been snuffed out. Nobody knew the exact figure because many bodies had been dragged away by other students. It was a shameful example of the real face of Communism, and what had been done in the name of 'democracy' was witnessed by the whole world. No longer could the Communists hide behind a 'bamboo curtain' as Mao had done. The indiscriminate, wholesale slaughter of the students is now known as the June the 4th Event in China and by the rest of the world as the Tiananmen Square Massacre.

Such high-handedness by the government caused a national outpouring of indignation against the Communist Party. But there was nothing anyone could do. The Party had the army, the police and the SSB. Anyone stupid enough to protest openly was arrested.

Photographs of ten student leaders were shown on television. They were wanted by the law as ringleaders of the gang who had organized the protest. They were all young, in their early twenties, and now, for daring to make peaceful, passive, unarmed protest, they faced a long term of imprisonment or even death. Fortunately they were helped by unknown sympathizers, and most escaped from China to the West.

However, the Party had to take revenge, so other students were rounded up and accused instead.

Throughout China, all university students, as well as many teachers and journalists, were forced to do self-criticism in their work units. Supporters of the students in TV stations were summarily sacked: television was the 'throat of the Party' so the Party could not allow people who were known to oppose the official line to be anywhere near a TV studio.

I, and everyone around me, was horrified by the bloody suppression. Estimates varied of the number of dead and wounded, but it had to be several thousand. China was shocked. The world was shocked. The change of attitude by the Chinese government to the student movement meant that many foreign investors withdrew their backing, forcing thousands of companies to close down. Among them was Tai-wen Toys. I was out of a job. My 'mud bowl' was broken.

I was back to square one but, strangely, I wasn't worried. I searched the newspaper advertisements – I was sure I could earn my living with my language skills. English was in demand so I knew a job was waiting for me just round the corner. And I was right: I became an amateur guide for an American travel company. They didn't care what kind of political trouble I had been in, they just used my English and Japanese. In fact, after the events in Tiananmen Square, my once shameful political status changed: foreigners looked at me with admiration and respect when they heard that I had been a political prisoner, and I exploited it for all I could get. 'Ah,' some said, 'this little woman is a brave freedom-fighter!' They were wrong, of course, but I didn't try to correct their mistake as they offered generous tips.

My new job was an easy and relaxed way to earn money. All I had to do was stay at home and wait for the telephone to ring. Whenever the company had tourists from the USA or other countries visiting Nanjing, I got a call and went to the airport to meet them. From there, I had to escort them to their hotel and see them safely settled in. Then, during their stay in Nanjing, I would accompany them when they went sightseeing. Sometimes I had to go with them to Shanghai. I only worked a few days a month but I earned more for that than I ever had before. Soon I had a bank balance of several thousand yuan – and a pile of American dollars hidden away at home.

I was a freelance and it was great. I was no longer under the control of anyone else and there was no political study, no shame, no humiliation. I answered to no one and I was free to contact as many foreigners as I wished. I kept up my correspondence with Joan and Gerald Sibthorp in Ramsgate without fear of being labelled a class enemy. Nobody bothered with me now, and that was how I liked it. Even in the community I was no longer regarded as a bad element.

I also did some translating at home. Many import and export companies needed help with their paperwork. My old classmate Tian had returned from Hainan and he made me his personal English interpreter. Every time he had a 'big-nose' client he gave me a call, and I would go to help him negotiate his deals.

Everything came full circle when Tian invited me to attend the Guangzhou fair that year. I took two large suitcases filled with clothes. When I first walked past the Sinochem stand, I stuck my head in the air and strolled by in a brand new pure silk pink suit with matching high-heeled leather shoes and handbag. I wore silk stockings, makeup, a pink pearl necklace, gold earrings and expensive rings. I felt wonderful as I went by, looking as if I owned the place. Every morning I deliberately passed the Sinochem stand wearing a different outfit. It was a sharp contrast to the plain clothes I had worn when first attending the fair in 1976. I knew they were watching and wondering. When, later, my old colleagues came to say hello, it felt good. It was also good to be meeting old clients. They still remembered me, even after the eleven-year gap.

At last I had regained my dignity and self-respect. And the knowledge that I had beaten the system was the cherry on the cake.

As our finances improved, Yan and I had a wonderful time. We went on shopping expeditions and bought new clothes, shoes and makeup. We were happy together. Yan was one of the top students in her school, and her eyes shone with health and happiness. My health improved, too: the Menière's disease never again plagued me after my hysterectomy – I have no idea why.

Little Yan now entered a college of hotel management. The entrance examination was difficult, and other standards had to be met – for example, fluency in English, being over 1.60 metres tall and having a good figure. After graduation, the students would work in the best Chinese hotels, which was, and still is, considered a good job in China, with excellent working conditions and high pay. Hotels preferred to recruit girls from this college, therefore once she had been accepted

Yan's future was assured. She had always been a self-sufficient, confident child and had picked this college and career by herself. It was a good choice and she did well.

At the end of June 1993 Little Yan completed her studies and was sent to Shenzhen where she and her classmates were to work in a large hotel. The whole class, accompanied by two teachers, travelled by train. Before she left home, we went on one last shopping spree. I bought her some new clothes and the suitcases to carry them in. The night before she left I helped her pack, and the following morning Tian came to help with the luggage. We went to the station by taxi.

Crowds of people were already on the platform: tearful parents, grandparents, brothers, sisters, uncles and aunts were grouped around each girl. For most of the youngsters, it was their first time away from home. Only Little Yan had been to Shenzhen before. To the other girls, leaving home was heartbreaking, as if they were parting from their families for ever. In her first letter, Little Yan told me that most of them had cried for a large part of the journey. Only when she started telling them about the wonders of Shenzhen did they begin to cheer up.

I didn't cry and neither did Little Yan. Her leaving could never alter our relationship. I was sad, though, not just because I was saying goodbye to my daughter but because I was losing my child. She was an adult now. My job as a parent had changed. I had done my best under difficult circumstances and, luckily, Little Yan had grown up into a beautiful, intelligent and independent young woman. I was proud of her. I knew she would be all right on her own.

Tian and I, with the other families, watched the train pull out of the station. Heads and waving hands stuck out of every window. Little Yan, in the green dress I had just bought for her, was waving a crimson scarf, chosen so that I could still see it long after all other details had faded into the distance. Eventually Tian and I left the station. He said, 'You are a strong woman, Little Gao. My wife could never do what you have done. It is hard to see one's only child embark upon her own pathway through life.'

I had a deep affection for this tall, thin man, whom I was proud to call my friend. He knew everything about me, yet he had always been around when I needed him. 'All children must leave home sometime,' I said, but inside I had a big empty hole. When I got home I felt lonely. Little Yan and I had been devoted to each other. I missed her terribly.

Two days later, she telephoned from Shenzhen and I was relieved to learn that everything was fine. She was not quite eighteen, and earning her own living. An image of Little Yan as a baby came to my mind. Her birth seemed to have happened only yesterday. I could still see the little pink face and tiny fingers of my new-born baby daughter.

Almost eighteen years had gone like a flash. She had been forced to learn at an early age to look after herself, shopping in the market at nine and learning to cook at eleven. She had always kept up with her studies, and had passed her exams with high marks, enabling her to go to good schools without the need of a 'back door'. And, above all, she had always behaved like a true filial daughter by never giving me the slightest reason to worry about her behaviour. Now she was gone and I cried big lonely tears.

It took me a while to adjust to living alone. By now I was working at a Japanese joint-venture garment factory. I worked hard and was promoted to manager of the import and export department. However, all the while, my long-held desire to get out of China niggled at me. I continued to write regularly to my friends in Ramsgate. I told them that although my life was going well now, there was always a danger that something bad could happen. I, and everyone else, always had to be on guard against revealing our inner thoughts. Just one careless moment could mean trouble.

It was nice to talk to them through letters. They wrote long descriptions of what it was like to live in Britain, and the biggest surprise was that they criticized their politicians. I thought, How can that be? Ordinary people cannot say such things about their leaders so openly. It is impossible.

To cope with my loneliness, when I wasn't busy translating I read newspapers and magazines. That is how I discovered that a senior Russian ophthalmologist had come to Nanjing for three months to perform eye operations using the latest techniques. Short-sighted people would be able to see again without spectacles. I had worn glasses for over twenty years and was eager to get rid of them, so I decided to ask if she could help me. Yes, she could. After a careful check of my eyes, she brought me into hospital. I stayed for four days, then bade goodbye to my spectacles when I got home. I found a letter from Gerald waiting for me. This was a chance to test my new eyesight, and I was delighted to be able to read it easily without glasses. Unknown to me, he and Joan had decided to help me find a pen-pal in Britain and had placed an advertisement in an English magazine. 'A lady from the East seeks genuine male pen-pal aged over fifty.' It was early December 1993. They had written: 'Merry Christmas, Annie. This is our present to you.'

Two weeks later the first replies arrived at my home. Three letters. The next day four more came, and six the next. In all, Gerald forwarded twenty-four letters, most with photographs. He said they were the best of the fifty who had bothered to write in response to the advertisement. I was confused. After reading the letters, I put them in a pile on the table. So many! How to choose? I read them again and again. Gerald and Joan had been right to suggest this idea. It would be nice to have my own special pen-friend, someone to talk to. But I could only have one. The trouble was, which one?

In the end I selected the one who had written me the longest letter and sent me the biggest photograph. He seemed a decent fellow. He had nice blue-grey eyes, straightforward and direct. I decided I liked the look of Harry. I wrote to him, enclosing a few snapshots of myself. Soon we were writing to each other several times a week, and it wasn't long before we felt special to each other.

Harry was a good descriptive writer. Sometimes he sat on a seat in the park and described his surroundings. Or he would stop his car at the end of a road and write about that. I began to know, in my mind's eye, exactly what he could see from the window of his second-floor flat in London. From his letters, I learned about the fickle English weather and the changing seasons. He made me happy and sad. He made me laugh. He made me feel important.

In February 1994 a Valentine card arrived from him. Instead of his usual signature, he simply wrote, 'To dear Annie – from your own running dog.' Oh! What a pen-pal. I felt a warm current run through my body and into my heart. Suddenly I realized that through our letters we had been building a bridge to our happiness. My long-dead husband had never shown me any affection so if Harry was to open his heart to me, why shouldn't I take it? I must not lose this chance of happiness.

In his next letter he wrote many pages, telling me how he felt about me. In my reply, I told him he was loved too. But how could we meet? We were thousands of miles apart, and I was locked behind the Communist shield. There were other considerations. Even though life in China had improved in recent years, it was frowned on for a girl to marry a foreigner, and even worse if she was a mature widow of forty-five.

I didn't care. I had suffered enough. I would not give up this chance of happiness. There must be a way. Harry was fifty-eight, so we had little time to waste. I wrote to my daughter and told her everything. I copied bits of Harry's letters and sent them to her. And she gave me her approval, especially when Harry wrote directly to her and asked for her blessing. 'You must take this chance, Mummy,' she wrote to me. 'Harry seems exactly what you need. I have always wished for you to have a happy marriage. Daddy and you were never happy. Don't let anything stand in your way.'

Despite our cultural differences, we discovered much common ground. We shared each other's sorrows and placed our hope in the future. I felt sad for him when I learned that his ex-wife, whom he had loved dearly, had divorced him and married another man. He felt compassion for me when he heard my sad story. He told me he had just lost his job. 'Redundancy', he called it, and said he had nothing to offer me but his whole heart. I wrote back: 'Harry. What else on earth do I need more than a real priceless heart? The only thing in this world that cannot be bought is a genuinely loving heart of another human being.'

It seemed as if we had been brought together by some unseen being. We now believe someone must have led the way. Harry recalled a visit to a gypsy woman, 'for a lark', he said. She had told him he would marry a lady from another world. As he was happily married at the time, he had just laughed and forgotten all about it. Until, one day, when he was writing to me, the memory returned.

Both of us wanted to end our past lives and begin afresh. Harry was important to me for two reasons: first, I cared for him and longed to have him by my side; second, he was my passport out of China. He was no fool. He had already guessed about the second and said he would try his best to help me fulfil my promise to myself to leave China one day.

By early spring 1994 we were desperate to meet. Harry booked a flight from London to Nanjing via Beijing for mid-May, and we waited impatiently for that day to come. But good things often bring problems: Harry hurt his back a week before he was due to travel and had to postpone his trip for six weeks, which seemed unbearably long to me.

Fortunately my dear sister Andong, her lovely husband Zhan and their daughter Zhao-zhao came back to Nanjing. Earlier in the year I had paid a visit to an old family friend, Hui Yu-yu. In 1959 he had helped my mother host the banquet held to honour the visit to Nanjing by Ho Chi Minh of North Vietnam, and had regained the post of governor of Jiangsu Province after the end of the Cultural Revolution. Now he was honourably retired. We had a lovely chat over dinner. In conversation, he asked how we children had got on after the death of my mother. I told him a little about myself, leaving out the distressing bits. Then I told him my brother was doing well in the army, and that Pei-gen and I had lost touch. Finally I told him about Andong being exiled to Inner Mongolia for over twenty-four years. The old man nodded as I told him of her wish to return to Nanjing.

Soon afterwards I had a happy letter from Andong saying they were coming home. Apparently, old Hui had written a letter to his younger brother, who was the principal Party secretary in Inner Mongolia, asking him to give permission for the transfer of Andong and her family to Nanjing. And, as if that wasn't enough, the old man arranged to have good jobs waiting for both her and Zhan.

We had a happy reunion. The People's Government of Nanjing, at the request of Mr Hui, gave the returning exiles a nice two-bedroomed flat, which would normally have been reserved for a government employee.

When they had moved in and settled down, I told Andong and her husband my whole story. They were indignant when they heard about my unfair imprisonment and all that had happened afterwards. Andong scolded me for not telling her sooner, but she stopped when I told them how kind life had been to me since leaving Sinochem. And she glowed with pleasure as I related the story of Harry.

During the weeks I was waiting for Harry, she came to keep me company almost every day. Her hard life in exile had ruined her health, and she was allowed to retire from work with a small pension. But it was not just her body that had been damaged. Her personality had changed too. I noticed it straight away. When she left Nanjing, she had been good-natured and sweet. Now, at the smallest annoyance, she flew into an uncontrollable rage. Her face would redden, then turn purple. She would foam at the mouth and her eyes would seem as if they were about to pop out of their sockets. Nothing would pacify her. It was a fearsome sight. I was frightened of her, and for her.

She was different in other ways too. She had become acquisitive. Everything she laid eyes on in my home, she coveted. If she hadn't got one she wanted mine, and when I refused, she flew into one of her rages until I let her have it. I lost a stereo music centre, cassette tapes, crockery, clothes, shoes and many other things. The Andong who had come back to me was not the one who had left. Her husband and daughter had a hard time coping with her.

She had also become very talkative. At first I thought it was because she was so excited about her return to Nanjing but, as time went by, I knew that she was suffering from a serious psychiatric disorder. Sometimes we went out together to visit our old friends and school-teachers. They, too, realized something was wrong with her, because when she started talking, she never let others speak. And she had sudden mood swings, from quiet to noisy, placid to angry, happy to miserable and back again. I was sure she needed help. I urged her husband to consult a doctor, but when Andong heard about it she flew into a rage, saying she was not sick, not at all. And because it was so difficult to pacify her, we gave in, with the result that she never received proper medical help.

In June, I went to Beijing for a week to attend a Sino-Russian trade conference, and afterwards stayed on in a hotel . . . because Harry was due to arrive in China a few days later. The morning he was expected, I checked out of my hotel early and went to Beijing airport to await his arrival. I was very impatient and found it hard to sit still. I prowled the public areas of the airport, trying to make the time pass more quickly. The clocks seemed to have stopped. Every minute seemed a year to me until at last the information board said his aeroplane had landed.

I stood and waited, and waited, and waited. An hour passed, and still he hadn't emerged from the arrivals hall. I cursed Customs and Immigration. Why should they check the passengers so slowly? I scanned every face. Another minute passed, then another. I saw many passengers coming out and into the arms of their dear ones waiting all around me. More minutes passed and disappointment crept into me. He hadn't come! Something had happened. His back had gone again. He had changed his mind at the last minute . . . There! There! Is that him? Yes, it is him, looking exactly like his photographs, but not quite so tall as I had imagined him to be – and his belly much bigger!

I stood still, holding my breath. I watched him slowly walk towards another exit. This way, please. Look this way! His eyes searched the crowds and met mine. Speechless, he came up to me and, from behind the rail, he stretched out his arm and gently circled my neck as he gave me a soft warm kiss on my cheek. He stepped out from behind the rail and I slipped my hand into his as naturally as if we had been old friends lost in darkness for a long, long time and now we had found each other again.

We flew on to Nanjing together. Thousands and thousands of words we thought to speak to each other melted in our silent smiles. He held my hand tightly throughout the flight, and it felt good. When we arrived at my home, all he could say was, 'If I say I love you, do you mind?' My eyes gave him his answer and he took me into his arms.

The following two weeks were the happiest of my entire adult life. Andong came every day in high spirits and on her best behaviour. We went out sightseeing all over the city. Andong and I showed Harry the places where the remains of my father's handwriting still existed and took photographs. We took him to every place of interest we could think of. He still had some back pain but he never complained as we jumped on and off buses or trams. Often we had to stand as the vehicle jolted us to our destination but all he said was that he was enjoying himself. Harry spent his fifty-ninth birthday in my little flat. Andong and Zhan bought him a big cake with lots of candles, and my home was full of laughter.

All of my friends were happy to meet him. His quiet smile charmed them, and they quickly accepted him as a friend. They liked his sincerity, and his love for me. During his first short stay in Nanjing he was invited to dinner almost every day. I took him to visit the factory where I worked. My general manager and he got on so well that my boss laid on a big banquet for us, and invited the rest of the factory directors and the Party secretary of the local county town.

Harry ate everything. All kinds of traditional Chinese dishes were put in front of him, and he enjoyed every morsel. Many of the foods were new to him, such as snake soup, fried fruit-bat, eel and tortoise. He refused nothing. The most delicious dish, he said, was the donkey-meat, ordered especially for him by my friend Little Zhu and her husband. That evening we ate in the faculty restaurant of Nanjing Normal University. Jokingly, Harry said, 'If you Chinese can eat it, so can I.' Which was a challenge to us food-conscious Chinese. We fed him everything and he ate it up with gusto. Only afterwards would we tell him what it was. He just shrugged his shoulders and said how much he had enjoyed it.

I came to adore him. His ability to set everybody at their ease was amazing. I had never seen any big-nose do this before. It didn't matter to him who they were. We had dinner with the top leaders one day and with a poor market-trader the next. My neighbours soon began to treat him as an old friend, and an old lady on a lower floor of my block smiled every time she saw him – which surprised me, because in all the years I and Little Yan had lived there, she had never once smiled at us. Children tried out their classroom English as we walked to and from my home and he would go down on one knee and talk to them. Market-traders outside my block of flats shouted, 'Hey, English!' as they tried to sell him something. Never did I expect such a thing to happen. Times had changed. Talking to a foreigner was no longer the sin it had once been.

On his last day in Nanjing, Andong and I took Harry to meet our beloved Auntie Shi, who was now living comfortably in retirement. Auntie Shi's husband, Wang Ye-xiang, had been the one to sponsor my father into the Communist Party in Yan'an, way back in 1938. Both Auntie and Uncle had been betrayed by Mao and branded capitalist roaders during the Cultural Revolution, so Andong had stayed in their home for a long time, helping them to write their self-criticisms. In fact, she stayed with them right up to her marriage to Zhan and the move to Inner Mongolia.

Since Uncle Wang's death Auntie Shi had lived in the best part of Nanjing in a nice house with a garden. She welcomed us with open arms. I was happy to see that she and Harry liked each other. As we were leaving, she embraced Harry, which was a surprise, because she was usually quite cool to foreigners. Then she turned to me and nodded her approval. Everything was going to be all right. I had expected opposition but instead we had the blessing of everyone who mattered to me. During our last night together, Harry whispered his proposal of marriage and I accepted.

He went back to England the following day, determined to sort out the necessary paperwork. He wanted to return quickly and make me his wife. I, too, had to make arrangements and was surprised how easy it was.

Andong continued to call on me most days but she became more and more depressed. She envied me my happiness and the fact that I had found a western husband. About two weeks after Harry had left for England, in one of her rages, she astonished me by blurting out that she wanted a western husband too! I couldn't believe my ears as she ranted on about her plan to divorce Zhan, whom she had loved so deeply for so many years. 'I'm going to marry a westerner,' she shouted, 'or a pop star!' At first I laughed, thinking she had made a joke, but she hadn't.

I was shocked. Zhan was kind and caring. He and Andong had gone through life together for over twenty-six years. Now, out of jealousy, she wanted a divorce so that she could marry a foreigner and escape from China. I couldn't believe it. I tried to reason with her and asked her to think it through but she stormed out of my home.

There was no changing her mind, and anyone who tried to do so became her enemy. She lost her temper constantly, and when her husband and daughter kept silent and let her shout, she became even angrier and began to smash things. In the end, she refused to allow them to live at home, and drove them to his factory collective dormitory. She broke off her friendships with everyone, even her old teachers, because no one could agree to her absurd ideas. All of us were terribly worried about her but could do nothing to stop her.

At the end of August, Andong paid me a surprise visit. She barely gave herself time to cross the threshold before she was talking about her divorce plans. I said I did not wish to hear about such things. Andong stopped in mid-sentence, because my words shocked her. As her younger sister, she expected me to listen quietly, without interrupting. Then she began to scold me. She called me a bad sister and accused me of not caring about her. I had found my happiness and now I didn't want to help her to be happy too.

I said she had a wonderful husband, a lovely daughter and nice home. What more did she want? Andong said she deserved to get out of China more than I, because she had suffered a much harder life. I told her not to talk rubbish. We had both been victims, I said. But I protested in vain. Andong was shouting insults at me as she walked out of my flat, banging the door behind her. The last thing I heard was: 'As from today, I have no sister!'

When Harry came back to Nanjing on 15 September 1994, Andong and I were still not talking. I didn't give her much thought as he and I busied ourselves with the complicated formalities of our wedding. I had to get a full Chinese passport, an exit permit to leave China and an entrance visa into Britain. The next day, we got up early to go to the marriage registration office. I wanted to be his wife, and I thought I had taken care of everything, but to my disappointment, when I handed over both sets of papers to the clerk, we were faced with further formalities.

We had to have a complete medical check by an approved doctor at the same hospital where I had undergone my hysterectomy. After that, it would take at least a week to get the necessary papers saying we were fit to marry. I dragged Harry off to the hospital. We both passed and the doctor stamped 'Can Marry' on our papers. We had one fright: Harry's blood pressure was a bit high, but the doctor accepted my explanation that he had just flown in from London and was jet-lagged. Then we went to another part of the hospital for blood and urine tests. Everywhere we went, money changed hands. Harry could understand nothing of what was said, so all the while I had to translate. He was surprised at how much everything cost. I explained that I was being charged at twice the usual rate because he was a foreigner.

After a week we returned to the hospital and collected the reports, with their official red stamps. Off we went again to the marriage registration office. We had a long wait as there were many before us. Some emerged from an inner office, happily married; others, like us, were going through the formalities. At last our turn came and I passed over the paperwork. Yes, it was all in order, but now the English papers Harry had brought with him from England must be translated into Chinese. 'I can do that,' I said. But, no, we had to go to the officially approved translator to get them done. So off we went across Nanjing to the address given me by the clerk.

The translator had a small, dingy office. He asked for our papers. 'How can I translate these?' he asked me. 'I don't understand them.' So, while Harry sat quietly, I helped the translator. It was quite a while before I succeeded in making him understand what we wanted. He had the cheek to ask for his fee, and told us to return in a week.

Another week later, after collecting the papers from the translator, back we went to the marriage registration office. It was even busier this time. We awaited our turn and I handed over the papers. 'Yes, fine, all in order,' said the clerk.

'Good. Now you can marry us?' asked I.

'No,' she replied, 'the papers must go to the next higher leadership for approval. Come back in a week.'

Four weeks after Harry had arrived in Nanjing, we were registered as married. We had to sign some forms with a blue ballpoint pen, then put our fingertips into red ink and leave our prints underneath our signatures. The official shook hands and took two photographs of us with a Polaroid camera, one for us and the other for them. She told us Harry was the first Briton to marry a Chinese in Nanjing since records began in 1949. Could she put our photograph on the office wall? We agreed.

The appearance of my old classmate Greg added to my joy at being married at last to Harry. After nine years in the United States, he had come back to see his mother and to do some research for his doctorate. He and Harry soon began to talk to each other as if they had known each other for years. It wasn't long before they got into politics and world affairs and, as they spoke in English, they soon left me far behind.

Then Harry said, after about half an hour, it was time for Greg and me to catch up on old times. So he stayed silent to allow us to gossip away in Chinese. Such consideration for my feelings was something I had never encountered before, and it made me feel good. It was then I realized that, in marrying Harry, nothing of my own life had to be sacrificed. I had answered the right letter.

It was time to make a decision. For years I had fantasized about leaving China and now I had the opportunity. However, in recent times life had been good to me so my need to leave had dulled. Should I stay in China, near my friends, everything I knew, and, most importantly, near my daughter? Or should I start a new life in Britain?

I talked to Little Yan on the telephone and by letter. She said I should go. So did Auntie Shi and the judge. In the end it was the memory of Yellow-teeth punching my face that decided me. I had lost confidence in the Communist Party. The memories of Tiananmen Square were still fresh in my mind and demonstrated that little had changed politically in China since Mao's time. I decided to follow my heart and my inclinations. I would go with Harry to his country. After all, hadn't I always wanted to go there?

It took another month and a pile of money to have our marriage certificate notarized, a passport obtained for me and an exit permit issued. Money was the key that unlocked the door to my freedom. Without it, I would have had no chance. Slowly I collected all the documentation I needed, and in late October we flew to Beijing for our most difficult confrontation: with the British embassy.

In the embassy we were questioned separately. I was asked forty-five questions, and Harry about thirty. Our questioner was a cool, detached young man. I felt that nothing in this world, not money, not politics or anything else, would influence him in his decision. Only the truth would do. And as Harry and I had decided only to speak truthfully, we must have answered to his satisfaction. His main concern, as far as I could see, was that our marriage was a genuine love-match and not a business transaction. I had never heard of such a thing, but apparently it was quite common for Britons to be paid large sums of money to marry foreigners and take them to the West, where they separated.

In the end, our questioner caught us by surprise by asking to see at least ten of my letters to Harry, which were lying in a drawer in Harry's flat in London. Harry was angry, and I caught his mood, but there was nothing for it but to do as our interrogator asked. He had to return to the UK immediately to post the letters off – and I was forced to go back to Nanjing alone and wait.

I received my visa in the mail on 22 November. That night, for the first time since Harry left, I fell into a sound sleep, to be awakened early the next morning by my telephone. It was just after five o'clock and pitch dark outside. I hurried from my cold bedroom into the freezing living room, wearing just my nightdress and slippers, to answer it. It was Zhan, Andong's husband. His voice shook. 'Anhua? It's Zhan. Andong . . . she's dead . . . hanged herself from the door last night. Please come.' I put down the telephone, at first unable to take in the news. Then I dressed hurriedly, went outside and hailed a taxi.

When I arrived, Zhan took me directly to see Andong in her bedroom. I looked down at my dear sister. She was lying in bed now, her mouth wide open and her face paper-white. The living room had already been transformed by Zhan and Zhao-zhao into a mourning hall. A large photograph of Andong, framed in white wood and draped with black ribbons, sat on a table against a wall with a pot of incense burning in front of it.

'How could it happen?' I asked, and burst into tears. The real Andong had been such a lovely person. Now we would remember the mad woman she had become. I tried hard to remember her before she had gone to Inner Mongolia: loving, kind, fiercely loyal and a wonderful sister and friend. She had shown her loyalty by following Zhan when he had been exiled by the Party. She had suffered all kinds of hardships there but had never thought of suicide. There had been no hint of it in any of the hundreds of letters she had written to me. Only after her return to Nanjing, when she had come up against the wide social and political gap between herself and some of the people she had once known, had her mind snapped.

Andong couldn't accept her blessings. She had a loving, faithful husband, who was still a Party member and on the rise. She had a beautiful daughter. They had been given a big new flat with all modern facilities, such as air-conditioning, automatic washing-machine and a refrigerator. But in Andong's muddled mind, none of that mattered. Only status was important. We could only conclude that her overwhelming jealousy had driven her to kill herself.

Zhan needed to talk. He had to unload his grief on someone, and I understood because I had undergone a similar experience when my Lin had died. He told me that Andong had gone through with the divorce, forcing him to sign the papers. Also, in her madness, she had made Zhao-zhao leave home and she was now living with her boyfriend. Andong had broken off all her friendships and had even destroyed her personal address book. Then she had locked herself away at home.

It was Zhan who had found her. Although they were divorced, he went to visit her every other day. On 22 November, Zhan had had a bath after returning home from his shift. On his way to see Andong, he had purchased two dishes from a kerbside restaurant. When he arrived at his old home, he went in (he still had a key) and found Andong hanging from the door between the living room and the bedroom. She had been dead for some time. Poor Zhan. He felt guilty, and blamed himself for her death. If only he had been firmer with her, if only he had insisted on her having medical help. If only, if only, if only . . .

I, too, felt guilty. If I had been more understanding the day she stormed out of my home, her death might have been avoided. I should have gone to see her and comforted her. What kind of sister had I turned out to be? If I had behaved as a true sister should, perhaps she would never have thought of suicide. I felt sad, and alone.

The leaders of Andong's working unit came that morning to discuss the funeral arrangements. Although Andong had been on permanent sick leave, her work unit was still responsible for her because they held her personal file. Wei-guo arrived about an hour later. It had been eleven years since we had last seen each other, at the funeral of my husband. He had broken off all contact with me after my brush with the law.

I couldn't talk to him; it was too late for us to mend any fences, for he had hurt me too much when I so badly needed his support. Zhan had also sent a telegram to Pei-gen, informing her of Andong's death. She didn't come, or send a message of condolence. I was glad: I had no wish to see her again.

We all agreed that we should follow the example of Premier Zhou. After her cremation we would drop Andong's ashes into the waters of the Yangtze to find their way over the soil of her Motherland. The memorial meeting was held in the Pebble Hill Funeral Parlour two days after her death. As we walked around her body, I took a last look at my dearest supporter and friend. Memories came flooding back . . . Andong and I playing in the Orchard, the 'terrible stink' of the chamber-pots we had investigated as tiny girls, her boundless love for us all, and the way she had stood up to Lin. 'Andong,' I whispered, 'be at peace. I am going to miss you for the rest of my life.' As I bent over to kiss her cheek, my tears fell on to her lifeless face.

Her body was cremated when everyone had paid their last respects. About an hour later, Wei-guo collected the ashes. They had been put into a red silk bag. They were still hot. Then we followed her leaders to the Yangtze River by minibus and taxi. I did not stop sobbing all the way to the river. Only recently Andong had been so alive and happy upon her return to Nanjing; now she was ashes. I felt so ashamed. I knew, deep down, I could not have helped her because the damage had been done long before she had come home, but if only . . .

We boarded a small ship that plied up and down the river. Andong had always loved the Yangtze. In her letters, she often wrote how much she missed walking beside it. She had even insisted on Harry being taken for a walk across the long bridge. Wei-guo and Zhan tied one end of a long strip of red ribbon around the bag containing Andong's ashes. The other end was tied to two large stones. When the ship was out in mid-river, they dropped the bag into the water. It disappeared immediately. My heart seemed to sink with it. Andong was gone for ever.

Zhan, Zhao-zhao, Wei-guo and I returned to Andong's home. Zhan had invited us to dinner in a restaurant that evening. By this time my brother had heard about my marriage to a westerner and my impending move abroad, so it came as no surprise to me when he became friendly and talked to me a lot during the return journey. He recalled the times when we were little and reminded me that our parents had loved us, so we should unite as one and keep in close touch.

I kept silent. I thought, Rubbish! Rubbish! Rubbish! I remembered his pompous attitude towards Andong and me the day he had strutted in front of us in his new army uniform, and the way he had turned his back on me when I was in great trouble. At that time, he had drawn a clear line between himself and me. Now I was married to a westerner, and he wanted us to be closer. I knew why: there might be some advantage in it for him.

Zhan suggested we all go to the eastern suburbs on the Sunday following Andong's funeral to visit the places where my parents had once worked. Wei-guo took his little son with him. He had divorced and was a single parent. The boy was a sweet eight-year-old and my heart softened when I saw him. He was my nephew, and he looked like his grandfather, my father.

What was left of our family was split into pieces, never, it seemed, to reunite. All because of the cursed politics. At that moment, while my nephew was with me, I could have forgiven my brother if he had only said, 'I'm sorry,' to me. If he had, the ice surrounding my heart would have melted clean away. But he did not. He only repeated that we should be good friends.

On the Monday I purchased my plane ticket from Nanjing to London, via Beijing, for 15 December. Little Yan arrived by aeroplane from Shenzhen so that we could spend our last few days together. We met the judge for a goodbye lunch. Tian ordered a farewell banquet for me on the evening before I left. He brought his family, and Greg was there too. Other friends came, and so did my brother. I was sad to be leaving, but excited too. We talked a lot while we ate, as if time was running out – as, of course, it was.

The presence of Greg and Tian warmed my heart. Our life at middle school flashed through my mind. We three had been together in the Youth League, and all of us had solemnly pledged to join the Communist Party when we were old enough. They had, I hadn't. Now, none of that mattered. Their continued friendship was what was important. The Party had never opened the door for me and I had been branded a class enemy. Tian was successful in his chosen field, and Greg had made a new life in the United States. My brother had become a colonel in the army, and even Pei-gen had risen a little up the Party ladder.

I looked lovingly at my daughter. So young, so beautiful, so brave. I prayed silently to Buddha that she would have a better life than mine. Leaving her was going to be the hardest thing I had ever done. I stood up, tears in my eyes, and proposed a toast: 'To you all, the foundations upon which my life has stood. Without you, my life would have been nothing.'

Early the next morning, Tian came to my home to help me carry down the big suitcases. He had arranged for a company car to take me to the airport. We shook hands and said goodbye. Little Yan and I got into the car. As it slid away Tian waved until he was out of sight.

I was in the queue to have my ticket and passport checked at the barrier at Nanjing airport. Suddenly Little Yan cried, 'Mummy, Uncle has come!' I turned round, and there was Wei-guo. He had come to see me off, and I could read in his face 'I was wrong'. He came over to me and said, 'Have a happy life, Anhua.'

I smiled, turned to my daughter and said simply, 'Take good care of yourself, darling.' Then I entered the large new waiting room. I knew

Wei-guo was still there, looking at me. Suddenly I saw my ten-year-old little brother walking beside me to school. Tears filled my eyes and all my resentment against him flowed out and away.

I knew what it meant. Wei-guo and I had been separated by the merciless unseen political fence a long time ago. He had been on his side, and I on mine. In her first letter, Little Yan wrote that he waited until he saw my plane climb into the sky and disappear before he left the airport. When he turned to her, he had tears in his eyes.

At two p.m. on 15 December 1994, I climbed the steps to board the Air China Boeing 747 bound for the United Kingdom, soon to be my second Motherland. I was flying to a land where there was no State Security Bureau, no 'unseen eyes' ever ready to betray the unwary, a land where I would no longer be frightened of political victimization or of what I might say, or even of what I might think.

Harry would be waiting, in the Land on the Edge of the Sky.